# The End of Liberal Ulster

# The End of Liberal Ulster
## Land agitation and land reform
### 1868–1886

## Frank Thompson

ULSTER
HISTORICAL
FOUNDATION

Frontispiece: Eviction scene (Royal 1767) by William Lawrence, courtesy of the National Library of Ireland

This book has received support from the Cultural Diversity Programme of the Community Relations Council, which aims to encourage acceptance and understanding of cultural diversity. The views expressed do not necessarily reflect those of the NI Community Relations Council.

First published 2001
by the Ulster Historical Foundation
12 College Square East, Belfast BT1 6DD
www.ancestryireland.com

Printed by Creative Print and Design Wales

*To Margaret,*
*Cormac, Aidan, Helen*
*and Carol*

# Contents

# Acknowledgements

I am extremely grateful to the staffs of the various repositories and institutions where I used material, especially the staffs of St. Mary's University College Library, the Public Record Office of Northern Ireland, Queen's University Library and the Linenhall Library, Belfast. I would like to express my gratitude to Professor David Harkness who supervised the doctoral thesis on which this book is based. I would also like to thank the following people who helped in various ways at different stages in its research and production: Professor Peter Jupp, Mr Alistair Cooke, Professor Paul Bew, Dr Eamon Phoenix, Dr Bill Crawford, Professor Ronald Buchanan, Mr Shane McAteer, Mr Fintan Mullan, and my former colleagues in St Mary's College, Mr Michael Millerick, Dr Jim Grant, Dr Brian Feeney, Dr Harry McKeown, Dr Peter McPolin and Mr John Rafferty. I am greatly indebted to the late Jack Magee for his friendship and counsel over the many years we worked together. Finally, I would like to record a more personal debt to my wife Margaret and my children Cormac, Aidan, Helen and Carol. This book is dedicated to them.

# Abbreviations

The following abbreviations have been used in the notes:

| | |
|---|---|
| B.F.P. | *Ballymoney Free Press* |
| B.M.N. | *Belfast Morning News* |
| B.N.L. | *Belfast Newsletter* |
| B.U. | *Banner of Ulster* |
| C.C. | *Coleraine Chronicle* |
| C. Const. | *Coleraine Constitution* |
| F.T. | *Fermanagh Times* |
| Gladstone Mss. | Gladstone papers, British Museum Additional Manuscripts |
| I.H.S. | *Irish Historical Studies* |
| I.R. | *Impartial Reporter* |
| J.S.S.I.S.I. | *Journal of the Statistical and Social Inquiry Society of Ireland* |
| L.G. | *Lisbellaw Gazette* |
| L. Journ. | *Londonderry Journal* |
| L. Sent. | *Londonderry Sentinel* |
| L. Stand. | *Londonderry Standard* |
| N.W. | *Northern Whig* |
| PRONI | Public Record Office of Northern Ireland |
| U.E. | *Ulster Examiner.* Published as *Daily Examiner*, Nov. 1870–1872 *(D.E.)* |
| W.N.W. | *Weekly Northern Whig* |

# Introduction

Much has been written on the Irish land question in recent years, and the traditional view of landlord–tenant relations in the post-Famine period has been subjected to radical reinterpretation by modern historians. Ulster, however, does not figure prominently in these studies, and in some of them it is scarcely mentioned.[1] While providing in the Ulster tenant-right custom the model for the main legislative attempts to solve Irish land tenure problems, the province itself — up to 1886 at any rate — has generally been considered to have been outside the main arena of events.

This failure to include the land question in Ulster in the broader national canvas is at least partly explicable. Northern tenants shared many common problems with those in the south, but landlord–tenant relations in Ulster were not subject to the same tensions, and Ulster tenants, enjoying as they did in varying degrees the benefits of the tenant-right custom, did not necessarily feel the same sense of oppression as tenants elsewhere in the country. Indeed, the very existence of tenant-right suggested both at the time and since that the land problem in the north was a good deal less acute than in the rest of the country: in many respects a different kind of problem altogether. Further, Ulster tenants are commonly seen as having played only a passive role in the campaign for land reform, lending no more than occasional vocal support to the agitational efforts of tenants in the south and west.[2]

Yet, if the land agitation in the north never reached the same level of intensity as it did, for example, in the west of Ireland between 1879 and 1882, there was for much of the period covered by this book a land movement in Ulster more active, more continuous, and better organised than could be found in any other part of the country. This was the Ulster tenant-right movement, which succeeded in making land the paramount issue in Ulster politics during the 1870s and 1880s, determining the political pattern of the province and bringing about fundamental changes in its political and social structure. In particular, land provided the dynamic of growth of the Liberal party in the north, with the result that while Liberalism was in terminal decline in the three southern provinces, Ulster increasingly appeared to be defining its own distinct political identity through adherence to the Liberal party. At the same time, the land question helped to undermine the Tory landed ascendancy which, in contrast to what had happened elsewhere in the country, had remained virtually unchallenged in Ulster during the previous two decades.

The impact of the Great Famine had been less severely felt in most parts of Ulster than in the south and west of Ireland. Nevertheless, no county in Ulster escaped its effects. The border counties of Cavan, Monaghan, Fermanagh and Donegal were most seriously affected, but there were communities in every county that endured great hardship and distress. The people who suffered most were the labourers, cottiers and small farmers, those most dependent on the potato and with fewest resources to fall back on. Larger tenants — those with upwards of twenty acres[3] — escaped more lightly, often managing to offset losses in potatoes with sales of grain and dairy produce, and able in many cases to expand their farms at the expense of less fortunate neighbours.[4] However, no class emerged unscathed. The Famine was also a crisis for landlords. All landlords — even those in less seriously affected areas — were faced with reduced rents and increased expenditure on rates, and for many landlords in the north, as well as in the south and west, the Famine delivered the final push into bankruptcy and the encumbered estates court.[5]

Landlord suffering, of course, was relative — 'no landlord', it has been pointed out, 'is known to have starved during the Famine'[6] —

and landlords in the north generally were under less pressure because the crisis in those parts was less acute. This was particularly true of the north-east, where the proximity of Belfast provided alternative forms of employment — the crucial factor in these years — and where the presence of domestic industry meant that landlords did not have the same difficulties in collecting rents or paying high rates as landlords in the south and west.[7] Thus financially they suffered a good deal less than the latter and were in a better position to respond constructively to the crisis. Moreover, apart from the poor law unions in the north-east being more prosperous, the electoral divisions on which the rates were based were often coterminous with estates so that landlords in these areas also had a greater incentive to provide private relief.[8] Of course, the part played by landlords in mitigating the effects of the Famine varied from estate to estate, but northern landlords generally do not appear to have been subjected to the same criticisms for their failure in this respect as landlords elsewhere in the country. The common perception was that they had done more to live up to their traditional responsibilities.[9] Ulster landlords, in fact, emerged from the Famine not only in a relatively strong economic position but also with less damage done to their moral credibility.[10]

The period 1848–52, however, saw a major challenge to their political power. This came not from those most severely affected by the Famine, but from large farmers who were increasingly concerned about the value and security of their tenant-right. Attempts by a number of landlords after 1845 to curtail the Ulster custom and the overwhelming defeat of a bill to legalise it had created tenant fears for its future, while the collapse of agricultural prices from 1848 threatened to undermine its value.[11] This led to the formation of a number of tenant-right societies in Ulster which joined with tenant protection societies in the south to form a new national organisation, the Irish Tenant League, in August 1850. The campaign in the south was stimulated by the furore over the ecclesiastical titles bill of 1851 (prohibiting the use of territorial titles by prelates of the catholic church), and in the general election of 1852 — largely because of the intensity of religious feeling — forty-eight independent MPs were returned for southern constituencies.[12]

In Ulster, however, the alliance with militant catholicism compromised the movement, whose impetus was already waning with the revival of agricultural prices and tenant-right values from 1851. Only one independent was returned in the election in Ulster (for the borough of Newry). Independent candidates had gone forward in seven of the Ulster counties, but all were defeated.[13] Although the religious factor undoubtedly contributed to their defeat, the main reasons were the reviving prosperity and the strength of landed influence. What the election of 1852 demonstrated was that, despite the trauma of the Famine and the tenant-right agitation of 1848–52, landed hegemony in the north in the post-Famine period was still as powerful as ever.

It was nearly two decades later that a movement of comparable significance emerged to challenge the landed ascendancy in the province, but these decades were not uneventful or unimportant in the history of the tenant-right movement. It was the social and economic developments during these years that provided the basis of success of the new agitation in the 1870s and 1880s. Chapter 1 examines the nature of landed influence in Ulster and shows how the traditional community of interests between landlords and tenants in the province began to break down under the pressure of these developments in the post-Famine period. A new, more assertive rural bourgeoisie emerged with social aspirations and economic fears, fears which were attached mainly to the greatly enhanced value of their tenant-right investment in the soil. Chapter 2 analyses the Ulster custom and discusses the factors which made tenants apprehensive about its future — basic insecurity of tenure (despite the relatively low number of evictions), increases of rent, the enforcement of estate rules, and especially, it is argued here, the sales of estates in the landed estates court. It was their fears for the future of tenant-right rather than the pressure of existing grievances which prompted Ulster tenants to join in the agitation for land reform in 1869 and which, indeed, sustained the tenant-right movement during the 1870s.

Chapter 3 examines the circumstances in which the tenant-right movement was established in 1869. The Land Act of 1870 and its effects on landlord–tenant relations in the north are discussed in chapter 4, which shows that the act was a good deal more successful in Ulster than has generally been allowed, although the main beneficiaries tended to be large rather than small tenants, for many of whom the benefits conceded were barely adequate compensation for the goodwill and social favours withdrawn. Nevertheless, it did not give even the larger tenants the full protection they had hoped for, and with landlords after 1870 more inclined to stand on their legal rights, it became more essential than ever from the tenants' point of view to have tenant-right put on a comprehensive statutory basis. Thus the tenant-right movement continued to flourish during the 1870s.

However, the ramifications of the movement went well beyond the tenant farmers and tenant-right. Much of its leadership and support was provided by the presbyterian urban middle classes, who had close social and commercial relationships with the tenant farmers and who had themselves deep-rooted social, religious and political grievances against the landed classes. These relationships and grievances are explored in chapter 5, which shows how the land question was used as a unifying issue for all the forces opposed to the landed ascendancy and how it led to the consolidation of these forces behind the Liberal party. As explained in chapter 6, it was the Liberal party's identification with tenant-right that enabled it to win unprecedented successes in the general election of 1874 and to enjoy continuing growth after this date. The landed classes were not unaware of the importance of the tenant-right question and, in the best traditions of pragmatic conservatism, were prepared to make timely concessions. It is argued here that the land question was allowed to assume the proportions it did in Ulster not because of any short-sightedness on the part of the Ulster Tories, but because of the intransigence and indifference to their special needs of their party leaders at Westminster.

The effects of the agricultural depression of the late 1870s and the course of the land war in Ulster are examined in chapters 7 and 8. Small farmers and labourers were particularly severely affected by the depression, but it was the larger tenants, fearful of the effects of the depression on their standard of living and more especially on the value of their tenant-right, who took the lead in the agitation for rent abatements at this time. Although many landlords responded generously to the needs of the tenants in the crisis, others refused to make allowances, and landlords as a whole lost a good deal of their social credit as a result of the events of these years. The general election of 1880 in which the landed Tories lost control of the majority of the county seats, the degree of protestant support for the Land League at the end of 1880, and the high level of evictions in 1880 and 1881 all revealed how far landlord–tenant relations in the province had deteriorated by this stage. But the northern tenants' perception of their own needs still differed markedly from that of tenants in the south, and although the Land League won protestant support in Ulster it did so only by adjusting its policy and tactics to suit northern conditions.

The landlords for their part tried to defeat the league by reactivating the Orange Order as a political force, but mainly they were anxious to have the land question settled, and it is argued in chapter 9 that the Ulster Tories played a vital role in helping to bring about the settlement of 1881. Chapter 10 shows that the act did not, as they had hoped, restore landlord–tenant relations to what they had been in the past, and tenant-right activity continued in Ulster after the act had been passed. The 1881 legislation had, however, removed some of the most serious causes of friction between landlords and tenants, with the result that when the National League began to campaign in the north from 1883 the different protestant interests in Ulster could more easily coalesce behind the Tory party. The final chapter shows how events after 1883 ended the primacy of the land question, aborted the growth of Liberalism, and enabled the landed classes — with the support of the Orange order and the assistance of the Conservative constitutional associations — to re-establish their position as leaders of Ulster's loyalist community. Land continued to be a divisive issue and a potential threat to protestant unity after 1886, but the fundamental cleavage in Ulster society was now between those who supported and those who opposed the union with Britain.

# 1
# Landlords and Tenants

The landed classes emerged from the Famine in as formidable a position as ever. Land ownership in Ireland was still heavily concentrated in the hands of a very small and privileged minority. This was particularly true of Ulster, where a higher percentage of the land and a larger total area were controlled by proprietors of 2,000 acres and upwards than in any other province.[1] There were about 500 such landlords, and between them they owned three-quarters of the entire province, with the forty largest proprietors controlling no less than 27 per cent of the total area. It was these 500 individuals — members of the landed aristocracy and larger landed gentry, owners of estates of 2,000 acres and upwards, and, with only a handful of exceptions, Tory in their politics — who, on the basis of their interest in the land, claimed and were usually conceded the right to dominate the social and political life of the province.[2]

In spite of a gradual encroachment by the state in such areas as health, poor relief and education, the landed classes continued up to the end of the nineteenth century to control practically every aspect of local government and administration, their members dominating either directly or indirectly the grand juries, the baronial presentment sessions, the bench and, as *ex officio* members, the boards of poor law guardians.[3] They also dominated the parliamentary representation of the province, with most of the boroughs as well as the counties being under their control. In 1865, of the twenty-nine Ulster MPs sitting at Westminster, twenty-five belonged to landed families, twenty-eight were members of the Church of Ireland, and all but two were Tories. Such indeed was the Tory, landed, and episcopalian dominance of political life in Ulster that, apart from 1852, it went virtually unchallenged until 1874. Between 1852 and 1868 only 34 per cent of all elections in Ulster were contested, and if Belfast, Derry and Newry — the three most distinctly urban constituencies — are excluded the proportion falls to 28 per cent. Landed control of the county elections was even more marked, with less than one election in four being fought between the same two dates. The 1868 general election reflected both the pattern of the previous decades and the strength of the entrenched interests, with only one county contest in the whole of the province, and with all eighteen county representatives being members of landed families and all but one being Tory.[4]

Up to 1868 at any rate the landowning interest in Ulster had found it less difficult than in the rest of the country to maintain their traditional supremacy. The radical and tenant-right press, of course, alleged that this landed dominance was based on coercion, and much of the campaign against the landed classes rested on the assumption that if tenants were given legislative protection for their interests, landed influence would diminish and eventually disappear. Certainly many landlords attempted in one way or another to reinforce what the British Liberal leader Lord Hartington spoke of as the 'legitimate influence which a popular and respected landlord must exercise in his neighbourhood', and instances of landlord coercion — as, for example, in Lisburn in 1852 and Antrim in 1869 — were often highlighted by the tenant-right press. However, J.H. Whyte suggests that the number of authenticated cases of intimidation or victimisation is 'remarkably small' and that 'only a minority of landlords tried to coerce their tenants'. K.T. Hoppen, on the other hand, rightly believes that coercion was 'much more widespread' than Whyte allows.[5]

It is, in fact, a mistake to attempt to measure the extent of landlord intimidation by the number of precise allegations or proven cases. It might, indeed, be argued that the small number of instances in which a landlord found it necessary either explicitly to threaten or to take action against recalcitrant tenants was in itself a reflection of how successful and deeply entrenched the whole system of intimidation was. 'The dread of being on bad terms with the agent', it was observed, 'exercises a potent influence upon minds more accustomed to view things from a selfish than from a patriotic point of view. There are so many ways in which an agent can make a refractory tenant's lot disagreeable that, unless he is actuated by a high sense of moral and public duty, he will not run the risk of incurring such a hardship.'[6] Tenants who displeased the office could suffer in many ways short of eviction or increase of rent: the right of turbary could be withdrawn; liberty to sell the tenant-right of a farm could be withheld or, if granted, the highest bidder not accepted; or allowances and accommodation given to other tenants, for example in such things as the provision of timber and slates for building or abatements of rent, could be withheld.

Landlord practices varied. A number, such as the Marquis Conyngham, prided themselves on allowing their tenants to exercise their vote freely. Others, such as John Hamilton of St Ernan's estate in Donegal, believed they had a 'duty' to advise their tenants.[7] Many landowners, however, while not overtly practising intimidation, clearly expected their tenants to support their nominees, and the use of circulars advising tenants how to vote was widespread throughout this period. Plainly these landlords assumed not only that their tenants would follow their political lead, but that they as landlords had a right if not a duty to give such a lead: 'I have yet to learn', said one landlord spokesman in 1872, 'that it is an offence for a landlord ... to send round either his agent or his bailiff to civilly request the tenant to vote for him.'[8]

'Civil' requests, however, often had implicit warnings for tenants. As the *Ballymoney Free Press* observed, 'it is well-known what a landlord means when he intimates that he is desirous for the return of a certain candidate'.[9] With a land system in which the tenant was totally dependent on the goodwill of the landlord and with the tenant's interest, up to 1870 at any rate, completely unprotected by law, tenants simply could not afford to run the risk of antagonising their landlords. And the more valuable the tenant's interest was, the less inclined he was to take such a risk: as James McKnight, editor of the *Londonderry Standard* and one of the founders of the tenant-right movement, pointed out, the despotism of the rent-office over tenants was 'in direct proportion to the amount and value of their unsecured interest in the soil'.[10]

Yet, if in the final analysis there was no basic distinction between 'legitimate' and 'illegitimate' influence, the ease with which the landed classes dominated politics in Ulster makes it clear that their influence was not based on coercion alone. Religious and racial divisions between landlords and tenants in the north were not as clear-cut as elsewhere in the country. Practically 50 per cent of Ulster tenants were protestants, nearly 30 per cent of them presbyterians, who generally held the better land and who were represented disproportionately in the electorate.[11] Although protestants were in a clear majority in only three counties — Antrim, Down and Derry — they dominated the electorate in all Ulster counties save Cavan.[12] Most of these tenants shared the same political views as their landlords, and readily accepted their political leadership so that there was not the same potential for friction as in the southern constituencies. Even the tenant-right advocates acknowledged that landlord–tenant relations in Ulster were good by any standards,[13] and tenants regularly gave expression to their feelings of affection for their landlords. Births, the attainment of majorities, marriages, deaths, and homecomings after prolonged absences in landed families were all marked by displays of loyalty and respect by the tenants.[14]

Such events were not entirely irrelevant to the tenant's own position — the birth of a son or a good marriage, for example, could help ensure that an estate remained in the same family — but manifestly there was an element of sycophancy and self-interest in the tenant's part in these proceedings. H.S. Morrison tells the story of a headstone erected by the Ironmongers tenantry in Aghadowey parish churchyard to Henry Anderson JP, agent of the estate, paying tribute to his conscientious discharge of duties and his generosity; Anderson was in fact to be succeeded by his son as agent, hence the memorial 'to an agent whose reputation for harshness and domineering tyranny are fresh in the parish to-day'.[15] Similarly, a tenant on the Hertford estate admitted that he and many others subscribed to a collection for a £500 silver plate service for the agent on the occasion of his marriage in 1852 only because they were afraid not to.[16] Yet it would be a mistake to explain all these demonstrations of loyalty in this way, or to understate the genuine regard which many tenants had for their landlords and, indeed, for many of the agents. Landlord–tenant relations in Ulster were good, and this helps to explain why the Liberal and tenant-right parties had such difficulty in weaning tenants from their traditional loyalties.

The truth was that the political and social dominance conceded to the landed classes was part of a complex and reciprocal relationship, and for the tenants an occasional vote and general compliance with the estate owner's wishes was a small price to pay for the benefits received. In return for social deference and political votes, landlords undertook to respect the interests of their tenants, and not to press to the full their rights under a law which up to 1870 denied the tenants any rights at all. Many landlords plainly saw the tenant's vote as a *quid pro quo* for a liberal policy of estate administration; as the agent of the Hertford estate explained, Hertford had increased his rents in Lisburn in 1852 because his tenants had opposed his nominee in the election, and 'people who were so independent could not expect special favours'.[17] It was not only that the majority of landlords were content with something less than a full competition rent; they were also expected to see tenants through difficult periods by not pressing for rents — or occasionally by making abatements — and it was unusual for a tenant to be evicted for arrears of less than two or three years.[18] There were in addition 'blankets and warm clothing', food parcels in times of need, money handouts, and occasionally pensions and cottages, as well as subscriptions to orphanages, infirmaries and schools, and other contributions to the general well-being of the community.[19]

Quite clearly these concessions were of much more importance to the small tenant, who needed something to cushion him in time of need, than to the larger, wealthier tenant who obviously had more to fall back on. And, equally clearly, the interests of these tenants were not the same; for the former, the establishment of landlord–tenant relations on a more strictly defined legal basis would protect an interest and an investment which was growing annually in value during this period; for the latter it would mean the withdrawal of benefits, a more precarious existence and, on balance, a worsening of his position. As some landlords were not slow to point out, many tenants could not survive without the support of the landlord.[20] In a society where nothing stood between the destitute and starvation but the workhouse and private charity, such security as the tenant had — and admittedly it was limited and insufficient — was often provided by the landlord and the estate. Part of the reason why proportionately much higher prices were paid at times for tenant-right than for the fee-simple of farms[21] was that the purchaser was purchasing a good deal more than the mere occupancy of the farm: he was also buying into a social institution — the estate — and the whole system of social concessions that went with it. Likewise, part of the initial reluctance of tenants to purchase their farms in the 1870s and early 1880s resulted from their realisation that as proprietors they would be deprived of the protective security of the estate. When tenants of the Ahoghill glebe in Co. Antrim were offered their holdings by the church commissioners, they petitioned the local landlord, Lord O'Neill, to purchase the land, expressing the opinion that 'they would be much better off under a good landlord like him than as owners of their own farms'.[22]

These multifarious landlord activities did not arise from purely philanthropic motives; they helped to legitimise the landlord's social and political pre-eminence. When Charles Wilson, a native of Broughshane who had made a fortune in Australia, went forward as Liberal candidate in Antrim in 1874, his candidature was questioned on precisely these grounds: 'What had Mr Wilson done for that county? Had he ever spent a shilling on it? Where were his subscriptions to the institutions of this county? If he intended to stand for the county he ought to have earned a name for himself there by assisting their benevolent institutions.'[23] And, similarly, neglect of these functions by prominent local landed families could weaken their influence in the area. The failure of the Earl of Ranfurly's family to live up to their obligations in Dungannon, for example, was made the basis of the linen manufacturer Thomas Dickson's opposition to them in the election of 1874:

> Mr Dickson has done much for Dungannon; the Ranfurly family have done nothing ... The two great local matters in which the prosperity of Dungannon is deeply involved at present are the collieries and the railway to Cookstown. In both Mr Dickson is the leading power and moving spirit: to neither have the Ranfurly family contributed one farthing of encouraging support.[24]

Dickson's candidature for Dungannon was part of a general challenge to the landed classes which came mainly in the 1870s. But in the 1850s and 1860s — and indeed for a long time after — politics in Ulster continued to be group- rather than class-oriented, and the majority of voters tended still to behave as members of hierarchical communities, in the tenants' case the community being the estate. Thus it was only natural that those tenants in Ulster who were not separated from their landlords by religious barriers should, unless there was a specific reason not to, continue to look to the leader of the hierarchy for example. Protestant tenants in Ulster, much to the frustration of the Liberal and tenant-right parties, did not necessarily see any conflict between their interests and those of the landlords. Assuredly there was at times resentment against the high-handed actions of some landlords, but there was little sign among the tenants of any bitterness of feeling against the landlords as a class. 'It has seemed wise to God', farmers at a meeting in Ballycastle were reminded, 'to compose society of different grades and orders — rich and poor, learned and unlearned. It is right in the poor man trying to become rich and the ignorant instructed; but there is no necessity for the one to envy the other.'[25] Tenants accepted the social values of landed society, and therefore continued to defer to the superior status of the upper classes in politics as in everything else, and continued to see politics and political leadership as the function of the landed classes.

If political leadership was still seen by the tenants as a function of the upper classes, it was a function which the latter took seriously. And, given the expense of elections, the property qualifications for

MPs, and the need which they had of both leisure and independent income, it was a function that few outside the landed classes could afford to undertake. The election of Viscount Castlereagh for Co. Down in 1878, for instance, cost £14,000, while Sir William Verner spent nearly £10,000 in the Co. Armagh election of 1880 and was still paying off his election debts five years later.[26] While these were substantially greater than the average expenses for county elections, they were a measure of how potentially costly such a contest could be. Hugh Montgomery, one of the small number of Liberal landlords in Ulster, estimated that '£2,000 or £3,000' was 'the lowest figure at which one could stand for a county'.[27] A petition against the result — not an unusual occurrence in Ireland — could more than double that amount, even after 1868 when petition trials were held in the constituencies instead of London; their average cost was estimated at £2,500 and the cost could often reach twice that figure.[28] Quite obviously if the landed classes were allowed to dominate politics, they were expected to be able to pay for the privilege.

In return for this expenditure and effort, the landed proprietor could expect an enhancement of his status in the local community and social, perhaps even economic, advancement. In a society preoccupied with rank and precedence, the position of parliamentary representative carried great social prestige. Moreover, political work could increase the patronage of a landed family and create opportunities for honours, titles, or promotions within the peerage. Certainly many of those who involved themselves in politics expected to be rewarded in some way for their services. A few aspired to political office, and for some of those who made a career in politics the monetary rewards could be substantial. The publicity attached to political activity was, of course, of immense value to lawyers, who might also aspire to any one of about sixty different legal offices in Ireland, offices which, it was generally recognised, were rarely filled on merit.[29]

Most Ulster landed representatives, however, were neither lawyers nor career politicians, and their ambitions tended to be social rather than economic. Some, indeed, went into politics only reluctantly and out of a sense of duty. Lord Edward Hamilton, the youngest son of the Duke of Abercorn, for example, was 'thrust, an unwilling victim', into the North Tyrone seat in 1885, found his time at Westminster excruciatingly boring, and gratefully retired from politics after one full parliament.[30] Hamilton's aversion to politics was not, however, shared by the vast majority of landed representatives; these entered political life willingly and expected to have their efforts acknowledged. Lord Arthur Hill-Trevor thought his thirty-five years' service as Conservative MP for Co. Down entitled him to have the viscountcy of Dungannon revived, though he eventually settled for being made Baron Trevor in 1880.[31] Others were less successful. Lady Constance Leslie campaigned unsuccessfully for a peerage for Sir John Leslie, who was, she claimed, 'too modest' to ask for himself; the basis of the claim was that the Leslies had 'represented County Monaghan for over 100 years' and that Leslie himself had sat in the Conservative interest from 1871 to 1880, and had then undertaken three further 'hopeless contests' against the nationalists.[32]

If Sir John Leslie was 'too modest' to ask for a peerage, not many other politicians were similarly inhibited, though few indulged in the crude bargaining attempted by Sir Samuel Wilson, who was prepared to petition against the Liberal success in Co. Derry in 1881 only if it was 'clearly understood that I am to have a peerage when next the Conservatives come into power'.[33] But the papers of the British party leaders abound in repetitive and supplicatory letters from local politicians and public figures seeking honours of one sort or another. Charles Lewis, Conservative MP for Derry city from 1872 to 1886, felt not a little peeved at being passed over for a baronetcy in 1886: 'I have spent from first to last nearly £20,000 in and about the Derry seat and this is the treatment I receive'.[34] It took a baronetcy in 1887 to mollify Lewis and induce him to go forward in the Conservative interest in North Antrim. This undignified scramble for honours was, of course, shared by the Liberals. Sir Shafto Adair, owner of an estate outside Ballymena and never one to underestimate his own importance, thought his unsuccessful efforts in Antrim and Suffolk entitled him to a peerage, while the Belfast merchant Thomas McClure successfully requested a baronetcy after his defeat in the election of 1874.[35]

Nor was it only titles or promotions in the peerage that were looked for. Prestigious positions in the county, minor places in government, and paid posts at home and abroad were all sought. Stuart Knox, who represented Dungannon from 1851 to 1874, asked for the post of inland revenue commissioner after his defeat in the latter year.[36] William Johnston was the subject of numerous appeals to Disraeli and other leading Tory politicians after 1874 until he was finally given the post of inspector of fisheries in 1878.[37] The Earl of Ranfurly and Lord Arthur Hill asked for colonial governorships in recognition of their services to the unionist cause.[38] Thomas Dickson believed he had strong claims on the Liberal leaders in 1885 when he asked for a position in the land court, and even stronger in 1892 when the Irish appointments came to be made by the new Liberal government (though Dickson had no illusions about Gladstone's attitude to his Ulster presbyterian followers):

> I sacrificed everything in separating myself from all my friends and association in Ulster. I have fought more elections than any living member of parliament and spent in contests alone over £16,000. I know too well by experience Mr Gladstone's, Lord Spencer's and John Morley's antipathy to Ulster presbyterians, but it might be well for the new government to recognise for the first time the claims of one who has been loyal to Liberal principles and never absent from one party division for 19 years.[39]

While men such as Dickson and Johnston might look for places and official appointments, or even like Lewis aspire to a baronetcy, the more prestigious county positions or honours such as the Patrick or Garter were reserved for substantial and well-connected members of the landed classes. But here, too, party service was important. The Earl of Belmore, asking Salisbury to approve his appointment as lieutenant of Co. Tyrone, reminded him that his family had represented the county in the Irish and imperial parliaments for five generations.[40] However, political service was only one of the criteria used in such appointments. The size of a candidate's property, his place of residence, his rank in the county, and his involvement in county affairs were also important, and an appointment made on purely political grounds and ignoring these other considerations could lead to great dissatisfaction in the county. Even the appointment of Thomas McClure as vice-lieutenant of Co. Down in 1872 led to an outcry by the Conservative press, which maintained that McClure's appointment was an insult to the county families: 'It does not follow that his success as a merchant is evidence of his fitness to govern the gentry and people of the great County Down'; if a Liberal had to be appointed, argued the *News Letter*, why not Major Crawford, 'a member of one of the oldest county families'?[41]

These appointments and honours were widely reported in the local press, which presented them as tributes not only to the immediate recipients, but to the support they represented. Thus in giving a peerage to Adair and a baronetcy to McClure, Gladstone was acknowledging not only their services, but also those of 'the independent electors of Ulster' who were obviously supposed to get some kind of vicarious satisfaction from Adair's and McClure's promotions.[42] The fact was that the government awards of places and honours were part of a general system of patronage, which helped to lubricate the whole political machine and served to consolidate party support at all levels.[43] Party activists in the localities expected to be rewarded for their party loyalty and services,[44] and MPs and leading government figures were inundated with requests and applications for all kinds of appointments and places. W.A. Dane, a solicitor with considerable influence in Enniskillen, thought his services to the Conservative party entitled him to a tax-mastership worth £500 a year (though it was less his contribution in the past than his potential for mischief in the future that encouraged the Coles of Enniskillen and Colonel Edward Taylor, the Tory chief whip, to support his claims).[45] The Duke of Abercorn's brother wanted a local presbyterian supporter appointed to the clerkship of the crown in Co. Derry, partly in order to reward his past services to the Tory party, partly because it would give great satisfaction to the presbyterians, and partly because it would strengthen Hamilton family influence.[46] Tax-masterships in chancery, clerkships of the crown, resident magistracies, crown solicitorships, stamp distributorships, clerkships of the peace, inspectorships of prisons, church livings and numerous other places and offices — these were all part and parcel of the system of patronage.

One of the most important appointments at constituency level — and the highest honour to which most middle-rank or middle-class party supporters could aspire — was the commission of the peace. This was the main patronage link between the national parties and the local leaders, and MPs were expected to use their influence to secure such appointments. 'I am literally overwhelmed with letters from Derry and Donegal with respect to the commission of the peace', Richard Dowse, the Liberal MP for Derry city, told Thomas O'Hagan, the Irish lord chancellor, in 1869. 'I have had letters from laymen and clergymen of both the great churches, catholic and presbyterian, complaining of the present state of affairs and asking me to send in names to you for the commission of the peace.'[47] The problem for Dowse and other Liberals, however, was that the magistrates had first to be nominated by the county lieutenants, who were almost invariably Tory, landed, and episcopalian; and these — while occasionally bowing to pressure from either above (the lord chancellor) or below (memorials from interested parties) — were notoriously reluctant to recommend the appointment of any but their own kind to the bench. 'Our complaint', wrote one Liberal paper, 'is that in certain high quarters the qualifications deemed essential for appointments to the magisterial office are: in religion the candidate must be an episcopalian, in politics a Conservative, in social status the owner of broad acres, or a receiver of rents.'[48]

It was not only that magistracies were important honours in themselves; the magisterial bench and the grand juries — also dominated by the landed classes — had at their disposal much of the small change of patronage in the constituencies. 'The haughty magistrates of counties', the *Northern Whig* complained, 'dispense the patronage of jails and infirmaries and lunatic asylums with an exclusive regard to the advancement of their own political interests and ... perpetuate jobs freely with other people's money.'[49] Equally the grand jury system was operated to the same end: 'Every little post in the gift of the grand jurors is reserved as a reward for political service, and thus a large amount of this sort of work is procured without costing a penny to the gentry.'[50] The result was that at constituency level in Ulster the whole system of local government and patronage tended to be dominated by the Tory landed classes, with presbyterians and catholics almost totally excluded.

This state of affairs was bitterly resented by a growing section of the presbyterian commercial and professional classes, and it was probably this more than anything else, especially after Irish church disestablishment in 1869, that stimulated their opposition to the Tory episcopalian and landed ascendancy. This ascendancy, however, could not be broken until the allegiance of the tenant farmers to the landed classes and their dependence on them began to weaken. In the decades after the Famine, economic and social developments in Ulster caused this to happen, and provided the presbyterian middle classes with an opportunity to harness to their cause the support of an increasing number of tenant farmers.

AGRICULTURAL DEVELOPMENTS

The period from 1851 to 1876 was, apart from a few years in the early 1860s, one of rising agricultural prosperity in Ireland.[51] This was based on an expanding market in Britain[52] which was reflected in steadily increasing prices for Irish farm products. Thomas Barrington's review of agricultural prices shows both a general rise in agricultural prices in the 1850s and 1860s and a clearly discernible movement in favour of animal products.[53] Beef and store cattle in particular enhanced their price position in relation to all other agricultural products. What this meant was that while all tenants stood to gain from the relative improvement in agricultural prices, those who could shift the bias on their farms to livestock production stood to gain most. This development was also encouraged by a shortage of labour, especially from the 1860s. The number of agricultural labourers had fallen steeply as a result of the Famine and the subsequent heavy emigration — by more than half between 1841 and 1871[54] — so that by 1870 farm wages were between 50 and 100 per cent up on what they had been in the 1840s.[55]

The combined effect of these factors was to encourage a move towards livestock farming, though the proportion of land given over to tillage in Ulster remained consistently higher than in the three southern provinces.[56] Although there was only a fractional decrease in arable land between 1851 and 1876, the acreage of cereal crops went down by nearly 30 per cent, while root crops increased their acreage by over 10 per cent and the acreage of meadow and clover virtually doubled.[57] This shifting emphasis in arable farming was accompanied by a simultaneous increase in the number of livestock, with the number of cattle going up by 25 per cent, sheep by 80 per cent and pigs by over 50 per cent.[58] Again, the overall figures tell only part of the story. Whereas in 1854, 48 per cent of the cattle were milch cows, by the mid-1870s this had fallen to 41.5 per cent.[59] In other words, even within the livestock sector increasing emphasis was being placed on beef rather than dairy farming. There was, moreover, an increased rate of turnover as a result of the killing and export of animals at little more than half the age that had formerly been the case;[60] thus, while the number of cattle over two years increased by 11 per cent, the number under one year increased by 74 per cent and those between one and two years by 23 per cent.

What was happening over this twenty-five year period was that the Ulster farmer was deriving more and more of his income from livestock products, in particular beef, and was tending therefore to concentrate on the production of crops for animal foodstuffs. Even in those areas such as the Ards peninsula, the Braid valley and other parts of the province where more land continued under the plough than was usual, most of the cereals and root crops that were produced were for feeding stock. This is not to say that cash crops ceased to be important. Both oats and potatoes, the two main crops, were still grown partly as cash crops, while flax — in spite of occasional claims that Ulster was 'flaxed out'[61] — continued to be a cash crop of great importance throughout the period. The comparative prosperity of the northern province can be attributed at least partly to flax, but it was a difficult crop — 'a greedy dirty crop that impoverished the soil and left it full of weeds'[62] — and its acreage fluctuated continuously in response to changing economic conditions. The highest figures recorded for it had been reached during the American civil war when the cotton trade was disrupted, but its acreage declined from 245,356 in 1866 to 147,065 in the early 1870s.[63] In the main, therefore, agriculture in Ulster was increasingly geared to pastoral farming with the emphasis in arable farming moving towards the production of animal foodstuffs, and while the area was still — and was to remain — a mixed farming area, Ulster farmers increasingly derived their income from livestock and livestock products.

Not all the Ulster counties were influenced to the same extent by these developments, and indeed sections of the presbyterian press tended to deplore the growing reliance on animal farming, implying that it represented to some extent a departure from what they saw as the northern and protestant virtue of hard work.[64] But neither the moral disapproval of the press nor the frequently expressed fear that livestock farming might lead to depopulation and unemployment[65] deterred tenant-farmers from responding to market conditions, and every northern county shared in the general agricultural trends of the period.

How far each county adjusted depended on local conditions, but one overriding factor was that with over three-quarters of farms in the 1870s still under thirty acres and 50 per cent under fifteen acres, only a comparatively small number of Ulster farmers had the acreage necessary for complete specialisation in any one product. Thus, even though agriculture was increasingly based on livestock and livestock products, the predominant type of farming continued to be mixed. This not only allowed full and more efficient use to be made of family labour, but also enabled a greater number of livestock to be maintained on the average size Ulster farm than would have been possible had the whole of the land been given over to pasture; the average value of livestock per acre on farms of under thirty acres in 1871 was about one and a half times the average on farms of over thirty acres.[66] James Godkin, for example, claimed that the very small farms in the barony of Fews in south Armagh had been 'so well drained, cleared, sub-soiled, and manured that the occupier is able to support on one acre as many cattle as on three acres when grazed'. The green crops, he said, were 'so timed as to give a full supply for house-feeding throughout the year'.[67]

With tillage being made to complement livestock in this way, the areas in which arable farming could be carried on most successfully were the very areas which were able to take greatest advantage of the swing to livestock. And these, generally speaking, tended to be in the east of the province where, additionally, there was readier access to the growing urban market in Belfast so that it was farmers on this side of the province and also in parts of Derry, Tyrone and more limited areas of other counties that benefited most from the changes in agriculture over these three decades. John Murphy contrasted this part of Ulster with the rest of the country, while William O'Connor Morris, travelling through Ulster in 1869, found Derry 'a very progressive county' and thought that Antrim and Down were 'in a special manner progressive counties'.[68]

These agricultural developments were accompanied by a decline in the number of holdings. Although the effects of the Famine were less severely felt in most parts of Ulster than in the rest of the country, it precipitated here as elsewhere the ruination and hegira of thousands of smallholders so that one third of the holdings of between one and fifteen acres and nearly half of those between one and five acres disappeared in the years 1845–51.[69] During the same period the number of farms of over thirty acres increased by more than a third. This rate of consolidation and enlargement could hardly be maintained but, while it eased off considerably in the 1850s, it did continue and it continued also to be more marked in Ulster than in the rest of the country. Between 1851 and 1881 the number of holdings of between one and fifteen acres decreased by 21.4 per cent in Ulster as against a decrease of 14.7 per cent in the remainder of the country. To put it another way, more holdings of between one and five acres and between five and fifteen acres disappeared in Ulster during these three decades than in the other three provinces put together.[70]

The average-sized holding in Ulster had always been smaller than in the rest of the country. According to one recent estimate the mean farm size in Ulster on the eve of the Famine was twelve acres as against a national mean size of fifteen acres.[71] Part of the reason for this was the prevalence of handloom weaving in the north, which enabled the occupiers of small holdings to supplement an agricultural income which on its own would scarcely have enabled them to survive. But this was already in decline in the border counties before the Famine, and the introduction of power-looms from the 1850s — the number of power-looms in operation in the country increased from 58 in 1850 to over 3,500 in 1859 to nearly 15,000 by 1871[72] — led to it being ousted in the north-eastern areas. In the ten years from 1861, the decade during which power weaving expanded most rapidly, the number of holdings of between one and fifteen acres in Ulster decreased at a rate three times greater than that of the previous decade. In some areas the presence of larger industrial enterprises eased the situation and allowed many small farmers to maintain their position. Of some 4,000 hands employed in five mills at Newry and Bessbrook, over 1,000 were the sons and daughters of small farmers in the neighbourhood.[73] Other factories in such places as Banbridge, Lisburn, Cookstown, Ballymena, Ballymoney and other centres assisted the farming community in the same way. But such assistance was extremely limited, and isolated industries such as the potteries at Belleek or McDevitt's woollen and tweed factory in Glenties could do little to relieve the hardship of smallholders in counties such as Fermanagh and Donegal.[74]

Generally then, the pressure of economic forces was towards consolidation, and only the introduction of land purchase legislation from the 1880s prevented the process from going further and radically transforming the whole structure of agricultural holdings in Ulster. Nevertheless, the large-scale reduction in the number of holdings and the continuing emigration and decline of population meant that the increasing rural wealth of this period was being shared by a progressively smaller number of people. In other words, the quarter of a century after the Famine saw a dramatic increase in both productivity and *per capita* income in Ulster. Not everyone shared in this or shared in it to the same degree. By and large, how well one did depended on how much land one had.[75] Ulster farms continued in the 1870s to be on average smaller than those in the rest of the country; of the 196,000 holdings in the province in 1871 exactly half were under fifteen acres. James Tuke was one of many observers who maintained that such farms were too small to support a family:

> It matters not whether a man has fixity of tenure, or being a peasant
> proprietor has no rent to pay, he cannot, unless he has some other source
> of income, live and bring up a family on the small farms under ten or
> fifteen acres of land, which form so large a proportion of the
> holdings in the west of Ireland.[76]

Tuke was referring particularly to the smallholders in west Donegal,
where farm sizes remained virtually unchanged between 1851 and
1881.[77] But even in east Ulster, despite its natural advantages, the
presence of manufacturing industry and the profitability of the widely
grown flax crop, life was difficult for the small tenant. Thomas
Shillington, a prominent tenant-right advocate, told the Bessborough
commission that 'if you take away the handloom weaving that is
rapidly leaving the country, the farmer cannot survive on ten acres'.[78]
Shillington's pessimistic analysis of the condition and prospects of
these small farmers is corroborated by a survey of rural life in
Northern Ireland in the 1940s which shows how, even with a system
of quotas and subsidies, they could still hardly make ends meet.[79]
Thus it is highly questionable whether any change in market conditions
or prices could ever have enabled smallholders along the west coast
of Donegal or in the hill country of Armagh, Tyrone and other
counties to attain any more than a frugal level of subsistence. For
them the prosperity of agriculture during the quarter of a century
after the Famine meant merely an easing of the relentless struggle to
hold body and soul together. And in times of crisis it was difficult to
imagine what would have been required in the way of legislation to
compensate such tenants for the loss of the goodwill of an indulgent
landlord.

On the other hand, the larger farmers — and even smallholders in
the most fertile areas — undoubtedly benefited from the new rural
prosperity. And by the 1870s there were more of them: between
1845 and 1881 the proportion of holdings of over fifteen acres
increased from one-third to over a half of the total. More significantly,
nearly a quarter of holdings by 1881 were over thirty acres, and with
a number of farmers having more than one holding the proportion
was almost certainly higher.[80] But consolidation combined with higher

agricultural prices, increased productivity and more livestock farming meant more than an increasingly prosperous tenantry: it meant also the emergence of a more numerous rural bourgeoisie who rapidly acquired both the paraphernalia and the ambitions traditionally associated with members of that class.

## THE RISING STANDARD OF LIVING

A number of developments testify to the general prosperity and advance in living standards of the tenant farmers during these years.

Deposits in all kinds of banks moved positively upwards from the 1860s. Both post office savings banks from their inception in 1862 and trustee savings banks, after suffering initially from the competition of post office savings, showed a steady yearly rise in deposits from 1866.[81] It was joint stock banks, however, which proved most popular with the tenant farmers — as many as 90 per cent of their depositors, it was claimed, were farmers[82]– and deposits in these provide a more accurate barometer of the state of agriculture and the general prosperity of the farming classes. Deposits and cash balances in these banks, after going down from £16 million to £13 million in the three years up to 1863, showed a continuous advance in every year after that up to 1876, when they reached nearly £33 million.[83] This prodigious increase in bank deposits may be partly explained by the growing confidence of rural society in the banking system.[84] But it is clear that Irish agriculture was generating increasing wealth during this period and that much of this was being accumulated in banks.[85] The growth of the dowry system — in general practice throughout Ulster by the 1860s[86]– reflected at one and the same time the changed economic conditions since the Famine and the greater wealth and higher expectations of the farming classes.

There was also during this same period a striking improvement in the general standard of rural housing. Table 1.1 shows that whereas in 1841 only about 20 per cent of families lived in first- or second-class housing, by 1881 every second family was accommodated in either a first-class or a second-class house with anything from five rooms upwards. Advertisements in the local press regularly detailed the good dwellings available with farms being offered for sale, and solid slated farmhouses with four, five and six bedrooms along with drawing room, parlour, kitchen and pantry for farms of twenty to thirty acres were not uncommon.[87]

Table 1.1 Number and percentage of families residing in each class of accommodation in the rural districts of Ulster 1841–81[88]

|      | 1ST CLASS | | 2ND CLASS | | 3RD CLASS | | 4TH CLASS | | TOTAL |
|------|-----|-----|-----|-----|-----|-----|-----|-----|-------|
|      | NO. | % | NO. | % | NO. | % | NO. | % | |
| 1841 | 3,582 | 0.9 | 78,522 | 19.9 | 173,009 | 43.9 | 139,398 | 35.3 | 394,511 |
| 1851 | 6,013 | 1.8 | 100,543 | 30.6 | 181,853 | 55.4 | 39,682 | 12.1 | 328.091 |
| 1861 | 7,550 | 2.4 | 112,138 | 35.2 | 172,800 | 54.3 | 25,679 | 8.1 | 318,167 |
| 1871 | 8,446 | 2.9 | 107,543 | 36.7 | 131.160 | 44.7 | 46,259 | 15.8 | 293,408 |
| 1881 | 11,433 | 4.3 | 117,696 | 43.9 | 129,822 | 48.4 | 9,236 | 3.4 | 268,187 |

Not only was the rural population of Ulster better housed by the 1870s, but the houses themselves were generally better furnished and equipped than they had been in the past. The contents of the dwelling on a twenty acre farm held at will outside Glenavy and offered for sale by an executor in 1872 included 'a rosewood cottage piano; walnut chiffonier; Spanish mahogany sideboard; a mahogany dining room suite upholstered in real leather; a handsome suite of walnut drawing room furniture upholstered in green silk; mahogany bookcase; walnut inlaid centre and occasional tables; a set of telescope dining tables; oil paintings and engravings' as well as tapestry, carpets, wardrobes, an eight-day clock, a barometer and a host of other items.[89] This was hardly typical of the household possessions of all farms, but similar lists appeared with such frequency in the local press — and indeed often with more numerous and more luxurious contents[90] — that one can come to the general conclusion that Ulster farmhouses were often extremely well furnished by any standards and that the material welfare of the tenant farmers, as measured by their possessions and the degree of comfort in which they lived, had greatly improved over the previous two decades.

Better housed, the farming classes of the 1870s were also better clothed and better fed than their predecessors of the 1840s and 1850s. William Prendergast, a public works inspector whose district included Fermanagh, Cavan and Monaghan — not by any means the most prosperous of the Ulster counties — reported in 1870 that 'among the farmers generally there is a taste for better clothes, food and furniture than were even thought of twenty years ago. The consumption of tea, coffee and sugar, as well as of bread and meat, has immensely increased'.[91] Prendergast was not alone in these views. Both James Godkin and William O'Connor Morris, who as special correspondents of the *Irish Times* and the London *Times* respectively travelled through the greater part of Ulster in 1869, also commented on the growing prosperity and more affluent lifestyle of the tenants; over the previous twenty years, O'Connor Morris observed, 'the consumption of almost every article that forms a luxury for the humble classes has increased in an extraordinary degree'.[92]

Support for these findings is provided by the expansion and increasing variety of retail businesses in the country towns, where 'the wonderfully multiplied shops' were said in the 1870s to be displaying 'articles of luxury in the way of food and dress which were undreamt of twenty years ago'.[93] In Coleraine, for example, the editor of one of the local papers claimed in 1871 that the farming prosperity had had the affect of 'doubling rents in our best business streets — the old effete shops giving place to more extensive improvements, and one vieing with another in chaste and costly designs of street architecture'. The upsurge in the business life of the town, he maintained, was clearly 'occasioned by a better and a more enlightened system of agriculture, as little of the increase of imports and exports can be attributed to an extension in our manufactories'.[94] This picture was repeated all over the province: Ballymena, Lurgan, Portadown, Ballyclare, Newry, Lisburn, and other towns were reported to be benefiting from the agricultural prosperity.[95] 'Commercial travellers that I have met for years at the same hotels in country towns', wrote William Prendergast, 'tell me that the shops depending on the rural population are doing an excellent trade.'[96] Even the seaside resorts shared in the general benefits as the rural classes began to make use of their gigs and jaunting cars in combination with the recently developed railway lines to take days and longer holidays at resorts such as Portrush, Newcastle, Rostrevor and Ballycastle. Portrush, for example, 'a fishing village of a dozen houses' in the early 1860s, had no fewer than six hotels by 1875.[97] And by the 1870s we are told that at Bundoran 'hundreds of women of the farming classes are seen bathing daily on the strand under the rocks at the north side, without any bathing boxes'.[98]

Other forms of entertainment also increased in popularity as the farming classes developed their own range of social activities. These included subscription balls — and later barn dances — concerts (professional and amateur), soirées, spelling bees, lectures, amateur drama, readings, recitations, bazaars and a host of other entertainments. 'The farmers' ball', Florence Mary McDowell tells us, 'was only one of the many dances during the Ballyclare Season ... Guests arrived on foot, in traps, side-cars and gigs.'[99] Dress was formal as fitted the occasion, with the girls in evening gowns and white gloves, while as time went on white ties for the men became more and more *de rigueur*. Classes for 'dancing, deportment and calisthenic exercises' were frequently advertised in the local press and regularly held in different parts of the province to prepare farmers' children for their new social roles: 'Each week the dancing master arrived ... and the children of minor gentry and of farmers round about congregated ... to learn their one-two-three-and-a-hop, or their simple one, two, rise.'[100] Nor were these dances purely frivolous forms of diversion: 'the young ladies knew very well that they were there not merely to dance, but to put their feminine charms in the shop window'.[101] And labourers — urban or rural — were of course rigorously excluded.[102] Even the small farmers held themselves superior to and apart from the labouring class, and marriage between the two classes was, to say the least, not encouraged.[103]

Concerts of all kinds proved increasingly popular with the farming classes. Amateur concerts were held all over the province by such societies as the Coleraine Choral Society, the Ballymena Choral Union, the Limavady Choral Society and the Coleraine Harmonic Society. Nor was it unusual for special trains to be arranged from towns such as Lisburn, Carrickfergus and Bangor calling at all stations in between for opera at the New Theatre Royal or grand vocal and orchestral concerts in the Ulster Hall in Belfast. Musical entertainment was an important part of the programme at various soirées held by different societies as well as recitations, readings and — a great favourite during the 1870s — spelling bees. Spelling bees, or competitions, originated in Cleveland in America in 1874 and quickly caught on in Ulster after their introduction here in 1875.[104] Not only were they a popular form of entertainment — often carrying as prizes such things as writing desks and other pieces of furniture — but they were also found to be both 'instructive' and 'very useful in stimulating to study'.[105]

This desire for self-improvement was a feature of much of the social activity of the period, and the very names of most of the societies which organised these functions reflected the serious nature and purpose of the people behind them: the Macosquin Mutual Improvement and Temperance Society, the Kilrea Literary Society, the Ballymoney Temperance and Benefit Society, the Stranocum Reading Society, the Coleraine Literary and Scientific Association, the Garvagh Young Men's Mutual Improvement Society, the Clogher, Comber and Portrush Mutual Improvement Societies — these were some of the plethora of societies which appeared from the 1860s. Farming societies also abounded and apparently felt obliged not only to promote ploughing matches and better farming, but also to arrange lectures and entertainment for their members. In short, the new agricultural prosperity from the middle of the century helped to stimulate both the social and the cultural aspirations of the farming classes, and the proliferation of literary, reading, scientific, choral and mutual improvement societies was a response to this.

The main avenue of social advancement for many was still of course through the more formal kind of education. Much of the credit for the decline of illiteracy in Ireland must be attributed to the national system of education introduced by the Whig chief secretary Stanley in the 1830s. Originally conceived as a non-denominational system, it had by the 1850s, largely as a result of persistent and at times fierce pressure from the protestant churches, especially the presbyterian church, begun to develop along denominational lines.[106] Despite the protestant opposition, however, and despite the growing reservations of the catholic hierarchy as the protestant demands were met, the system flourished and nowhere more than in Ulster where, after it had been remoulded to their liking, the presbyterians took full advantage of it to multiply the number of schools under their control.

As shown in Table 1.2, the number of national schools in Ulster virtually trebled between 1841 and 1881, while over the same period the number of pupils on their rolls increased fivefold. The rise in the number of pupils between 1851 and 1861, however, is inflated by the fact that whereas up to 1856 the number of children on the rolls was computed as of a specific date in the year, from 1857 the practice was adopted of calculating the returns on the basis of the total number who appeared on the rolls at any time during the school year.[107] Moreover, the average attendance figures, which are available only after 1855, make one cautious of overstating the degree to which education was reaching the mass of the population. Nevertheless, even allowing for the continuing inadequacies of the system — including irregular attendance, early leaving and an acute shortage of trained teachers — the table clearly reveals the rapid expansion of educational provision which took place in the middle decades of the century. It equally clearly shows the decisive impact of the system on the rate of illiteracy in the province: in 1841 some 41 per cent of all people of five years and upwards in Ulster could neither read nor write; by 1881 this figure had been cut by more than half, to just over 20 per cent.

Table 1.2. The number of national schools, the number and
average daily attendances of pupils and the rate of illiteracy
among five-year-olds and upwards in Ulster, 1841–81.[108]

| | NO. OF NATIONAL SCHOOLS | NO. OF PUPILS ON THEIR ROLLS | AVERAGE DAILY ATTENDANCE | % OF PEOPLE OF 5 YEARS AND UPWARDS WHO COULD NEITHER READ NOR WRITE |
|---|---|---|---|---|
| 1841 | 1,005 | 77,783 | | 41.0 |
| 1851 | 1,878 | 148,927 | | 35.0 |
| 1861 | 2,153 | 278,049 | 92,902 | 30.0 |
| 1871 | 2,561 | 360,027 | 122,075 | 26.4 |
| 1881 | 2,890 | 376,289 | 151,438 | 20.3 |

It is impossible to estimate — perhaps impossible to overestimate
— the effect of the spread of education on social relationships in
nineteenth-century rural Ireland. Admittedly the emphasis in the schools
was on obedience, discipline and hard work; 'their lessons', said one
of the commissioners of national education, were to 'prepare for
labour and direct to industry'.[109] But they did more: they taught people
to read, to write, perhaps to read newspapers — the number of
provincial papers nearly doubled between 1850 and 1880[110] — and
in many cases they taught them (quite accidentally, judging by the
methods used) to think. 'Modern education and modern journalism',
said John Carey, a prominent benefactor of the people of Toome,
'have taught the people that they should be more than serfs, more
than slaves.'[111]

Many farmers, however, had ambitions for their children which
ranged beyond reading newspapers or merely ceasing to be serfs. In
some cases the national schools appear to have given to those who
wanted it a good deal more than a basic grounding in the 'three Rs';
James Shanks, who was the leading light in the Portaferry tenant-
right association, attended the national school in Portaferry until he

was eighteen years of age and, according to his biographer, received an education up to the level of that given in the secondary schools.[112] But the development of 'higher tops' in Irish national schools to cater for those wanting to do secondary work appears to have been rare,[113] and well-to-do farmers, wanting more than an elementary education for their children and yet neither anxious nor wealthy enough to send them to English schools, looked rather to private schools to meet their educational needs. By 1881 there were 182 of these schools in Ulster, some more efficient than others, but all of them at least holding out the promise to farmers of enabling them to realise the social ambitions they had for their children.[114] Florence McDowell describes the early beginnings of one such school and, acutely perceptive as always, emphasises the social rather than the educational purpose of the establishment: in the village hall in Doagh, she says, 'was established by the Misses Douglas, the ladies' (or social climbers') School. Here for one pound per quarter, the children of the more pretentious parents learned English, Latin, Algebra and Superiority. This private school was later taken over by Miss Aiken, moved to Ballyclare, and developed into Ballyclare High School.' She noticed the same social pretension at the Private Collegiate School in Limavady, where she taught for a year.[115]

But, however much Florence McDowell might despise the shallow snobbery and social affectations of such schools, they were part of a general response to the demand for a higher and qualitatively different type of schooling to that provided by the national system.[116] The foundation in the second half of the nineteenth century of schools such as Coleraine Academical Institution (1860), Methodist College (1868), Princess Gardens School in Lisburn (1869, later moving to Belfast), St Dominic's High School (1870), Watt's Endowed School in Lurgan (1873), Bangor Grammar School (1876), Sullivan Upper in Holywood (1877), and Rainey Endowed at Magherafelt all reflect the same growing demand;[117] and so too does the rapid increase in entrants for examination under the new Intermediate Education Board set up in 1878 — within two years the numbers presenting themselves for examination had virtually doubled.[118] Part of this growth was vocational — with the civil service reforms in Britain, the establishment of the General Medical Council and similar bodies in other professions all setting new standards of entry — but the social factor was never absent, and it is hardly too much to assume that these schools and the education they provided helped both to fuel and to satisfy the social aspirations of the rural middle class.

Not all tenants shared in the general advance of living standards, just as not all benefited to the same extent, or in some cases at all, from the increased rural prosperity. The highest proportion and the highest number of first-class houses were still to be found in Counties Down and Antrim just as they had been in 1841; some 60 per cent of all houses in Down and over 50 per cent of those in Antrim were either first or second class by 1881. On the other hand, Donegal, which had the worst housing in 1841, was still bottom of the housing league in 1881, with over 60 per cent of its houses being third class and 65 per cent falling into the bottom two categories. Similarly Antrim, Down and Derry, which had the lowest rates of illiteracy in 1841, still had the lowest rates in 1881, while Donegal had the most serious problem in this respect with its rate of illiteracy in 1881 being practically twice that of Antrim in 1841.[119]

In short, those areas which had made the greatest advances by 1881 were the same areas where living standards were, relatively speaking, already high in 1841. And, not unexpectedly, these turn out to be the areas which were benefiting most from the new agricultural prosperity. Just as some regions still had a predominance of small tenants barely scraping a living from the soil, so too there were places — almost always the same places — where poor housing, illiteracy, poor diet and the absence of virtually all the material comforts continued to be the norm. James Tuke found tenants' dwellings in Donegal which his friends, who had had no experience of the west of Ireland, couldn't believe were human habitations, often with no furniture at all except straw or 'a miserable heap of rags' to sleep on.[120] Nonetheless, Tuke noticed that even in west Donegal, 'except in the very small farms, there are signs of real and permanent improvement in the country'.[121]

The fact was that while many tenants in different parts of the province remained poor and dependent, there had clearly emerged in Ulster a tenant class which was rapidly acquiring all the accoutrements of middle-class life; it is significant that in spite of the shortage of agricultural labour and the general decline of population there were still in Ulster in 1881 practically as many domestic servants as there had been in 1841.[122] Yet far from the tenants' material prosperity making them more content, the opposite proved to be the case. One tenant-right paper explained:

> Year after year servants' wages have been increasing. Food and clothes have become more expensive. The habits of society exact respectable dress and generous hospitality ... Though for a long time a slave in politics, the Ulster farmer is independent in social life. Each is inspired more or less by a sort of undefined feeling that he is as good as his neighbour. Hence spring laudable emulations — well-kept farms, clean and well-furnished houses, spruce jaunting cars, furbished harness, sleek horses, and the various home and personal belongings which are reckoned among the indispensable necessaries of well-to-do people and those who have kindred aspirations. The man who cannot procure them to his heart's content is in danger of falling a victim to discontent. He grows dissatisfied with his lot, especially if he has a young family anxious to push their fortune elsewhere.[123]

It was not only that expectations were rising. There was also and always the feeling of insecurity. The paradox was that the more tenants had the more they stood to lose, and nowhere was this more truly the case than in Ulster; here tenant farmers stood to lose not only their tenure, but also a tenant-right investment in the soil which by the 1870s was estimated to be worth not less than £20 million and possibly as much as £35 to £40 million.

## 2
# Tenant-right and Tenant Fears

The system of tenant-right — i.e. the right of an outgoing tenant to sell his interest in his holding — was not confined to Ulster; analogous customs were to be found in different areas and on many of the larger estates in the south.[1] But nowhere was tenant-right as strongly entrenched or as valuable as in the northern province, where tenants claimed a proprietorial interest in the soil on the grounds that it was they and not the landlords who had reclaimed and cultivated the land and made it what it was.[2] Thus in Ulster tenants looked on tenant-right as a disposable property to the extent of bequeathing it in wills and charging it with dowries and portions for younger children.[3] Even here, however, the practice varied from one part of the province to another and, indeed, sometimes from one estate to the next. But, as a general rule, it was to be found in its strongest and most comprehensive form in the north-eastern counties of Antrim, Down and Derry, and in an increasingly attenuated form as one moved south-west into mid-Ulster and the border counties of Fermanagh, Monaghan and Cavan.

There were occasional estates in Antrim and Down where the custom was not allowed, and others where its price was severely restricted. But recognition in this part of Ulster was almost universal, and tenant-right on some of the larger estates sometimes reached what seemed to outsiders to be astronomical figures.[4] It was also firmly established in Donegal, Derry, Tyrone and Armagh, where it again sold for fairly large sums of money.[5] This was not the case in Fermanagh, Monaghan and Cavan, where tenant-right existed only in a more modified form and where those landlords who allowed it did so only under certain well-defined restrictions. Frederick Wrench, who was land agent on several properties in Fermanagh, told the Bessborough commission that he didn't know of any estates in his neighbourhood where full tenant-right was permitted.[6] Similarly in Monaghan and Cavan, although there were occasionally estates where the full custom was found — as, for example, on the Clonmel and Verner estates in Monaghan — it was by no means universally recognised. 'Here it is altogether of a more modified and permissive character', reported the poor law inspectors, 'and is subject to much greater control and restriction than in the more northern counties.'[7]

The fact was that there was no single 'usage' or custom in Ulster, rather a variety of usages extending over the width and breadth of the province. Not surprisingly, then, contemporary definitions of the custom varied.[8] However, they usually contained part or all of the three main elements of 'continuous occupation, free sale and fair rents'. The 'right of free sale' was generally recognised as 'the fundamental principle' of tenant-right.[9] What the tenant was selling, however, was more open to dispute. Most people accepted that the tenant when selling his interest was selling more than his improvements, and many cases were quoted of farms being sold — sometimes for high figures — on which no improvements had been carried out, and even in some cases where the land had been impoverished.[10] Robert Johnston, the chairman of Co. Down, who had wide experience of the operation of the Ulster custom, maintained that improvements made up only part, and not the most important part, of the tenant-right claim.[11] According to Johnston — and this was a view which was shared by Lord Dufferin, Fitzherbert Filgate (the Marquis of Downshire's agent), and others — the incoming tenant was purchasing also the goodwill and the right to 'the peaceable enjoyment of the farm'.[12]

The right to continuous occupation was also widely regarded as an essential part of the custom.[13] The value of such occupation to the tenant depended of course on the rent he was paying. Hence the claim of the tenant-right advocates was almost invariably for continuous occupation at a fair rent. What a fair rent was, however, was more difficult to say, and it was in this area that most allegations about encroachments on the custom were made and most disputes arose. Tenants never disputed the right of landlords to make periodic revisions of rent,[14] and rents in Ulster do not appear to have been on average any lower than those in the rest of the country.[15] The only condition was that such revisions should not encroach on the tenants' interest. Yet it was widely acknowledged by both landlord and tenant representatives that the value of tenant-right varied proportionately to the rent, the common belief being that one shilling on the rent knocked twenty shillings off the value of the tenant-right.[16]

Some contemporaries, indeed, defined tenant-right as the capitalised value of the difference between a competition rent and what the tenant was actually paying: the difference, according to Lord Dufferin, 'between a fair rent and a rack rent'.[17] But most interested — or even hostile — observers were reluctant to define it only in these terms. Even where rents were known to be high, tenant-right sold, and the sums paid for it at times, especially on some of the smaller holdings, were obviously in excess of what the land was worth at any rent.[18] Manifestly, such purchasers were paying for more than exemption from a full rent; they were paying for the right of occupation, for security, for the actual possession of the land and all that went with it, including whatever social favours the landlord normally allowed.

It does not seem unreasonable to suggest that the custom was too complex to be defined in terms of rent alone, or to suggest that, consisting as it did of different elements, the value of these elements themselves should vary from time to time and from area to area. Thus in west Donegal, where the pressure on land remained intense and where prices were inflated, the payment was primarily for the possession of the land, and such possession or occupation sold at a high figure nearly regardless of the condition of the farm or of the improvements that had been made on it. In other areas, such as on the large estates of the Downshire family or Hill-Trevor in Co. Down or Lord Waveney's estate in Antrim, tenants were paying for security at comparatively low rents and often for improvements which had been carried out by their predecessors.

Certainly what is known about the origins of the custom indicates that something more than exemption from competition rents was being sought. Modern research suggests that the custom developed in the late eighteenth and early nineteenth centuries out of the practice of selling the remaining terms of a lease and the preference given to sitting tenants at the end of a lease.[19] As leases became less and less popular in the uncertain economic climate after 1815, landlords were prepared still to acquiesce in the sale of farms by one tenant to another as long as their rents were maintained. From the landlords' point of view, this had the added advantage of facilitating the removal of tenants in difficulties and of ensuring that all arrears were paid.

The change in market conditions from the 1830s and more particularly from the 1850s influenced the situation in two ways: first, the tenant-right itself became more valuable; and secondly, landlords increasingly saw it as an obstacle to both the maximisation of rents and the consolidation of farms. With the prosperity and rising agricultural prices of the post-Famine period, tenant-right rose steadily in value so that by 1877 it was estimated to average between seventeen and twenty-five years' purchase, as opposed to between ten and fifteen years' purchase at the time of the Devon commission.[20] William Shaw, Lord Annesley's agent, told the Bessborough commission that tenant-right on the Annesley estate had gone up from £10–15 per acre to £25–40 per acre over the previous twenty years.[21] On the Hertford estates in Down and Antrim, where small shopkeepers as well as farmers competed for holdings, it was reckoned in the 1870s to be worth three times what it had been worth in 1845; and on the Fishmongers' estate in Derry it was claimed to have doubled in value over the same period.[22]

Numerous other examples of the enhanced value of tenant-right by the 1870s could be given, varying like the custom itself from area to area; but there was practically unanimous agreement on the one central fact that its value — i.e. the value of the tenant's interest in the soil — was substantially greater by the 1870s than it had been in the pre-Famine period. Gladstone in introducing his land bill in 1870 put its value at £20 million, but this was a figure which had been quoted by John Hancock, Lord Lurgan's agent, some twenty years beforehand, and Robert Donnell, a leading tenant-right lawyer, claimed in 1874 that tenant-right in Ulster was worth between £35 and £40 million.[23] In 1869, James Godkin, on the basis of estimates given by the agent, calculated that tenant-right on the Hertford estate alone was worth between £500,000 and £600,000.[24] There is, of course, no way in which the exact value of tenant-right in Ulster can be computed, but what is clear is that by the 1870s the tenants had an interest in their farms which was too great to be left dependent on the goodwill of the landlords. There was, moreover, mounting evidence that such goodwill could no longer be relied upon, and that landlords in general were anxious to curtail if not abolish the custom.[25]

Not all landlords, however, shared in this antipathy to tenant-right. Many were prepared to support it because they believed it contributed to good landlord–tenant relations. Others were less circumspect in their judgement, attributing to it not only the tranquillity but also the prosperity of the northern province.[26] Ellison Macartney, independent Conservative MP for Tyrone from 1874 and owner of estates in Tyrone and Antrim, claimed that 'no district in the north of Ireland where tenant-right did not exist was superior in any way to any district where it did exist'.[27] And the Marquis of Headfort's agent, Major Dalton, attributed the greater prosperity of one of two adjoining estates which he managed to tenant-right, which was not permitted on the other less thriving property.[28] In short, many landlord representatives were at one with tenant spokesmen and others in believing that tenant-right conferred advantages on landlord and tenant alike; it gave tenants a sense of security, stimulated improvements, secured rents for the landlord, produced contentment and social harmony, and was generally held to be responsible for the superior economic condition of the northern province.

However, this view of the merits of tenant-right was not held by the majority of landlords in Ulster. 'It is unquestionable', wrote one poor law inspector in 1870, 'that the result of the experience landlords have had in Ulster of the practical operation of the tenant-right custom, has been to render them, generally speaking, more or less adverse to it.'[29] The Marquis of Dufferin, for example, thought that the custom was prejudicial both to rents and to the general prosperity of the province, often causing the incoming tenant to exhaust what capital he had or encumber himself by paying an excessive price with money borrowed at an exorbitant rate.[30] Other landlords simply looked on it as an impediment to consolidation and economic rents.[31] It was widely believed that the presence of tenant-right on an estate materially diminished its value, and the potential for increasing rents at the expense of tenant-right was often held out as an inducement to purchasers in the landed estates court.[32]

But landlords, however hostile to the custom, were hesitant about directly interfering with it, deterred, it was claimed, by 'the pressure of public opinion'. No doubt many landlords were unwilling to court the loss of popularity, respect and perhaps political influence that went with disregard of tenant rights, but 'the pressure of public opinion' was often merely a euphemism for the threat of agrarianism. 'There can be no doubt', reported the poor law inspectors, 'that any systematic attempt on an extensive scale to destroy the Ulster tenant-right would be attended with serious danger to the tranquillity of the country.' This echoed earlier evidence which had been given to the Devon commission and was a view widely held in Ulster.[33]

Yet, though few landlords dared defy public opinion by openly denying tenant-right, at the same time many tried to weaken and undermine it in more gradual ways. Tenant-right spokesmen dated the first systematic encroachments on tenant-right from the 1830s,[34] and the fact that it was in 1835 that the first attempt was made to secure some kind of legislative protection for the tenant interest would suggest that this date was not an arbitrarily chosen one. Certainly from the 1830s Ulster landlords had more reason to want to curtail the custom: in the first place the abolition of the forty shilling freehold franchise in 1829 and the introduction of a higher qualification supplied a political motive for the amalgamation of farms; and, secondly, the movement of agricultural prices from that time encouraged livestock farming and consolidation. There was, too, the additional factor from the 1840s that the burden of rates was thrown wholly on to landlords in the case of holdings valued at under £4. In these circumstances, it was understandable that an increasing number of landlords should want to get rid of small tenants, consolidate farms, and share in the greater prosperity of agriculture. Tenant-right, as we have seen, was regarded by many landlords as an obstacle to the attainment of all these objectives.

But while it was increasingly in the interests of landlords to curtail the custom, landlord encroachments before 1845 were not such as to provoke general unrest among northern tenants; none of the three tenant compensation bills introduced by Sharman Crawford between 1835 and 1843 evoked much interest among the Ulster tenantry.[35] This situation was changed by the Devon commission which first focused attention on tenant-right, highlighting the dangers it presented to the property interests of landlords and making it the subject of public debate in both England and Ireland. James McKnight and others believed that Ulster landlords began after the Famine to act on the advice of the Devon commission, and that from that time efforts were made, more determinedly than ever before, to curtail and restrict tenant-right.[36] Lord Bessborough, too, in his report accepted that the campaign against tenant-right became more systematic after the Devon report.[37] What is certain is that after Devon and after the overwhelming defeat of Crawford's bill to legalise tenant-right in 1847, Ulster tenants suddenly became aware of the weakness of their position, and this along with the fall in agricultural prices in the late 1840s gave rise to the formation of tenant-right associations and the tenant agitation of this period.[38]

This campaign was not sustained, declining as it did with the new prosperity of the 1850s. But complaints about landlord encroachments on tenant-right continued over the next two decades. W.D. Henderson and other tenant spokesmen claimed that it was in this post-Famine period, and especially during the 1860s, that 'much of the former good feeling between landlord and tenants in Ulster had disappeared' and that the most serious infringements of tenant-right had been made.[39] The main dangers to tenant-right, as the tenants saw it, were evictions, increases of rent, the introduction of estate rules, and finally, and perhaps most important, the sales of estates in the landed estates court. All of these threatened the greatly enhanced investment which tenants had in tenant-right by the 1860s and lie at the root of much of the tenant unease of this period.

## EVICTIONS, RENTS AND ESTATE RULES

Of all the threats to the tenant's interest, eviction was far and away the most drastic, the most sensational, and the most emotive. Yet evictions in Ireland were infrequent after 1854, and there were fewer in Ulster than in the rest of the country. It was noticeable that northern tenant witnesses to the Bessborough commission hardly mentioned evictions as a grievance, and when questions were asked of others, there was almost unanimous agreement that tenants were only put out of their holdings if they failed to pay their rent.[40] The land act of 1870 had, of course, made it that much more difficult for tenants to be summarily evicted, but even before 1870 there was general agreement that, except for accumulated arrears of rent, evictions were uncommon.[41]

A parliamentary paper which was issued in 1881 gave for each province and county the total number of evictions that had come to the notice of the Royal Irish Constabulary in each of the years from 1849 to 1880.[42] This shows that the number of evictions declined sharply after 1850, reaching a more even level from 1854. A note on the return states that the readmissions given for the years 1870–80 refer exclusively to those readmitted as tenants and do not include those who went back into their holdings as caretakers. If we accept Barbara Solow's estimate that a third of those evicted in the 1870s were readmitted as caretakers,[43] we arrive at a total of 2,973 permanent evictions in Ulster for the period 1854 to 1879, or 114 evictions per year. Even allowing for the fact that not all evictions were brought to the notice of the constabulary and that Solow's estimate of the number readmitted as caretakers may be high, this indicates a fairly low rate of eviction, and suggests that for the huge majority of tenants in Ulster the loss of a holding in this way was an unlikely and remote possibility for most of this period; in fact, the chances of an Ulster tenant being evicted in an average year were less than one in a thousand.

The return also shows that the rate and number of evictions in Ulster — up to 1880 at any rate — were consistently lower than in the other three provinces. Whereas holdings over one acre in Ulster made up 36 per cent of the total for the entire country, less than 17 per cent of all evictions took place in the northern province. Although readmissions in the north were proportionally lower — 18.6 per cent as against 24.4 per cent for the remainder of the country[44] — Ulster still had an eviction rate of less than half the national average. Part of the reason for this lay in the greater prosperity of the province, part in the better landlord–tenant relations, but part also lay in the fact that tenants in the north were often — perhaps usually — allowed to sell their tenant-right before the actual eviction took place. On the Marquis of Waterford's estate outside Limavady, for example, evictions were 'unknown', but only because if a tenant did fall badly into arrears proceedings were taken against him and he was forced to sell out. This was the practice also on the Downshire and Annesley estates and indeed on most of the large estates in Ulster.[45]

Within Ulster the number and rate of evictions varied broadly from one county to another. An examination of the number of evictions in relation to the number of holdings shows that the lowest rates of eviction were in Down, Derry and Antrim, the three strongest tenant-right counties and the three most prosperous, while the highest rates were in Donegal, Cavan and Fermanagh, the last two probably the counties where, along with Monaghan, tenant-right was weakest. Evictions in general, of course, tended to go up in years of agricultural difficulty, and in west Donegal times were always difficult and the small tenants, living perilously close to subsistence level even in good years, were always more likely to fall into arrears than elsewhere. Father John McFadden, parish priest of Gweedore, addressing a tenant-right demonstration at Letterkenny in 1870, claimed that he himself had conducted over 1,300 people to the emigrant ships: 'Some people will say evictions are rare. I say that in Donegal it is not so'.[46]

Evictions, then, were more frequent in Donegal than in any other northern county. But evictions anywhere and anytime cast long shadows, and the years of the Famine period and events such as the notorious Derryveagh clearances of 1861 were not easily forgotten. Moreover, if tenants were only occasionally evicted, the continuing use of notices to quit — even after 1870 when they had to carry a 2s 6d stamp — meant that they were never allowed to forget the insecurity of their tenure. It was this sense of insecurity, this liability to eviction and to the threat of eviction, which constituted one of the principal grievances of the tenants.

The main complaints in Ulster were not against what the landlords did, but against what they had the power to do. It was generally accepted by tenants and tenant-right advocates that northern landlords rarely abused their powers, and most tenant-right speakers paid tribute to the general restraint of landlords in the matter of evictions. The evil, it was felt, lay 'not in the exercise, but in the possession of this power on the part of the landlords'.[47] The tenants' primary concern was that they had 'capital and interest in the land estimated as high as £30 million' which 'lay at the mercy of the landlords, with nothing to prevent them appropriating it to themselves but their own sense of justice, the force of custom, and the power of public opinion'.[48] Appropriation by eviction may have been rare, but it was always a possibility — perhaps a remote possibility, but still a possibility. Tenants with limited resources were always at greater risk. But no tenant could have full peace of mind until the absolute powers which landlords had in such matters were curtailed.

Of much greater concern to the larger and more prosperous tenants was the threat posed to tenant-right by increases of rent. 'Disturbance of tenancy by ejectment', it was maintained, 'is not the first evil of Ulster. The first evil of Ulster is disturbance of the tenancy by adding to the rental.'[49] This was a recurrent theme in tenant-right speeches throughout the 1860s and 1870s, and tenant representatives in their evidence to the Bessborough commission dwelt on the general uneasiness and sense of insecurity induced by the raising of rents. Arthur McMurrough Kavanagh, an Irish landlord member of the commission, was convinced by this evidence that in Ulster at any rate 'the exercise of the power of raising rent on the part of landlords, where unduly used, was the grievance most severely felt'.[50]

Yet William O'Connor Morris, touring Ireland in 1869, found rents in the north 'decidedly on a low average', and 'heard hardly a single complaint of rack-renting'.[51] And Samuel McElroy, editor of the *Ballymoney Free Press* and a leading tenant-right activist, told the national land conference meeting in Belfast in 1874 that 'on the whole, rent in Ulster is moderate'.[52] The poor law inspectors also reported that rents on average were reasonable and that there was little evidence of rack-renting. This was the conclusion also of the Bessborough commission.[53] Modern research has more or less confirmed these findings. Barbara Solow maintains that rents were moderate and fairly stable in the quarter century after the famine and that rents in Ulster were slow to rise and were felt to be low or reasonable by many tenants'.[54] W.E. Vaughan has also argued that Irish rents including rents in Ulster were not exorbitantly high, that rent increases were not frequent and, furthermore, that whereas the value of Irish agricultural output rose by 70 per cent between the early 1850s and 1870s, rents were increased by only 20 per cent.[55]

Although these general conclusions have been disputed by Cormac Ó Gráda and Michael Turner,[56] all the qualitative evidence is that the tenants were doing better in the post-Famine period and taking a bigger share of agricultural output than they had in the past. Nevertheless, rents still absorbed a very high proportion both of the value of agricultural output (according to Vaughan, some 44 per cent in the 1850s, 33 per cent in the 1870s) and of the tenants' income. Moreover, while landlord investment in Ireland generally was low, investment in Ulster, where landlords feared that their improvements might be sold as part of the tenant-right, was lower than the national average.[57] Tenant-right was a disincentive to landlord investment, and this in itself lent credence to the tenant belief that it was they 'who had brought the barren waste of Ulster into cultivation' and made the province what it was.[58]

There were, however, more specific grievances with regard to rent. When Samuel McElroy in his address to the national tenant-right conference in 1874 said that 'on the whole, rent in Ulster is moderate', he went on to qualify this by stating that 'in this case, as in others, the exceptions are grievous and unbearable'.[59] There were properties where rent raising was arbitrary, frequent and often excessive, and there were cases of rent being imposed on improvements carried out by the tenants.[60] And while the national average increase of rent in the quarter century after the famine may have been modest — 20 per cent according to Vaughan — there were estates and holdings within estates where increases were substantially greater than this. Rents on the Leitrim estate in Donegal went up by some 60 per cent, while over half the increases of rent on both the Gosford and Hall estates in Armagh and Down were over 40 per cent.[61] And rents on Major Gray's estates in Antrim were put up by well over 50 per cent in 1875, with the rents on some of the farms being more than doubled; one rent for instance went up from £24 to £66, another from £42 to £92.[62]

The main point is that while rents may on average have been moderate, the level of rents was uneven, falling more severely on some tenants than on others, and rent increases were in many cases arbitrary and irregular. Northern tenant representatives made few complaints to the Bessborough commission about the general level of rents; they dwelt rather on rent increases and the effect these were having on the value of tenant-right. This was their primary concern. For a tenant on a tenant-right estate, a rent increase was a bit like a person having his mortgage repayments increased and his house devalued at one and the same time. The evidence of Thomas Shillington, chairman of the Armagh Tenant Farmers' Association, was typical:

> You think that the effect of raising rents in the north has been more or less to interfere with the tenant-right? The effect has been to reduce the value of the tenant-right, and it has interfered with the comfort and contentment of the farmers and made them discontented, and produced a great deal of agitation and discontent with the existing state of things.[63]

Northern tenants were also particularly worried about what they claimed to be the new and growing practice of increasing rents at the time of sale. This had obviously a direct and harmful effect on the value of tenant-right, taking, according to McElroy, 'from ten to twenty per cent out of the tenant's pocket at one haul'.[64] One witness after another gave examples to Bessborough of rent being raised at the time of sale, thus lowering the value of the tenant's interest.[65] The perennial fear was that if the landlord's power to do this was not controlled in some way, then it would merely be a question of time before the Ulster custom disappeared altogether.

In one sense, recent research has simply confirmed what was well known at the time: that the majority of landowners were not rack-renting and avaricious. These findings were clearly stated in the Bessborough report and were acknowledged by many of the leading tenant-right advocates of the day. It was not the majority of landlords in Ulster that the tenant-right party was concerned about; it was the minority who abused their position and, more particularly, a system which allowed them to do so. What the Ulster tenants were objecting to was not the general level of rents, nor even the fact that these were periodically increased, but rather the tendency of landlords to increase them at the time of sale and, secondly, their liability to have them increased at any time. Their prime consideration was the value of their tenant-right which was totally dependent on the goodwill of the landlord. The examples of rack-rents and untimely and excessive revisions of rent, which the northern tenant representatives quoted at meetings and gave to various investigatory commissions and committees, were never intended to prove either that rents in general were exorbitant or that landlords in general were greedy and rapacious — indeed, the complaints were often accompanied by unsolicited testimonials to the generosity and indulgence of most landlords — rather they were intended to illustrate the defects in the system of land tenure and to show how vulnerable the tenants were under the system. 'Our complaint', said one tenant, 'is not of the landlords, it is of the land law; it is in an unsettled state, and it gives to one man the power of appropriating to himself in one way or another our property.'[66] This was the essence of the problem: rents were directly related to the value of tenant-right, and because of this they were perhaps an even greater source of grievance in Ulster than they were in the rest of the country.

Estate rules were also seen as a major threat to the tenant's tenant-right investment in the soil. Virtually all landlords tried — in the interests of themselves, their estates, and indeed their tenants — to exercise at least some control over sales of tenant-right; almost all these attempts were seen by tenants as encroachments on the Ulster custom and almost all of them affected to some degree its value. Broadly speaking, estate rules can be divided into those which set out the conditions of sale of tenant-right, and those which more directly limited its price.

It was common practice even in the strongest tenant-right counties for the incoming tenant to be approved by the landlord. Many proprietors also insisted that sales of tenant-right should be by private treaty rather than public auction and that the right of pre-emption should be given to adjoining tenants.[67] Taken together, all these conditions of sale could seriously restrict tenant-right, even on those estates where it was otherwise openly acknowledged. Landlords who imposed such rules were trying to prevent the worst abuses of tenant-right without at the same time destroying it altogether. On the one hand, they stopped short of specifying an upper limit for tenant-right and thus removing all incentive to improvement. On the other hand, they hoped that by controlling the price indirectly through various conditions of sale, a situation would be created in which the tenant could be rewarded for his industry and his improvements without at the same time exacting a price from the incoming tenant which would subject the latter to the equivalent of a rack-rent.[68]

Other landlords, however, were more hostile to the whole principle of tenant-right and more open in their opposition to it. These, while finding it impossible to abolish the custom altogether, often sought to limit its price, and it was this practice which above all others caused the most serious discontent among the tenants, representing in their view a direct and unjustifiable attack on their interest in the soil.[69] Setting a ceiling on the price of tenant-right was common practice in Fermanagh, Monaghan and Cavan, but it was also present — and, according to tenant spokesmen, being increasingly adopted — throughout the rest of the province. In Derry, for instance, the Ironmongers' company introduced a rule in 1860 restricting prices to ten years' purchase. There was a £15 per acre rule on the Hall and Close estates in Counties Down and Armagh. In Co. Down, tenant-right was limited to £10 per acre on Lord de Ros' estate and to £5 per acre on Lord Bangor's estate, and in Co. Antrim several landlords tried to introduce a £10 limit.[70]

These attempts to limit the price of tenant-right were not always successful, being frequently defeated by the practice of making *sub rosa* payments. This, according to Thomas Shillington, was the 'ordinary practice on estates where such a rule exists'.[71] Nevertheless, unsuccessful or not, the attempts to control prices were seen by tenants as a threat to their tenant-right interest. Tenants paying part, and often a major part, of their money outside the office did not have the same security for their investment as those whose purchases were given the official approval of the landlord or his agent. But, apart altogether from this consideration, the increasing efforts being made to curb tenant-right prices were seen by the tenants as evidence of the general hostility of landlords to the custom and of their determination to seize every opportunity to restrict it. 'There appears', reported one poor law inspector whose district comprised the main tenant-right counties, 'to be a growing feeling amongst the tenantry in some districts that there is an increasing desire on the part of some landlords to curtail the custom.'[72] It was not only the tenants who believed this; William O'Connor Morris noticed 'a general tendency to abridge the right gradually', while the poor law inspectors themselves found that landlords generally looked on the custom with disfavour and were anxious to end it.[73]

Not unnaturally, such attempts to restrict tenant-right and the growing belief that landlords in general were averse to it led to increasing alarm amongst the tenants; as O'Connor Morris pointed out, it took only two or three instances of landlord encroachment or indeed just the rumours of such cases to cause widespread discontent.[74] In one sense, the actual infringements were less important than the fears and insecurity they created. Security and harmonious landlord–tenant relations were the usual concomitants of tenant-right, but they weren't necessarily corollaries of the custom. In fact quite the reverse: the confusion of landlord and tenant interests in the soil should in theory have led to more tension and uncertainty. The successful working of tenant-right was based on a tradition of good landlord–tenant relations, and the custom could only work when landlord–tenant relations were good. Once suspicions began to grow about landlord intentions, and once some landlords, even a minority, began to attack the custom, the confidence of the tenants and the social harmony between them and the landlords, without which the custom could not work, began to diminish. In short, any violation of tenant-right or even the suspicion that landlords wanted to destroy it had, from the tenant's point of view, serious implications for a custom based essentially on trust, and rendered it essential for them to secure some kind of legislative protection.

## THE LANDED ESTATES COURT

In the parliamentary debates on Gladstone's first land bill in 1870 several speakers, including Gladstone himself, referred to the stimulus given to the land agitation in Ireland by the operation of the landed estates court, and William Johnston, the independent Orange MP for Belfast and self-appointed spokesman for the Ulster tenants in the land bill debates, identified the sale of estates through this court as the greatest single source of danger to the tenant-right custom in Ulster.[75] Tenant fears with regard to infringements of tenant-right or its abolition through eviction, increased rents or the introduction of office rules were, it was generally believed, more likely to materialise on estates sold in the landed estates court.

Established in 1849, the encumbered estates court, as it was then called, was intended to facilitate the transfer of bankrupt estates to new and more efficient landlords, many of whom, it was expected, would come from England with the capital and skill necessary to revitalise Irish agriculture.[76] These expectations proved to be ill-founded. The act did not result in the infusion of new capital, the vast majority of purchasers being not British capitalists but Irishmen;[77] nor did it have any palpable effect on the overall standard of Irish agriculture. It did, however, facilitate the sale of estates and over the next three decades land changed hands in Ireland in substantial quantities. By the beginning of the Land League crisis in 1879 property to the value of £50 million had been sold through the landed estates court.[78] A large proportion of this was in the northern province where, with the prospect of new owners either ignoring or restricting tenant-right, tenants had a great deal more to fear from such sales than those in the south. Between 1865 and 1875 over 28 per cent of all land sold in the landed estates court was in Ulster — altogether about a quarter of a million acres or about 5 per cent of the total landholdings in the province.[79] Taking into account the heavier sales in the years immediately following the court's inception, it can be calculated that nearly 25 per cent of all land in Ulster changed ownership in the period 1849–1879. Many of the properties sold were comparatively small, but the occasional sale of larger estates such as the Mountcashel estate in Antrim, the Conolly estate in Donegal, the Waterford estate in Derry, and the Ker and Dufferin estates in Down showed that no estate and no landowning family was immune from the pressures of time or economics. Given the implications of these sales and what the tenants had at stake, the rate of transfer of land in Ulster during this thirty-year period can hardly have been reassuring to tenants whose interest in the soil depended almost entirely on the goodwill of the landlords.

Conflicting opinions are held as to the character of the men who purchased these lands. The traditionally most widely held view was that they were for the most part local speculators, shopkeepers and traders who had done well out of the Famine and whose first object was to get the best return they could on their money. More recently, however, it has been suggested that a large proportion of the land, perhaps the bulk of it, was bought by solvent landlords, and that the new owners were neither better nor worse agriculturists or landlords than their predecessors.[80]

What is certain — and what was perhaps more important both at the time and in the context of the argument being put forward here — is that these new landlords were believed to be more greedy and ruthless than the old landlords. Their estates were singled out by representatives of all shades of opinion as those on which landlord powers were most likely to be abused and tenant-right ignored.[81] It was not only tenants and tenant representatives who held these views; they were shared by journalists, by independent observers, by judges and by government officials alike. James Godkin reported that 'the best and most indulgent landlords, the most genial and generous are unquestionably the old nobility ... The worst, the most harsh and exacting, are those who have purchased under the landed estates court — strangers to the people, who think only of the percentage on their capital.' Finlay Dun discovered that it was these estates which illustrated 'all the evils of extravagant rents, insecurity of tenure, and ruthless appropriation of tenants' improvements'.[82] A.G. Richey, William O'Connor Morris, Barry O'Brien, Hugh de Fellenberg Montgomery, George Shaw-Lefevre, John Stuart Mill and numerous others all subscribed at one time or another to the same view.[83] And the poor law inspectors, in their report on landlord–tenant relations in 1870, repeatedly drew attention to the unsatisfactory position of tenants on these estates: 'Upon no other point is the testimony of all classes so unanimous as that the greatest hardships, both as regards evictions and exorbitant increase of rents, have been inflicted by purchasers in these courts.'[84] Even the Irish Land Committee added to the chorus of condemnation of these parvenu landlords whose acts had brought discredit and opprobrium to the whole of the landowning class.[85]

These new landlords were, of course, convenient scapegoats for the misdeeds of the landed class especially as, strictly speaking, many of them did not themselves belong to this class at all. Yet the allegations made against them were so frequently voiced and came from so many quarters that one can hardly doubt that they had some basis of truth. Many of them were, at any rate, well authenticated. The poor law inspectors reported specific cases of rent being doubled and trebled by the new owners, of tenants being deprived of the value of their improvements and of tenant-right not being recognised.[86] Finlay Dun found that many of those who had purchased parts of the Conolly estate in Donegal had 'repeatedly raised' their rents, 'sometimes to much more than double their former figure'.[87] Other cases were reported in the local press, some receiving wide publicity at the time, many others coming to light only in the hearings to fix judicial rents under the land act of 1881. In some the main complaint was that the new proprietors had directly prohibited the sale of tenant-right on their properties; A. Collum and C.W. Ogilby, for example, had each purchased part of the Belmore estate in 1851 and 1853 respectively, and both had refused to allow tenant-right even though unrestricted right of sale had formerly been the custom on the estate.[88]

But the main charge levelled against purchasers in the landed estates court was that they strove to maximise the income from their investment in land as they would from any other purely commercial undertaking, and that this was done at the expense of the interest and the improvements of the tenants. A typical example, which was widely discussed in the papers in 1866–7, was that of the Crossley estate, a small estate in Co. Down which was bought in the landed estates court by John Finlay, a merchant of Ann Street, Belfast. Virtually all the improvements on the estate had been carried out by the tenants and the price of tenant-right on the property was put at nearly £30 an acre. As soon as Finlay took possession, he increased the rents from between 31 and 36 shillings to 50–60 shillings an acre and instituted eviction proceedings against those who refused to pay; apart from this he took very little interest in the estate, visiting it only five times in fifteen years.[89]

Other purchasers showed an equal determination to enhance the return on their investments. Joseph Biggar, the father of the nationalist MP, purchased an estate in Co. Antrim in 1864 for £7,900 and immediately put the rents up by nearly 45 per cent, thus giving himself an annual return of 7.5 per cent on his investment instead of the original 5 per cent.[90] John Raphael purchased two townlands of the Broadisland estate of D.S. Ker, on which tenant-right sold at about £20 an Irish acre, and promptly served the tenants with notices that the rents were to be raised by some 30 per cent.[91] George Graham paid £2,300 for one of the townlands on the Mountcashel estate in Antrim, which was sold in 1850 and on which many of the tenants held leases. As the leases expired Graham pushed the rents up so that by the late 1870s he was getting an annual return of nearly 18 per cent on the original investment as against about 5 per cent at the time of purchase.[92] Tenants on this property were among the first to apply to have judicial rents fixed under the land act of 1881 and had their rents reduced by 35 per cent, the sub-commissioners concluding that they 'were satisfied that the tenants of these holdings have been severely rack-rented, and that the increased rents which they have been forced to pay to a large extent represent the reclamation and drainage improvements which they have, unaided by the landlord, effected upon their holdings'.[93]

Of course, as against those who abused their position there were many purchasers who respected the tenants' interests, although, not surprisingly, less was heard or written about these. Some, such as Charles Deazley, a doctor from Pembroke who bought the 5,500-acre Lettermacard estate on Gweebarra Bay from Thomas Conolly in 1867, generally let things go on much as they were on the estate.[94] In other words, Deazley was neither better nor worse than his predecessors. Then, too, there were others such as J.G. Richardson, the linen manufacturer who purchased Lord Charlemont's Bessbrook estate in 1865, and John Young, a leading Ballymena merchant, whose father had purchased part of the Mountcashel estate in 1850, who acted in the best traditions of hereditary ownership, taking an active interest in the general welfare of their tenants, making abatements of rent and providing work for them in the difficult years at the end of the 1870s.[95]

Two of the largest northern purchasers in the landed estates court were James Chaine and James Musgrave, both from manufacturing backgrounds. Chaine paid £64,000 for the Cairncastle estate at Larne in 1864 and £22,000 for a second estate at Oldstone, Killead, and over the next two years invested large sums of money in developing Larne harbour. By 1871 he had, at his own expense, built two new quays and was largely responsible for the establishment of the Larne and Stranraer packets. He also promoted at his own cost a new railway from Larne to Ballyclare and was the principal contributor to another line from Larne to Ballymena.[96] Similarly heavy expenditure was undertaken by James and John Musgrave, wealthy Belfast iron-founders, who bought four Donegal estates in the landed estates court during the 1860s and 1870s. In all, their property covered some 52,000 acres in south-west Donegal with a population of over 8,000 people. Up to August 1879, the Musgraves spent about £12,000 on the building of piers, the reclamation of land and various agricultural improvements, with about half of this going directly on wages. And over the following three years they laid out another £10,000 with an additional £8,000 coming from public money as a result of their efforts and subscriptions. Within a period of fifteen years, they had been either directly or indirectly responsible for the expenditure of some £30,000 on improving these estates, making them more accessible and creating employment for the inhabitants without at any stage increasing the rents.[97]

The Musgraves were classical examples of manufacturing wealth moving into the country. They, like Chaine, or John Mulholland the linen manufacturer who bought estates in Antrim and Down, or William Tillie the Derry shirt manufacturer who purchased six townlands of the Waterford estate near Limavady, or Thomas McClure the Belfast merchant who purchased the Belmont estate, were investing primarily in authority, prestige and status, perhaps even the makings of a political career or, more ambitious still, the first step towards a public honour if not a knighthood. Thus they were prepared to accept lower returns from their land purchases than they would have expected from any other form of investment. Other smaller, less affluent purchasers in the landed estates court, like the smaller landlords among the old landowning class, could afford neither to entertain the same ambitions nor to show the same generosity towards their tenants. Generally speaking, the smaller the purchaser the less considerate and more exacting he tended to be. At the other extreme to the Musgraves were those who purchased land in almost minute portions, often the residues of estates containing sometimes the holdings of the smallest and poorest tenants. The people who purchased these tended to be local traders, shopkeepers and petty capitalists, the so-called 'gombeen' men who above all others had the reputation of exacting the last penny and more from their tenants; they were, said Judge Flanagan, 'the most merciless, the most avaricious, and the worst class of landlords that can by possibility be put over an unfortunate class of tenants'.[98]

No doubt many of these men were every bit as despotic as Flanagan described them. But, for the majority of purchasers in the landed estates court, the desire to make their investments pay was not necessarily a dishonourable one, and it was understandable that they should be anxious to raise rents above levels which had already in many cases bankrupted the previous owners. Clearly changes in ownership of land were not always for the worse and were frequently for the better, and the more perceptive of the contemporary observers of the Irish land question recognised and acknowledged this. Finlay Dun wrote in 1880:

> Facilities for the acquisition of land during the last twenty-five years have, however, also introduced in many districts a most valuable race of landlords, who by precept and example have done much to improve the country. They have ... demonstrated how much can be done by judicious outlay, not only in developing the resources of the land, but in finding the much-wanted regular employment for the labouring population, and in advancing their social condition.[99]

The fact was that the new landlords, like the old landlords, were a mixture of good and bad, and it is perhaps safer and more accurate to generalise about large and small landlords than about old and new. It is significant in this respect that the poor law inspectors and others when discussing estate practices tended to group 'small and newly purchased estates' into one and same category.[100] Smaller landlords, even among the established landowning class, tended to be more commercial and to appear more grasping simply because they generally could not afford to be as benevolent or altruistic as the larger landowners. Smaller owners predominated among the new landlords, and this, at least partly, explains their reputation. Few self-made men had the capital to purchase on the same scale as the Musgraves, and the result was that when extensive properties were sold off they were usually divided into a number of lots as happened, for example, in the case of the 37,000-acre Waterford estate at Limavady which was sold in 1871 in 148 separate lots, or the Meredith estate in Down which was sold in 1869 in fifty-seven lots.[101] During the first eight years of operation of the act the 3,000 estates sold had passed into the hands of nearly 8,000 purchasers.[102] Thus for many tenants the sale of their estate in the landed estates court meant not only a different but a smaller landlord, and smaller landlords no matter what their background were notoriously less indulgent than their aristocratic predecessors. The smaller the estate, the more frequent the rent increases, the higher the rent and the lower the value of the tenant-right. It was widely acknowledged in Ulster that rents were usually higher and tenant-right usually less valuable on small estates than on large — whereas tenant-right on the likes of the Downshire, Londonderry, Ker and Hill-Trevor estates sold for £30 to £40 an acre, on adjacent smaller properties it averaged only between £15 and £20 an acre.[103]

What made the situation more alarming for the tenants was that, up to 1870 at any rate, purchasers in the landed estates court purchased 'the absolute ownership of the land, subject only to the existing tenancies' and without regard to the claims or interests of the tenants.[104] James Godkin commented in 1869 that 'the legislature were guilty of a strange oversight, or deliberate injustice, in the passing of the incumbered estates act ... They made no provision whatever for the protection of the tenants, or of the property which those tenants had created on these estates.'[105] Thus up to 1870, the law having recognised neither tenant-right nor any legal claim by the tenants to improvements made by them, estates were bought and sold 'as though no Ulster custom and no right to any claim for improvements existed'.[106] In other words, with no distinction being made between the landlords' and the tenants' interests, landlords were selling what from the point of view of the tenants they had no moral or equitable right to sell at all. More, the existence of tenant-right on an estate and the improved condition of the estate were regularly put forward in advertisements for sales of property in the landed estates court as an inducement to purchasers, the clear implication being that the estate was rented well under its full market value.[107] And a sufficient number of new owners did come in and immediately raise rents — indeed, in a number of instances rents were increased before the sale in order to enhance the value of the estate[108] — to cause general disquiet among the Ulster tenantry. Shaw-Lefevre discovered from an enquiry made through the constabulary in 1870 that of 1,225 properties purchased under the encumbered estates act of 1849, rents were 'considerably raised immediately after purchase in 533 cases'.[109]

Thus while Ulster tenants had serious misgivings about the general antipathy of the older landlords to tenant-right, they were even more concerned about what might happen if these landlords were superseded by other new men less inhibited by traditional ties and obligations. 'They had no fault to find with their landlords there', said Dr Hume, chairman of the Crumlin Tenant Farmers' Association. 'Better could not be found in Ulster, but they also knew that over the province, property was going through the landed estates court. It passed from the old families, who respected the tenants, into the hands of new men — Belfast merchants and Derry merchants — and a great many of these men had no respect for the old families. Other pharaohs were arising who knew not Joseph.'[110] The fact was that the sales of estates through the landed estates court were such that no tenant could be confident that the estate on which he held his tenancy would not change hands.

In these circumstances, the concern of the tenants for their tenant-right was understandable. What the landed estates court had done above all else was to undermine the traditional relationship and the traditional feelings of trust between landlords and tenants in Ulster. These had already been weakened by the Deasy act of 1860, which had attempted to place relations between owners and tenants entirely upon the basis of contract: 'Henceforth, the landlord was to differ from the village baker, butcher, grocer or publican, merely in the nature of the article in which he traded'.[111] In fact, after 1860 landlord–tenant relations on the vast majority of estates had remained unchanged, but the act of 1860 and the general *laissez-faire* thrust of government policy on land could not help but make the tenants more aware of the precariousness of their position, and make that position, in the legal sense at any rate, more precarious in itself. More even than before, tenants depended on the goodwill of their landlords in not taking a strictly legal view of their relationship.

This situation was greatly exacerbated by the cumulative effect of sales in the landed estates court. As early as 1854 Lord Dufferin, in a speech in the House of Lords, had drawn attention to the fundamental change which was taking place in landlord–tenant relations in Ireland as a result of these sales:

A great change is taking place in the proprietary of Ireland; and though an understanding did once exist between the landlord and his tenants, this understanding is no longer sufficient to afford the requisite security. Old families are disappearing, new men have purchased their estates with business-like habits and advanced views respecting the management of property, who look, as they ought to look, to making their estates pay ... In consequence of the great revolution and the breaking up of the old state of things which has taken place ... semi-feudal and ill-defined understandings, which once existed between a former race of landlords and their tenants, are no longer found to give the necessary security, and the tenantry are, therefore, anxious to substitute for an equitable right under an uncertain custom a legal right under a definite law.[112]

This effect which Dufferin had so clearly identified in the mid-1850s was a great deal more pronounced by the late 1860s. Both landlords and tenants recognised that landlord–tenant relations were in a state of transition and that traditional relationships, with their tacit and reciprocal obligations, were rapidly changing. 'Our old aristocracy have been leaving us, with their parental care,' a tenant meeting at Moira was told, 'and the land has been taken up by mercantile men who, with mercantile ideas, are exacting to the utmost their legal rights, and forgetting the claims of feudal obligations.'[113] These new men had 'neither the hereditary prestige, nor the easy or proudly benevolent notions of the old territorial aristocracy'; they had 'none of the hereditary feelings to the tenants felt by the present proprietors', 'none of the old attachments ... none of the old moral responsibilities'.[114] In their case there were no 'deterrent social influences'; they 'came into possession of the estate unhampered by those ties which exist under an old regime; there could be no intimate friendly regard, because there had been no intercourse, no fellowship, no sympathies developed by long existing and mutually recognised interests'.[115] All in all, it was agreed, 'the operation of the landed estates court has been utterly fatal to the old relations of confidence and security' which had existed — and which doubtless appeared stronger in retrospect — in Ulster up to the 1850s.[116]

Legislation had accelerated the collapse of the semi-feudal system of the past, and the tenants now looked to the state to provide them with an alternative form of security. No doubt such a demand would have come sooner or later in any case, but there can also be no doubt that the operation of the landed estates court had played an important part in precipitating that demand, especially in Ulster where tenants had so much more to protect and so much more to lose. It was, said the *Northern Whig*, 'the operation of the landed estates court which rendered a measure to protect the interests of the tenants absolutely indispensable'.[117] The irony was that it was concern for the future of Ulster landlords and fears as to their ability to survive which helped to create tenant unease and stimulate the demand in Ulster for greater legislative protection for tenant interests.

3

# The Tenant-right Movement and Land Reform 1868–70

Land agitation was slow to start in the north. Ulster's part in the Tenant League and the earlier tenant-right activity of the post-Famine period had virtually ended with the defeat of the independents in the general election of 1852. Although occasional tenant meetings were held during the 1850s,[1] no real effort was made after 1852 to resurrect the movement, and with the collapse of the independent party and the increasing prosperity of the period, discussion of the land question became less urgent.

Yet interest in the question never disappeared. At elections in Ireland, both north and south, candidates still apparently felt obliged to make non-committal and imprecise statements about supporting a settlement on terms equitable to both landlords and tenants; while at Westminster bills continued to be introduced with almost monotonous regularity — but with little likelihood or even expectation of success — during the 1850s.[2] The improving conditions and greater social stability in Ireland convinced English opinion that the Famine had successfully dealt with the problem in the manner long advocated by the classical economists — 'removal of the cottiers, increase in the size of farms, and more capitalistic methods of farming'[3] — and government policy after 1848 was to leave the solution of the question to *laissez-faire* principles. Thus such legislation as was passed — most notably the cncumbered estates act of 1849 — was directed towards establishing free trade in land. This policy culminated in the Cardwell and Deasy acts of 1860 — the first giving tenants a right to compensation for certain improvements carried out with the approval of the landlords, the second attempting to establish landlord–tenant relations on a basis of contract — and these were seen by British politicians at the time as 'a final treatment of a vexed question'.[4]

The depression of the early 1860s, however, shook British complacency and stimulated public discussion of the issue once again. The National Association in Ireland made land reform in the shape of compensation for tenants' improvements one of its three main objectives in 1864.[5] And from 1865 the Fenian movement added urgency to the question so that several bills, including ministerial measures from successive Liberal and Conservative governments, were introduced in 1866 and 1867. By this stage it was obvious that the policy of *laissez-faire* in land had not been a success, and in December 1867, only a few days after the Clerkenwell explosion, Gladstone, who had up to this time shown no special discernment of the Irish land problem, spoke for the first time of the need for agrarian reform in Ireland. Although Gladstone himself approached the question without any preconceived ideas, the greater part of informed opinion in England by this time was agreed that a good deal more than compensation for improvements was necessary to solve the problem and satisfy Irish opinion.[6] Moreover, with the landed classes in Britain feeling 'peculiarly exposed' after the parliamentary reform act of 1867, many of these too were little disposed to defend the Irish landed interest and were, like *The Times*, anxious to neutralise the Irish land question as an issue in British politics.[7] The question now was not whether a land bill would be passed, but how far beyond compensation for improvements it would go.

All these developments were assiduously reported by the local press in Ulster, where they were watched with careful interest rather than enthusiasm. The lukewarm response of Ulster tenants to the various legislative proposals of these two decades is easy to understand.

None of the measures introduced between 1852 and 1867 went as far as Sharman Crawford's tenant-right bill of 1852, and none of them therefore was likely to advance in any way the interests of tenants in tenant-right areas.[8] Of the ministerial bills — and these were the only bills ever likely to be passed — only one, that of the Tory Irish attorney-general Joseph Napier in 1852, recognised the principle of retrospective compensation for improvements. The others, including the Liberal chief secretary Chichester-Fortescue's proposals in 1866, allowed only for prospective improvements, generally subject to the approval of the landlords and even then usually hedged in with various safeguards and qualifications designed to protect the interests of the latter. But even legislative compensation for past improvements had little attraction for northern tenants who already had in most cases a good deal more than this.

Interest quickened to some extent in Ulster in 1866–7. Towards the end of 1866 John Bright, in two speeches in Dublin, put forward for the first time his proposals for tenant purchase. Bright's speeches were widely and mistakenly interpreted as a demand for the compulsory sale of the estates of absentee owners and, according to Thomas MacKnight, 'excited much attention … among the Ulster tenant farmers'.[9] His views were immediately challenged by Lord Dufferin, who, in a series of letters to *The Times*, replied to Bright's criticisms of Irish landlords, denying that the system of land tenure was responsible for Ireland's economic problems and reiterating the conventional arguments against fixity of tenure. These letters gave rise to wide comment in the press but they evoked no positive response from the Ulster tenants.[10] And although the demands of the southern representatives at Westminster were rapidly escalating to the point where northern as well as southern tenants stood to gain if they were conceded — whereas in 1865 the demand had been for compensation for improvements, by 1867 it was for fixity of tenure[11] — these were denounced as 'wild', 'mischievous' and 'impracticable' by the tenant-right press in Ulster which, after the withdrawal of the Conservative proposals in 1867, increasingly turned its attention to the question of the Irish church.[12]

The joint campaign of the National Association in Ireland and the

Liberation Society in Britain had made the Irish church a front-ranking issue in British politics, and it was primarily on this question that Gladstone appealed to the electorate in 1868. While it may be safely assumed that Irish tenants, both north and south, attached a great deal more importance to the land question, Gladstone's priorities in the matter of Irish reform had the full support of the Liberal press in Ulster which, controlled as it was mainly by the presbyterian middle class, was anxious to strike a blow against what it saw as one of the main pillars of the episcopalian and landed ascendancy. Thus the question of Irish church disestablishment dominated the election of 1868 in Ulster as elsewhere.[13]

The Conservatives, of course, appealed for protestant unity, exhorting the presbyterians to defend protestant endowments and claiming that the proposals for disestablishment were part of a 'jesuitical conspiracy' against Irish protestantism of all shades.[14] Their task was not made any easier, however, by the record of their own members on Monsell's English burials bill of the previous session,[15] nor by the persistent refusal of Derby and Disraeli — in spite of appeals from both the presbyterians and the Ulster Tories themselves — to increase the *regium donum* (the government grant to the presbyterian church).[16] Thus, while the majority of presbyterians voted Conservative and while the bulk of the Liberal votes in Ulster in 1868 came from the catholics, such Liberal successes as there were — in Derry city, Newry and Belfast — could not have been won without a substantial degree of presbyterian support.[17]

The Ulster Tories also faced difficulties with their Orange supporters arising from the Conservative government's seemingly one-sided administration of the party processions act[18] and their apparent willingness to endow the catholic church and give a charter to a catholic university in Ireland.[19] Discontent was brought to a head in 1868, when William Johnston of Ballykilbeg, a small landowner and maverick Orange radical, was sentenced to two months' imprisonment for marching in defiance of the processions act from Newtownards to Bangor, and much of it was directed against the local Tory and Orange leaders, who were reluctant to embarrass the Tory government and who failed to support Johnston and the rank and file in what was seen as a time of crisis.[20] Consequently, there was an Orange revolt against the Conservative party in Belfast, where an independent Orange organisation was established, and Johnston and the Liberal, Thomas McClure, were returned in preference to the two official Tory candidates.

But the dissatisfaction extended well beyond Belfast, with the result that Orangemen in various parts of the province failed to respond with their customary enthusiasm to the cry of 'the church in danger'.[21] It was not only that rank-and-file Orangemen were lukewarm on the church issue: the Orange dissentients threatened at one stage to make land a real issue in the election. In September 1868, following a speech by Isaac Butt to a tenant demonstration in Limerick, the Rev. Thomas Drew, one of the most prominent Orange figures in the province and William Johnston's father-in-law, sent a *frisson* of alarm through Conservative ranks by writing a public letter to Butt endorsing the latter's views on the need for land reform, condemning the electoral dependence of tenants, and claiming that there were 'estates in the north where the screw is never withdrawn from its circuitous and oppressive work'.[22] What made Drew's intervention more alarming to the Tory landlords was the fact that speakers at independent Orange meetings in the rural districts had already begun not only to show an unprecedented interest in the land question, but to make demands far in advance of those made by the tenant-right press. Some months earlier, for example, Orangemen of the Ballymoney, Rasharkin and Dervock districts, meeting at Dervock in support of Johnston, had pledged themselves to use every legal means to procure for the tenant farmers fixity of tenure.[23] But while Drew's action caused something of a minor sensation in the north and while speakers at several meetings in support of Johnston echoed his criticisms of the land system, the threatened Orange revolt did not materialise at this time outside of Belfast, and Drew's intervention failed to shake the primacy of the church question over all other issues in this election.

The Conservatives, therefore, continued to give prominence of place to the church question and, in view of the potentially divisive nature of other issues such as land and party processions, it was clearly in their interest to do so. The Liberals, in circumstances more favourable to their cause than any since 1852, entered candidates in only six constituencies, four of them boroughs. The fact that the Tory and landed control of the counties went virtually unchallenged in this election was a measure both of the weakness of Liberalism in the province and of how little progress had been made on the land question there. While all the Liberal candidates included support for land reform in their manifestos and campaign speeches, their demands were always limited and never explicit. Basically their position was one of support for the policy of Gladstone, who had given no indication of how far he would go on this question, and it is clear that as a party they not only attached more importance to the church issue, but had not as yet realised the full potential of the land question.[24] Thus while they were able to take advantage of Conservative divisions to win a seat in Belfast and managed also to return members for Newry, Derry city and one for Cavan — where the sitting members, both belonging to prominent local families, were returned unopposed — these successes were a result mainly of Conservative divisions and the paramountcy of the church question, and owed virtually nothing to the issue of the land.

THE BEGINNING OF THE TENANT–RIGHT MOVEMENT

Preoccupation with the church question continued into 1869. Once the church question was safely settled, however, there was increasing concentration on land.[25] This was certainly the case in the south and, indeed, even in England, where the appointment in May 1869 of William O'Connor Morris as a special correspondent of *The Times* to report on the land question was a measure of the interest being taken in it.[26] In southern Ireland, farmers' clubs — sporadically active during the early 1860s — had been campaigning in many areas during the election of 1868, and by September meetings were being held all over the country and steps were being taken to establish a tenant league with Isaac Butt as president.[27]

In Ulster, however, apart from a single privately convened meeting held at Ballymoney in February, and despite repeated promptings, warnings and complaints from the tenant-right press,[28] no action was taken until the middle of October. The reticence of the northern tenants, however, was the result of neither the indifference nor the 'stupid blindness' with which they were reproached by correspondents in the local press; tenant farmers in Ulster did not have to be told by newspaper men that they 'had just as strong an interest in a fair security of tenure, and a proper compensation for unexhausted improvements as any of the catholic farmers south of the Boyne'.[29] But Ulster tenants did not see their interests as being identical with those of tenants in the south, and many of them were in fact suspicious of the agitation in the south and especially of what they mistakenly saw as its close association with the campaign for an amnesty for fenian prisoners.[30] Moreover, there were certain practical difficulties in launching a movement in Ulster: first, whereas in the south the farmers' clubs already provided the nucleus of a tenant organisation, there was in the north 'an absence of organisation among the rank and file of the people, and, therefore, no means of arranging meetings';[31] and secondly, while tenants in the south had leaders for such a movement in MPs such as Gray and Maguire, who had already been leading a campaign for reform at Westminster, and in national figures such as Butt, who not only knew the land question but knew what the tenants wanted and needed, there was no such obvious leadership in Ulster.

At any rate, the position of tenants in the north was fundamentally different from that in the south, and tenants there had less reason for agitating and more reason for caution. Not only were landlord–tenant relations better in Ulster and grievances less acute, but the greater interest which northern tenants had in the soil through their tenant-right made them both more vulnerable and more hesitant about jeopardising what they already had. Apart from the fear of landlord reprisals,[32] there was the danger that legislation might actually leave northern tenants in a weaker position than they were already in. Isaac Butt said that he had

> found in the north an apprehension, I must say, not altogether unfounded, that any legislation that is likely to pass will only have the

> effect of placing the northern tenant in a worse position than he would be without legislation if the Ulster custom of tenant-right were not disturbed. In other words, that if legislation were to confer any new rights upon the tenants, the landlords would find in this an excuse for substituting the new rights for the old advantages which were secured to the tenants by the custom of tenant-right.[33]

Although Butt went on to advise northern tenants that they could not avert this danger simply by remaining quiescent, many tenants clearly preferred to leave things as they were rather than run the risk of getting a land bill which would not necessarily improve and which might, indeed, adversely affect their position.

Part of the problem was that those who were trying to stimulate the agitation in Ulster were, up to the end of 1869, outlining demands which, even if conceded, were unlikely to advance the tenant's legal position beyond what it already was by convention. The tenant-right press which took the lead in the movement in Ulster reflected above all else the views of the presbyterian middle classes, and these, while anxious to strike a blow against the landed ascendancy, had, like the nonconformist middle classes in Britain, serious reservations about advocating reforms which would in any way infringe on the rights of property, even the property of the landed classes. What they wanted was to curtail the political and social influence of the latter without interfering with their economic or property interests. And the way to do this was to dismantle what remained of the semi-feudal system in the counties, and establish in its place one based on ideas more fitting to the capitalist society of the Victorian age. Their ideal was to have affairs 'regulated on the plan of fair money equivalents, a clear bargain, and no favour'.[34] 'The serfdom of the tenant franchise', contended James McKnight, 'is a necessary consequence of the insecurity of tenant property, and would disappear even without the ballot were our economic relations established upon a proper foundation'.[35]

Hence the demands of those who had appointed themselves tenant-right spokesmen in the north — and the expectations of Gladstone's supporters in the province — were extremely limited. Long after the south had adopted the cry of fixity of tenure, the demand in the north was still for compensation for unexhausted improvements and the settlement of landlord–tenant relations on an equitable basis.[36] There were of course frequent references to an undefined security of tenure, but none of the tenant-right papers spelt out what this meant or how it might be secured. Moreover, these demands were accompanied by repeated warnings against 'unreasonable expectations'.[37] Even the *Derry Journal*, more radical in its opinions than most northern papers, warned that it was 'useless to advance wild and extravagant demands, involving a sheer and indubitable confiscation of the property held at present by landlords, and they are not the friends of the tenantry who sanction and support such unreasonable claims'.[38]

In these circumstances, with a programme promising the tenants little and accompanied by warnings not to expect too much, it was hardly surprisingly that there was little response from the farmers. Towards the end of 1869, however, the situation changed. This change was brought about partly by the Antrim by-election of August 1869 which, according to MacKnight, 'powerfully stimulated the agitation on the land question',[39] and partly by a general rise in expectations which was being encouraged by discussion on both sides of the channel.

The Antrim election affected the question in two ways. First, the meetings during the campaign created an opportunity for the public discussion of land reform which up to this time the absence of tenant organisation in the north had prevented, and tenant-right quickly emerged as the main issue in the election.[40] Second, and perhaps more important, the demonstration of territorial influence and power during the election was such that it effectively convinced the Liberal middle classes that landed political predominance would continue unless the tenants were given full security of tenure. Thus it reconciled many to a more radical settlement of the land question than they would otherwise have supported. The election, the *Weekly Whig* claimed, showed plainly that 'without the settlement of the land question any freedom of election in the Ulster counties is hopeless'.[41]

Not only did the zeal for reform increase, but so too did the demands. An indication of how far these had advanced over the previous six months is given by comparing the demands put forward at the two tenant-right meetings in Ballymoney in February and in October; whereas the meeting in February demanded only legal protection for tenant improvements, that in October passed a resolution expressing the belief that 'any legislation which failed to embrace fixity of tenure and compensation for permanent and unexhausted improvements would fail to give satisfaction to the people'.[42] Only the Belfast press lagged behind, still warning against the 'delusive' phrase 'fixity of tenure' and against creating expectations which could not be satisfied. Nevertheless, it too was now spelling out demands more specific and radical than it would have contemplated at the beginning of the year — legal protection for tenant improvements, security against arbitrary eviction, compensation for disturbance, courts of arbitration, and facilities for tenant purchase.[43]

These more radical demands not only promised a positive gain for Ulster tenants, but reflected the general rise in the level of expectancy which was taking place in both Britain and Ireland. Even Conservative spokesmen were now talking freely of compensation for improvements, with some even hinting at the legalisation of the Ulster custom and its extension to the rest of Ireland.[44] In these circumstances interest among the tenant farmers in Ulster quickened, and they began to realise that with reform coming at any rate they ran the risk of having their interests neglected by not speaking out.[45] What made it all the more imperative for tenants to let their views be known was the apparently widespread assumption in Britain that the 'northern province is all prosperity and happiness with scarcely a land grievance to be complained of'. Thus there was the danger — or so the Liberal and tenant-right press claimed — that Ulster might be neglected in the coming enactment in the belief that no more than the existing custom was necessary.[46] There was evidence, too, that some landlords — including the Earl of Leitrim and Lord Dufferin — were already taking steps to protect themselves by forcing agreements and leases on their tenants in anticipation of Gladstone's legislation.[47]

Not all Ulster tenants were influenced by these considerations, but tenant feeling and interest had developed sufficiently by October to provide the basis of support for a campaign in the province. All that was required was organisation and leadership, and this was now provided by a small number of tenant-right activists, not all of whom were primarily interested in land. The decision to form the first tenant association in the province — the Route Tenant-Right Association — was taken as a direct result of the Antrim election and chiefly for political reasons. Samuel McElroy, who was to become the secretary of the new association, describes its formation as follows:

> After the defeat of Sir Shafto Adair, this question arose, what is to be done? It was soon answered — Start a tenants' defence association. The advice of Dr McKnight was sought, and he advised this course.[48]

Consequently a small group of presbyterian businessmen and large farmers in and around Ballymoney decided to take the initiative. A preliminary meeting was held in Ballymoney town hall on 12 October, and a week later the Route Association was established with the object of settling 'the land question on a firm and permanent basis, having due regard to all just interests'.[49]

This marked the beginning of the tenant-right movement in Ulster, and from Ballymoney it gradually spread to other parts of Antrim and to other counties. In the first week of November the campaign was launched in Co. Derry with a meeting of 1,000 — 'mostly tenant-farmers' — at Magherafelt where John Glover, a local solicitor, had long been active in gathering complaints against the London companies and trying to stimulate the tenants to action; and tenant meetings were held at Scotstown in Monaghan and at Cavan, where a county league was formed following a meeting of, it was claimed, 20,000 people.[50] During November, a public demonstration attended by 'upwards of 1,000 farmers' was held at Ballymoney, and preliminary meetings were held for the formation of tenant associations in Ballymena, Coleraine, and Castlefin in Donegal.[51] In December, major demonstrations were organised at Newtownlimavady, where 'a good attendance of tenant-farmers' was reported, and at Coleraine, where the meeting was claimed to be 'essentially representative of the intelligence and respectability of the tenant farmers in the neighbourhood', while a conference on tenant-right was held under the auspices of the Ballymena Tenant-Right Association and attended by representatives from Counties Antrim and Derry.[52] Other bodies were also taking up the question and making their voices heard on behalf of the farmers; resolutions in favour of land reform were passed at meetings of the Omagh and Cookstown town commissioners, and at a conference of the catholic clergy of Down and Connor held in Belfast in November.[53] Perhaps even more significant as a measure of the growing support was the address in favour of legal protection for tenant interests issued by the Grand Lodge of the Independent Orange Association in the following month.[54]

The new year of 1870 saw no let-up in the campaign. Between 1 January and the introduction of Gladstone's bill on 15 February there was further activity in Counties Antrim and Derry, with meetings at Larne, Newtownards, Toome and Newtownlimavady.[55] The agitation also spread into Tyrone with demonstrations at Castlederg, where 'upwards of 5,000' attended, and Cookstown, where an estimated crowd of 10,000 'including a great many tenant farmers' gathered, and into Donegal, with meetings of 5,000 at Ballybofey, 10,000 at Letterkenny, and at Eglinton where 'those taking part were, with few exceptions, farmers of good standing in the district'.[56] Tenant organisation too continued to spread, so that by the time of the provincial tenant-right conference in Belfast at the beginning of March the organisers could claim that no fewer than seventeen tenant-right societies from the six counties of Antrim, Down, Armagh, Donegal, Derry and Tyrone were represented.[57] In the six months from October to March a tenant-right movement of some significance and strength had finally taken root in the northern province.

The demands of the tenant-right advocates, also, had advanced in clarity since the inauguration of the movement. The recommendations put forward at the earlier demonstrations in Ulster had varied from area to area; some, such as those at Magherafelt and Cavan, had passed resolutions in favour of fixity of tenure at fair rents; others, such as that at Ballymoney in November, had coupled tentative demands for security with resolutions repudiating any desire to infringe upon the just rights of landlords.[58] The *Northern Whig* in particular continued to deprecate the advocacy of fixity of tenure, and at the Ballymena conference at the end of December, at which the editor of the *Whig* moved one of the main resolutions, a definition of the Ulster custom was put forward which included only buildings and improvements.[59] The provincial press, however, took up the cry of fixity of tenure, and meetings during January and February went almost without exception for the Ulster custom in its fullest meaning. Demands for fixity of tenure, fair rents to be settled by arbitration, and free sale of the tenant's interest in his holding were repeated at meetings at Eglinton, Castlederg, Ballybofey, Larne, Letterkenny, Cookstown and Toome.

What the tenants and tenant-right press were now demanding was the legalisation of the Ulster custom, not as it was practised in various parts of the province, but in its integrity. More than this, the tenant movement in the north had apparently at last caught up with the demands of the tenant league in the south so that, with Gladstone's measure imminent, it no longer seemed sensible to stand wholly apart from the south on the question. The suspicion of the southern movement continued, of course — more pronounced in some quarters than in others — but a number of delegates from Ulster attended the national land conference in Dublin at the beginning of February, which reiterated the claims now being made at tenant meetings throughout the country. Thus on the eve of Gladstone's bill, north and south were united in their demand for 'a thoroughly equitable and comprehensive' measure of land reform.[60]

THE PASSING OF THE LAND BILL

Expectations were running high in Ulster when Gladstone introduced his land bill in the House of Commons on 15 February 1870 and, in the circumstances, it was almost inevitable that they would be disappointed. Yet, although the bill conceded neither the fixity of tenure nor the arbitration of rents demanded by the Dublin tenant-right conference, the immediate reaction in the north was not unfavourable. What Gladstone proposed to do was to give Irish tenants a measure of security, firstly by legalising the Ulster custom in the northern province and analogous customs elsewhere in the country, and secondly by providing for compensation for disturbance and for improvements for those tenants whose holdings were not subject to such customs.

If Gladstone's proposals met with 'almost instant condemnation' in the south,[61] their reception in Ulster was much more cordial. Here the bill was welcomed as one of 'immense progress', 'a good and equitable measure', and 'one of advanced statesmanship conferring large and important privileges upon the occupiers of the soil'.[62] The *Coleraine Chronicle* was gratified 'to find that the Ulster tenant-right, in its integrity, is to receive the sanction of the law', while Dr James McKnight of the *Londonderry Standard* believed that 'at length we have lived to see in near prospect the realisation of a large amount of our life's labours'.[63] 'I think on the whole', Richard Dowse, the Irish attorney-general, reported to Gladstone, 'public opinion in the north approves of the land bill'.[64]

This initial euphoria soon passed, however, and closer and longer examination of the clauses of the bill gave rise to serious doubts and criticisms. A week after acclaiming the bill as 'a good and equitable measure', the *Coleraine Chronicle* had come to the conclusion that 'the clause with reference to Ulster is lamentably defective. It defines the custom partially and legalises it questionably'. The *Londonderry Standard* too was having second thoughts, and on 23 February — only four days after welcoming the measure — claimed that the first clause as it stood would legalise not the genuine tenant-right custom, but all the variations. 'The more we see of the tenant-right bill of the government', said the *Northern Star*, 'the less we like it ... It is essentially a bad bill ... It opens the way to endless squabbles and endless litigation.'[65]

Only the *Northern Whig* continued to defend the measure, claiming that it conferred great advantages on all the tenant farmers of Ireland, but especially on those in Ulster, securing to them 'all that they have really desired'.[66] Yet the letters from tenant farmers and other interested parties in the *Whig*'s own columns controverted its view that the bill gave tenants all that they wanted.[67] It was in fact felt to be deficient in three main particulars. First, it made no provision for the fair valuation of rent and thus left undiminished the landlord's power to raise rent and so ultimately destroy the tenant-right value. Secondly, it failed to include a proper definition of the Ulster custom and this, it was feared, would give the force of law to all the violations of the custom. And finally, it failed to assume that all holdings in Ulster were subject to the custom, and thus left upon the tenants the responsibility of proving the nature and extent of the custom in every case of dispute; this, it was pointed out, would be nearly impossible to prove on farms which had often been held for three and four generations without purchase or sale of any kind.[68]

These criticisms were repeated in letters to the press, in press editorials, and at tenant meetings throughout the province as well as at meetings of the independent Orange association in Belfast.[69] Even the *Northern Whig* by the third week of March was voicing its concern that landlords would still be allowed arbitrarily to raise rents and that the burden of proof with regard to the existence of tenant-right was being left to each tenant individually.[70] The rather ambivalent attitude of the northern farmers and tenant associations to the bill was probably best summed up by the series of resolutions passed by the conference of tenant-right associations meeting in Belfast at the beginning of March. While conceding that the bill was 'an honest and earnest attempt to settle the Irish land question', the conference demanded a comprehensive list of far-reaching and radical amendments — that 'the Ulster tenant-right should be fully defined … in the bill'; that rent disputes should be submitted to arbitration; that the presumption of law should be that every holding in Ulster was subject to tenant-right; and that the principles of the Ulster custom should be extended to the rest of the country.[71] Basically what the Ulster tenant associations were seeking was not the legalisation of tenant-right as it actually operated at this time, but its uniform enforcement throughout the whole province.

These amendments — and similar proposals from other tenant-right meetings — were sent to Gladstone in the form of a memorial, but to no avail; Gladstone refused to go further — indeed, in the circumstances of the time, could not have gone further — than his original proposals.[72] A deputation from the northern tenant-right associations, like an earlier deputation from the south, met with a similarly negative response.[73] Worse still, such amendments as were carried in committee weakened rather than strengthened the bill from the tenant point of view.

The bill went through its second reading, accepted in principle by both sides of the house, and opposed only by a handful of the more advanced southern members and by two British Conservatives, one of whom was James Lowther who later became Irish chief secretary. In the committee stage, however, several important amendments were carried. Of these, undoubtedly the most significant from the Ulster point of view was the substitution in the first clause of the plural 'usages' for the singular 'usage' thus, according to William Johnston who vainly opposed the change, legalising 'all the encroachments of the landlords on the tenant-right custom'.[74] Although this amendment was proposed by an English Tory MP, the government readily accepted it, Chichester Fortescue pointing out that it was 'only a fair and honest recognition' of the fact that the custom differed 'in its form and also its amount on various estates'.[75] A subsequent attempt by Johnston to have Sharman Crawford's definition of the Ulster custom incorporated in the enacting clause was opposed by Liberals and Tories alike and easily defeated.[76] Johnston did succeed, however, in persuading the government to amend the clause so as to allow tenants the option of forgoing their claims under the Ulster custom, and claiming instead compensation under the other sections of the act.[77]

Overall, the bill which emerged from committee was a good deal less satisfactory from the tenant point of view than the original version. The change of 'usage' into 'usages' in particular had, according to the *Coleraine Chronicle*, 'blasted the hopes of the Ulster tenantry ... and largely nullified any beneficial features the clause possessed'. The *Ballymoney Free Press* thought that the bill left tenants in the north 'in a worse condition than formerly'.[78] There was, in fact, 'deep and general dissatisfaction' with the bill even as it left the commons, and when it was emasculated by the House of Lords — by, for example, reducing the scale of compensation and limiting it to tenants of holdings under £50 rather than £100, reversing the presumption that improvements had been carried out by the tenants, and reducing the leases under which landlords could exempt themselves from the provisions of the bill from 31 to 21 years — the tenant-right press and speakers at tenant-right meetings began to urge its rejection.[79]

Even the *Northern Whig*, which had consistently defended the government efforts and had tried to moderate the expectations of the tenants, was forced to admit that 'the bill, as amended by the lords, has become utterly unacceptable'.[80] The *Whig*, however, refused to accept that it would be better to reject the bill altogether. By this stage some of the tenant-right papers and associations were making the point that rather than accept a half-measure at this time, it would be better to continue the agitation for another year and secure something worthwhile.[81] But, as the *Whig* forcefully and rightly reminded tenants, matters could not remain as they were, indeed could never be the same again:

> It is well that the tenants should understand that they cannot now choose between the present bill and the old system of no legal protection. The present system is at an end. It can never be restored. Never again will the landlords allow vague and illimitable claims to accumulate ... They will always have the fear of a coming land bill before them ... If they resist the present measure, it is not with any intention of continuing the present system. It is to gain time, in order that they may take means to secure themselves from the effects of a future bill ... The landlords know that a land bill is inevitable ... It is folly, therefore, for tenants to talk of remaining as they are. They cannot remain as they are. Their position must either be made better by immediate legislation, or be infinitely worse than in Ulster, at least, it ever was before. The days of kind, indulgent landlords, with 'moral' but no legal obligations to their tenants, are over. Every man will henceforth look to his bond.[82]

In the event, the House of Lords — 'under the private tuition of the Ulster landlords', it was claimed[83] — realised the dangers of their tactics and suddenly abandoned their most restrictive amendments so that the bill eventually went through in more or less the same form as it had left the commons. And, despite the earlier criticisms of the measure and although it was still considered by some to be a lame and impotent conclusion to all the agitation, it was fairly unanimously welcomed in Ulster as an honest attempt to solve a difficult question. It had not of course given the tenants all they wanted, but it was, with all its shortcomings, 'a substantial instalment of justice' far in advance of anything that had been proposed in the past, giving, as it did, legal protection to the Ulster custom where it had been observed, and enabling the tenants to claim under the other provisions of the bill where the custom had atrophied. The Rev. Archibald Robinson, presbyterian minister of Broughshane and a prominent critic of the bill when it was first introduced, summed up the general feeling of Ulster tenants and tenant-righters at a meeting of the Route Association at the beginning of December:

> His impression was that it was a good and great act, though not up exactly to what they had been expecting ... He thought they must admit it was a most decided advance upon anything heretofore proposed in parliament — upon anything the most sanguine tenant-righter expected to receive ... It was more than even Sharman Crawford asked for (Applause).[84]

4
# The Land Act of 1870

EARLY SUCCESS

Whatever its ultimate failure or its immediate defects, the land act of 1870 finally marked the abandonment with regard to Irish land of the British policy of *laissez-faire*, and recognised that tenants, as well as landlords, had an interest in the land. The act had two main objectives: first, to provide greater security of tenure; and second, to secure for the tenant the value of his improvements, thus removing what was considered to be a serious disincentive to tenant investment. Section 1 legalised 'the usages prevalent in the province of Ulster, which are known as, and in this act intended to be included under, the denomination of the Ulster tenant-right custom'.[1] Section 2 legalised similar usages in other parts of the country. In each case the tenant was given the option of claiming either under the custom or under the general provisions of the act, but tenants claiming under the custom were not entitled to compensation under any other part of the act. No definition of the Ulster custom or other custom being given, the proviso was included that the claimant must prove 'the usages pertinent to him'.

Tenants of holdings not subject to the custom — and this applied to many of those in Ulster — and tenants of holdings on which the landlord had purchased the tenant-right could claim compensation for disturbance and improvements under the remaining sections of the act. The most important of these — and for tenants outside

Ulster the most important part of the act — was section 3, which enabled the tenant to claim compensation for disturbance. The compensation varied inversely with the valuation of the holding, ranging from a maximum of seven years' rental in respect of holdings rated at £10 or less to a year's rental for holdings of £100 or more, with a maximum of £250 in all cases. Tenants holding leases for 31 years or more, occupiers of demesne lands and townparks, and those who subdivided or sublet without the consent of the landlord were excluded from the act, while tenants of holdings valued at £50 or more were allowed to contract themselves out of it.

Sections 4 and 5 of the act reversed the presumption of law with regard to improvements and entitled a tenant upon quitting his holding, either voluntarily or involuntarily, to claim compensation for improvements made by him or his predecessors. Certain exceptions were made to this as, for example, in respect of improvements prohibited in writing by the landlord, while claims for improvements made twenty years before the passing of the act were limited to permanent improvements and reclamation of wasteland. The amount of compensation, like so much else in the act, was left to the discretion of the court. Indeed, one of the features of the act was the power given to the civil bills courts which were to administer it, so that it could have been foreseen even in 1870 that there would be a good deal of controversy in the future. A court of appeal was vested in two judges of the assize, and a final appeal might be made to a special land court sitting in Dublin.

Finally, in deference to John Bright, some provision was made for tenant purchase (though Gladstone saw purchase as having but 'a very small' part to play in settling the question).[2] Clauses were included which empowered the Board of Public Works in Ireland to lend tenants up to two-thirds of the money required to purchase their holdings, to be repaid at 5 per cent over thirty-five years. In the event, the board of works made little effort to give effect to this part of the act, and this, combined with the complicated and expensive process of sale, meant that the Bright clauses failed almost totally (only 877 tenants purchased their holdings under the act).[3]

Such then were the main provisions of the land act of 1870, which has generally been considered by historians to have been an almost complete failure. Certainly it fell far short of satisfying tenant demands in the south, where failure to control rents and to concede fixity of tenure were pinpointed as its two main weaknesses. Compensation for improvements and for disturbance, while recognising the tenant's interest in his holding, were negative rights realisable only when the tenant left the holding. What the tenant wanted was security, not a pecuniary compensation which, it was pointed out, 'was nothing in comparison to the loss of his home, and the destruction of his business'.[4] Thus one historian has concluded that 'for much of rural Ireland, the act was a monumental failure'.[5]

This was not the case in Ulster, however. Here, for a time at any rate, the act worked well and worked to the general satisfaction of the tenants. Tenants in Ulster made greater use of the act than those in the south and derived a great deal more benefit from it. Between 1870 and 1878, 61 per cent of all cases brought under the act were in Ulster and 54 per cent of the total awards made under the act went to tenants in Ulster. The average value of each award in Ulster was also usually higher than the average for the south; in 1871, for example, the average award in Ulster was £81 as against an average of £69 for the country as a whole, or £49 for the three southern provinces, and, though it dropped below the national average in 1872 and 1873, in every other year it was higher.[6]

Northern tenants and tenant-righters had of course certain reservations about the act. They shared, for example, the fear of the south that the landlords' power of raising rent would be used to defeat the purpose of the act. And then, too, there was the fact that the tenant-right custom had been left by the act 'in a state of remarkable indefiniteness'.[7] With no definition of the custom included in the act, it was left to the courts to determine where and to what extent it applied.[8] What this meant was that the degree to which the act would satisfy tenants — and landlords — in Ulster, the degree to which in a sense it would work in Ulster, would depend on the decisions of judges who up to this time had, if anything, been identified with the landed class.[9]

The indeterminate nature of the first clause also meant that there would — almost inevitably — be a greater amount of litigation under the act in Ulster, and that cases brought on the grounds of tenant-right would be surrounded with more uncertainty than those brought on other grounds. Thus tenants claiming in Ulster often filed two claims — one under the Ulster custom, and the second under the other sections of the act. In 1870–1, in only seventy-two of the 287 cases brought in Ulster was tenant-right made the sole ground of the claim; in 110 other cases where tenants claimed under tenant-right they filed parallel claims under the other sections for compensation and disturbance; and in the remaining 105 cases no attempt was made to claim under the first clause at all.[10] The high proportion of cases in which claimants made no attempt to prove tenant-right gave rise to much comment in the early 1870s.[11] But with the tenant-right custom often difficult to prove, it was understandable that many tenants should rely rather on clause 3, and throughout the 1870s a high proportion of the compensation awarded in Ulster was awarded on grounds other than tenant-right; in the first six years of the act's operation an average of 50 per cent of the awards in Ulster were for tenant-right, the remainder for improvements and disturbance under sections 3 and 4.[12]

Nevertheless, in spite of the difficulty of proving tenant-right and in spite of northern tenant reservations respecting both the vagueness of the first clause and the failure of the act to control rent, the act was accepted as, and undoubtedly represented, a substantial advance in the position of the tenantry. If it did not establish the Ulster custom in its full integrity throughout the province, it did at least promise to safeguard the custom where it had been observed, and arrest its deterioration and destruction in other areas. James McKnight frankly acknowledged its value in this respect: 'It will preserve to Ulster tenants the existing remains of their provincial rights and immunities … In no case will Ulster landlords, after the passing of the bill, be able to reduce the value of the tenant-right property below its present standard'.[13] At the very least, even where the custom could not be proved, it secured for the tenants a measure of compensation, and every decree obtained in favour of tenants under the new legislation represented so much money of which the tenants, before the passing of the act, would have been deprived.

But the act did a great deal more than this. By giving the Ulster custom the force of law and ending a situation in which it was merely a thing of grace, totally dependent on the whim of the landlord, it both enhanced the value of tenant-right — without, the tenants claimed, affecting the value of the fee-simple[14] — and gave tenants a degree of security which they had never had in the past. 'I find that there is a difference already in the minds of the tenantry', Edward Gardner, a tenant-right solicitor from Downpatrick, told the Chelmsford committee — a committee of the House of Lords — in 1872. 'They seem to feel more secure, and deal with more confidence.'[15] Others confirmed Gardner's testimony, and most agreed also that tenant-right — at least partly because of this — was increasing in value more rapidly after 1870 than before; from Armagh, for example, it was reported that sales of tenant-right were bringing 'prices hitherto unknown in this district', while sales in Antrim were said to be illustrating 'in a striking manner the confidence with which farmers now invest their savings in land, compared with the hesitation shown previous to the passing of the land act'.[16] The *Belfast Newsletter* denied that the higher value of tenant-right was a result of the act, but the evidence — both from newspaper reports of sales and from testimony given to the Chelmsford committee and the Bessborough commission — that such an increase was taking place was convincing.[17]

Not only was tenant-right going up in value, but the fact that it had now become a legal security enabled tenants to raise money and secure credit more easily than had been possible before 1870. Ideally this credit should have been used to invest in the soil and improve the efficiency of farming, and, of course, it sometimes was; but the general consensus was that it was used mainly to purchase articles for consumption[18] so that, while this contributed to the greater material comfort of tenants during the 1870s, many tenants found themselves in the crisis at the end of the decade under greater pressure from shopkeeper creditors than from landlords. A sheriff's officer from Donegal told the Bessborough commission in 1880 that 'I suppose I have for execution at present in the district nearly 150 decrees for shop debts outside rent. It is seldom we get a decree for rent'.[19]

Nevertheless, tenant investment does appear to have increased after 1870. The tenant-right press claimed that improvements had 'commenced on a scale quite unprecedented' and that the tenants had been 'inspired with a new spirit of enterprise', and were 'investing with confidence they never had before'.[20] Tyrone, in particular, was singled out as a county in which the act had had a most salutary effect.[21] On the other hand, there were counties such as Donegal and Antrim where some early — but temporary — dissatisfaction with the act's administration was supposed to have initially discouraged improvements.[22] But, on the whole, it was generally accepted that the act had stimulated tenant improvement in Ulster, and even those who were critical of the act, and who denied that it had had any palpable effect on tenant improvements elsewhere in the country, were generally prepared to concede that it was beneficial in this respect in Ulster.[23] Yet, manifestly, the extent of the improvements was not such as to have any major impact on the general level and standard of Ulster agriculture, and evidence to the Bessborough commission suggested that whatever stimulus the act gave to improvements in the early years, these were gradually checked with the returning sense of insecurity as the defects of the measure became more apparent.[24]

At all events, if the act encouraged tenant improvement, it has been argued that it had precisely the opposite effect on landlord investment. Greater landlord reluctance to invest after 1870 is perfectly understandable: in the first place, landlords were naturally loath to make improvements which might later be used to enhance tenant claims for compensation; secondly, in many areas such as west Donegal where improving an estate almost inevitably meant — as a preliminary at least — consolidating farms, landlords could no longer make the same free use of notices to quit for such purposes;[25] and finally, landlords were more inclined after 1870 to take a more strictly legal view of their relations with their tenants, which meant that they no longer felt the same obligations to assist with such things as slates and timber for the building of cottages, or grants towards drainage and fencing, or even abatements for reclamation. Thus numerous witnesses to both the Chelmsford committee and the Bessborough commission claimed that the 1870 act had discouraged landlord improvements, and the Bessborough report concluded that while 'the land act seems at first passing to have stimulated tenants, especially in Ulster, to improve ... landlords' improvements were checked by it'.[26] On the basis of this evidence, Barbara Solow has maintained that the act 'put an abrupt stop to landlord improvements'.[27]

Although more recent research has effectively refuted the suggestion that landlord improvements halted in 1870,[28] there can be little doubt — in view of the contemporary evidence — that landlords were less inclined after 1870 to spend money on improvements. As against this, however, two points need to be borne in mind: first, landlord investment in Irish agriculture had never been heavy at any rate;[29] and second, it had been more limited still in Ulster where landlords had always been afraid of their improvements being sold as part of the tenant-right.[30] The decrease in landlord investment in Ulster, therefore, could hardly have been of major significance to the tenantry.

Nevertheless, the increased reluctance of northern landlords after 1870 to help tenants with improvements reflected a more fundamental change in landlord–tenant relations; it was not only that they invested less in their estates, but they were, it was believed, more inclined, in their relations with their tenants, to stand on their legal rights. According to Hugh Montgomery, 'some landlords, who had been tolerably considerate before the land act passed, seem to have considered that, law having taken the place of custom and mutual confidence, they were at liberty to get all the law allowed them out of the tenants'.[31] Lord Antrim, for example, widely regarded as a munificent landlord before 1870, was accused by the *Ballymoney Free Press* of doing precisely this when, after 1870, he took advantage of the act to disallow tenant-right on townparks.[32] Lord Lifford, too, after 1870 withdrew the free turbary concessions traditionally made to tenants on his estate, and began charging ninepence per perch and upwards for all bog cut by them.[33] Landlords generally, it was believed, were more cautious and less indulgent with tenants after the act was passed, and the Bessborough commission later concluded that some landlords plainly 'judged that their former forbearance was not suitable to the new relations which legislation had established between themselves and their tenants'.[34]

Tenants also were supposed to have become more independent and assertive as a result of the act which had, it was claimed, created 'exaggerated expectations' among the farmers and given rise 'to unreasonable and extravagant pretensions on the part of a certain class of tenantry'.[35] Certain rights such as, for example, the right to game and the right to cut turf, which had been universally admitted by tenants in the past were, after 1870, sometimes disputed. One incident which was widely commented on at the time was the refusal of the tenants of W.H.M. Style, the owner of an estate at Glenfin, Co. Donegal, to allow Style to let the shooting rights on his land, though they were prepared to allow Style himself a day's shooting should he so wish.[36] More serious disputes — frequently resulting in litigation, and in a number of instances on Lord Lifford's Donegal estate eventually in the eviction of tenants — arose over turbary, especially in Donegal.[37] The problem for the landlord in such disputes was that if he did resort to the traditional remedy of serving a notice to quit, he left himself open to having to pay either compensation for disturbance or, more seriously, a 'ruinous' amount in compensation for tenant-right.

Thus, landlord spokesmen contended, 'exaggerated expectations' and growing self-confidence on the part of the tenants, increased and increasing litigation, and disputes over game and turbary, all threatened to destroy the harmonious relations which had formerly existed between landlords and tenants in Ulster.[38] Yet such strictures clearly overstated the change which had been brought about in landlord–tenant relations by the act. Complaints about the 'unreasonable' and 'exorbitant' demands of tenants came only from a handful of proprietors, while disputes over turbary and game were confined mainly to Donegal; indeed, the very publicity given to the opposition of Style's tenantry to his letting the shooting rights reflected how unusual, almost unique, such an occurrence was. Robert Wilson, guardian of Stranorlar union, 'never heard of a single instance' of tenant interference with shooting rights 'excepting in the case of Mr Style'. Turbary disputes were common even before 1870 and Wilson had not noticed 'any material increase in claims or disputes of that sort since the act passed', except in the case of Lord Lifford.[39] Certainly tenants did not suddenly acquire a new independence overnight as a result of the act. Indeed, one of the problems in administering it in the north was the reluctance of tenants to come forward to give evidence as to the existence of tenant-right customs on their estates for fear of antagonising the landlords.[40]

The fact was that, on the surface at any rate, relations on most estates continued as they had been: not only relations, but — and this was one of the problems of the act — practices as well. What the act had done, as was so frequently pointed out by representatives of both sides, was to legalise both good and bad landlordism, thus in a sense punishing the former and rewarding the latter. John J. Rowan, whose father owned a large estate in north Antrim and who supported tenant-right and tenant-right demands, said it was 'an unjust act inasmuch as it now gives by law to the tenant what formerly the good landlord granted him through a sense of justice; while what the bad landlord formerly withheld is now to some extent withheld by law'. 'In short', Rowan concluded, 'in the north it has left us pretty much where it found us'.[41]

Such a conclusion, however, was not strictly accurate. On the surface things may have continued as they were, and this was especially true on the larger estates where few disputes arose,[42] but underneath the surface things were not the same and could never be the same again. The tenants had in fact made important gains. 'It did not require a land bill to settle the tenant-right question on the Belmore estates', claimed the *Tyrone Constitution*, 'the Belmore tenants always enjoyed tenant-right, and we believe they will admit that the land bill has not improved their condition in the slightest degree'.[43] Perhaps the act had no palpable effect on the Belmore estate, but what it did was ensure that the Ulster custom would continue to be recognised on the estate regardless of any change of circumstances or ownership in the future. 'Tenants', said the *Ballymoney Free Press* in 1874, 'are no longer uneasy as to whether some future king may arise ignorant of their existence and claims'.[44] Moreover, the litigation under the act — in itself a deterring influence on landlords — meant that during the 1870s a great body of land law was gradually being built up, which was increasingly providing a strong barrier against future invasion of tenant rights.

The fact was that the 1870 act gave tenants additional security on estates where the Ulster custom was recognised, and gave them a measure of protection on others where it was not. Speakers at the annual meeting of the Ulster Land Occupiers Association in May 1871 were unanimous in their view that the act was 'of immense value to the tenantry of Ulster'.[45] The *Northern Whig*, towards the end of 1872, smugly described the change which had taken place in the attitude of the northern tenant-righters:

> When the measure was before the legislature, we incurred much obloquy by advising the tenant farmers to accept it, because it really gave them all that they could reasonably expect ... The act has not been two years in operation, and in Ulster it is found to give, as we said it would, practical security and virtual fixity of tenure ... It is felt to be a great and most valuable law. It is now as popular with tenant-right associations as it once appeared unpopular ... The wonder is, not that it has some imperfections, because they were necessarily inevitable in such a complicated piece of experimental legislation, but that it does so much, and that it does it so well.[46]

Even the initial reservations which Ulster tenants and tenant-righters had with regard to the act being administered by the county chairmen had largely disappeared by this stage.[47] All in all, as the *Spectator* pointed out in 1872, the success of the act in Ulster had 'notoriously been beyond what anyone could have foreseen'.[48]

LANDLORD ATTACKS

If Ulster tenants were generally satisfied with the act in its first years, this was not the case with many of the landlords, who looked on it as an encroachment on their rights and who, as we have seen, claimed that it had destroyed the traditionally good landlord–tenant relations in the north. On a number of estates landlords attempted to impose agreements on their tenants which would have virtually deprived them of benefits under the act. One such document, for example, stipulated that on giving up possession of his holding, the tenant should not be 'entitled to any compensation or allowance for what is usually known as tenant-right, or for improvements, save and except such permanent improvements as shall be made by me under special written agreement hereafter made between us'.[49] By 1872, tenant associations throughout the province were warning tenants not to sign any agreements or leases without first seeking legal advice.[50]

For some, however, these warnings came too late. The Earl of Leitrim, for example, after an unfortunate case in which he had to pay forty-one years' compensation to an evicted tenant, enforced agreements on a number of tenants on his Fanad estate; the result was that when one of them, a certain James Carr, was evicted in 1873, his claim for compensation under the Ulster custom was dismissed on the grounds that he had signed an agreement in 1871 that his holding was not subject to tenant-right and disclaiming all right to compensation under the first and second sections of the act.[51] In other cases the vigilance of the tenant associations paid off and attempts to impose agreements on, for example, the Clough estate of David Ker were abandoned as a result of organised tenant opposition.[52] Not all tenants, however, had the self-confidence to withstand office pressure, and, faced with the choice of either signing away part of their rights under the act or giving up their farms and claiming compensation, many of them quietly submitted.[53] In any case, on many estates the owners or agents went about their task more insidiously by confining the agreements to incoming tenants. After John Robinson of Portadown had agreed to buy the tenant-right of a 20-acre farm on the Ranfurly estate for £20 an acre, the agent tried to get him to sign an agreement 'that if, at any time, we require it we will get it, and all you will receive is £10 an acre'. Robinson refused to purchase on these terms, and the holding remained unsold.[54] The Fishmongers' company similarly tried to make incoming tenants sign a deed of covenant releasing all claims to tenant-right, although this was abandoned in face of tenant resistance.[55]

Confiscatory agreements were only part of the landlord campaign against the act. The main landlord attacks — and it should be emphasised that a minority of landlords were involved — focused on the administration rather than the principle of the act. Early attempts to form associations to protect landlord interests under the act came to nothing,[56] and although it seems clear that some of the first appeals against the decisions of the county chairmen were fought as test cases by groups of landlords — the case of *Menown v. Beauclerc* was a case in point — the majority of landlords were prepared to accept the changes brought about by the act and realised the danger of reopening the question. Thus the landlord campaign, such as it was, consisted mainly of individual criticisms through the press and in parliament of the decisions of the county chairmen who, it was contended, were abusing their powers and destroying landlord rights.[57] A particular case which alarmed many landlords in Ulster was one in which Lord Leitrim was obliged to pay the equivalent of forty-one years' purchase of the rent as compensation to an evicted tenant. Although the appeal judge ruled that the special circumstances of this case justified the award, the case was widely quoted by landlord spokesmen as evidence of the way in which the act was being abused and landlord rights endangered.[58]

This campaign against the act culminated in 1872 in the appointment, at the instigation of Lord Lifford, of a select committee of the House of Lords under the chairmanship of Lord Chelmsford to investigate the working of the act and examine in particular the charge that 'the diversity of judgements' by the chairmen of the counties rendered 'the primary tribunal unsatisfactory'. Ulster tenants were understandably concerned at this development, especially as Lifford, in moving for the appointment of the committee, made it clear that such objections as landlords had to the administration of the act were largely confined to Ulster, and were therefore directed mainly against the decisions in favour of Ulster tenant-right; his particular grounds of complaint were the excessive sums being awarded for tenant-right by the Ulster chairmen.[59] Thus the appointment of the committee was met with a storm of protest from tenant associations throughout the province, and public meetings were held in virtually every county expressing approval of the working of the act, of its 'cheap, simple, and expeditious procedure', and of 'the impartiality and equity' of the tribunals which administered it.[60] Even the grand juries in a number of counties joined in the public outcry, presenting addresses to various chairmen complimenting them on their equitable and beneficent administration of the law.[61] The strength of feeling shown in Ulster plus the weight of evidence given to the committee by barristers, solicitors and judges convinced the members of the inadvisability of recommending any change at that time either in the constitution of the primary tribunals or in the procedures under the act.[62]

Nevertheless, although the primary tribunals were completely vindicated, the appointment of the Chelmsford committee had given rise to serious disquiet among Ulster tenants who realised, some of them for the first time, how hostile a number of landlords were to the act and how vulnerable they themselves still were under it. It was from this time too that basic deficiencies in the measure began to appear.

EMERGING DOUBTS

There had earlier been a scare about how far tenants on estates sold in the landed estates court were protected by the act. This had arisen out of a judgment given by Lord Justice Christian in a case brought by tenants on the Waterford estate in Co. Derry, which had been put up for sale in 1870. The trustees of the estate in advertising the sale simply stated that the tenants held from year to year, and the tenants made an application to the court to have their claim under the Ulster custom set out on the rental of the estate. What the tenants wanted was an authoritative declaration that such a notice was unnecessary and that claims under the Ulster custom were not barred by a landed estates court conveyance.[63]

The judges of the landed estates court refused the application of the tenants on the ground that their claim was one which did not need to be noticed in the conveyance and that their rights under the Ulster custom could not be affected by the conveyance.[64] Both judges in the court of chancery appeal affirmed this refusal, but on diametrically opposed grounds. Lord Chancellor O'Hagan concurred in the view taken by the judges of the landed estates court that the tenant-right would not be affected by the conveyance. But the Lord Justice of Appeal, Judge Christian, took the opportunity to launch an attack on the act itself, and gave as his judgment that the claim made by the tenants would be beyond all question defeated by a landed estates court conveyance. Christian's judgment — which virtually deprived tenants on estates sold in the landed estates court of the protection supposedly afforded by the 1870 act — caused widespread consternation in Ulster. At Westminster Gladstone explicitly declared that the government would if necessary introduce further legislation to make good the intention of the land act, but maintained that such legislation was unnecessary. However, Lord Cairns, the former Conservative MP for Belfast, promptly introduced a bill in the House of Lords which finally removed all doubts on this particular point, and the immediate crisis passed.[65]

The alarm excited by Christian's judgment had scarcely subsided when tenant confidence in the adequacy of the first clause of the land act was again shaken by the decision given by the chairman of Co. Derry, James C. Coffey QC, in the case of *Austen v. Scott*. Thomas Austen held the lease of a farm of some eleven acres on the estate of Major Scott, a small estate in the barony of Kennaught. When the lease expired in 1871, Scott served notice of eviction on Austen, who claimed £250 under the Ulster custom. Coffey's opinion, however, was that the covenant in the lease requiring the tenant to give up possession on the termination of the term — such a surrender clause being a common feature of all leases — abrogated the tenant-right custom, and while he awarded Austen £55 this was only because this figure had already been offered by the landlord.[66] This decision naturally caused immense apprehension, especially on estates such as those of the Fishmongers' and Drapers' companies where tenants held under leases which were due to expire in the 1870s. In the event, the decision was reversed on appeal by Chief Justice Monahan, who refused to accept that the surrender clause in a lease overruled the tenant-right. Monahan based his decision on two grounds: first, he could see no difference in the abstract between a tenant who held under lease and a tenant who held from year to year, and who had obviously entered into an express or implied agreement with his landlord to surrender his holding at the end of the year in the same way as leaseholders agreed to surrender their premises at the end of the lease; and secondly, the evidence presented to the court by the owners and agents of some of the principal estates in Derry attested to the fact that no distinction was made in the matter of tenant-right between leaseholders and yearly tenants.[67] Thus the alarm caused by Coffey's decision passed.

The *Austen v. Scott* case, however, was only the first of a series of cases involving leasehold tenant-right and the beginning of a dispute which was to continue for the remainder of the decade. The question was important, affecting as it did some 35,000 holdings in Ulster, the value of tenant-right on which was estimated by Robert Donnell at about £5.5 million.[68] Most of the large landowners were, in fact, quite prepared to accept the view that tenant-right did apply at the end of the lease — and indeed prior to 1870 this had rarely been questioned[69] — but the problem arose, as always, not on the big estates but on the smaller properties where the new owners in particular were more inclined to challenge such an assumption. Thus this was to emerge as the first major area of dispute under the new act, and by mid-1872 the question of leasehold tenant-right was being widely and keenly contested in courts throughout the province.

Earlier decisions in the courts tended to be mixed and only added to the general confusion. In April 1872 Sir Francis Brady, chairman of Tyrone, ruled in the case of *Burns v. Ranfurly* that the lease did not affect the tenant-right of a farm.[70] This followed the ruling of Chief Justice Monahan in the *Austen v. Scott* case, and so too did the almost simultaneous decision of Robert Johnston, chairman of Down, in the case of *Menown v. Beauclerc*.[71] On the other hand, Johnston disallowed leasehold tenant-right claims in at least two cases — *Johnston v. Torrens* and *Wallace v. McClelland* — claiming that the usage had not been proved in either case, while the chairman of Donegal likewise dismissed a leasehold claim in the case of *Ellison v. Mansfield*.[72] Up to this point, while there was mounting concern among the tenants, those claims that were dismissed were being dismissed for lack of proof rather than on any ground of law, and tenants still assumed that neither the act nor the tribunals were making a distinction between leasehold and yearly tenancies.

All these cases were appealed, and the appeals went, almost without exception, against the tenants; the decisions in *Burns v. Ranfurly* and *Menown v. Beauclerc*, for example, were reversed, while those in *Johnston v. Torrens*, *Wallace v. McClelland* and *Ellison v. Mansfield* were affirmed. *Menown v. Beauclerc* in particular was looked upon as a test case of the first importance — being one in which the landlord directly challenged the claim that tenant-right existed at the end of a lease — and it 'excited the most extraordinary interest in the neighbourhood, and, indeed, throughout Ulster'.[73] Menown had claimed £2,000 under the Ulster custom for a farm of about 70 acres, which his forefathers had occupied under a lease of three lives since 1778 and which they had greatly improved. Beauclerc, who was anxious to include the farm in his own demesne, had claimed that, as the farm was under lease, no tenant-right existed. The chairman of Co. Down had found in favour of the claimant and awarded him £1,400, ruling that tenant-right could exist at the end of a lease.[74] Beauclerc appealed the decision, and the case came before Judge Barry at Downpatrick assize, who decided that no tenant-right was proved on the estate at the expiration of a lease and that all Menown was entitled to was compensation for improvements.[75]

Barry's decision was not a decision against leasehold tenant-right as such; indeed, he fully concurred with Chief Justice Monahan's ruling that a lease did not in itself nullify the tenant-right. According to Barry, the question on the expiration of a lease, as on the termination of a yearly tenure, was to be decided by the evidence. But this was precisely what worried northern tenants about this case and why Barry's decision caused such excitement and dismay; the evidence in this instance, they believed, had been overwhelmingly in favour of tenant-right at the end of a lease, and the feeling was that no more convincing evidence would be likely to be produced.[76] The main problem was that tenant-right on leasehold farms was more difficult to prove, for the very simple reason that the sale of tenant-right at the close of a lease was an extremely rare occurrence; after the *Burns v. Ranfurly* claim was dismissed on the ground that the custom had not been proved on the townland, Samuel McElroy pointed out that on some townlands no such sales had taken place for half a century or more.[77] The problem, said W.D. Henderson, a Belfast banker who played a leading role in both the tenant-right movement and Ulster Liberal politics, was not that the judges actually refused leasehold tenant-right, but that they required proof 'which was very difficult to give'.[78]

Thus it was mainly the tendency of chairmen and judges — especially chairmen and judges with conservative predilections and landed connections — to look for 'impossible evidence' which rendered leasehold tenant-right cases under the act extremely hazardous, and it was mainly in this sense that leasehold tenant-right became a major grievance. This was in spite of the fact that the great majority of landlords — certainly of the larger landlords — freely acknowledged the tenant's interest in his holding at the end of a lease, subject only to an equitable increase of rent; tenant-right at the end of a lease, said Marcus Gage, the agent of the Abercorn, Ker and other estates, 'was the custom on nearly all the Conservative estates in Ulster'.[79] But while a minority, even a small minority, of landlords contested such rights and while land courts were ambiguous and demanding in their attitude to such claims, tenants could not feel totally secure, and leasehold tenant-right remained an unsettled question and a potential source of grievance even in the late 1870s, by which time landlords themselves were joining in the campaign to have the issue unequivocally settled in the interest of the tenants.

By this time, too, other defects in the act and its administration had emerged. Robert Donnell listed tenant complaints in a paper read to the British Association in 1874: 'restrictions on tenant-right; deficient protection to leaseholders; inadequate awards even when the custom is proved; the roundabout and ineffective process of adjusting rents; and the confiscation of tenant-right in townparks'.[80] As with leasehold tenant-right, these problems arose partly from the actions of a minority of landlords, and partly from the sometimes narrow, unpredictable and inconsistent administration of the act. Initially, for example, it was assumed that occupiers of townparks could claim under the Ulster custom in the same way as occupiers of other agricultural holdings provided that that was the custom on the estate,[81] and in several early cases various chairmen upheld this view, ruling that section 15 of the act — which excluded townparks from claims for compensation under the general provisions of the act — did not apply to claims under the Ulster custom.[82] But then at the beginning of 1873, the court for land cases reserved gave a decision in the case of *Wilkinson v. Antrim* that the 15th section applied to tenant-right claims and that occupiers of townparks were therefore excluded from compensation under the Ulster custom.[83] To such tenants — and there were a large number of them — it seemed that the land act had suddenly deprived them of a tenant-right which they had enjoyed up to 1870.[84]

Other grievances were more serious in that they affected, at least potentially, a much greater number of tenants. How far estate rules were legalised by the act was a question of pressing interest and importance to most tenants. Early decisions in the courts, however, set at rest some of the fears in this respect, with the county chairmen generally overruling the more recently introduced infringements of the custom. The chairman of Derry, for example, ruled that full tenant-right prevailed on the Clothworkers' estate which Sir Hervey Bruce had purchased in 1871, despite the fact that the Clothworkers' company had attempted to enforce a five years' limit since 1859.[85] And in the *Leitrim v. Friel* appeal case, Judge Lawson, affirming the decision of the Donegal chairman, similarly ruled that tenant-right obtained on Friel's holding even though Leitrim, who had succeeded to the property in 1854, had refused from that date to allow tenant-right.[86] A great many other restrictions were similarly declared illegal in the land courts, such as in the cases of the McGeough estates in Armagh, the Archdall estates in Fermanagh, the Ogilby estate in Tyrone — where Ogilby had disallowed tenant-right since he had purchased the property in 1853 — and many others.[87]

On the other hand, decisions were given which upheld what, from the tenants' point of view, were clearly infractions of the custom. In the case of *McCausland v. McCausland*, for example, proof of the existence of the custom on neighbouring estates was given, but evidence was produced on behalf of the landlord that during the previous twenty years the usage had prevailed on his estate of allowing only two years' purchase. Coffey, the Derry chairman, decided in this case that the usage having prevailed for such a period was legalised by the act.[88] Similarly in the case of *Keown v. de Ros*, Robert Johnston, the chairman of Down, dismissed the claim of Keown, the tenant of a townpark, because de Ros was able to prove that in 1825 he had established a rule on his estate that townparks were not subject to tenant-right;[89] Johnston took the view that 'whatever practice prevailed for any reasonable time previous to the passing of the act, and not imposed in contemplation of the act, was the tenant-right legalized upon the estate, no matter what the tenant-right might be in the district round about'.[90]

Moreover, there was considerable confusion as to whether proof was required of tenant-right on the estate or in the district. Hugh Law, Liberal MP for Co. Derry and attorney-general in Gladstone's first government, said that when the act first came into operation,

> it was the custom of the judges to allow the custom to be proved, not merely by evidence relating to the particular holding or to the estate of which it formed part, but relating to neighbouring estates. It was, however, successfully contended that you must confine the evidence either to the holding itself, or to the estate of which it formed part.[91]

Robert Johnston told the Chelmsford committee that he looked to the usage of the estate rather than the district, and after Judge Barry's judgment in the cases of *Menown v. Beauclerc, Johnston v. Torrens* and *Wallace v. McClelland* in 1872, the *News Letter* commented, 'one thing appears to have been decided, and that is, that the custom claim is limited to the estate'.[92] This in fact was not strictly true, for proof of tenant-right in the district was still accepted in a number of cases, but where proof on the estate was required, it was not always easy to find, especially on the smaller estates where most of the cases tended to arise; and on all estates, as Robert Johnston admitted, there was the problem of getting tenants to give evidence against their landlords.[93]

The main point is that claims under the custom were surrounded by a great deal of uncertainty, and the high number of claims brought under sections 3 and 4 of the act in Ulster was a measure of the lack of confidence of Ulster tenants in claiming under the Ulster custom. In 1873 only 28 per cent of the amount decreed by the county chairmen in Ulster was under section 1, and the tenant-right press was claiming that 'the Ulster custom is being gradually dropped in the land courts, owing to the difficulty of proving it'.[94] And although in subsequent years the amount decreed under section 1 never fell below 50 per cent of the total awarded in Ulster, the uncertainties of litigation were such that few tenants could bring claims with any degree of confidence. By 1876, for example, following a series of complaints from tenants about the decisions of the Co. Antrim chairman, the *Weekly Whig* was maintaining that 'farmers are afraid to bring land disputes before him for adjudication. They complain that he does not attach due weight to the evidence; that it is almost impossible to remove his preconceptions'.[95]

Moreover, even where the custom was established, the county chairmen were often reluctant to award what the tenants believed to be the full market value. William Montgomery, a prominent tenant-right advocate, claimed after the act had been in operation for a year that in no case had he heard of the full benefits of the Ulster custom being granted to a claimant.[96] 'The county court judge', Richard Dowse later agreed, 'rarely gives the full market value of the tenant-right.'[97] Part of the problem was that the chairmen in assessing the value of the tenant-right usually heard contradictory evidence from conflicting sources so that they tended to strike a medium which, by its very nature, was a good deal less than the tenants would have obtained by free sale to the highest bidder in the open market. Some chairmen, indeed, made no attempt to hide their hostility to the whole custom of tenant-right or their reluctance to award the full claims under it. Thomas Lefroy, chairman of Armagh, openly denounced 'the reckless and absurd value which, sessions after sessions, he heard set upon what was called the tenant-right under the Ulster custom',[98] while Robert Johnston admitted to the Chelmsford committee that he would 'feel very much embarrassed' if a case from one of the leading estates came before him because the tenant-right sold for such high amounts. He had, he said, refused to give £30 an acre in one case though the evidence was that that was what the tenant-right sold for;

Johnston took it on himself to limit the award to £20 an acre.[99]

With this uncertainty of administration and with awards under the act apparently depending on the predilections and whims of the residing chairman, tenant dissatisfaction increased. Even the *Whig*, which had consistently defended the act, was by the middle of the decade beginning to admit that the tenants had genuine fears and grievances under it: 'Farmers were growing distrustful of the land courts. Litigation was so expensive and the result so uncertain that they were becoming more and more disposed to bear all their ills until a new act could be passed'.[100] Indeed, in many cases — as, for example, where the landlord either refused the right of sale or refused to accept an incoming tenant, but where no notice to quit had been given — tenants were uncertain how far the act applied at all.[101] Chief Justice Whiteside stated in the case of *O'Brien v. Scott* in 1875 that he would decree against a landlord who 'capriciously' refused to accept a purchaser of the tenant-right interest. Yet when Catherine Hart, a tenant on Robert McGeough's estate in Armagh, claimed under the Ulster custom after McGeough had, without giving any reason, objected to the purchaser of her tenant-right, the chairman dismissed the claim, ruling that 'a claim, in the absence of some act evidencing the intention legally to terminate the tenancy, could not be sustained under the act'.[102]

It was the question of rent, however, which, more even than the ambiguities of administration, gave rise to increasing tenant complaints after 1870. 'In my opinion it was shown', said Arthur McMorrough Kavanagh, a landlord member of the Bessborough commission, speaking of Ulster, 'that the exercise of the power of raising rent on the part of the landlords, where unduly used, was the grievance most severely felt.'[103] One of the main tenant reservations about the act in 1870 had been its failure to control rents, and tenants repeatedly claimed during the 1870s that the intentions of the act were being flagrantly defeated by persistent increases of rent which were virtually confiscating the tenants' property. The Bessborough commission, on the basis of evidence presented to it, concluded that the act had failed to afford tenants adequate security against unreasonable increases of rent, which had 'in some cases ... almost "eaten up" the tenant-right'.[104]

Rents in Ulster may on average have been moderately set,[105] but landlords after 1870 were, it was believed, more inclined to stand on their rights and look for a higher return from their estates than they had in the past. W.E. Forster, after making enquiries for Gladstone about rent increases in Ulster after the act, reported to him that 'in one respect, matters are worse than they were before the act, because the legalizing of the custom has induced the landlord to test his legal powers', while the Bessborough report stated that 'some landlords, who previously were content to take low rents, appear to have begun a system of rent-raising when the land act was passed'.[106]

Yet, while tenants may have believed — or claimed — that rent increases were higher or more frequent after 1870, the act did, at least indirectly, exercise some kind of control over rents. Although it gave county chairmen no jurisdiction over rents, many chairmen found themselves — reluctantly, but to the immense satisfaction of the tenants[107] — having to decide at times whether rent increases were exorbitant or not. In a number of cases where tenants had refused to pay what they claimed were unreasonable increases of rent and consequently had notices to quit served on them, the county chairmen accepted that such increases were tantamount to disturbance of occupation under the act and awarded the tenants their full claims under the custom. The first important decisions in this respect were given at the Ballymena Land Sessions early in 1872 when the chairman of Antrim, J.H. Otway QC, ruled that the rent demanded by Archibald Hamilton of two tenants on his Ballinaloob estate was excessive and would in great measure destroy the tenant-right: 'In my opinion, judging solely from the evidence before me, the rent demanded is exorbitant and extortionate. Had the landlord been more reasonable and proposed a reasonable rent, I believe I should have dismissed the claim.'[108] In the circumstances, Otway awarded the tenants the value of their tenant-right and by doing so had, it was believed, 'established a precedent of incalculable value to the tenant-farmers of Ulster'; 'in every case of increased rent', it was claimed, 'the tenant has only to show that it encroaches on his property, and he will recover its value to the uttermost'.[109]

Such decisions exercised some kind of control over rents. But the problem with these claims, as with others under the act, was that the tenancy had still to be terminated and, as one tenant advocate pointed out, 'many farmers would submit to a most unreasonable tax rather than be evicted out of their holdings, submit to what would not only represent the fair value of the landlord's interest, but also encroach on the property of the tenant'.[110] Even when the tenant was successful in his claim, he was still turned out of his holding; in other words, the act gave him compensation for the loss of his tenant-right when what he really wanted was to continue in occupancy at a fair rent. Moreover, tenant spokesmen claimed that in many cases where landlords were forced to pay compensation they were able to recoup their losses from the increased rents paid by the incoming tenants.[111]

At any rate, even if the act did provide some kind of indirect deterrent against excessive increases of rent, landlords soon found a way round it, and that was by raising the rent at the time when the tenant-right was being sold. 'Before the land act', Forster was informed in 1880, 'the time of sale of a tenant's interest was not generally selected by landlords to raise the rent; now it is often so selected.'[112] Numerous complaints were made on this score to the Bessborough commission which, on the basis of the evidence presented to it, concluded:

> This practice appears to be a comparatively new one, since the land act of 1870. Before that time there was a delicacy in meddling with sales of tenant-right ... After the land act, a demand for an increase of rent, if followed by a notice to quit, became liable to the inconvenience that a tenant might refuse to pay, and might serve a claim for compensation for his tenant-right. In this way the landlord, if he persisted in his notice to quit, might be forced unexpectedly to pay down a large sum of money, when he had only calculated on receiving an increase of rent. To wait for a sale of the tenant-right, and then announce the increase, was a course which made it in the highest degree improbable that any resistance would be made to the landlord's demand.[113]

Such untimely increases of rent had obviously a direct and damaging effect on the value of tenant-right and, while Ulster tenants had few complaints about the general level of rent in the province or even about periodical revaluations of rent, this new and growing practice of raising rents at the time of sale had emerged by the late 1870s as one of the leading tenant grievances in the province.

It would be a mistake, however, to conclude that the land act of 1870 had been a failure in Ulster; as the *Weekly Whig* commented in 1877:

> Take the act with all its errors of administration, and it must be prized as one of the most valuable boons ever conferred upon Ulster. It would be superfluous to draw a comparison between the condition of the custom now and its condition before 1870. Then it was a thing of grace, subject to every whim of the landlord, whether feudal, political or selfish; now it has acquired the force and dignity of law, being no longer the shuttlecock of circumstances but the acknowledged basis of the relations between landlord and tenant.[114]

Nevertheless, in spite of its merits and in spite of what it had achieved for Ulster tenants, it had not given tenants all that they had wanted, and as time went on its defects became more apparent: it had failed to control rents, to provide adequate protection for leasehold tenant-right, to prevent leases and agreements being imposed on tenants, or to prevent the confiscation of tenant-right on townparks; then, too, there was the expense of litigation, the inadequate awards even when claims were proved, and the general uncertainties of the act's administration. In these circumstances, tenants were increasingly anxious for amending legislation. In one sense, with the old traditional relationships between landlords and tenants already disturbed, and with an increasing number of landlords standing on their rights, it was essential for the legislative protection partially given by the act of 1870 to be completed. 'We have shifted our moorings, and we cannot remain where we are', one speaker told a meeting of tenants in Moira in 1874. 'It is quite evident the guardianship of feudalism will afford us no further shelter, and the protective wing of British law has not yet taken us in.'[115] What the tenants wanted was the legalisation of the Ulster custom in its integrity, with tenant-right preserved at the fall of a lease and with rent differences settled by an independent tribunal. It was these demands which were articulated by the tenant-right associations during the 1870s, and it was the failure of the Conservative government to meet them after 1874 which provided the dynamic of growth of the Liberal party in the province during this decade.

# 5
# The Tenant-right Movement 1870–74

DEVELOPMENT

The passage of the land bill through its final stages was immediately followed by a change in the nature of the tenant-right movement. The original purpose of the movement had been to support the agitation for reform, to give expression to the views of the northern tenants, and hopefully to influence the shape of whatever legislation was passed.[1] If the passing of the bill rendered societies created for such purposes redundant, it created an even greater need for them in another respect. The degree to which the act benefited tenants in Ulster was going to depend on its interpretation by the courts, and the first decisions under the new law were going to be absolutely crucial in this respect. What the act had done was create a situation in which a decision about a single holding could have repercussions for every other holding on the estate or in the district, or even indeed in the province.Not all tenants had either the courage or the will to stand alone against their landlords; and not all of them could afford the expense or the risk of litigation, especially litigation which might involve appeals through the higher courts. In these circumstances it was essential for tenants to combine to watch over the operation of the act and sustain tenant claims brought under it 'so as to prevent erroneous decisions from becoming legal precedents'. The clause concerning Ulster was so indefinite, said James McKnight, that associations of this kind were 'imperatively necessary at least for a few years, until the true interpretation of the law shall have been authoritatively settled by the superior judges, so as to rule in future all similar cases which may be brought before the courts'.[2] Thus the passing of the act in August 1870 gave the tenant associations a new and in many respects a more vital role, and stimulated both the reorganisation and the growth of the tenant movement in the province.

In the initial agitation leading up to the land bill, the main areas of tenant-right activity had been in north Antrim, north Derry, east Donegal and east Tyrone, all wealthy farming regions and strong tenant-right areas — those areas in fact where tenants had most to lose or gain from legislation — and it was in these same areas that the tenant-right movement was best organised. North Antrim in particular took a leading part in the campaign, and the most powerful tenant organisation in the province was the Route Tenant-Right Association centred on Ballymoney; but strong tenant-right associations were also formed at Ballymena and Ballyclare, with another less active society at Larne. In County Derry, the Derry, Eglinton, Kennaught and Coleraine tenant-right societies were all prominent in the early agitation, while in Donegal those at Letterkenny, Castlefin and Ballybofey played an equally important part in stimulating tenant interest and support.

No other counties were as well organised as these. There were important tenant-right associations in Tyrone at Dungannon and Cookstown, but the county generally was not well organised. And although there were four societies in Down — at Newtownards, Comber, Downpatrick and Killyleagh — agitation in the county was muted, and the only effective organisation in the sense of undertaking any kind of sustained activity was the Newtownards Tenant-Right Association; Comber, Downpatrick and Killyleagh were generally represented at the main tenant-right conferences of this period, but otherwise appear to have been almost totally inactive. Armagh tenants were slow to organise and the only important society here was the Portadown Tenant-Right Association, although another short-lived association was formed at Armagh itself. In Monaghan and Fermanagh there was little activity, while the County Cavan Tenant

League identified itself more with the National Tenant League of the south than with the tenant-right movement in Ulster.

After 1870, while the intensity of activity varied — peaking at certain times as, for example, in 1872 when the Chelmsford committee was appointed and again in 1873–4 when the movement was heavily involved in electioneering — and while societies were sometimes formed during periods of excitement only to become inactive or even disappear after the immediate crisis had passed, the main areas of activity remained largely the same. But many of the existing societies acknowledged their new function by changing their names from tenant-right associations to tenant defence and protection associations. Hence the Ballymena Tenant-Right Association was reconstituted as the Ballymena Tenants' Protection Association, the Route Tenant-Right Association as the Route Tenants' Defence Association, the Kennaught Farming Society as the Kennaught Farmers' Defence Association, and so on.[3] New societies, too, were formed at Lisburn and Ballycastle in Antrim, Saintfield, Banbridge and Newry in Down, Claudy in Derry, Tandragee in Armagh, Donemana, Castlederg and Omagh in Tyrone, and Carrickmacross in Monaghan. But all of these bodies, whether reconstituted or newly formed, had the same purpose, namely to protect tenant rights under the act and give legal protection to their members.

In most cases their intentions were general, but in some their formation was a response to a specific incident or threat. The chairman of the Ballycastle Tenants' Defence Association, for example, admitted that the association would not have been formed had it not been for the refusal of Alexander Stewart to approve the sale of the tenant-right of one of the holdings on his estate at Ballycastle, an action which caused 'a sense of uneasiness to extend throughout the entire neighbourhood'.[4] Similarly, the formation of the Claudy Tenant-Right Defence Association was a direct result of the attempt of the Fishmongers' Company to increase rents and impose new agreements on their tenants, thus threatening the tenant-right interests not only on the Fishmongers' estate but also, it was felt, on neighbouring estates.[5] The Newry Tenant Farmers' Defence Association too was originally established because of a dispute on the McGeough estate, while the Tandragee Tenants' Defence Association was formed mainly in order to contest the imposition of a £5 rule on the Manchester estate.[6] And what was to become one of the most important associations in the whole movement, the Down Farmers' Union, was a direct result of the *Menown v. Beauclerc* case.[7] Mainly, however, the societies were formed for the general purpose of watching over the administration of the act and ensuring that section 1 was properly interpreted in the tenant interest.

Much of this early development after 1870 took place under the auspices of the Ulster Land Occupiers' Association, an umbrella organisation formed at the end of September 1870 following meetings in Ballymoney and Belfast. The stated objects of the association were to defend tenant interests under the land act, and to reform the grand jury system 'upon the principles of local self-government and representation by taxation'. It was agreed at the inaugural meeting that the funds of the association should be used to finance all legal proceedings in which its members were involved with landlords, and that the subscription rate should be 2s 6d for tenants whose valuation was below £10 and at least 5s for all others. A permanent committee was to be established consisting of two members from each local association which had subscribed £5 to the parent body.[8]

The need for such a provincial organisation in the new situation created by Gladstone's act had been strongly urged by the tenant-right press, and many of the existing tenant-right societies such as the Route, Ballymena, Kennaught, Cookstown, and Castlefin associations welcomed its formation and became affiliated members. Its leaders also, especially its chairman W.D. Henderson and its secretary William Montgomery, did a great deal of work in promoting the formation of branch associations — as, for example, at Magheragall, Banbridge and Donemana — so that by mid-1871 it could claim to represent tenant societies in Antrim, Down, Derry, Donegal, Armagh and Tyrone.[9] But these early efforts were not sustained, and the Belfast-based organisation never became, as its leaders had hoped, the 'Anti-Corn Law League' of the tenant-right movement.[10] Although it began in 1871 to publish edited reports of cases under the land act as a guide to farmers, its direct involvement in such cases and in local disputes appears to have been limited, and its activity — much of it in the first year or so directed towards securing grand jury reform — did not extend beyond the end of 1872.

It was, in fact, through the local societies rather than the provincial organisation that the main work of the movement was carried on. It was, for example, the Kennaught Farmers' Defence Association which took up and successfully carried the appeal in the case of *Austen v. Scott*; the chairman of Derry's decision that the surrender clause in a lease abrogated the tenant-right custom affected tenants not only on Scott's estate, which was a small one, but on the larger surrounding properties so that there was an immediate response to the Kennaught society's appeal for funds to fight the decision.[11] Likewise, when William Fleck was ejected from his holding on Lord O'Neill's Braid estate near Broughshane in 1871, the Ballymena Tenants' Protection Society fought the case for him, and successfully appealed the decision when it went against Fleck.[12]

Other examples of actions taken on behalf of tenants can be quoted, but it should not be assumed — and the societies were at pains to point out to their members that they should not assume — that the associations were prepared to support their members in all legal proceedings arising out of the act. Benjamin Barfoot, chairman of the Cookstown Land Occupiers' Association, defined the general policy of the tenant societies when he emphatically warned his members that they would not necessarily have the support of the association in every legal dispute; the committee, he said, would fight no case where they did not expect a tenant victory or where some vital principle of the bill was not involved.[13] 'They were not law lovers', said Joseph Perry, explaining the work of the Down Farmers' Association. 'In the course of four years they had been solicited by fifty or sixty tenants to take up their cases, but they had never interfered except one, and that was the now celebrated case he had referred to. They had now taken up another case, that of *Wright v. Montgomery*.'[14] The 'celebrated case' to which Perry had referred was that of *Menown v. Beauclerc* in which, as in the cases of *Austen v. Scott*, *Fleck v. O'Neill* and *Wright v. Montgomery*, an important principle was at stake.[15] Other associations found themselves more heavily involved in litigation; the Route association, for example, had fought no fewer than seven cases by the beginning of 1873,[16] while the Kennaught Society undertook several important legal actions under the act in its first years of operation.[17] But all associations were prepared to take legal action only as a last resort, and the legal activity of most societies consisted mainly of securing legal advice for their members; indeed, in the majority of cases referred to the associations this was all that was required.

There was, then, no justification for landlord allegations that the tenant-right societies were deliberately encouraging litigation. But while membership of a tenant association did not give tenants a licence to seek disputes with their landlords, it did mean that if such a dispute arose they did not have to stand alone against their landlord. Belonging to a tenant organisation gave the tenants a security under the act that they would not otherwise have had, and enabled them to resist encroachments by landlords on their tenant-right in a way that they could not have achieved as individuals. The refusal of Alexander Stewart to approve the sale of the tenant-right on one of the holdings on his north Antrim estate was quickly withdrawn after the intervention of the Ballycastle Tenant-Right Defence Association.[18] Likewise, under pressure from the Claudy and Kennaught associations, the Fishmongers' company gave up their attempt to impose new agreements on their tenants and reduced their proposed increases of rent.[19] And where the refusal of tenants to pay what were apparently exorbitant increases in rent did result in notices to quit and legal action, the tenant societies were generally prepared to give their members whatever support was necessary; hence, the Portadown Tenant Farmers' Association took up the case of tenants on the Macnaughten estate in Armagh where refusal to pay 20 per cent increases of rent had led to a number of ejectments, and the Newry, Ballymena and Coleraine associations took up similar cases for tenants on the McGeough, Gray and Bruce estates in their respective areas.[20] The tenant societies, in fact, did what they had set out to do, viz. give tenants legal protection under the act and enable them to enjoy its full benefits, and much of the success of the measure in the north owed not a little to their work and activity.

This legal and protective work, undertaken at a time when there was a high degree of tenant satisfaction with the concessions won in 1870, constituted the main function of the tenant-right movement in 1871–2, and indeed continued to be carried out during the remainder of the 1870s. From 1872, however, circumstances changed in Ulster, and several developments combined to shake tenant confidence in the act of 1870 and to bring about a perceptible and growing change both in the direction of the tenant-right movement and in the nature of its activity. First, the appointment of the Chelmsford committee threatened for a time to reopen the whole land question, and provoked the tenant organisations into a flurry of renewed agitation directed this time not to the protection of tenants under the act, but to the defence of the act itself and of the primary tribunals which administered it. However — and perhaps partly as a result of the determination shown by the associations — neither the fears with regard to Chelmsford nor the threat of a concerted landlord attack on the act — of which the appointment of the Chelmsford committee had appeared to be part — materialised. Secondly, and more seriously, the series of legal decisions referred to in the previous chapter went against the tenants and raised questions once again as to the value of the protection afforded by the act. Cases such as *Burns v. Ranfurly*, *Menown v. Beauclerc* and *Ellison v. Mansfield* raised serious doubts about the position of leasehold tenant-right, while almost simultaneously the townpark tenant-right interest was put in jeopardy by the decision in *Williamson v. Antrim*.[21]

The most important of these cases, and the one which received widest publicity at the time, was that of *Menown v. Beauclerc*, in which Judge Barry reversed the earlier decision of the County Down chairman and disallowed the leasehold tenant-right claim of Menown. Although, as we have seen, Barry's decision was not a decision against leasehold tenant-right in the abstract, it seemed to demand proof for leasehold claims which tenants felt it would be impossible to give and it caused widespread apprehension throughout the province. In Co. Down it led directly to the formation of what was to become one of the strongest tenant organisations in the province, viz. the

Down Farmers' Association. This was a significant development in itself because landlord–tenant relations in Down were traditionally the best in the province, and such agitation and activity as there had been in the county up to this had been half-hearted and sporadic. When the claim was first made, W.J. Moore, who was later primarily responsible for the formation of the Down Farmers' Union, had taken an active part and met great difficulty in getting up witnesses for Menown. After the initial success at the quarter sessions, Moore had received information that the landlords were intending to challenge the decision of the county chairman and he, along with Joseph Perry, a local farmer of some 130 acres, had set about forming the Down Farmers' Union to assist Menown. At first, however, this covered only the Downpatrick area, and it was only after Barry's decision that a sufficient stimulus was given to the movement in Down to transform the Downpatrick body into the County Down Farmers' Association with branches in various parts of the county.[22] It had, in fact, taken the Barry judgment to shake the county out of its complacency.

The repercussions of this judgment, however, extended well beyond Down, and in many respects it represented a turning point in the history of the tenant-right movement. It was the first case in which serious and lasting doubts about the value of the 1870 act were raised. And when it was followed by other, from the point of view of the tenants, questionable decisions with the county chairmen apparently looking — partly, it was felt, as a result of the Chelmsford committee and pressure from the landlords — for more demanding proof in all claims, disillusionment and dissatisfaction with the act began to set in. More frequent complaints began to be heard about other aspects of the act's administration, especially with regard to the insistence of some chairmen that tenant-right be proved on the estate rather than in the district, and increasingly about the failure of the act to control rents.

For the first time serious demands began to be made for amending legislation. The *Coleraine Chronicle* in an editorial entitled 'The insufficiency of the land act' claimed that 'the Ulster clause' was 'misleading and defective', and called for the introduction of perpetuity of tenure and the establishment of a legal tribunal for fixing rents.[23] A tenant conference held in Ballymoney in February 1873 — the most important of the demonstrations held at this time — went further and demanded legislation embracing the '3Fs' — fixity of tenure, free sale and fair rent.[24] These demands were quickly taken up by the other tenant associations. Only the *Northern Whig* struck a cautionary note, warning against reopening the question 'in pursuit of a visionary and mischievous theory', and claiming that the 'extreme demands' made at Ballymoney could never be conceded 'by a responsible government and legislature'.[25] In spite of such warnings, however, meetings at Newry, Downpatrick, Ballycastle, Magheragall, Coleraine, Dungannon, Portadown and other centres passed resolutions condemning the deficiencies of the act of 1870 and demanding its amendment along the lines promulgated at Ballymoney.

These new demands in Ulster were an echo of those which were being increasingly made in the south, and one of their immediate effects was to bring the Ulster tenant associations into line with tenant societies in the rest of the country for the first time since the 1870 act had been passed. Although southern tenants had been left without any form of national organisation after the collapse of Butt's Tenant League in 1870, the local farmers' clubs had continued in existence, while the support given by home rule candidates to tenant-right in by-elections up to 1874 testified to the continuing importance of the land question.[26] By 1872 the shortcomings of the act had been clearly illustrated in the south and moves were afoot to rejuvenate the tenant-right movement on a national basis. These developments were welcomed by the northern tenant-right press which, apart from the *Northern Whig*, urged unity between north and south in the common cause, and supported the call for a national conference.[27]

Not all the tenant associations in Ulster responded to the call for national unity, and at the Dublin tenant-right conference in April only the Ulster Land Occupiers' Association and the Route, Ballymena, Lisburn, Portadown, Banbridge and Cavan associations were represented. Nevertheless, the conference was generally regarded as successful, with the southern delegates studiously avoiding all references to home rule, and all delegates unanimous in their opinion that the 1870 act had failed in its objects, that it had not imposed any real check on evictions or the exaction of exorbitant rents and that it had failed to give adequate protection to the Ulster custom. The only remedy for the land problem in Ireland, it was agreed, was to give to all tenants 'the full rights of the Ulster custom — undisturbed possession at a fair rent to be fixed from time to time with the right to sell his interest at the highest price he can obtain'.[28]

These resolutions were reaffirmed at another national tenant-right conference in Belfast in January of the following year. As one would expect, this conference was much better attended by delegates from Ulster with at least nineteen northern associations represented, but there was also a large delegation from the south with representatives from Counties Wicklow, Leitrim, Dublin, Cork, Kilkenny and Queen's County and from Kanturk, Mallow and Athy.[29] Again there was unanimous agreement that nothing less than the complete legalisation of the Ulster custom and its extension to all parts of Ireland would suffice to solve the land problem.[30]

Thus by 1874 the northern tenant demands appeared to have been subsumed in a broader national programme. In reality, however, this was far from being the case. Although the growing dissatisfaction with the act in Ulster prompted co-operation with the south at this time, and although this co-operation continued on an occasional basis up until the emergence of the Land League in 1879, the relationship between north and south was never — in spite of the goodwill and efforts of certain individuals on both sides — a truly harmonious or close one. Northern tenants always suspected the association of the southern farming clubs with home rule[31] — though there were few enough grounds for such suspicion — so that, even before the emergence of the Land League, there was never more than a tenuous and superficial unity between the two movements.

A much more significant consequence of the revival of tenant discontent from 1872 was the change it brought about in the direction and nature of the tenant-right movement in Ulster itself. Once the need for amending legislation was realised, the movement almost inevitably assumed a political dimension and became more directly and increasingly involved in political activity. Practically from the start of the dispute about leasehold tenant-right, speakers at tenant-right meetings began to urge the return of independent representatives to parliament, and from the beginning of 1873 this advocacy became more strident. At meetings of the Newry, Portadown, Coleraine, Dungannon and Magheragall associations, resolutions were passed advising members not to vote for any candidate in the forthcoming election who would not pledge himself to promote the amendment of the land act.[32] And at the Ballymoney conference in February, every single speaker emphasised the importance of returning to parliament men who would represent their views on the floor of the House of Commons.[33] Nor did the political interest of the associations end here. On the day after the Ballymoney conference, McElroy tells us, a meeting of 'deputies from several tenant-right associations was held with reference to the parliamentary representation of County Antrim ... [and] arrangements were made for organising the county'.[34] In Co. Down, the Down Farmers' Union was working along the same lines. Some time later, W. J. Moore explained how Sharman Crawford had come to be elected as the tenant-right representative for the county:

> After the decision of Judge Barry in Menown's case, the Down Farmers' Union held a meeting at Downpatrick, at which Mr Crawford presided. It was then first mentioned that Mr Crawford should be made their member ... Had it not been for Mr Godfrey Lyle [Beauclerc's land agent] there would be no tenant-right association in the County Down, and Mr Crawford would be sitting then in Rademon House [Crawford's Co. Down residence].[35]

Likewise in Tyrone, where a vacancy occurred in the county representation in February, notices appeared in the local papers informing tenants that a tenant-right candidate would be put forward and advising them to keep themselves free to support him.[36]

Increasingly from this date attempts were made by the associations, especially those in Down and Antrim, to organise committees in the various polling districts to look after the registration of the tenant farmers, who had clearly been given a new and greater political influence by the introduction of the ballot in 1872.[37] Yet, if by this stage tenant-right was again becoming a political question and being rapidly and inexorably pushed by the tenant-right associations to the centre of the political stage in Ulster, the tenant-right leaders still insisted that it was not a party question. 'We care for no man's politics at present', said Joseph Perry, 'but we want farmers to be in the position to return tenant-right candidates, be their politics what they may.'[38] These views were stated more fully by Thomas Swann:

> We have nothing whatever to do with politics, and the tenant-right society that starts into existence as a political body could scarcely be considered in union with the other tenant-right associations in Antrim or Down ... Tenant-right societies to be of any working value must remain free, independent, and totally unpledged to any side in politics, for if the Conservatives will not do our work and secure us in the one or two thousand pounds which each of us has invested in tenant-right, then we must ask the Liberals, and if the Liberals deceive us, we must go back to the Conservatives. But ... we will not be made party tools to do the work of any particular party.[39]

Swann and Perry were large farmers — and Swann was clearly addressing an audience in which such people predominated — and their views on the political role of the tenant associations were not necessarily shared by other tenant-right leaders. But while these statements were a fair definition of the political policy of the tenant-right movement and of the public stance taken by it in 1873–4, there were many in the movement — not all of them directly connected with land themselves — who welcomed its more immediate involvement in politics, and who looked on it as a means of securing more fundamental changes than a reform of the land laws.

## LEADERSHIP AND SUPPORT

As already suggested, one of the most consistent features of tenant-right activity in Ulster was its distribution. In spite of the vitality of the tenant-right movement in certain areas, tenants in the north generally were never widely nor well organised, and the sustained campaigning in places such as north Antrim, north Derry and later Down was in marked contrast to the sporadic and ephemeral nature of the agitation in other counties. But even in strong tenant-right areas, tenant-right leaders often found the response of the tenants disappointing. With no records of the membership of any of the associations surviving, it is impossible to estimate either how large the membership was or to what extent it was made up of tenant farmers; but the overall evidence suggests both that the actual membership was limited and that the farmers never joined the movement in any great numbers. Twelve months after the Magheragall branch of the Ulster Land Occupiers' Association was formed it had just over seventy members. The Moira Tenant-Right Association had about 100 members. Others of course were more successful; there were, for example, about 400 members enrolled in the Tandragee Tenants' Defence Association, while the Route association — the most consistently active of all the tenant societies during this period — claimed a membership in 1880 of close on 1,000.[40]

Not all of these members were necessarily tenant farmers, and complaints were frequently made about the failure of tenants to subscribe to a movement which was primarily intended to protect their interests. Even at the height of the land bill crisis in 1870, the tenant-right associations were reported to 'have been anything but influentially supported by the class they profess to represent', and three years later complaints were still being made that while 'almost every important town has its tenant farmers' association', the tenants themselves were refusing to join.[41] Nevertheless, without at least a degree of tenant support the movement could neither have survived nor enjoyed the success it did, and while the numbers who actually became members of the associations may have been only a fraction of the whole, it is clear that the rank and file membership of most associations was made up predominantly of farmers.[42]

The tenant-right press were, of course, at pains to emphasise the extent of tenant support for the movement, if only to refute Tory and landlord allegations that 'tenant leaguers have no land and know nothing about land'.[43] Certainly many of the meetings were well attended by farmers and also frequently addressed by them. But the degree of tenant interest naturally depended on the circumstances of the time. Thus in the agitation preceding the 1870 bill there was a good turn-out for land meetings and reports claimed attendances of 1,000, 5,000, 10,000 and even in one instance 20,000, the majority of those present being tenant farmers.[44] Likewise at other times of excitement as, for example, on the appointment of the Chelmsford committee when, it was claimed, the tenants were 'thoroughly aroused', tenant-right activity was both more intensive and better supported by the farmers.[45]

Tenants generally, however, were most likely to respond when their own interests were directly threatened. The most successful meeting ever held by the Ballyclare Tenants' Protection Association, for example, followed an attempt by Major Gray to raise the rents on his estate outside the town, so that William Gault, one of the committee members, suggested they should propose a vote of thanks to Gray for the stimulus he had given to the tenant-right cause in the district.[46] Many associations indeed — as we have already seen — owed their very formation to the threat posed to tenant interests by some specific incident or landlord action rather than to any general desire to protect tenant-right in the abstract. Apart from such cases, however, the tenants generally were reluctant to organise or to agitate and the picture as a whole is one of tenant apathy. 'It must be confessed', said the *Northern Whig*, 'that hitherto they [the tenants] have generally shown but little public spirit. Even during the recent agitation on the land question they have been only too ready to call on Mr Gladstone and the government to do everything for them, while scarcely doing anything for themselves'.[47] These views were reiterated by tenant-right editorials and by tenant-right activists at meetings throughout the province; virtually every speaker at the Ballymoney land conference of February 1873, for example, excoriated the farmers for their servility and their failure to do anything to help themselves.[48]

The fact was that the majority of tenants — and this applied in particular to the smaller tenants — were unwilling to organise or campaign against their traditional benefactors, even after they had been given a degree of protection and security by the act of 1870.

Samuel McElroy himself pointed out that it was not reasonable to expect the tenants of a landlord 'who had given them continuous occupation, the right of free sale and charged fair rents' to agitate or vote against that landlord; 'they say that he has treated them justly and kindly all his days, and that to turn against him now under a new order of things would be ungrateful'.[49] No doubt the smaller tenants attended public demonstrations in considerable numbers, especially at times of crisis when excitement was running high, but, given the paucity of entertainment and events in rural areas, it was not surprising that they should do so. But in so far as tenants took a leading or active part in the movement, it was the larger tenants who did so; indeed, the participation of these tenants and the respectability of their position was something that the tenant-right press was only too anxious to underline. Those who attended the Eglington meeting in January 1870, for example, were 'farmers of no common order, being men of social mark, distinguished for their high intelligence and their resolution'.[50] At Toome 'the platform was filled with some of the most substantial tenant farmers in the neighbourhood', while a meeting of the Coleraine association was 'essentially representative of the intelligence and respectability of the tenant farmers in the neighbourhood'.[51]

An analysis of the occupations of forty-four leaders of the movement — including the chairman and secretary of twenty associations and the chairman or secretary of four others[52] — shows that 25 per cent of those taken for the sample were tenant farmers, 27 per cent were shopkeepers, merchants or publicans with a further 7 per cent being manufacturers, 11 per cent professional and financial, 11 per cent presbyterian ministers and 5 per cent landowners, with some 14 per cent unidentified (Table 5.1).

Table 5.1.The occupations of the chief officers of twenty-four
tenant-right associations in Ulster[53]

| | ANTRIM | ARMAGH | DOWN | DONEGAL | DERRY | TYRONE | TOTAL | % |
|---|---|---|---|---|---|---|---|---|
| Farmers | 5 | 1 | 1 | 1 | 2 | 1 | 11 | 25 |
| Shopkeepers | 1 | | 1 | 1 | | 2 | 5 | 11.4 |
| Merchants | 1 | 1 | 1 | | 2 | 1 | 6 | 13.6 |
| Publicans | | | | 1 | | | 1 | 2.3 |
| Manufacturers | | 2 | 1 | | | | 3 | 6.8 |
| Bank Managers | | | 1 | | | | 1 | 2.3 |
| Business Agents | | | | | 1 | | 1 | 2.3 |
| Professionals | 2 | | 1 | | | | 3 | 6.8 |
| Presbyterian Ministers | 2 | | 1 | 1 | 1 | | 5 | 11.4 |
| Landowners | | | | 1 | | 1 | 2 | 4.5 |
| Unknown | 1 | | 3 | 1 | 1 | | 6 | 13.6 |
| TOTAL | 12 | 4 | 10 | 6 | 7 | 5 | 44 | |

This is not, of course, an exact measurement of the involvement of these occupations in the tenant-right movement or its leadership, and it is not being suggested that Table 5.1 gives any more than a general indication of the main social groups from which the leadership was drawn. But several points do emerge: first, the tenant-right movement in Ulster was clearly led by an alliance of tenant-farmers, presbyterian ministers and town commercial and professional classes; secondly, and equally clearly, the tenants themselves were heavily involved at leadership level. Townspeople of course were in a better position to undertake organisational activities, but it seems quite evident that tenant farmers played a good deal more than a supporting role. Indeed, the 25 per cent may well understate their involvement; an examination of the membership of the committee of the Route association in 1870 shows that whereas the three officers of the association — the chairman, secretary and treasurer — were all townspeople, over half of the membership of the committee as a whole were tenant farmers. And the probability is that those leaders who could not be identified in the original sample of forty-four also belonged to this class.

One of the problems here is that tenants are the group that is most difficult to identify. Townspeople can be reasonably easily traced through the directories and landowners through the so-called Domesday survey of 1876 and Bateman's *Great Landowners*. But an attempt to trace farmers through the valuation records proved so tedious and time-consuming that it was finally abandoned, and reliance was placed on the local press. Press reports of meetings frequently identified tenant-right officers as belonging to particular social groups and sometimes gave general indications of their relative position within those groups; thus Benjamin Barfoot, chairman of the Cookstown association, was described as 'an extensive tenant farmer' and William Gault, secretary of the Ballyclare society, as 'another fine type of successful Antrim farmer'.[54] Gault and another tenant, J.J. Kirkpatrick, chairman of the Ballyclare society, were also listed in the directories under the category 'gentry, clergy etc', indicating that they were figures of some social standing in the locality. Additional information on the occupations and the size of the holdings of tenant officers was also sometimes given to the Bessborough commission: Thomas Swann, secretary of the Lisburn association, identified himself to Bessborough as a tenant of seventy acres on the Yarmouth estate, and Joseph Perry, founder and chairman of the Down Farmers' Union, as a farmer of 130 acres.[55] Thus of the eleven office-holders identified in the sample as tenants, five were clearly what could be described as large farmers, and it can be stated with a fair degree of certainty that tenant leaders of the movement were generally men of some substance. This is borne out by such evidence as has come to hand about the holdings of other tenant leaders not included in the sample.

A number of prominent tenant-righters, indeed, combined tenancies with ownership of land. James Ferguson, for example, one of the leading lights in the Ballyclare association, held at least three separate farms, including one of over eighty-two acres, as well as owning 336 acres of land himself, and Nelson Ruddell of Lurgan and W.J.

Devlin of Cookstown similarly combined ownership with large tenancies on neighbouring estates.[56] Landowners generally, of course, held themselves aloof from the movement, though there were a number of exceptions. James Sharman Crawford, the tenant-right MP for Down, belonged to a prominent landed family, and John Young DL, who owned over 2,000 acres outside Ballymena, appeared regularly on the platform of tenant-right meetings in the area. Another landlord, Edward Maguire DL — owner of 1,000 acres near Swanlinbar — chaired the inaugural meeting of the Cavan Tenant League, while Sir Shafto Adair, Thomas Elliott and Charles Dunlop, all landlords, were presidents of the Ballymena, Castlefin and Newtownbreda associations respectively.[57] Such landlords, however, were in a minority, and landlords generally and not surprisingly failed to transcend their social backgrounds and class and personal interests so that, with the agricultural labourers also showing little inclination to support tenant demands, rural support for the movement came almost exclusively from the tenants, with those who had larger holdings tending to be most actively involved.

The larger farmers had, of course, a greater interest in the success of the movement. Less dependent on the landlord, socially ambitious with a large investment in the soil, and concerned about the transfer of land through the landed estates court, they were increasingly anxious to secure full legal protection for their tenant-right. They had, too, the additional grievance of the grand jury cess — 'decidedly the most unjust and disgraceful of local taxes'[58] — which fell heavily on the tenants, though they had practically no voice in its distribution or allocation. County expenditure was controlled by the grand juries and initiated by the presentment sessions, and while cesspayers were supposed to be represented on the latter, these were, like the grand juries, completely dominated by the landed classes.[59] Still more objectionable than the unrepresentative nature of county government was what the tenants saw as the jobbery and unnecessary extravagance involved in it. From the tenant point of view, the salaries of all county officials were excessive, but they reserved their most bitter criticism for the baronial high constables or cess collectors who were frequently paid 9d or 1s in the pound for the collection of cess, and equally frequently delegated the work to others at a lower rate; this, they maintained, was 'an utterly useless office ... a convenient sinecure, by which an office flunkey or favourite can be rewarded for services rendered in the interests of the grand jury class'.[60]

County cess, then, was a standing grievance with the larger farmers, and local government reform ranked second among the major objectives of the class; it was significant that once the question of land reform appeared to be settled in 1870, the tenant-right associations immediately turned their attention to the question of local government reform, demanding that ratepayers be given more control over county administration and expenditure.[61]

The second major group identified in the sample were the urban commercial and professional middle classes. The population of the majority of country towns in Ulster steadily increased in the years after the Famine — excluding Belfast and Derry, town population in Ulster increased by 16 per cent between 1851 and 1871[62] — and much of the growth came from migration from the rural areas, thus providing the tenants with urban supporters who had often carried their own land grievances with them.

Townspeople, of course, were better placed than farmers to organise local group activities, and it was they who, in many instances, provided the initiative to start and the support necessary to sustain the local associations. Michael Martin, a grocer, and John McKelvey, a publican, for example, were primarily responsible for launching the agitation in Ballybofey.[63] W.D. Henderson, who founded the Ulster Land Occupiers' Association and was later president of the Lisburn Tenant-Right Association and deputy president of the Antrim Central Tenant-Right Association, was a leading Belfast merchant and banker who had no direct connection with land at all.[64] Dr Hume of Crumlin was not only 'the parent and founder' of the local association, but was primarily responsible for sustaining its activities during the 1870s.[65] The success of the Newtownbreda Farmers' Association was attributed to Dr Gawn Orr, a local GP, that of the Route association to Samuel McElroy, an auctioneer and editor of the *Ballymoney Free Press*.[66] The support of newspaper editors such as McElroy, Dr James McKnight of the *Londonderry Standard*, A.J. McKenna of the *Northern*

*Star*, Moses Irwin of the *Ballymena Advertiser*, J.H. Farrell of the *Portadown News*, John McCombie of the *Coleraine Chronicle* and others was crucial to the success of the movement, and it would be difficult to overestimate the influence of their papers in disseminating tenant-right propaganda, prompting the tenants and the middle classes to campaign, and generally educating the tenants to a new level of social and political awareness.

Many of those townspeople who did involve themselves in the tenant-right campaign were already prominent local figures — many indeed had participated in the earlier tenant campaign of the 1850s[67] — and were often members of the town commissions. The letters TC appear frequently on lists of committees of the tenant-right associations given in the local press, and some such as Stewart Hunter of Coleraine and Thomas McEldery of Ballymoney were chairmen of both their respective town commissions and their local tenant-right committees. Other chairmen of town commissions like John Patrick of Ballymena, Arthur Thornton of Portadown, George Harrison of Newtownards and many others, while not directly involved in running the tenant-right associations, regularly chaired public tenant-right meetings and demonstrations.

Nor was it only that the municipal representatives felt obliged to appear on tenant-right platforms; in many areas where no tenant-right organisation existed, the town commissions as bodies took up the cause, passing resolutions in favour of tenant-right and sending delegates to the provincial and national conferences. The town commissions of Omagh, Cookstown, Castlederg, Enniskillen, Cavan and other towns spoke out at one time or another in favour of tenant demands and were represented at conferences in Ballymoney, Belfast and Dublin. With many towns still subject to county administration, town commissioners sometimes had a direct grievance against landed control of county government and resented what they saw as landed neglect of town interests,[68] but mainly it was their close social and commercial links with the tenant farmers rather than the common dissatisfaction with county administration that tied the town commissioners and other townspeople to the tenant-right cause — as one correspondent said of the Strabane town commission, 'there are in Strabane twenty-one town commissioners, who, from the chairman down, have sprung from the tenant class, and in a great degree are dependent on that class for their support'.[69]

Many of the urban leaders, in fact, came from a rural background and were either farmers' sons or one generation removed from the land, and their views were often coloured more by the grievances of their fathers than by the realities of the situation as it was in the 1870s. What stood out in their minds was not the interdependence of rural relationships, but the sense of social subordination and humiliation. 'Though I am now a Belfast man', wrote one tenant-right supporter, 'I am the son of a County Derry farmer, and my early experiences of the relations of farmers to their landlords has left on my mind an impression of shame and degradation which I find it impossible to efface.'[70] 'He was sprung from a race of tenant farmers', Dr Motherwell, a local GP, told a tenant demonstration at Castlederg, 'and in his earliest childhood the rights denied that class in the community continually rang in his ears.'[71] J. B. Armour, presbyterian minister of Ballymoney and an acerbic critic of landed pretensions, had, in his childhood, 'learned at first hand the difficulties of the Irish farmer',[72] and many others, like Armour and Motherwell, early had instilled into them a sense of the grievances of tenant farmers and of the principles and importance of tenant-right. As a child, James Rentoul accompanied his father to tenant-right meetings, and although he later became Unionist MP for East Down and a prominent member of the Unionist establishment, he never lost his sympathy for the tenant-right cause.[73] Professor Richard Smyth, twice moderator of the presbyterian church and the son of a prosperous Co. Antrim farmer, 'was early instructed in the principles of tenant-right ... I learned its doctrines first of all from a father who still lives to take an interest in its fortunes, though he has for years ceased to be an occupier of land'; and John Young of Ballymena also explained that he had 'been brought up in an atmosphere of tenant-right. I have learned the doctrines of tenant-right from my father'.[74]

The interest of the urban middle classes in the land question, however, was not purely one of sentiment based only on parental indoctrination and childhood memories: there were sometimes more material considerations. The publicity attached to campaigning in a popular cause was obviously of immense value to solicitors and barristers, who clearly had a vested interest in encouraging tenants to stand for their rights under the legislation of 1870. 'There is a class of attorneys', Salisbury suggested to the land agent and landlord spokesman Courtenay Newton, 'who make a great deal of money out of those land cases and who stimulate them.'[75] Newton, who happened to be an attorney itself, indignantly repudiated the suggestion — although he himself claimed that the tenants were 'driven on by people in towns, generally engaged in trade'[76] — but there was no doubt that prominent tenant-right solicitors such as Alexander Caruth of Ballymena, John Dinnen and Hans McMordie of Belfast, John Glover of Magherafelt, Edward Gardner and William Russell of Downpatrick and R.C. Martin of Ballymoney — all leading figures in the movement — had a professional interest to add to whatever other factors influenced them.

The same was true to perhaps an even greater degree of the merchants and traders in the towns. Samuel McElroy explained the support for tenant-right in Ballymoney as follows:

> The intercourse between town and country was mutually beneficial and agreeable. The farmers' custom was a benefit to the town, and it was natural that appreciation on both sides should prevail. Besides, many of the Ballymoney merchants, when young men, had come in from the country, keenly dissatisfied with the land laws, and ready to join in the movement for their reform. Not all, however. Some of the foremost merchants held aloof, but reform was in the air, and in due course they cast in their lot — there were still a few exceptions — with the industrious tenants.[77]

The fact was that many of the commercial people in the towns were dependent on the farmers, so that even those who had otherwise little disposition to support the tenant agitation were eventually forced by local social and economic pressures to do so. The growing prosperity of the tenant farmers from the 1850s had created a new and expanding market for town and village traders and merchants, and by the 1870s there was a greater commercial interdependence between the two interests than there had ever been in the past. As one tenant pointed out,

> if farmers are impoverished, the merchants and artisans of Coleraine
> and of all boroughs in the same position must suffer in consequence,
> and if farmers are prosperous, merchants and artisans will have good
> trade, just as naturally as effect follows cause. Nothing can be clearer
> than that the prosperity of a borough like Coleraine depends upon
> the prosperity of the country.[78]

Thus when shopkeepers and traders were accused by the Tory press of meddling in questions that did not concern them, their reply was that the land question concerned everyone. And, indeed, they were prepared at times to undertake the agitation of the cause even where the tenants themselves showed little interest, maintaining that where tenants were too timid to do anything for themselves, it was the duty of the commercial interest to act for them. 'We have been twitted that this is a meeting promulgated by shopkeepers — not occupiers of land', John Stevenson Riggs, chairman of Armagh town commission, told a tenant-right demonstration in the town. 'Well, my answer to that is, that although the landholders did feel strongly on the subject, they are not in a position to identify themselves with us and therefore it is our duty, as we sympathise with the farmers, to take the matter in hand.'[79]

The interest of the town merchants during the 1870s, however, went beyond mere sympathy or even, indeed, trade. The extension of credit by traders to farmers after 1870 on the basis of the latter's legalised tenant-right meant that, as time went on, many traders began to have nearly as great an interest in the capital investment of some tenants as the tenants themselves. When Lord Annesley threatened in 1879 to seize the farms of any tenants who became bankrupt, it caused as much alarm among local traders as it did among the tenants on the estate.[80] Town traders, it was claimed, had

> just as great an interest, directly and indirectly, in tenant-right as the
> farmers themselves. Auction the book-debts of your merchants against
> farmers now, when we have tenant-right, and they would realise 95
> per cent by a solvent merchant. Repeal the land act tomorrow, and no
> sane man would offer them 20 per cent.[81]

But what the middle classes wanted was not only greater protection for tenant-right, but also an end to the law of distraint which gave landlords priority in the settlement of debts; landlords, said James McKnight,

> ought to be placed on the same level with all other trading and commercial interests in society, so far as the legal recovery of debts is concerned. In a word, landlords ought to be obliged to recover rent arrears in the civil courts by the ordinary law process made and provided in relation to other classes of debts, instead of being enabled, by an exceptionally unfair law, to cheat all other outstanding creditors out of their common share of any assets which an insolvent tenant debtor may possess for the discharge of his collective liabilities.[82]

Understandably, this particular middle-class grievance was not widely voiced at tenant-right meetings, but here was a symbol of landed privilege which had a direct bearing on the commercial classes themselves and increasingly so as the 1870s progressed.

Moreover, with most towns still subject to county administration, the middle classes in towns such as Portadown, Coleraine, Newtownards and Newtownlimavady had, like the larger tenants, an interest in ending landed control of county government and reforming in particular the grand jury system, which was looked upon as 'one of the chief means of maintaining a class ascendancy of the most mischievous kind'.[83] In some towns, too, there was resentment against the refusal of certain landlords to grant building leases; landed influence, it was claimed, had prevented towns such as Toome and Lisburn from growing in the way they should.[84] In Co. Derry in particular it was felt that the attitude of the London companies had suffocated commercial and manufacturing development: 'There are no manufactories on any of the estates, and very few towns, for the companies seem to discourage the growth of both, by persistently refusing to give long leases, or freehold leases for building in towns'.[85] The paramount objection to the policy of the Irish Society in Derry city, for example, was its failure to give 'equitable building tenures', the refusal of which, it was believed, was responsible for the comparative retrogression of the city as against

Belfast, where Lord Donegall had granted perpetuity leases.[86]

The commercial classes in the towns, then, had a vested interest in the economic well-being of the tenantry and had themselves direct grievances — economic, social and political — against the landed classes. The presbyterian ministers, on the other hand, claimed to be more interested in the moral welfare of the farmers, and in their emphasis on this, and with their traditional influence and importance in the northern protestant communities, they helped to raise the campaign to levels it would never otherwise have attained.[87] The catholic clergy too played their part, chairing and speaking at meetings in different parts of the province, frequently sharing platforms with presbyterian ministers, and occasionally filling offices in the local associations; at the Letterkenny demonstration of February 1870, for example, there were no fewer than seventeen catholic parish priests and curates 'on and around the platform', while the Ballybofey, Farney and Clogher tenant associations were all presided over at one time or another by the local priests.[88] But, as already suggested, the tenant-right movement tended to be strongest in the more prosperous parts of the province where tenant-right itself was most firmly established, and these areas were mainly presbyterian rather than catholic. Thus, while catholic priests occasionally appeared on tenant-right platforms in places such as Larne, Portadown and Banbridge, the clerical presence at these and at most tenant-right meetings tended to be predominantly presbyterian.

There was, in fact, hardly a single tenant-right meeting in which presbyterian ministers did not play a leading role as chairmen or speakers. And this, it was claimed, was how it should be:

> There is no section of the community in Ulster more deserving of being heard on the land question than the presbyterian clergy. By birth, by local knowledge, by long experience and observation, they are intimately acquainted with the habits, thoughts, feelings, and wrongs of the tenant farmers ... the great majority of them have for years been earnest advocates of a reform in the land system.[89]

With most of them being 'either farmers' sons or more remotely the descendants of farmers', and with the tenants making up 'the backbone' of the presbyterian church,[90] it was only natural that the presbyterian ministers should have strong sympathies with the class from which they came; as the Rev. Moore of Ringsend explained:

> My answer to those who want to know why I took part with the tenants in this struggle is that I am a farmer's son myself, born and brought up on a farm; I love my neighbours and I am anxious to see justice done them ... Besides, my people are almost all farmers, and their interests are my interests and I stand here at their request and at the request and entreaty of hundreds of tenant farmers of all denominations.[91]

But the interest of presbyterian ministers went well beyond the material welfare of the tenants. From the point of view of many of them, the land question was a moral question and one which legitimately concerned them as Christian ministers. To them the dependence and servility of the tenants was an affront to all the virtues of manliness, self-respect, self-reliance and independence which they held so dear. 'Far larger interests', asserted the Rev. J.B. Armour, were involved in the land question 'than the bare money interests of the farmer. The social and moral interests of the community are involved in it.' The land system as it stood was 'not only the negation of justice, but so battered the moral qualities out of men that they could not look their fellow mortals in the face without their hat in their hand nor speak save in a bondsman's key.'[92] In such circumstances, it was argued, presbyterian clergymen had not only a right, but a duty to support the tenants in their cause.

However, it was not only the presbyterian tenants who suffered from the deleterious effects of the land system; their dependence and the influence which landlords had over them were, it was believed, used 'in the interest of episcopacy',[93] providing the basis of the episcopalian and landed ascendancy and depriving the presbyterian church and its members of their rightful place in the political and social life of the northern province. 'The truth is', said James McKnight, 'that the unsecured tenant-right of Ulster is the grand instrument of Ulster's political bondage.'[94]

Although the Irish church had been disestablished in 1869, past persecutions were not forgotten and the traditional divisions and ill-feeling between episcopalians and presbyterians largely continued.[95] The latter believed that the disendowment carried out in 1869 was a good deal less than complete and that 'the vested interests of the disestablished clergy were carefully preserved'.[96] Provision had been made in the act for compensation for the new life interests of presbyterian ministers in receipt of the *regium donum* as well as for those of the clergy of the Church of Ireland, but the total amount of compensation paid to the disestablished church — based on the commuted value of the life annuities of its clergy plus bonuses and compensation for private endowments — was of course immeasurably greater than that paid to the presbyterian body — over £8.5 millon as against some £620,000 for the latter.[97] Moreover, the presbyterians resented the fact that the Church of Ireland was allowed compensation for 201 curates appointed between the passing of the act and the date when it came into operation, a concession which the presbyterians were denied and which, they alleged, the episcopalians abused.[98] Thus the disestablishment act in 1869, while removing one bone of contention between protestants, in some ways created new grievances for the presbyterians. William Latimer's account of the settlement, written some thirty years after the event, reveals the lingering bitterness which presbyterians still felt over its terms:

> The episcopal body as usual obtained special advantages. Their curates were permitted to commute, although paid by their rectors, while no provision was made for licentiates of the presbyterian church who discharged similar duties. Besides, curates who were in office before the 1st January 1871 obtained compensation, while that right was denied to presbyterian clergyman ordained after the passing of the act. The episcopal church took advantage of the additional time to manufacture about 400 curates, many of whom had never passed through college, but who were able to claim a vast amount of their life interests. Even the parish clerks received large sums as compensation for the supposed loss of salaries which they still continued to receive.[99]

Moreover, although the Church of Ireland ceased to be the state or established church, the old episcopalian and landed ascendancy continued, with landed episcopalians dominating the social and political life of the province to the near total exclusion of presbyterians. Even at the end of the century Latimer could write that

> there is, doubtless, in aristocratic circles the same tendency to maintain the social limitations of dissent, and to exclude presbyterians from intercourse with that class, who imagine they occupy a high position in society because they live on the earnings of others rather than their own earnings.[100]

What made this grievance more galling was the fact that some wealthy presbyterians were, as a result, inclined 'to qualify themselves for social greatness by adopting the principles and joining the church of those who persecuted their forefathers'.[101]

These social barriers were mirrored politically, with the presbyterians excluded from parliament and from the whole system of local government and patronage, deliberately kept, as Armour put it, 'in political degradation'.[102] Up to 1874, and with certain exceptions after 1874, 'the power of the Tory episcopal landlords was too strong in the northern counties to permit presbyterians to elect candidates of their own religion'.[103] The Rev. William Johnston, moderator of the general assembly, claimed in 1874 that

> the presbyterian church occupied a prominent place in the land. It had a right, on the ground of intellect, property, and population, to a fair share in the representation, and to have its voice heard in the council of the nation. But while they had often heard of the Ulster twenty-nine, not one of them was a presbyterian. The aristocracy of Ulster had ignored the element of presbyterianism.[104]

Johnston's statement was not strictly accurate — McClure, the Liberal MP for Belfast, and Lewis, the Tory representative of Derry city, were both presbyterians — but his main point generally was correct, and that was that the representation of the province — more particularly, that of the counties — was monopolised by 'a particular religious creed'. In Antrim, for example, the most presbyterian county in the country with presbyterians making up over 50 per cent of the population and some 66 per cent of the electorate,[105] 'not one presbyterian was ever sent by the landlords to the House of Commons',[106] and the same was true for virtually every other county.

This same policy of exclusion was practised at every other level of politics and government: 'everywhere', the presbyterians complained, 'the subordination which is reflected in the parliamentary representation is distinctly visible'.[107] Out of seventy-two resident magistrates in Ireland there was not a single presbyterian, while in the constabulary force it was claimed that presbyterians were 'systematically kept down in the lowest ranks'.[108] In the counties, they, like the catholics, were shut out of 'every office almost, either of honour or profit'. In Co. Derry, for example, where presbyterians constituted over a third of the total population and members of the Church of Ireland less than one fifth, not one of the twenty-four most important offices in the county from the county lieutenant down to the barony cess collectors and sub-inspectors of constabulary was held by a presbyterian. Membership of the board of the county gaol — whose members were appointed by the grand jury — was exclusively episcopalian, while of the twenty-seven governors of the district lunatic asylum only two were presbyterians; and all the paid officials of both institutions with one exception — a catholic — were episcopalians.[109]

Part of the problem was the refusal of county lieutenants — all of them episcopalians — to appoint presbyterians to the bench, which, as the *Derry Journal* pointed out, exercised a vast, almost unlimited, influence over county affairs:

> They are the channels through which the law of the land, whether well or ill-administered, chiefly operates upon the people ... But their influence does not end here ... With some exceptions every magistrate is an *ex-officio* guardian of the poor, while it is a well-known fact that most of the elected guardians are the nominees of the *ex-officios*; thus the whole poor law patronage may be said to be at the disposal of the magistrates. They constitute the grand jury, and their influence permeates the course of appointments to the petty jurors' roll. They preside at road sessions, where their will is law; it is true, they are assisted by 'associated cesspayers', but the paucity of such associates,

compared with the number of magistrates, and their dependent condition render the 'assistance' of these reed-like functionaries quite ridiculous. The appointment to clerkships of petty sessions, which they conduct after their fashion of exclusiveness, rests with them too.[110]

Thus the magistrates were the key figures in much of the government and patronage of the county, and the huge majority were members of the privileged church. In Antrim, for example, there were 105 episcopalian and twelve presbyterian magistrates out of a total of 127; in Derry, eighty-seven episcopalian and seven presbyterian magistrates out of a total of ninety-seven.[111] This pattern was repeated over the province, with a parliamentary return in 1884 showing that 73 per cent of all magistrates in Ulster were Church of Ireland, 14 per cent presbyterian, and 8.5 per cent catholic.[112]

This state of affairs was keenly resented by the presbyterians, who indignantly repudiated the suggestion that their social position ill-fitted them to fill these and other places. It was the presbyterians, they claimed, who had made Ulster what it was, who had created an industrial oasis in the north and turned the province from 'a barren waste into a fruitful field';[113] 'they possess nearly all the wealth, energy, and commercial industry, while the episcopalian body are for the most part a lingering fabric of an antiquated aristocracy'.[114] What kept them down was not any kind of social or intellectual inadequacy on their part, but rather an 'official favouritism' towards the episcopalians and 'an intolerant bigotry' which had 'lowered their social standing, and made them, as it were, "hewers of wood and drawers of water" to the noble upholders of a most aristocratic church'.[115]

However, presbyterians, it was argued, had it in their own hands to remedy this state of affairs; they had 'only to become thoroughly independent to cause their power on all political questions, and on all questions of patronage to be fully respected'.[116] Their subordinate position in local and county affairs was, it was contended, 'the offspring of their inferior parliamentary position';[117] 'if they had more representatives in parliament, they would have more weight with the government, and their claims would have a better chance of being fairly answered'.[118] But this could only be done if the presbyterian tenants were made totally independent of their episcopalian landlords. The process had already begun in 1870, but the dependence and the deference continued even after the introduction of the ballot in 1872. In other words, presbyterians could only assume their rightful place in Ulster society and politics when the system of semi-feudal relationships in the counties was completely dismantled. To the presbyterian ministers and to many of the presbyterian commercial and professional classes, tenant-right was part of a broader cause and that cause was the cause of presbyterianism. The identification of the two was clearly drawn by the *Weekly Whig*:

> In parliamentary, grand jury, presentment sessions, and poor law matters, the presbyterian element occupies a subordinate role. From a tenant point of view these things may not be immediately involved in the settlement of the question; but they form part of that system which has striven, and is now striving with increased energy, to keep the farmers out of their rights.[119]

Thus, while Ulster tenants themselves rarely looked beyond their own immediate interests, the land question in Ulster provided the focus for a wide range of political, social, commercial and religious grievances. These had centred first on the church question and then in 1869–70 on land. With the apparent success of Gladstone's land act of 1870, local government reform had been singled out as the next objective, and between 1870 and 1872 many of the tenant-right associations under their presbyterian middle-class leadership had turned their attention to this question, demanding that ratepayers be given more control over county administration and expenditure.[120] But as dissatisfaction with the administration of the land act set in after 1872, priority was given once again to the question of tenant-right, and by 1874 this had become the cardinal issue in Ulster politics.

Although tenant-right leaders, as we have seen, claimed to be prepared to support tenant-right candidates of either party, in practice it was the Ulster Liberals who generally and almost exclusively got their support. This was welcomed and encouraged by many of the presbyterian middle-class leaders of the movement who were already themselves prominently involved in Liberal politics. It is doubtful if the support of the tenants for Liberalism ever went beyond concern for their tenant-right, but for the presbyterian middle class the Liberal party was the vehicle for presbyterians' ambitions and objectives, and its identification with the tenant-right cause gave it a potential for growth in Ulster which its members had scarcely dreamed of in the 1860s.

6

# Liberals, Conservatives and Tenant-right

LIBERAL DIVISIONS

Liberalism in Ulster in the 1860s was at a low ebb. Subjected to scurrilous abuse by Tory papers and Orange clergymen on the one hand, and with Dr Cooke, the most influential and the most Conservative presbyterian minister of his time, still using his influence against them on the other, the Ulster and Belfast Liberals 'seemed utterly cowed'.[1] Describing the electoral prospects of the party as they appeared in 1866, Thomas MacKnight, editor of the *Northern Whig*, wrote that 'it was felt that to return a Liberal candidate was almost hopeless in the great borough, and quite hopeless in the counties'.[2] In the general election of 1859 Liberals had contested only three of the nineteen constituencies, and although a Liberal was returned for Derry city, this seat was lost in a by-election in the following year so that from 1860 until 1865 the party had not a single representative at Westminster. Eight seats were contested in the general election of 1865 but only two Liberals were returned, both prominent episcopalian landowners distinguishable by party label only from the province's other members. In 1868 the number of contested constituencies was reduced to six, and although the Liberals won four seats they lost two of these in subsequent by-elections before 1874.

Dismal as this record was, however, the picture was not entirely black. When MacKnight came to Belfast to take up his post as editor of the *Northern Whig* in 1866, he found a general air of expectancy in Liberal circles in the north with 'the Ulster Liberals ... full of hope and confidence for the future'.[3] At Westminster a new leader held out the promise of new policies. And in Ulster the formation of the Ulster Liberal Society in 1865 provided moral and legal support for Liberals throughout the province, and resulted in them playing a more active and effective role in revision courts in various constituencies.[4] The most important work of the society was in the field of registration, and between 1865 and 1868 — and indeed up to 1874 — its main efforts in this respect were directed towards the borough constituencies which, especially after the extension of the borough franchise in 1868, offered the Liberals their best chances of success.

The reform act of 1868, by lowering the occupying franchise in the towns from an £8 to £4 valuation, increased the number of electors in the nine borough constituencies outside Belfast — a special case by any criteria — by practically 40 per cent. But the effect varied from borough to borough, ranging from a 5 per cent increase in the electorate of Downpatrick to a 70 per cent increase in Derry city.[5] The act broadened the social basis of the electorate and made the boroughs more independent of landed control.[6] But it had a special significance in constituencies such as Derry and Newry, where the episcopalian proportion of the population was low and where catholics, who could be expected to be anti-Tory, sharply increased their share of the votes; in Newry, for example, the proportion of catholics in the electorate went up from 39 per cent in 1866 to 46 per cent in 1868.[7]

Thus the franchise reform of 1868 enhanced in varying degrees the Liberal prospects in different borough constituencies. The Liberals did not take full advantage of these changed circumstances until the general election of 1874, but they did make some gains in 1868. Altogether six Liberal candidates went forward, four of them in the boroughs, and all of them, with one exception, campaigning mainly on the platform of church disestablishment. The exception was in Co. Cavan where Colonel Edward Saunderson, the sitting Liberal member, a prominent and popular local landowner, was returned unopposed.[8] A Liberal candidate also went forward in Monaghan in 1865, but he was late into the field, secured the support of only a minority of catholics, and was easily defeated.[9]

It was, in fact, in the boroughs that the Liberals enjoyed what success they had. In Belfast the Orange revolt against the Conservative government's administration of the party processions act gave them an opportunity to return a candidate where, in normal circumstances, they would have had little chance of success.[10] They were also successful in Newry, where the presbyterian merchant William Kirk defeated Lord Newry, and in Derry city, where Richard Dowse QC defeated the sitting member, Lord Claud John Hamilton. And although the Liberal John Collum was narrowly defeated in Enniskillen, the success of M.R. Dalway, an independent Orange candidate, against the official Conservative in Carrickfergus was seen as the next best thing to a Liberal victory.[11] Out of six contested constituencies the Conservatives had lost control of four, and it seemed for a time that their hold on the province was weakening.

The Liberals were naturally euphoric. 'Wherever a seat had been challenged in Mr Gladstone's interest', wrote MacKnight, conveniently forgetting the Liberal setbacks in Monaghan and Enniskillen, 'it has been won by one of his followers'.[12] The Liberal press saw the successes as an 'indication of a strong and rising tide of Liberal feeling in the north of Ireland', and looked forward to a land bill to provide them with further victories in the counties.[13] Although Sir Shafto Adair was heavily defeated in Antrim in 1869, this was put down to the 'unscrupulous use of the office screw', and Richard Dowse's second victory in Derry city in 1870 after his appointment as solicitor-general for Ireland was seen as further evidence of the growing attachment of Ulster to the Liberal cause.[14]

However, hopes of a Liberal revival in the north were premature, and the successes of 1868 and 1870 proved only temporary. In 1871 the Conservatives regained Newry without a contest, and in 1872 they recaptured Derry city so that by 1874 the Liberal representation in Ulster had been reduced once again to only two members, one of whom — with the Tories and Orangemen in Belfast already reconciled — was plainly destined to lose his seat at the next election.

What by-elections between 1868 and 1874 had chiefly shown, in spite of the success in Derry in 1870, was the limitations of Liberal support in the north and the fragility of the alliance on which the Liberal party was based.

Traditionally, Liberalism in Ulster was identified with the presbyterians, many of whom supported it for precisely the same reasons as they supported tenant-right; for many presbyterians these were symbiotic movements with the same objective and that objective was the overthrow of the Tory landed and episcopalian ascendancy. Their radicalism, says one recent writer, 'was rooted in centuries of opposition to an establishment which was economic and political, and of which the landlord class and the Church of Ireland were seen as two aspects of the thing'.[15] Opposed on historical, theological and social grounds to this establishment, their opposition found expression in their support of the Liberal party, and to many presbyterians the Liberal cause was virtually synonymous with the cause of presbyterianism. Throughout the electoral campaign of 1868, presbyterians were reminded that it was their duty as presbyterians to support the Liberal candidates, and certainly the return of Thomas McClure for Belfast and William Kirk for Newry were seen in presbyterian circles as presbyterian rather than Liberal victories.[16]

But not all, or even a majority of, presbyterians were Liberals, and presbyterian electors in both the counties and the boroughs continued for the most part to return Tory episcopalian representatives. Recent analyses of the poll in Newry in 1868 show that only 15 per cent of presbyterian electors voted for the Liberal Kirk, while the remainder gave their support to his Conservative opponent Lord Newry.[17] In Derry city in the same election a higher proportion, but still a minority, voted for Dowse, who got 163 presbyterian votes as against 259 given to the Conservative Hamilton.[18] And again in the Derry city by-election in 1870, a majority of the presbyterian votes — 248 against 141 — went to Robert Baxter, a London solicitor, who was totally unknown in the constituency up to his nomination as Conservative candidate.[19]

The support of presbyterian tenants for Tory candidates in the counties was attributed to landlord intimidation and tenant social and economic dependence. But manifestly this neither explains the strength of Toryism in the counties nor the pattern of presbyterian voting in the towns. The fact was that many of the presbyterian laity were never as acutely conscious as the presbyterian ministers and sections of the presbyterian middle classes of the divisions between the protestant churches, and the opposition of many presbyterians to the Tory episcopal ascendancy was more than balanced by their fear of catholicism. The presbyterian small farmers and working men, said Latimer, 'led by the influence of the Orange society, were enthusiastic Conservatives. Aware that the church of Rome claims infallibility and universal authority, they feared popery more than they hated landlordism; and they were told that the interests of protestantism were not so safe with Liberals as with Conservatives.'[20] Presbyterians, complained the *Northern Whig*, had 'sacrificed their own independence to the lowest and most subservient sectarianism'.[21]

The fact was that Liberalism as a political creed and as a party was supported by only a minority of presbyterians, and these were largely ministers and members of the professional and commercial middle classes. Although a majority of presbyterians voted Conservative in the Derry city election of 1868, seven of the eight presbyterian ministers on the electoral register supported Dowse, and Dowse himself later described his main supporters in Derry as 'not mere nobodies, not mere men of straw; they were your large and influential manufacturers, your large and influential traders, and your rich and substantial shopkeepers'.[22] And of the thirty presbyterians who supported Kirk in Newry in 1868, only one occupied premises valued at under £8;[23] in other words, those Presbyterians who voted for Kirk tended to belong to the wealthier commercial and professional classes. But even for many of these people the 'emancipation from traditional bondages and restraints', which Liberalism traditionally stood for, was primarily an emancipation for presbyterians with only what has been described as a 'general but rather vague sympathy' for catholic grievances.[24] Later in 1880, Charles Russell had first-hand experience of the limitations of presbyterian sympathy when they refused to accept him as Liberal candidate for Monaghan; Russell bitterly concluded that the incident illustrated the real 'narrowness and bigotry of the presbyterians, who are always talking of their liberal principles'.[25]

Yet it was catholic support which gave Liberalism much of its success in Ulster. 'In the face of obloquy and danger, of contumely and persecution', declared the catholic *Northern Star* after the election of 1868, 'the catholics of Ulster have been true, loyally true, to the Liberal principles.'[26] It was generally recognised that without catholic support McClure would not have been elected for Belfast.[27] In Newry, where Kirk was returned by a small majority of seven votes and where only thirty presbyterians supported him, his total poll of 386 votes included 341 from the catholic electors. Likewise in Derry city, out of 704 votes cast for Dowse in 1868, 501 came from the catholics, while in 1870 in a smaller poll 511 catholics contributed to his total of 681 votes.[28] In short, Liberal successes in Ulster between 1868 and 1872 were based on an alliance of catholics and a minority of the presbyterian middle classes, with the bulk of the support coming from the catholics.

The Liberals themselves recognised and at times acknowledged their dependence on catholic votes.[29] But the alliance was never completely harmonious, and the catholic commitment to the Liberal party, like the Liberal support of catholic claims, was always less than total. Although catholic papers such as the *Derry Journal* and the *Belfast Morning News* gave a fairly consistent backing to the Liberals throughout this period, the *Ulster Examiner*, from its inception in 1868, pursued a persistently critical and hostile attitude towards the party.[30] The *Examiner* was the paper of Dr Dorrian, catholic bishop of Down and Connor, who had a deep suspicion of the Liberals and of the motives of catholic politicians who supported them: 'I cordially hate Whiggery', he had written in 1865, and in 1868 he still believed that 'Gladstone is further from the Catholic view than Disraeli, and will never yield to the bishops' views as Disraeli is inclined to do'.[31]

Dorrian's suspicion was reciprocated by the Liberal and presbyterian press in Ulster and by many of the Liberal leaders. The *Northern Whig*, for example, clearly revealed its anti-catholic prejudice in its welcome of Judge Keogh's judgement in an election trial in Galway

— in which Keogh had made a virulent attack on the catholic clergy — as the 'just decision' of 'an able and independent judge' in language that was 'bold, honest, fearless, and true'. Later editorials qualified this approval by conceding that parts of Keogh's address were scarcely judicial, but rebuked the catholic church in Ireland for being ungrateful to the government and reminded catholic clergy that they had 'now more freedom in Ireland than in any other country in the world', adding as a final gratuitous insult the observation that the priest in Ireland was 'almost as provincial and narrow in his views as the peasants with whom he has been associated'.[32] The Co. Antrim grand jury under the foremanship of Sir Shafto Adair also quite unnecessarily applauded Keogh's judgment and address, Adair showing, according to Joseph Biggar, 'the basest ingratitude' towards those catholics who had supported him in the Antrim by-election of 1869.[33]

Most catholics, of course, were infuriated by Keogh's comments[34] and the affair served mainly to reveal some of the basic divisions between Liberals and catholics and expose the fragile nature of the Liberal–catholic alliance in the north. Other issues from time to time also threatened to disrupt this alliance. Opposing sides were taken, for example, on questions such as the party processions act and amnesty for the Fenian prisoners; while the presbyterian Liberal press supported repeal of the party processions act in 1869 in order to cement their alliance with William Johnston and the democratic Orangemen, the catholic view was that such repeal 'would be an act of manifest folly' and 'tantamount to a declaration of internecine warfare between the two communities';[35] and while northern protestant Liberals were strongly opposed to amnesty, the *Derry Journal* claimed that it would do more to satisfy the people of Ireland than either the church or land bills.[36] An even greater threat to Liberal prospects in Ulster emerged with the formation of the Belfast Home Rule Association in 1872 and attempts to promote home rule meetings in various parts of the province.[37]

Above all, however, there was the question of education, on which feelings ran extremely high among both catholics and protestants, and on which neither side was prepared to compromise. The formation of the National Education League — a largely presbyterian organisation supported by many leading Ulster Liberals — in 1870 to oppose the denominational proposals of the Powis Commission had already imposed a severe strain on the Liberal–clerical alliance.[38] With the Irish church disestablished and the land question apparently settled, education by 1872 had become the question of the hour. It was the paramount issue in a by-election in Derry in 1872 and it was in this election, the first held in Ireland under the secret ballot, that the conflicting forces and loyalties within Liberal ranks came to a head.

The vacancy in Derry occurred as a result of Richard Dowse's elevation to the bench. Dowse was succeeded as attorney-general by Christopher Palles, a catholic QC who was now put forward for the seat vacated by Dowse.[39] Palles, however, faced a formidable task. Although Gladstone in 1872 still largely enjoyed the confidence and support of Irish catholics, Palles's part as solicitor-general in the prosecution of catholic clergy — including the bishop of Clonfert — after the Galway petition judgment created a deep-seated hostility to his candidature among Derry catholics, and his inaugural meeting in Derry ended in disorder amid cries of 'no priest-hunter' and 'Palles, the place-hunter and government hack'.[40] The presbyterians, on the other hand, were unhappy with Palles's known support of denominational education, and the *Ballymoney Free Press* protested that his views on education made it impossible for the presbyterians to support him and that 'a gross blunder' had been made in putting him forward as the Liberal candidate.[41]

The Conservatives, who had at an early stage nominated Charles Lewis, a London presbyterian solicitor, as their candidate, were of course anxious to capitalise on this dissension in the Liberal camp, and presented the contest as essentially one between a presbyterian supporter of the national system of education and a catholic nominee of Archbishop Cullen.[42] The nomination of Joseph Biggar, a Belfast provision merchant, as a home rule candidate complicated matters, adding to Palles's problems and threatening to test even further catholic allegiance to the Liberal party. It was obvious, however, that Biggar had little chance of carrying the seat and that any serious division of the catholic vote would merely result in the return of Lewis.[43] In these circumstances, the catholic bishop and clergy of Derry, after initially refusing to intervene in the election, came out in favour of Palles.[44] Lewis, however, still won the election with a majority of eighty-five over the combined total of his opponents. Palles had clearly lost some catholic support,[45] but his defeat, as many of the Liberal papers acknowledged, was directly attributable to his views on education and to defections among the Liberal presbyterians.[46]

This election was a major setback to the Liberal party in Ulster. It had now been reduced once again to only two representatives and this had happened in circumstances which gave rise to much ill-feeling within the party itself. The election had shown that where presbyterian or protestant interests were felt to be at risk, the Liberal protestants were ready to abandon the party and coalesce with the Conservatives. Yet, even though the Liberals seemed to be back to square one after Derry, it was during these years that the basis of future Liberal growth in the province was laid, and this growth was directly related to the new situation which was emerging in the counties rather than to any particular efforts on the part of the Liberals themselves.

By 1874, we are told, 'a great change had come over Ulster ... The tenant farmers, with the protection of the land act and the ballot act, began to show unwonted signs of independence'.[47] The land act, as we have seen, gave tenants a greater degree of security than before 1870; but this in itself did not necessarily lead to more independent political activity. Tenant farmers, as so many contemporaries pointed out, were rarely actuated by any sense of public duty. 'They looked at political questions', says MacKnight, 'very much according to what they believed to be their own interests ... They considered every question from the point of view of their own farms.'[48] Thus if the land act had worked to their satisfaction, their greater independence under it would probably have meant little political change in Ulster. But the act fell short of what the tenants wanted and as its defects became more apparent, especially from 1872, the tenants became increasingly anxious for its amendment; indeed, as McElroy suggested, the failure of the act 'brought rights more prominently to the footlights'.[49] But dissatisfied though they may have been, the tenants were still reluctant to act openly against their landlords; the land act may have given them a certain protection against eviction, but they could still be subjected to rent raises, the withdrawal of privileges, and various kinds of social annoyance. It was only after the introduction of the ballot that tenants could be fully freed from landed control and tenant dissatisfaction channelled into political action.

The Tories, of course, opposed the ballot for precisely this reason, arguing, however, that it was unnecessary, that the coercive power of the landlord had already ceased with the passing of the land act, and that the ballot would only strengthen the political influence of the catholic clergy.[50] The Liberals, on the other hand, strongly supported it. Up to 1872 their successes had been confined to the boroughs, and they were long aware — the more so after the débâcle in Antrim in 1869 — that the territorial dominion in the counties could only be successfully challenged under the protection of the ballot.[51] Thus they gave an enthusiastic welcome to the measure.

It was somewhat ironic that in the first election held under it the Liberals should lose one of their gains of 1868, and there were some fears that the mark would remain 'after the manacle had been removed'.[52] But, generally, their expectations proved to be well founded. The ballot allowed electoral expression to be given to those tenant-right forces which had been gathering over the previous years. If Derry was a disappointment, the full potential of the new situation was clearly revealed in a by-election in Tyrone in the following year, and it was here that the first real demonstration of tenant-right power and the new political importance of the land question came.

## ELECTORAL IMPACT OF TENANT-RIGHT 1873–4

Tyrone was not the most obvious county for the tenant-right movement first to make its political influence felt. Dominated from time immemorial by the Corrys and Hamiltons, Tyrone was probably as closed a constituency as one could find in Ulster; it had been contested only once by the Liberals since 1832 and on that occasion, in 1852, the Liberal candidate had received only 13 per cent of the votes.[53] Moreover — and no doubt part of the reason for the easy landed control of the county — landlord–tenant relations were traditionally good; tenant-right was generally respected and, when put up for sale, regularly brought prices of over £20 an Irish acre.[54] The administration of the 1870 act had also given general satisfaction to the tenants, and Tyrone was often singled out as a county in which the beneficial effects of the act were most plainly in evidence.[55] Nor was the county especially well organised in the tenant-right cause. Tenant societies were active in and around Cookstown, Dungannon and Donemana, and an attempt was made in 1872 with the formation of the County Tyrone Tenants' Protection and Land Law Reform Association to establish a county organisation. But the tenant-right movement in the county was never as well organised as, for example, that in Antrim was or that in Down was to become. Indeed, in 1871–2 the main efforts of the Tyrone tenant associations were directed towards securing the reform of the grand jury system, and such activity in itself reflected the general satisfaction in the county with the land concessions won in 1870.[56]

As in the remainder of the province, however, the situation began to change in 1872. Tenants in Tyrone shared in the general apprehension which spread as a result of the appointment of the Chelmsford committee — of which the Earl of Belmore, one of the leading landowners in Tyrone, was a member — and of the general hostility displayed towards the act by a number of landlords and agents, some of whom, the Cookstown Land Occupiers Association complained in 1872, were attempting to impose agreements on their tenants precluding future claims for compensation, and others of whom were apparently determined to limit tenant-right by the imposition of estate rules.[57] One of the most persistent critics of the act was Courtenay Newton, a land agent who represented several estates in Tyrone and Donegal,[58] and it was Newton who — 'too hastily' and 'unfortunately' from the point of view of most landlords — precipitated a dispute with tenants on the Ranfurly estate near Dungannon, which probably more than anything else served to undermine landlord–tenant relations in the county.[59]

The most important of the cases arising out of this dispute was that of *Burns v. Ranfurly*, which involved leasehold tenant-right and which Newton rashly claimed to be fighting on behalf of all landlords.[60] When Burns's lease expired in 1872, he was offered a new lease at an increased rent, which he was quite prepared to pay provided it was agreed that tenant-right would exist at the end of the lease. Ranfurly, on the advice of Newton, refused to agree to this and Burns claimed under Section 1 of the act. Sir Francis Brady, chairman of the county, found in favour of Burns, but the decision was reversed on appeal, Judge Keogh deciding that while tenant-right might exist at the close of the lease, it had not been specifically proved in this case.[61] Other tenants on the Ranfurly estate quietly submitted after this case had been fought and lost, but the effect of the decision, especially when taken in conjunction with several almost simultaneous decisions against leasehold tenant-right elsewhere, was to spread alarm throughout the county so that by the time of the Tyrone by-election in 1873 the tenants had been thoroughly aroused; one prominent Tory, J.C. Lowry, for example, said he 'was quite startled and surprised at finding how great a spirit of discontent and dissatisfaction prevails in Tyrone'.[62]

It was against this background of tenant disaffection that the by-election was fought in 1873. As soon as the vacancy occurred it became clear that the tenants were determined to make use of the opportunity, and a notice appeared in the local press informing tenant farmers that a tenant-right candidate would be put forward and advising them to keep themselves free to support him.[63] As it happened, however, it was the Orangemen rather than the tenant associations that took the initiative. The Orange discontent which had first manifested itself in the return of Johnston for Belfast and Dalway for Carrickfergus in 1868 had not disappeared after the election, and the independent Orange movement to which it had given rise began from that date to spread into the rural areas.[64] The discontent had originally been caused by the equivocal attitude of the Tory leaders to the party processions act, and it was partly kept alive after 1868 by the insensitive expulsion of Dalway and a number of Johnston's supporters from the Orange order.[65] Moreover, many of the landed classes had failed even to keep up the pretence of identifying with Orangeism,[66] and there was a feeling among the Orange activists in Tyrone that their views and wishes had been ignored in the past and that they had been 'made the tools' of the 'small Orange clique' who normally controlled the political arrangements for the county.[67] But the independent Orangemen also took an early and increasing interest in land reform and the ballot, and it was these issues, especially the former, which provided the basis of their appeal to the protestant tenant farmers.[68]

The candidate selected by the Orangemen was James Ellison Macartney, a Co. Antrim landowner with family connections in Tyrone, who was known to support leasehold tenant-right and a more precise legal definition of the Ulster custom.[69] Macartney's candidature was immediately welcomed by the tenant-right press, which at the same time advised the Liberals against starting a candidate.[70] It soon became evident, in fact, that Macartney's commitment to tenant-right had secured for him the support of an unlikely combination of Orangemen, tenant-righters, Liberals, presbyterians and catholics; and during the campaign he wisely concentrated on tenant-right, prudently ignoring other issues such as education which were likely to divide his supporters.[71] And although the Conservatives tried in various ways to disrupt Macartney's ill-assorted alliance, it continued to hold together and polled well on the day.

In the event, the Belmore and landed influence, a heavy presence of landlords and agents at the polling stations, and certain polling technicalities and irregularities saw the Conservative candidate — the Earl of Belmore's brother, Henry Corry — through, but only by the slenderest of margins — 3,139 to 3,103, a majority of thirty-six in a surprisingly high poll of nearly 75 per cent. Corry's return was greeted with immense relief by the landed classes, but the contest had been 'too close to be pleasant', and the relief was tinged with anxiety for the future.[72] The tenant-righters, on the other hand, were elated, claiming that Macartney had gained 'a moral triumph'.[73] Macartney, it was pointed out, had been fighting under considerable disadvantages: new polling places which were supposed to have been provided under the recent reform act had not been arranged, and Corry's agents had dexterously engaged most of the conveyances in the county.[74] Even with these inconveniences, Macartney might still have won had it not been for some official blundering during the poll, in which the presiding officers at two polling stations had — inadvertently, it was supposed — put the number of the elector on the back of 187 ballot papers, an action which the returning officer — in the face of strenuous protests by Macartney's agents — ruled had vitiated the votes. Macartney's supporters claimed that 113 of these 187 votes were for Macartney, which if correct — and the figures were never seriously disputed by the Tories — would have given him an overall majority of three votes.[75] Much to the alarm of Belmore and Corry, who felt they could ill-afford the expense of another contest, Macartney lodged a petition against Corry's return but, with a general election impending, eventually decided against pursuing it.[76]

The election result, then, was allowed to stand, but the election was none the less significant for that. It clearly indicated the change which had been brought about in Ulster politics by the ballot and the tenant-right question. The ballot had given tenants an electoral freedom they had never had in the past, and Macartney could not have done as well as he did without it. But it was the tenant-right question which lay at the root of his near success in Tyrone and which was threatening to transform the whole political scene in the north.[77] The territorial and Tory ascendancy in Ulster had always been based on the close identity of interests between landlords and tenants, and this was now being subjected to intense pressure. What was particularly significant in Tyrone in 1873 was the way in which the county had divided; 'every landlord in the county', Belmore was told, 'was on Captain Corry's side, and the struggle was not merely one between Mr Macartney and your brother, but between gentry and farmers, landlord and tenant'.[78] What the ballot had done was to allow tenant grievances to come to the electoral surface and reveal the depth of the divisions between landlords and tenants. But it did not cause these divisions. They were the result, rather, of earlier economic and social developments and, more particularly, of the tenant dissatisfaction which had set in since 1870.

It was the Liberals who benefited most from these developments. If the Derry by-election had shown the fragility of the presbyterian–catholic alliance and the vulnerability of the Liberal party in Ulster once it departed from an anti-ascendancy programme, the Tyrone election demonstrated the political potential of the tenant-right question. The Liberals increasingly concentrated on this question, and it was this which was to provide the great unifying issue in Ulster Liberal politics over the next decade and the basis for future Liberal growth in the province.

A measure of the change brought about in Ulster politics by the land question and the ballot was seen in the general election of 1874. In the three southern provinces the election was fought largely on the question of home rule and was, on the surface at any rate, a sweeping success for the newly formed Home Rule League.[79] In Ulster, on the other hand, the home rule movement was not extensively or well organised,[80] and home rule candidates went forward in only two constituencies — in Monaghan where John Madden, a protestant home ruler, was narrowly defeated, and in Cavan where Joseph Biggar and Charles Fay defeated the sitting member Edward Saunderson, whose support of the established church had made him unacceptable to the catholic electors.[81] In the remainder of the province, home rulers and catholics, anxious to avoid a repetition of the fiasco in Derry in 1872, generally gave their support to Liberal and tenant-right candidates, and the election in Ulster was fought on the land question and along traditional party lines.

The Liberals, their expectations aroused by the land act, the ballot and tenant dissatisfaction, put forward fourteen candidates in twelve of the nineteen constituencies. Liberal party organisation, however, had not developed in step with the growth of Liberal support. The Ulster Liberal Society, as we have seen, played only a supportive role and that mainly in the field of registration, and outside of Belfast there do not appear to have been Liberal associations in any of the constituencies. Thus the management of electoral affairs and the choice of candidates were often left to groups of individuals or local committees, usually self-nominated and consisting of a handful of prominent local leaders, and it was these who took the initiative in most of the borough constituencies such as Dungannon, Armagh, Coleraine, Enniskillen and Newry. In the county constituencies, however, it was the tenant-right associations that took the lead, reflecting both the inadequacy of Liberal organisation and the close identification by this stage of the tenant-right movement with the Liberal party. In Antrim, Down, Armagh, Derry and Donegal, the Liberal candidates all went forward under the auspices of the tenant-right associations, while in Tyrone Macartney, standing again as an independent Conservative, got strong backing from the Cookstown Tenant League.[82]

With the tenant-right associations making the running in this way, it was hardly surprising that the Liberal and independent candidates in the counties should make tenant-right the first issue in their addresses and campaign speeches.[83] Some were quite explicit in their promises, saying they would vote for tenant-right at the expiration of leases and the uniform legalisation of unrestricted tenant-right, or promising to support the programme outlined by the national conference in Belfast; but most candidates in one way or another undertook to support amendments of the 1870 act so as to ensure that tenants got the security intended by the measure. Conservative candidates, on the other hand, generally dealt with the land question only in so far as they had to, and it was clear that in the early stages of this election many Conservatives did not fully realise the strength of tenant-right feeling in the province. The Conservatives would, in fact, clearly have preferred to have fought the election on a programme of protestantism and empire, and, indeed, the Tory press and a number of candidates tried in the early stages of the campaign to do this. Within days, however, they were forced to face up to the fact that the key issue in the election was going to be tenant-right.

This presented a real and obvious threat to the Tory position in Ulster, and the Tories tried to meet it in several ways. First, they made a deliberate attempt 'to confuse tenant-right, home rule and Rome rule';[84] tenant-right, it was claimed, was 'merely a pretext' for home rule, and tenant-right candidates the dupes of 'a designing clique' of 'radicals, revolutionists, Romanists, and unitarians'.[85] Second, the whole machinery of landed influence was used in favour of the Conservative candidates, amounting on some estates almost to a campaign of intimidation. The Liberal press claimed that the exertions of the landed classes on behalf of the Tory candidates were greater in 1874 than in past elections, and certainly there were reports from virtually every constituency of landlords and agents vigorously canvassing their estates, of circulars being issued by estate offices — even by landlords such as Lord Londonderry and Sir Richard Wallace who had never done so in the past — and of placards being posted by agents and bailiffs.[86] This activity was accompanied by assiduous attempts to sow doubts about the secrecy of the ballot, and from all over the province came reports that 'the most tremendous exertions are being made to induce the people to believe that, nothwithstanding the operation of the ballot, the landlords will know how they vote'.[87]

But, finally, the landed candidates themselves had to adjust their position on the question of tenant-right. Initially even where they did refer to tenant-right, they did so in very general terms (the significant exception was Tyrone, where the Conservatives had learned an early lesson). But the pressure of the tenant-right demand was such that candidates throughout the province found it increasingly difficult to ignore and were obliged during the campaign to explain their views, affirm their support for tenant demands and often issue supplemental addresses.[88]

Tenant-right did not figure as prominently in the borough contests. In Belfast, where William Johnston and his Orange supporters had settled their differences with the official Conservatives,[89] the Liberal, Thomas McClure — as expected — lost the seat he had won in 1868. Conservatives were also returned for Derry city, Enniskillen, Lisburn and Downpatrick. As against these successes, however, the Tories lost control of Newry, Coleraine and Dungannon, while M.R. Dalway, standing once again as an independent, successfully defended Carrickfergus. The results in Carrickfergus and Newry were not unexpected, but the Liberal successes in Coleraine and Dungannon were regarded as a real breakthrough in the boroughs. In Coleraine great emphasis was placed on the fact that Taylor, the Liberal candidate, was both a merchant and a presbyterian,[90] while in Dungannon there was a growing feeling that the Ranfurly family had forfeited their influence through neglect — the Conservatives in the previous year had anticipated difficulty in holding the seat[91] — while Dickson had emerged, as a result of his factory, as the borough's chief benefactor.[92]

The Liberal successes in the boroughs were, in fact, largely presbyterian and middle-class successes. Those in the counties, on the other hand, were clearly victories for tenant-right. In Down, where the election was fought almost exclusively on this issue, James Sharman Crawford, son of William Sharman Crawford, the veteran champion of tenant-right, became the first Liberal to be elected for the county since 1835.[93] The tenant-righters scored an even greater success in Co. Derry, where two Liberals were returned by almost two to one majorities.[94] In Donegal, the Liberals were only narrowly defeated by less than forty votes, while in Antrim the Liberal Charles Wilson lost by only 133 votes despite being a virtual stranger in the constituency.[95] Wilson's presbyterianism no doubt helped him, and attacks made during the campaign on his opponents' failure to support various burials bills since 1868 suggest that many of Wilson's supporters saw the contest as a campaign against prelacy as much as a campaign against landlordism.[96] But there was no mistaking the fact that, as Wilson himself said and as the two Tory candidates agreed, this was 'a purely tenant-right contest'.[97] In Tyrone, the tenant-right mantle was carried by the independent Conservative, J.W. Ellison Macartney, who not only topped the poll, but received almost twice as many votes as Lord Claud Hamilton, who lost the seat he had occupied for the previous thirty-eight years. Macartney, of course, took the Conservative whip, and in this sense his election represented no loss to the Conservative party. But it was a resounding victory for tenant-right and a measure of the progress made by the question and the change it had brought about in Ulster politics; as the *Northern Whig* put it, 'who could have believed five years ago that Lord Claud Hamilton could be not only defeated in Tyrone, but placed at the bottom of the poll?'[98]

The election of 1874 radically transformed the pattern of representation in Ulster; whereas on the eve of the election the Conservatives had controlled twenty-five seats and the Liberals two, with two independents, there were now nineteen official Conservatives, six Liberals, two home rulers and two independents. The Conservatives had regained Belfast, but lost the boroughs of

Coleraine, Dungannon and Newry, and, more significantly, lost county seats — up to this, the absolute preserve of the Tory landed classes — in Cavan, Down and Derry. Moreover, they had come within 133 votes of losing a seat in Antrim, within forty votes of losing one of the Donegal seats and within thirty votes of losing both Derry city and Enniskillen. The Ulster counties, it seemed, as well as the boroughs, were falling away from the Conservative party.

The Conservatives attributed their losses to apathy and poor organisation, and certainly the sudden dissolution had caught their supporters in most constituencies — the exceptions were Belfast, Armagh county and city, and to a lesser extent Derry city and Enniskillen — almost totally unprepared.[99] But there was more to it than this. The election in fact reflected the fundamental changes which had taken place in Ulster society — in the boroughs the growing dissatisfaction and self-confidence of the presbyterian middle classes (already evident in the Liberal successes of 1868), in the counties the gradual disintegration of the traditional community of interest between landlords and tenants, and the increasing independence of the tenants under the agricultural prosperity, the land act and the ballot. It may well be, indeed, that with greater effort on the part of the Liberals, or even with fuller confidence in the secrecy of the ballot, Conservative losses in this election would have been more serious. As it was, they held on to as many seats as they did — twelve of the eighteen county seats, thirteen if Macartney's is included — only by making concessions on tenant-right. The election was, above all else, a victory for tenant-right and the tenant-right movement. The main political beneficiaries were the Liberals. But even the Liberal press had few illusions about the nature of Liberal support in the counties:

> The counties are stirring with new life. The tenant farmers are now, independently of mere party politics, bent on asserting their own interests. We do not say that on all questions they take broad or thoroughly liberal views, but they do, at all events, desire to be represented by those who may assert their case, and not by landlords who have hitherto scarcely thought that they have a duty to the tenants

who gave them their votes. The movement now going on in Ulster may not in every respect be the best possible; but it is very much better than mere stagnation and servility.[100]

In short, the shape of county politics in Ulster in the future was going to depend on the response of the two main parties to the needs of the tenant farmers. The Liberals — surprised at the extent of their own success in the counties[101] — were, after 1874, more anxious than ever to consolidate their position as the party of tenant-right. But the Conservatives too were aware of the needs of the situation and were quick to respond, firstly by developing their organisation in the north[102] — in itself an acknowledgement of the changed social circumstances in the province and of the fact that deference and dependence were no longer sufficient in themselves to return landed representatives to parliament — and secondly by adjusting their position on the land question. But in order to convince the northern tenants of their good faith, they needed an accommodating government at Westminster. As it was, Conservative attention to organisation paid off in the boroughs in the election of 1880, but the Liberal and tenant-right cause continued to make progress in the counties, not because of any insensitivity on the part of the Ulster Tories, but because of the indifference and intransigence of the party leaders and Conservative government in Britain.

## CONTINUING IMPORTANCE OF TENANT-RIGHT

The Liberal successes in 1874 were acclaimed as 'the beginning of the end of the Tory domination in Ulster', the prelude to the emancipation of the entire province.[103] Yet if the Liberals anticipated further successes in the future, they seemed curiously reluctant to make any preparation for them. Apart from the Ulster Liberal Society which continued its work of registration, there was little evidence of Liberal organisation in the months and years after this election, and towards the end of 1877 the *Weekly Whig* was complaining that 'few Liberal associations undertake the duty of registration ... Liberalism in Ulster has yet to be developed by registration'.[104] Instead, the Liberal leaders — and the Ulster Liberal Society — sought to attach the tenant-right associations to the Liberal cause, and looked to these to organise the counties and take care of the registers;[105] and in so far as Liberalism developed between 1874 and 1880, it was a development which was prompted by and through the tenant-right movement and which was based entirely on the issue of tenant-right.

If the Liberals seemed content to rest on their laurels after the general election, this was not the case with the tenant-right associations. Their activity continued, and mainly in the areas where it had been carried on before 1874 — in Antrim, Derry, Donegal and to a much lesser extent in Tyrone and Armagh. But the most important new developments came in Down, where the Down Farmers' Union made a sustained and largely successful effort to organise branch associations in each of the polling districts of the county. By the end of 1874 the parent association at Downpatrick had become the centre of a network of no fewer than fifteen associations covering almost the entire county.[106] Credit for this development in Down must go to a handful of local activists, most notably Joseph Perry and William J. Moore, the founders of the Down Farmers' Association, and Edward Gardner, a Downpatrick solicitor, all three of whom tirelessly perambulated the county addressing meetings of farmers and setting up local societies.

But although great advances were made by the movement in Down, Antrim continued to be the best organised county in the province. Here there were fewer associations, but all of them showed a vigour and enjoyed a continuity which most tenant societies in other parts of the province did not have. There had always been close collaboration between members of the different associations in Antrim — and indeed between associations in different counties — and in 1876 it was decided to form a central association. Hence the Antrim Central Tenant-Right Association came into being, comprising the six associations of Route, Lisburn, Ballymena, Ballyclare, Crumlin and Ballycastle.[107] Attempts were made to launch county associations in Armagh, Donegal and Tyrone, but the results in each case were a good deal less successful than those in Antrim and Down. In Armagh, following proposals made at the annual meeting of the Newry Tenant

Farmers' Defence Association, the Armagh Tenant Farmers' Defence Association was established in February 1875, but it was never as active or as influential as the Antrim and Down organisations.[108] The Donegal Tenant-Right and Liberal Registration Association was founded immediately after the election of 1874 with the intention of establishing local societies in each polling district of the county, but little appears to have been done to implement these plans. And in Tyrone, the County Tyrone Tenants' Protection and Land Law Reform Association was formed in 1874, but seems to have met only occasionally, and by 1875 complaints were being made about the general apathy in the county.[109]

These county associations were generally formed, as the title of the Donegal body suggests, with a clear political purpose, and that was to organise the counties for the next election. The tenant associations continued, of course, to carry out the legal and protective work for which many of them had originally been formed; but increasingly the argument was that complete security could only be achieved by an amendment of the 1870 act and that this could only be procured by the return of their own representatives to Westminster.[110] Thus the efforts of the leading associations, especially in Antrim and Down, were directed more and more towards 'the registration of votes in the tenant-right interest' and the preparation of the constituencies for the next election, and certainly for many of the tenant-right leaders it was these activities rather than any others which were of paramount importance during this period.[111] The victories of 1874 had made them realise the political potential of the land question, and many of them were determined to use it. Thomas Swann of Lisburn plainly — indeed, bluntly — explained the change which had taken place in the nature of the movement:

> Tenant-right is at the present moment the key to the political situation in Ulster ... A couple of years ago, the tenant-right party never in their wildest moments dreamed of laying hold on the political power of the province. The defence of cases in the land courts and the general support of the Ulster custom were nearly the summit of their aims ... We have, however, arrived at this position in real earnest — that the

> tenant-right party are determined to control and direct, as far as their
> legitimate influence is concerned, the parliamentary representation of
> the province, as the only means now left of arriving at a solution of
> the difficulties now before them.[112]

Swann and others in the movement continued, however, to insist
that tenant-right was not a party question and that they were prepared
to support candidates of either side so long as they were pledged to
tenant-right principles. But, clearly, with the close co-operation between
the tenant-right movement and the Liberal party in 1874 and after,
and with so many of the leading figures in the movement also
prominent in the Liberal party — the presidency of Lord Waveney
of both the Antrim Central Tenant-Right Association and the Ulster
Liberal party symbolised the link between the two movements — it
was the Liberal party which stood to gain.

Such electoral gains, however, were in the future, and, in the
meantime, the tenant-right movement sought to keep the issue before
the public by continuing its campaign of meetings and by promoting
legislative attempts through its parliamentary representatives. During
the course of this parliament no fewer than twenty-three Irish land
bills were introduced at Westminster, many of them jointly supported
by northern Liberals and southern home rulers.[113] Delegates from a
number of the Ulster societies — from the Route, Down, Lisburn,
Ballymena, Clogher, Tandragee, and Farney societies — attended a
land conference in Dublin in January 1875, which produced a set of
resolutions reiterating the principles adopted at the Dublin and Belfast
conferences of 1873 and 1874 in favour of security of tenure, free
sale, the arbitration of rents, and the extension of the Ulster custom
to the rest of Ireland. A parliamentary committee appointed by the
conference to prepare a bill on these lines included nine northern and
nineteen southern representatives.[114]

Not all of the northern tenant-right supporters, however, were
happy about casting in their lot with the south; some, indeed, felt that
a premature and injudicious reopening of the question in a
Conservative-dominated parliament could jeopardise what had
already been gained; others, who were anxious to press for

amendment, believed that the basic differences between north and south were such that it was better for the Ulster tenants to look after their own interests.[115] Thus Sharman Crawford, contrary to the decision taken at the conference and contrary also to the express wishes of the Antrim tenant associations, introduced a separate bill for Ulster before the conference bill had been given its final shape. Crawford's bill, which sought to establish leasehold tenant-right, free sale either by public auction or private contract, and, most importantly, the presumption that every holding in Ulster was subject to tenant-right unless the landlord could prove otherwise, was of course easily defeated, and served mainly to alienate the southern tenants, who regarded it as a distinct violation of the pledge given at the Dublin conference.[116]

Relations between north and south did not break down entirely, however. Many tenant-righters in both parts of the country were anxious to preserve a united front, and a number of northern representatives attended further land conferences in Dublin in 1876.[117] But while these conferences agreed on a common policy embracing 'the full legalisation of the Ulster custom and its extension to the south of Ireland', and while various tenant-right bills continued to get the joint support of northern Liberals and southern home rulers, the dispute of 1875 had revealed the clear divergence of interests between Ulster farmers and those in the south. The grievances of the former during the 1870s were always less serious than those of tenants in the rest of the country, and there was always a deep-seated reluctance in the north either to tie their fortunes to a bill encompassing the whole country or to trust their cause to representatives who openly attached more importance to home rule than to land reform. The co-operation with the south, especially after 1876, never in reality amounted to much more than well-intentioned statements on both sides and, with attention in the south turning increasingly from 1876 to the struggle within the home rule party and with Butt apparently losing control of the party, even these came to an end.[118] 'The fact cannot any longer be disguised', observed the *Weekly Whig* in 1878, 'that practical union among the tenant associations in Ireland is broken. No organisation now exists for drawing them together either at a national conference or by any other means.'[119]

Apart from Crawford's bill of 1875, six other bills were introduced during this parliament by Ulster Liberals, all specifically dealing with Ulster. Crawford's bills in 1875, 1876 and 1877 and Taylor's in 1879 and 1880 tried to meet the general grievances of the Ulster tenants by reversing the presumption of tenant-right in favour of the tenant, granting the right of free sale and removing doubts about leasehold tenant-right; Professor Richard Smyth's bill in 1875 was an attempt to improve the Bright clauses of the 1870 act, while his bill of 1877 was intended to establish leasehold tenant-right. None of the measures was given a second reading, and in fact only two of them — Crawford's bills of 1875 and 1877 — were put to a vote.

The Ulster Conservatives also introduced a number of bills; four of these — Mulholland's in 1876, two introduced by Hill-Trevor in 1878 and 1879, and Belmore's in 1879 — dealt with leasehold tenant-right, while the remaining three, introduced by the Conservative tenant-righter Macartney in 1878, 1879 and 1880, were, like Crawford's, directed towards transferring the onus of proof with regard to tenant-right from the tenant to the landlord, establishing leasehold tenant-right, and abolishing estate rules which restricted the right of sale. All of these met the same fate as the Liberal measures, being rejected, counted out or withdrawn; Hill-Trevor's first leasehold bill did get as far as the House of Lords, but its relative success in this respect owed more to an impending by-election in Down than to any change of heart by the Conservative government.

These Conservative bills were — with the possible exception of Macartney's bills of 1879 and 1880 — generally more limited in scope than those of the Ulster Liberals, and on the occasions on which the Ulster Conservatives were put to the test on Liberal bills — on Crawford's bills of 1875 and 1877 — they voted almost to a man against the first, and 'were conspicuous by their absence' from the division on the second.[120] There was not necessarily any inconsistency here, nor indeed was their policy purely one of expediency. While most Ulster Tories were reconciled by the second half of this decade to accepting and even supporting the legalisation of existing practices, they argued, with considerable justification, that what Crawford's bills — and indeed Macartney's bills in 1879 and 1880 — proposed to do was to establish the strongest incidents of the Ulster custom in areas where they had never been, or at the very least had long ceased to be, recognised; what these bills were doing was not legalising but creating usages, and they were, therefore, from the Conservative point of view, a serious encroachment on the property rights of the landlords.[121] Mulholland's bill of 1876, Hill-Trevor's bills of 1878 and 1879, and Belmore's in 1879, on the other hand, were intended merely to remove existing doubts as to leasehold tenant-right, though even these measures were rendered unacceptable to the tenant movement by the inclusion in the first of a proviso that the judge in awarding compensation should take into account the length of time the lease had been enjoyed, and the inclusion in the others of a clause exempting leases which had an express covenant to give up the holding.[122]

But, generally, if support for leasehold tenant-right had been given only half-heartedly and under pressure in 1874, by 1876 most Ulster Conservative members recognised that in the interests of social harmony and their own political future such a measure would have to be passed.[123] Thus while they continued — at this time at any rate — to oppose any measure involving a sacrifice of territorial rights and while a number of them continued to have reservations about leasehold tenant-right, they were, as a body, genuinely and increasingly anxious to have this question settled. 'There was not a Conservative member in Ulster', stated the Hon. Edward O'Neill, the Tory MP for Antrim, in 1877, 'but wished that a lease should be made no bar to tenant-right.'[124] And, indeed, as this parliament drew nearer its end, a growing number of northern Tories realised that something more than leasehold tenant-right was required if they were to maintain their position in Ulster politics. There were others, of course, such as John Leslie, MP for Monaghan, and Lifford and Annesley in the lords, who continued to resist any further appeasement of the tenants; the assault on Hill-Trevor's bill in the House of Lords, for example, was led by Lifford, much to the exasperation of his own Ulster colleagues.[125] But by 1880 — indeed, by 1878 — Lifford and those of like mind were very much in a minority in the party.

The Conservative government, however, though not unaware of the pressures on their supporters in the north of Ireland, did not view the question with the same urgency and were, in fact, most anxious to disabuse tenants of the notion that 'the land act might any further be altered'.[126] The result was that, despite almost unanimous agreement among the Ulster political parties as to the need for amending legislation, and despite repeated requests from the Ulster Tories to their leaders at Westminster for such legislation, nothing was done in this parliament to satisfy even the minimum demand for leasehold tenant-right.[127]

In any case, events by the late 1870s had gone well beyond the point where the tenant-right movement would have been prepared to settle for leasehold tenant-right. What the tenant associations wanted — 'leasehold tenant-right, freedom of sale of tenant-right, arbitration as to rent, and security of tenure' — had not changed markedly since 1874, but what was new was their determination to settle for nothing less than this:

> There is one point on which the farmers will be wise to be careful — viz., not to be satisfied with anything short of their just rights, fair rents, free sale, and continuous occupancy. The constitutional tenant-righters, otherwise the landlords and their political allies, are making a great ado about tenant-right at the end of a lease, as if that were sufficient to quieten agitation and satisfy the farmers. But the farmers have put off their coats to the work now, and they will act very foolishly if they put them on again till their whole rights are won.[128]

Yet if the tenant associations were determined to accept nothing short of a full settlement of the question, it was becoming increasingly obvious that they could expect little from this particular parliament. Moreover, the Conservative landlords had learned their lesson in 1874, and after 1874 there were fewer attacks on the land act and a greater desire on the landed side to avoid litigation. In these circumstances, with no prospect of immediate legislation, with general agreement on both sides on the need to amend the 1870 act if not on the form the amendment should take, and with landlords carefully avoiding any kind of confrontation with their tenants, the campaign in Ulster became increasingly difficult to sustain. From 1877 there were fewer tenant-right meetings and the province, says MacKnight, 'began to feel something like comparative repose'.[129]

Tenant apathy was not the only problem facing the movement at this time, nor was it the only reason why the movement languished. Tenant-righters had pinned their hopes to the Liberal party and the return of Liberal MPs at the next election and, as we have seen, much of their efforts since 1874 had been directed to that end. These efforts were now put in jeopardy by the re-emergence of divisions which threatened to split the whole basis of support of the Liberal–tenant-right movement.

The Liberal–catholic alliance had earlier been severely shaken by the publication in November 1874 of Gladstone's pamphlets attacking the Vatican decrees of 1870. Gladstone's action seriously embarrassed his followers in the north of Ireland, and one prominent member of the party feared 'it will deprive us of all catholic support in Ulster, and we cannot beat the Tories without the catholics'.[130] The Ulster Liberals made a point of dissociating themselves from the views expressed by Gladstone and no actual breach occurred at this time.[131] Nevertheless, relations continued on a very uneasy basis, with the Liberals subjected to persistent attacks by the *Ulster Examiner* and home rule sympathisers such as Father Michael Cahill of St Patrick's in Belfast, who claimed that they had 'too often climbed to power on the shoulders of catholics' while at the same time totally ignoring catholic interests, and that tenant-right in Ulster simply meant 'the ascendancy of Whig-presbyterianism'.[132] Cahill was not alone in these views, and when a vacancy occurred in Donegal later in that year there were some fears that the catholic electors would follow Cahill's advice and vote Tory in the hope of concessions on education. But few catholics were prepared as yet to carry their dissatisfaction with the Liberal party to the point of supporting the Conservatives, and a meeting of the catholic bishop and clergy of the Raphoe diocese in Donegal decided, despite reservations about both candidates in the election, to come out in favour of the Liberal nominee.[133]

In fact, in this election the main defections from the Liberal side were not catholic but presbyterian. The Conservative candidate was

William Wilson, and from the point of view of meeting the tenant-right threat and dividing the presbyterians, a better choice could not have been made. Wilson was a respected local presbyterian solicitor and tenant farmer, and issued an address which promised to secure the full benefits of the Ulster custom for both leaseholders and yearly tenants and to support grand jury reform.[134] He also prudently ran a very low-key campaign, holding no public meetings, presenting himself as an independent Conservative and keeping his landed support very much in the background. Moreover, the Liberal candidate, Thomas Lea, a Kidderminster businessman, was seriously handicapped by the fact that he was a stranger to the constituency and a congregationalist rather than a presbyterian.

In the event, Lea was defeated by 1,975 votes to 1,876. Wilson clearly owed his victory to the fact that he was a local man, a presbyterian and a strong supporter of tenant-right, and, despite his victory, the election did not augur well for the future of landed representatives. The very choice of Wilson as a candidate was a measure of how far the Ulster Tories had shifted their ground from 1874 and especially from 1868, but the message was — and this was not lost on the Ulster Tory leaders — that further concessions were necessary. The Liberals were disappointed with the result, but they could claim, with some justification, that the election was in many respects a victory for tenant-right.[135] Moreover, while a number of presbyterians had voted for their co-religionist, the catholic support for the Liberal party — despite repeated allegations that Lea had voted for Newdegate's bill for the inspection of convents — had held firm.[136]

Yet scarcely a year later Thomas MacKnight was telling Gladstone that 'the Liberal protestants are almost now the only Irish Liberals'.[137] The reasons for the withdrawal of catholic support at this time were the usual ones of education and home rule. Butt's introduction of an Irish university bill in March 1877 re-opened the education question, and although Butt's bill was rejected, the indications were that Michael Hicks-Beach, the Irish chief secretary, while unwilling to act on land, was anxious to placate the Irish hierarchy by making concessions on secondary and higher level education.[138] The prospect of education reform, as always, tested Liberal–catholic relations; attention was now diverted from the unifying issue of tenant-right, and a series of catholic meetings urged an early settlement of the question of university and intermediate education.[139]

More important, however, were the developments on home rule. At the end of November 1877 at a meeting in St Mary's Hall in Belfast, the Ulster Home Government Association was launched as the first step in 'the organisation of Ulster in the home rule interest'. Moreover, the same meeting unanimously resolved that the creation of a peasant proprietary in Ireland was the only permanent solution of the land question, thus seemingly rejecting the programme of the tenant-right movement.[140] The Liberal and tenant-right press scornfully dismissed such proposals as being totally unrealistic, but they were fully aware of the threat this new home rule initiative presented to the unity of the Liberal and tenant-right movement.[141] As it happened, home rule efforts to organise the province never really got off the ground, but Liberal fears with regard to the unity of the movement were shown to be well-founded when, a few months later, the death of Sharman Crawford led to a by-election in Co. Down.

The Liberals faced a formidable task in this election. The Conservative candidate was Lord Castlereagh, heir to the Londonderry estate, one of the largest in the county and one on which tenant-right had always been fully recognised, and Castlereagh's own professions of support for tenant-right went every bit as far as those of W.D. Andrews, the Liberal nominee.[142] The Conservatives, moreover, were considerably better organised than in 1874, and Lord Londonderry was apparently prepared to spare no expense in order to secure Castlereagh's return.[143] The government, too, played their part by allowing a second reading to Hill-Trevor's bill, thus for once recognising the special difficulties facing their supporters in the north of Ireland.[144] But over and above all this, the Conservatives made a skilful and determined bid for the catholic vote, giving great prominence to the education question and the recently introduced intermediate education bill, which had been well received by the catholic clergy. Moreover, when the Ulster Home Government Association made representations to both candidates on the questions of self-government and education, Castlereagh was obviously prepared to give them more satisfactory assurances than Andrews with the result that the nationalist organisation urged its supporters to vote for Castlereagh in the election.[145]

In these circumstances, many of the catholic votes which had been given to Crawford in 1874 were transferred to the Conservatives, and although the total Liberal vote did not drop markedly from that of 1874 — the presbyterian Liberal vote evidently increased — Andrews was easily defeated.[146] The defeat was a serious blow to Liberal and tenant-right aspirations in Ulster, less serious in itself perhaps than in what it presaged for the coming general election.[147] The Liberal and tenant-right movement was now in total disarray, the unity between catholics and presbyterians on which it depended plainly shattered by the emergence of issues on which there could be no agreement. The situation at the end of 1878 was described as follows:

> It is to be deeply regretted that the dissensions which have arisen in the north render it difficult to settle any plan of united action. Tenant-righters cannot put confidence in the northern home rule vote. In the face of this obstacle tenant-right candidates hesitate to come forward in northern constituencies, and without the prospect of parliamentary contests the tenant-right associations do not seem inclined to carry on the movement.[148]

Scarcely had these words been written when a by-election in Co. Derry created an opportunity to test how serious or permanent were the divisions that had rent the movement throughout the previous year. Although the Conservative candidate matched the Liberal promises on land reform and made much of the Conservative intermediate education act, the majority of the catholics voted Liberal on this occasion and were, in fact, urged to do so by the Ulster Home Government Association which, in a manifesto to the catholic electors, explained that

> the limited state of the franchise precludes us from putting forward a candidate who would really represent the interests of Ireland, and,

under these circumstances, the only alternative left to us is to support the least objectionable candidate who is undoubtedly Sir Thomas McClure [ the Liberal candidate].[149]

This was a fair statement of the general attitude of many catholics towards the Liberal party, and plainly indicated what was likely to happen to that party once a viable catholic alternative emerged. In the meantime, although the catholic vote divided, the majority of catholics were again prepared to make common cause with the Liberal presbyterians so that the Liberals managed to retain the seat they had won in 1874, though with a reduced majority.[150]

The result was greeted with relief by the Liberal press. Fears that tenant-right was being superseded by what the *Whig* described as 'questions of less practical importance' now passed. The signs were that catholics and presbyterians were reuniting on the land question, which had been given a new urgency by the agricultural depression of the late 1870s. Tenant-right was still the key issue in Ulster politics. Moreover, it was becoming increasingly obvious that there would be no settlement of the question by this government. The Ulster Tories were ready, indeed anxious, to meet tenant demands — the Conservative candidate in Derry, for example, had been prepared to go as far as, if not further than, the Liberal in supporting tenant claims — but they were clearly powerless against the apparently implacable hostility of their own party leaders.[151] With a growing belief among tenant farmers that further concessions could only be obtained from the Liberals, this success in 1878 promised to be the forerunner of further Liberal victories in the counties.

All the developments seen in Derry in 1878 — the restoration of unity between catholics and presbyterians, the re-establishment of the primacy of the land question, the increasing disillusionment with the Tory government — were confirmed by a by-election in Donegal in 1879 following the death of William Wilson, who had won the seat in 1876. Thomas Lea once again contested the seat on behalf of the Liberals, and this time won a resounding victory. What was perhaps as gratifying to the Liberals — and as alarming to the Tories — as the capture of the seat was the size of Lea's majority, with his share of the vote going up from 49 per cent in 1876 to 59 per cent in 1879.[152] Lea had got the combined support of the presbyterians and catholics, with the Ulster home rule executive coming out strongly in his favour.[153] But undoubtedly the main factor in the size of the Conservative defeat was the persistent refusal of the Tory government to make concessions on land, and the imprudent and hostile comments made by the Tory leaders, most notably the chief secretary James Lowther, on both the 1870 act and tenant-right in general.[154]

Whereas in the first years of the ministry, Tory candidates, once they accepted the need to amend the act of 1870, could claim to be in a better position to do something about it, they were now, after five years of Tory rule, finding it increasingly difficult — in fact next to impossible — to convince the tenants that they, whatever their own readiness to make concessions, could influence the Conservative government to introduce remedial legislation. The Marquis of Hamilton warned the Tory leaders that, unless they were able before the general election to bring in a land bill, at least half the Conservative seats in Ulster would go:

There is only one subject that the tenant farmers in the north of Ireland at the present time care about and that is the land question. It is all absorbing to them. They care little about general politics or foreign policies, but the whole of their thoughts absolutely and without any exception is concentrated upon the land. Their argument is this — we want a new land bill to give us security of tenure and unlimited sale of tenant-right, and tenant-right at the end of a lease. The present government have been in office for six years. They have done nothing for us. Gladstone gave us one land bill and he will give us another, and so we will vote for him and his candidates ... The feeling of the people is intensely bitter ... I am not now referring to the Liberals and radicals who always will be Liberals and radicals, but to men who have hitherto been Conservative and who now, under the ballot, on account of this very question vote for the Liberal candidate. [155]

Hamilton had long been aware of the threat presented to the Conservative position in Ulster by tenant-right, but when he wrote this letter the question had been made a great deal more urgent by the downturn in Irish agriculture at the end of the 1870s and by the developments which were then taking place in the southern part of the country. These developments presented a new and potentially more dangerous threat to the position of the landed classes in Ulster, but, if they initially created new tensions in the north, they also eventually resurrected old divisions so that their ultimate effects there were to be vastly different from those in the rest of the country.

7

# Agricultural Depression and Landlord-Tenant Relations 1879–80

It is sometimes assumed that Ulster escaped the worst effects of the agricultural depression of the late 1870s, but in fact its impact was felt in every county, and in some districts in the north the consequences were every bit as serious as those in any part of the south. Small farmers who had shared marginally in the prosperity of the early and mid-1870s found themselves by 1879 once again on the verge of destitution, while larger farmers, who had enjoyed a steadily rising standard of living over the previous three decades, were confronted by a crisis which threatened not only to bring this to an end, but to destroy the value of their tenant-right investment in the soil. In these circumstances the nature of tenant agitation in the province changed and a new, more spontaneous and more desperate agitation took the place of the earlier organised activity of the previous decade.

From early in 1877 the nearly incessant rains were causing problems for agriculture. Farming operations were already reported to be in a 'backward state' in March,[1] and there was little improvement over the following months. The summer generally was cold and wet so that by September it had become apparent that virtually all the leading crops had been damaged.[2] At the beginning of November the RIC sub-inspectors reported crop failure in practically every district and every county in Ulster.³ Wheat, oats, barley, flax and turnips were all down on previous years (see Table 7.1), but the most serious failure was in potatoes, which had been planted late because of the wet spring and attacked by blight in many areas before they matured. The only exception to an otherwise disastrous harvest was the hay crop, which was 10 per cent up on the previous year.

A warmer spring and summer and less rain brought about a partial recovery in 1878. Yields everywhere were up on 1877 and the provincial returns were higher in every single crop than the average for the years 1871–76 (see Table 7.1). Certain crops in some counties fell below the average, but the harvest generally was good and all counties shared in the improvement.⁴

Table 7.1. Percentage differences between average crop yields
in Ulster 1871–76 and yields in 1877 and 1878⁵

|  | WHEAT | OATS | BARLEY | POTATOES | TURNIPS | FLAX | HAY |
|---|---|---|---|---|---|---|---|
| 1877 | −5.8 | −5.5 | −3.3 | −44.1 | −34.3 | +12.4 | +10.0 |
| 1878 | +14.4 | +6.3 | +13.8 | +5.9 | +4.3 | +23.3 | +10.0 |

As against this, however, and preventing a full recovery from the disasters of 1877, the prices of agricultural products were low as Ireland began to feel the full effects of American competition.⁶ Thus, while the harvest of 1878 was good, it was not sufficient in itself to compensate for the losses of the previous year. At the end of the year small farmers in different parts of the province were reported to be in a critical condition and shopkeepers, it was claimed, were finding it 'extremely difficult to collect their country accounts'.⁷

There was no improvement in the following year: in fact quite the reverse, the 1879 season being one of the coldest and wettest on record. Following an exceptionally hard winter of snow and frost — 'more severe and continuous than had ever been known'⁸ — there was scarcely any spring, while the summer months were characterised by high rainfall and low temperatures.⁹ Fears about harvest prospects set in early in the season and the continuing inclemency of the weather during the summer months — with flooding in many areas — caused mounting concern, and by September it was being predicted that the agricultural classes were going to be faced with a disaster of the same proportions as that of 1846.[10]

In the event, a providentially fine October saved the harvest from total catastrophe and the worst fears did not materialise. Nevertheless, all crops proved lamentably deficient and although not all areas were equally affected — crops on the lighter soils were well up to the mark — the decline in crop yields in Ulster as a whole was greater than the national average. As shown in Table 7.2, every crop was well below the average for the years 1871–76. The worst failures were in potatoes and turnips, each of them practically 70 per cent below the average. Even these figures hid the seriousness of the failure in some areas, where it was reported that the crop had rotted in the ground and was 'scarcely worth the digging'.[11]

Table 7.2. Percentage differences between the average crop yields in Ulster and Ireland for the years 1871–76 and the yields in 1879[12]

|         | WHEAT | OATS  | BARLEY | POTATOES | TURNIPS | FLAX | HAY  |
|---------|-------|-------|--------|----------|---------|------|------|
| Ulster  | −20.9 | −15.0 | −21.7  | −67.6    | −67.9   | −7.4 | −5.0 |
| Ireland | −16.8 | −12.0 | −23.4  | −60.6    | −50.8   | −7.7 | 0.0  |

If it was tillage which was most seriously affected in 1879, the livestock sector also fared badly (worse, according to some observers[13]). Both livestock and pastures suffered from the severe winter and late spring, while the continuing rainfall and low temperatures of the summer months caused further deterioration. Moreover, the prices of livestock products in general were well below the levels of the early 1870s; according to the Barrington index of prices, butter was down 22 per cent, wool 47 per cent, mutton 8 per cent and store cattle 7 per cent on the average for the period 1871–76.[14] Barrington's figures for store cattle, however, were taken from the reports of country fairs in May and June and clearly made no allowance for the fall in prices which took place after these months. 'Young cattle', it was reported in September, 'after being grazed all summer, are selling for from £1 to £1.10.0 a head less than they cost in April or May'.[15] Tillage prices held up better, but even here increasing foreign competition deprived farmers of the usual compensation of higher prices for low crop yields.[16] With the failure of potatoes and other crops, with stagnation in the cattle trade and with low prices, the farming classes in Ulster as in the rest of the country were faced with a crisis of alarming proportions.[17]

All rural classes in Ireland were affected by the depression, and rural incomes and social well-being in general were seriously reduced. Thomas Grimshaw, the Registrar-General estimated the depreciation in the money value of crops in 1879 as compared with 1878 at over £10 million.[18] Even large farmers suffered privation. Many were forced to draw on their capital to see them through the season, and deposits in joint-stock banks, which had reached a peak of £33 million in 1876, fell in 1880 to below £30 million for the first time since 1872.[19] But it was the small farmers and labourers who suffered most severely.[20] Turf shortages were reported in Donegal, Monaghan, Tyrone, Cavan, Down and other parts of the province,[21] while the generally poor harvest and retrenchment of both landlords and large farmers meant that there was little employment for agricultural labourers.[22] Small farmers, it was claimed, were even worse off. As a result of the failure of crops, especially the potato crop, many of them were forced further into debt. But the problem for others was that their credit — unduly extended during the good years — was, as a result of the previous bad reasons, already exhausted, some of them owing to 'shopkeepers and others four, five, six and even ten times the amount of their annual rent'.[23]

With the failure of crops, fuel and credit, the small farmers were in the early months of 1880, according to Thomas Dickson, 'in the deepest distress, bordering on starvation'.[24] A parliamentary return showed that at the beginning of March 1880 nearly 20,000 people were receiving poor law relief in Ulster, an increase of 26 per cent on the corresponding period in 1878.[25] But this seriously understated the true extent of the distress. In Donegal — the most distressed county in Ulster — the numbers in receipt of poor relief had increased only from 1,296 in March 1878 to 1,512 in March 1880; yet there were during the first six months of 1880 between 60,000 and 70,000 individuals on the relief lists of the Donegal Central Relief Committee.[26] Poor law guardians were prohibited by statute from granting outdoor relief to able-bodied persons, and small farmers and cottiers could only become eligible for relief by surrendering their holdings. But over and above these restrictions, which in themselves excluded a large section of those in want, the poor law guardians showed a notorious disinclination to spend money on relief.[27] Even after the relief of distress act in March 1880 gave permission to boards of guardians to grant outdoor relief to persons holding land, few boards took advantage of the new regulations and many were under severe pressure from ratepayers not to do so; in Carrickmacross in Monaghan, for example, the returning officer and master of the union had to seek police protection from a crowd of 300 ratepayers protesting against outdoor relief.[28] Out of eight scheduled unions in Donegal, only two put the relief of distress act into force and unions in other counties showed a similar reluctance.[29]

Yet distress in some areas in Ulster reached nearly famine proportions. Donegal, where pre-Famine conditions still existed, was worst hit and James Tuke, an English quaker who toured the county in the spring of 1880, found suffering and misery on a huge scale. The situation in Killybegs parish was typical, with 450 of the 600 families in receipt of relief from the local relief committee. Many of these people, Tuke was told, 'had formerly gained something of a livelihood from fishing, but the fish have nearly all left the bay'. The combined loss of fish and potatoes left them destitute, many of them so deeply in debt from potato failures of previous years that the shopkeepers refused to extend their credit.[30] It was the same in Glencolumbkille with 600 of the 800 families on relief, in Kilcar, Ardara, Gweedore and virtually every other district along the western side of the county. In addition to the failure of the potato crop and fishing there were the shortage of fuel and the collapse of the market for kelp.[31] And to cap it all, the poor harvests in England and Scotland deprived many of the small farmers of the income they would normally have received from seasonal work in these countries. Even the young people, who were usually taken on at 'hiring' fairs to work in other parts of Ulster during the summer months, found that there was no market for their labour.[32] This catalogue of disasters left smallholders and labourers in west Donegal in a critical condition, and by the early months of 1880, as already indicated, no fewer than 70,000 people were on the relief lists of the forty-six committees affiliated to the Donegal Central Relief Committee.

If Donegal was clearly the most stricken county in Ulster, there were districts in every county where the distress was acute. The Mansion House committee received urgent appeals for aid from all over the province. Cavan was the most seriously affected county outside of Donegal, with thirty-three local relief committees and 33,000 persons on the relief lists; 'many of the small farmers', it was reported in February, 'are destitute of food, fuel and clothing'.[33] The mountainous districts of Monaghan, where 7,500 were receiving reliefs, were described as being 'in a state of actual starvation'.[34] Small farmers in Tyrone at Carrickmore, Fintona, Gortin, Pomeroy, Kildress and other areas were reported to be in a pitiable condition. with some 12,000 people depending on relief provided by twenty local committees.[35] From Belleek, Derrylin, Derrygonnelly and other parts of Fermanagh came reports that the distress had 'assumed an alarming appearance' and that small farmers and labourers were 'in dire misery'.[36] In Armagh, some 10,500 people were receiving relief, mainly in the southern more mountainous part of the county. Even Antrim and Down were affected, with serious distress being reported in parts of south Down and in the Glens of Antrim.[37]

Clearly not every part of Ulster was equally affected by the depression and the province as a whole escaped more lightly than the south and west. Flax, while down in both yield and price from 1871–6 — by 7 per cent and 3 per cent respectively — was still highly remunerative and, with a greater acreage devoted to it in 1879 than in previous years, provided many of the small Ulster farmers with a cushion against losses in other agricultural products.[38] But flax alone could not compensate for other losses, and the distress in many parts of the province in 1879–80 was real and acute.

Both the English press and English politicians remained for long sceptical about the seriousness of the situation in Ireland, and government officials continued all during the summer and autumn months of 1879 to insist that it was less critical than 'in most other parts of the United Kingdom'.[39] This was in the face of mounting evidence to the contrary. All over Ireland newspapers, public meetings, boards of guardians, clergymen, politicians and prominent figures were increasingly urging on the government the necessity of taking immediate action. In November seventy Irish MPs, including both Liberal and Conservative representatives from Ulster, submitted a memorial to Beaconsfield emphasising the critical condition of the small farmers and labourers, and appealing to him to take immediate steps to prevent and mitigate the oncoming calamity.[40] The government, however, continued to procrastinate, and was encouraged to some extent to do so by the local government board which, while accepting that there would be considerable distress and destitution during the winter months, reported in November that there was no reason to believe that the existing system of poor law relief would be unequal to the demands likely to be imposed by the crisis.[41]

The only concession made by the government before the end of 1880 was a measure facilitating the borrowing of money — up to £250,000 to come out of the Irish church surplus fund — by landowners, boards of guardians and other authorities in the distressed districts under the terms of previous land improvement acts.[42] This project proved to be totally inadequate to meet the exigencies of the situation and finally, at the beginning of the new year, the government was forced to take more decisive action, authorising the extension of loans up to £600,000 to Irish landlords and sanitary authorities at one per cent interest.[43] Irish landowners hastened to take advantage of these terms, and by the end of March over £1,325,000 had been applied for and schemes totalling nearly £400,000 sanctioned, the figures for Ulster however being only £85,000 and £20,000 respectively.[44] But the problem was that some of the districts where the distress was most acute were precisely those in which the landowners were either unable to unwilling to incur loans on any terms and, in the result, no appreciable amount of employment was created where the need was greatest until the worst of the crisis was over.[45]

At the same time the lord lieutenant was also empowered to convoke extraordinary baronial presentment sessions in the distressed districts, and to make advances at one per cent interest repayable in fifteen years for such public works as the sessions might sanction. One hundred and six such baronial sessions were actually summoned — including four in Donegal, five in Cavan and three in Fermanagh — but once again in some of the most needy districts the justices refused point-blank to saddle bankrupt baronies with taxation, while in others the procedure involved was so long drawn out that the worst of the distress was over by the time they were implemented.[46]

Two further relief measures were passed by the government. First, the relief of distress act in March enabled guardians in the scheduled unions to grant outdoor relief to able-bodied persons and small farmers without the surrender of their holdings, but it proved impossible to spur the boards into any general system of outdoor relief.[47] And secondly, the seeds supply act allowed boards of guardians to borrow money without interest for the purchase of seed oats and potatoes to be issued at cost price and on reasonable terms of repayment to farmers rated at under £15. A greater number of unions in both Ulster and Ireland as a whole took advantage of this act, and nearly £600,000 was advanced under it, almost £316,000 of this going to some forty unions in Ulster.[48] But this was more important for the following season and, on the whole, the special measures adopted by the government failed to provide relief at the time it was most needed, with the result that the brunt of the responsibility fell on the charitable organisations and the landlords.

Indeed, in the first six months of 1880 it was private charity alone which stood between the people and actual starvation in many parts of Ireland. The two most important relief agencies were the Duchess of Marlborough's committee and the Mansion House Relief Committee under the presidency of the lord mayor of Dublin, although important relief work was also carried out by the Land

League, the Liverpool Irish Distress Fund, the New York Herald Committee and a host of other minor organisations and individuals. It was estimated that over £800,000 had been spent in charitable relief work in Ireland by October 1880, with at least another million pounds coming in remittances from Irish exiles in North America.[49] The bulk of these donations went to the south and west, but substantial amounts were also spent in Ulster. From January to the end of July, the Donegal Central Relief Committee besides distributing 'considerable quantities of food, seed and clothing' expended over £34,000, £14,000 of it coming from the Mansion House fund.[50] This organisation also contributed over £7,000 to relief in Cavan, over £3,000 in Fermanagh, and over £2,000 in each of Monaghan and Tyrone.[51]

Even with the efforts of the relief agencies, however, distress throughout Ireland would have been more serious had it not been for the exceptionally mild nature of the autumn and winter of 1879–80, and also for the fact that the seeds act ensured that a normal sowing of potatoes could take place early in 1880. But how far most tenants suffered from the depression would ultimately depend on how much forbearance landlords showed in not pressing for rents.

### THE CAMPAIGN FOR RENT ABATEMENTS

There had been isolated demands for rent reductions in 1877 and 1878, and in some instances concessions had been made,[52] but there had been no general campaign. This now started in 1879, slowly at first but with increasing intensity during the late summer and autumn months as the worst fears of the farmers materialised. Ulster tenants were faced in the crisis not only with diminished returns from agriculture, but also with a serious deterioration in their capital investment in the land. 'Not only is the Ulster farmer enduring the losses common to farmers throughout Great Britain and Ireland', the *Coleraine Chronicle* pointed out, 'but his tenant-right property is depreciated in value by more than one-third.'[53] This was obviously a primary cause of concern and underlay much of the tenant unease in

Ulster at this time. Bad harvests seemingly could be as destructive of tenant-right as bad landlords.

Larger tenants, of course, plainly stood to gain most from such allowances. A ten or twenty per cent reduction in rent meant very little to smallholders, who could barely afford to feed their families during the winter months and whose inability to pay any rent often deprived them of whatever concessions were going.[54] But it was what one Tyrone landlord described as an important and valuable 'discount for cash' for the larger tenants.[55] It was in fact the larger tenants, many of them — such as Samuel Black of Randalstown and J.C. Lendrum of Clogher — already prominent figures in the tenant-right movement, who took the lead in the rent agitation in different parts of the province; the first rent abatement meeting in the Bangor area, for example, was 'called at the requisition of a large number of respectable and influential farmers in the parish', and Hugh Montgomery's agent informed him that the people who were 'giving trouble' on the estates along the Tyrone–Fermanagh border were 'all of the class that the Lendrums and Browns are with you'.[56] But if it was the large tenants who stood to gain most, all classes of tenants could subscribe to a movement that promised them some relief, and the result was that the rent agitation was taken up on different estates and in different areas with a spontaneity and an enthusiasm that the tenant-right campaign had never had. 'This anti-rent agitation', Stuart Knox told David Plunket, the Tory MP for Dublin University, 'has found more sympathy among the Ulster farmers than any previous popular movement originating in the catholic provinces.'[57]

Yet the agitation in the north, apart from being slower to start, was altogether different in character from that in the south and never at any stage reached the same level of intensity or militancy. Although public meetings were held in several centres — at Monaghan, Toomebridge, Bangor, Carndonagh, Camlough and Ballymoney — they were limited in number, and there was no co-ordinated campaign as such in Ulster.[58] Rather the agitation tended to take the form mainly of estate meetings, the primary and almost exclusive purpose of which was to memorialise landlords for abatements of rent. Petitions to landlords began to appear in August, and by September, when the full extent of the depression had become evident, meetings were being held by tenants on estates throughout the length and breadth of the province, many of them clearly encouraged by the remissions of rent which some landlords had already made in the previous month.

None of these meetings — neither the estate meetings nor the larger demonstrations — were anti-rent or anti-landlord meetings as such, and none of them subscribed to the programme being promulgated at this time by the Land League in the south.[59] The memorials appealed directly to the goodwill of the landlords and were, almost without exception, couched in respectful and deferential terms, and, when concessions were made, they were gratefully received and profusely acknowledged. At the public meetings the resolutions were moderate and expressed in temperate language; generally they 'respectfully but earnestly' called on landlords to make 'liberal and generous reductions on rent' to help the tenants through the period of crisis, and supported land reform along the traditional lines of the 3Fs with, as time went on, an increasing emphasis on the extension of facilities for tenant purchase.[60] Speakers at the meetings strenuously denied that they were intended 'to promote socialism or invade the rights of property', and strongly advised tenants not to 'repudiate their obligations' and 'not to be led away by the wild theories that were being propounded by people in other districts of the country'.[61]

This advice was reiterated by the tenant-right press, which warned tenants against adopting revolutionary doctrines and making extravagant demands. Incendiary language and impracticable proposals to abolish landlordism and not to pay rents would, it was argued, antagonise not only the landlords but opinion at Westminster on which the settlement of the question depended. Rent was a debt like any other debt and had to be paid, while Land League proposals to abolish the landlords as a class and create peasant proprietors in their place were 'too ridiculous for serious discussion'.[62]

There was, in fact, a deliberate attempt in the north to dissociate the rent agitation from the campaign of the Land League, and tenant meetings in Ulster displayed little of the hostility to landlords as a

class which was so much in evidence in parts of the south. Nor was
there the same level of agrarian violence. There were occasional cases
of incendiarism, maiming of livestock and personal assault (mainly
on tenants who had broken ranks with others holding out for
abatements of rent). But the number of attacks on either property
or persons was negligible. The vast majority of agrarian offences
were cases of intimidation, of letters or notices either threatening
landlords who refused to reduce rents or warning tenants not to pay
rents until reductions were made. And while there was a marked
increase in the number of these offences in the later months of 1879
— 52 per cent of all the agrarian crimes in 1879 were committed in
the last three months of the year — the number still remained low
(the total number of outrages in 1879 was 111 as compared with
476 in Connacht, 147 in Leinster and 136 in Munster).[63] In December
1879, resident magistrates in Ulster, in reply to a query from Dublin
Castle as to the necessity of renewing the peace preservation acts,
stated almost without exception that their districts were 'peaceable':
'In all my time', said Moore Miller, R.M. of Armagh, 'this district has
never been marked by any of the offences alluded to — nor the
counties of Down, Tyrone, Antrim, Londonderry, nor the great part
of Donegal'.[64]

There were, of course, occasional instances of tenants refusing to
pay rents, but these were rare, and while arrears accumulated on
many of the northern estates these were more the result of tenants'
inability to pay than their unwillingness.[65] Even in the most distressed
areas tenants in general showed little disinclination to pay when they
were able to do so and provided proper allowances were made.
James Tuke found acute distress among smallholders in west
Fermanagh, but 'no one', he reported, 'refuses to pay his rent who
can do it'.[66]

All this is not to argue, however, that the rent movement in Ulster
was merely a matter of tenants going cap in hand to the landlord
and gratefully accepting whatever concessions he condescended to
give. If there were few absolute refusals to pay rent, tenants on a
number of estates tried to make payment conditional on rents being
reduced, and were frequently prepared to try to withhold rents until

reductions were given. One of Hugh Montgomery's neighbours got 'hardly any rent' at the appointed time, apparently 'because he had not announced that he meant to give an abatement'.[67] Montgomery's agent discovered that many tenants on different estates in the Fivemiletown area shared this attitude and were determined 'not to pay any rent as they are getting no abatement'.[68] Northern tenants may not have joined in the rent agitation with the same vigour as some of their southern neighbours, but they were unmistakably determined to make the landlords share their losses with them. The abatements asked for were at times quite substantial — 50 per cent was not unusual — and tenants were prepared to argue their case in detail and frequently through the press, drawing comparisons with rent levels on neighbouring estates and sometimes making pointed references to what was happening elsewhere in the country.[69]

Clearly tenants in the north were not unaffected by the excitement and expectations created by the anti-rent agitation in the south, and they were plainly prepared to use whatever means were available to them within the law to secure rent concessions. But equally clearly they were less inclined to go outside the law, and the rent-abatement campaign in the north — and this is what it was — was conducted in a lower key and without the same openly expressed bitterness towards the landlords as a class, and it was never, during the winter of 1879–80, nearly as militant, as violent, or as potentially subversive of the existing system as the campaign in the south.

THE RESPONSE OF THE LANDLORDS

All during the summer months the northern tenant press carried lists of abatements being made first in England and Scotland and then increasingly in the south of Ireland. But Ulster landlords generally were slow to respond. Few took advantage of the easier facilities for borrowing money introduced by the government in November, and most showed a greater reluctance than landlords elsewhere to reduce rents.[70] In truth, many northern landlords, like the government ministers, remained for a long time unconvinced of the seriousness of the crisis. One Ulster landlord claimed in September that it was being 'most shamelessly exaggerated … by the anti-rent agitators'; and as late as November Lord Lifford was still denying the existence of distress and maintaining that the only serious problem facing the people either north or south was the shortage of fuel.[71]

If, however, landlords in general were slow to respond to the distress, there were some who acted promptly and generously, and as the full extent of the calamity was realised an increasing number contributed in one way or another to relief. Apart from making remissions of rent, many landlords such as the Earl of Yarmouth and the Earl of Erne distributed food, clothing and fuel among their tenants, or like the Earl of Belmore and the Downshire trustees provided the poorer tenants with seed potatoes, or like Hugh Montgomery created employment to help some through the winter months, or even on occasions like John Richardson of Bessbrook simply distributed money.[72] A number also took advantage of the cheap loans provided by the government to create employment. By the end of 1880 some £70,000 had been borrowed by landlords in Donegal, Cavan and Fermanagh, although complaints were made that the loans were not always used in the best interests of the tenants.[73] Few, however, took advantage of the government schemes to the same extent as the Earl of Leitrim, who borrowed over £14,000 for drainage works, or matched the generosity of the two Musgrave brothers, who spent over £7,000 of their own money in relieving distress and creating employment in south-west Donegal.[74]

Not many landlords could afford expenditure on this scale, and some estates were so heavily mortgaged that the proprietors were simply unable to offer any financial assistance.[75] The number of landlords who took advantage of the cheap government loans was comparatively small[76], and numerous landlords, even when they had the money, showed little inclination to spend it on relief. The Duke of Abercorn, one of the wealthiest proprietors in Ulster, excused himself from subscribing to the Duchess of Marlborough's fund on the plea that he had already given £100 to local relief in Donegal.[77] Others, like the Earl of Charlemont, Lord Lifford and Murray Stewart, proprietor of the Ardara estate in Donegal where nearly half the families were on the relief lists, refused to make any contribution whatsoever.[78] Two representatives of the Liverpool fund travelling through Donegal got 'a very strong impression ... that the owners of land are doing very little for the poor'.[79] Hugh Montgomery was the only landlord about Fivemiletown who subscribed to the Fivemiletown Relief Committee; none of the other proprietors in the district, his agent told him, had 'contributed a halfpenny' and landlords such as Sir Victor Brooke and T.R. Browne had done 'next to nothing for the tenantry'.[80] All in all, in terms of providing relief the common impression was that Ulster landlords in general did a good deal less than might have been expected of them in a time of crisis.[81]

Charity and relief, of course, were mainly for the small farmers and agricultural labourers. Farmers in general were more interested in remissions of rent. Again there were some early instances of landlord generosity. In July the Earl of Erne, for example, announced a reduction of 10 per cent on the year's rents, and during August several landlords made similar abatements, some going as high as 20 per cent, but none at this stage matching the generosity of J.V. Porter who, at the beginning of September, remitted a full half-year's rent to his tenants at Lisbellaw.[82] From September notices of rent abatements began to appear with increasing regularity in the local press, most of them ranging from 10 per cent to 25 per cent — leaseholders generally excepted — and in one or two instances, as on the Westenra estate in Monaghan, going as high as 50 per cent.

The value of these varied from estate to estate and from tenant to tenant, depending both on the original level of rents and on the tenant's individual circumstances. A 10 per cent reduction on the Dunseath estate at Kildowney, for example, still left rents at over 20 per cent above Griffiths' valuation, whereas Sir William Verner made an allowance of 15 per cent on his Armagh estate where rents were already 8 per cent below the valuation.[83] Percentage reductions were at best a crude response to the needs of the tenants, generally conceding most to larger tenants who were suffering least. Some landlords such as Hugh Montgomery would have preferred to have made allowances according to the respective needs of individual tenants but, as Montgomery was advised, this was 'quite out of the power of any landlord to do fairly and every instance of injustice would cause endless bad feeling and lying'.[84] What many of the larger landlords did, however, was to relate the size of the remission to the size of the holdings. Thus William Archdall in Fermanagh offered a 10 per cent remission on all rents over £10, 15 per cent on rents between £5 and £10, and 20 per cent on those under £5 with special allowances to tenants whose lands had been flooded, while Montgomery himself, on the rents due in November, allowed 10 per cent on those under £10 and 5 per cent on those over that figure, and a further 30 per cent and 15 per cent respectively on the rents due on 1 May when, he believed, the relief would be most needed.[85] Some landlords such as Lord O'Neill in Antrim varied the remission according to how far the existing rents were over or under the government valuation, while others, such as Colonel J.G. Irvine in Fermanagh and Lord Rathdonnell, who had estates in Fermanagh, Tyrone and Monaghan, allowed larger reductions on those parts of their estates which had been flooded or most palpably affected by the depression.[86] Lord Erne, for example, cancelled the entire rent on flooded lands at, it was claimed, a cost of £1,000 to himself.[87]

Many of these abatements were made in response to tenant memorials. But a large proportion were unsolicited, some landlords undoubtedly actuated by a genuine concern for their tenants' welfare, others clearly attempting to pre-empt tenant demands. The publication of lists of abatements in the press had in itself a kind of snowball effect, unsettling tenants on estates where no concessions had been made, and forcing action on landlords who might otherwise have been prepared to sit tight. The Earl of Charlemont, for example, bitterly resented this practice although he refused to be influenced by it, and Montgomery's agent, while he doubted whether an abatement was actually needed by Montgomery's tenants, thought that 'in the end it will be necessary partly really and partly to avoid serious bad feeling if the other landlords do the same, and you see three of them Lord Ely, Lord Erne and Captain Archdale have already done so'.[88]

Abatements were, of course, one way of ensuring that at least part of the rental would be punctually paid, and the usual practice was to make them conditional on the rents being paid at the appointed time and on arrears being cleared. Tenants on Lord Lurgan's estates in Armagh were offered a remission of 12.5 per cent if they paid 'all rent and arrears due by them to the 1st November 1879 on or before the regular rent days in December 1879', 10 per cent if they paid a month later, and 7.5 per cent only if they paid by 1 February 1880.[89] Sir Richard Wallace's offer of a 7.5 per cent reduction on rents over £50 and 15 per cent on those under £50 also depended on arrears being cleared and rents being paid at the proper time, so that in the event comparatively few of the tenants in need were able to avail themselves of the offer.[90] Indeed, James Pomeroy, Montgomery's agent, saw as one of the advantages of the abatement scheme that it would 'ensure the payment of all arrears' so that Montgomery's income for the year would 'not be lessened'.[91]

If, however, some landlords imposed what the tenants saw as excessively stringent conditions, others, like the Earl of Charlemont and Sir Robert Bateson Harvey of Rasharkin, refused to make any concessions at all, or like Lord Leitrim and Sir Victor Brooke made only very minor concessions, Leitrim allowing only what amounted to a 5 per cent remission, Brooke merely postponing payment of a quarter's rent and charging 5 per cent interest on this until it was paid.[92] Part of the problem for many estate owners was that their rents were already low or their estates subject to heavy family charges and other pecuniary obligations; as one landlord spokesman explained, an allowance of 20 per cent could sometimes reduce a landlord's disposable income by half.[93] Some landlords like Lord O'Neill and Sir William Verner, each of whom had heavy settlements on his estates, still managed to offer abatements, but others simply refused to sacrifice their own interests.[94] A number, such as Lord Lifford, took the view that the crisis was not as serious nor the tenants as hard-pressed as was made out; others held that where tenant-right was selling at from twenty to thirty years' purchase there was little reason to give abatements.[95]

More commonly, landlords argued that as they had not increased rents during the years of high prices and tenant prosperity, they should not be expected to reduce them in years of depression. James Price of Saintfield, for example, owner of one of the most prosperous estates in Co. Down, thought that it was totally unreasonable of his tenants to expect him to lower rents which were already £1,000 under government valuation, while the Fishmongers' company reminded their tenants that 'their farms were generally held at rents very considerably below their actual value, a fact which is evidenced by the high prices the holdings have obtained on numerous sales which have taken place since the present leases were granted'.[96] Many of these landlords attributed such tenant distress as there was to the fact that so many tenants had paid ruinous sums for their tenant-right and had borrowed money in order to do so, and to the tenants' own extravagance during the good years; they were, as a result of these factors, it was argued, head over heels in debt to shopkeepers and money-lenders, and it was these people who were putting pressure on them and forcing them to seek remissions of rent from the landlords.[97]

It is impossible to estimate how many or what proportion of Ulster landlords granted abatements to their tenants, or how far they contributed to the relief of distress during this period of depression. Clearly many acted in the best traditions of their class. However, despite their generosity and despite the at times prodigious efforts of some of their number, there was a widespread belief that Ulster landlords had not done all that they might have done either in relieving distress or in remitting rents.[98] Moreover, although the vast majority of landowners showed restraint in not evicting tenants in arrears and although the total number of evictions was still comparatively low, there was a dramatic increase in their number, with twice as many evictions in 1879 as in 1878 and practically as many in the first six months of 1880 as in the previous two years put together.[99] Plainly at least some landlords were unwilling to make allowance for the special circumstances of this period, although the Conservative press contended that the properties on which evictions were taking place were those of the new mercantile landlords and 'not the old Conservative landed proprietors of Ulster'.[100] It may well be that the new owners were less sensitive to the needs of their tenantry, but it was not only against the new landlords that the criticisms were directed. Landlords in general, it was claimed, were showing a disposition 'to absorb the tenant's interest by the maintenance of a rent which the present prices of produce will not warrant'.[101]

In short, there was a general feeling in the north that landlordism had failed in many respects to live up to its traditional responsibilities. Although many Ulster landlords acted creditably at this time and although Ulster tenants eschewed the more militant tactics and more extreme demands of their southern neighbours, the crisis undoubtedly weakened landlord–tenant relations in the province and exacerbated anti-landlord feeling, and helped to prepare the ground for the more open confrontation of the following year. Evidence of some of its effects was to be seen in the more independent line taken by tenants in the general election of 1880.

### THE GENERAL ELECTION OF 1880

One of the most puzzling features of the rent agitation in Ulster was the fact that the tenant-right societies, which might have been expected to take the lead, played practically no part at all. 'We have been more than astonished, and all those interested in the welfare of the farmers have been more than astonished', commented the *Ulster Examiner* at the end of October, 'at the apathy displayed by men who arrogated to themselves the front rank in the tenant-right cause.'[102] The fact was that many of the tenant-right leaders did not agree with the concentration on the rent question, and were indeed suspicious of attempts to interfere with rents which were, after all, debts like any other debts. Their argument was that rent remissions could only be temporary palliatives when what was needed was a permanent remedy.[103]

The tenant-right leaders could not, of course, openly oppose appeals for rent abatements, but the truth was that such appeals reflected precisely the kind of tenant dependence and the kind of special estate relationships that the Liberal tenant-right movement wanted to end. Thus, whereas at tenant meetings organised independently of the tenant-right societies — and these were the only kind of meetings held in Ulster up to January 1880 — the demand for land reform was clearly subordinated to more pressing demands for reductions of rent, at tenant-right meetings, when they were eventually held, the order of resolutions was almost exactly reversed, with priority being given to the complete legalisation of the Ulster custom and the return of tenant-right representatives to parliament, with only perfunctory resolutions on rents and distress.[104]

If, however, the circumstances of the winter of 1879–80 made the tenant-right programme appear peculiarly irrelevant to the immediate needs of the tenant-farmers, the programme itself was in danger of being eclipsed by the more extreme demands being made in the south. Many tenant-righters were alarmed by the activities of the Land League, and believed that, in the circumstances, it was both inadvisable and pointless to add to the general level of excitement in the country by holding meetings of their own.[105] The tenant-right press condemned the 'revolutionary sentiments' and 'seditious doctrines' being expressed at league meetings and were anxious to dissociate their movement from them. It was not only that the Land League schemes were impracticable; they were also likely to damage the tenant-right cause by exciting 'a prejudice in the minds of sensible and moderate men on both sides of the channel' against the movement for reform and setting 'all independent opinion against the tenant farmers'. No government at Westminster could support such schemes and no programme of reform could be passed without such support.[106]

However, these sentiments did not necessarily reflect the views of all northern supporters of tenant-right. Many northern catholics — including Bishop Dorrian — approved of Parnell and the Land League programme, some of them explicitly repudiating the old tenant-right programme as 'now perfectly worthless'.[107] The *Ulster Examiner* made a vehement attack on the organisers of the Ballymoney meeting for failing to invite Parnell, dismissed the legalisation of the Ulster custom as 'a flimsy programme' and, more alarmingly, went on to intimate that if the Liberal tenant-righters were to continue to have catholic support on tenant-right, the catholics would expect reciprocity on self-government and education.[108]

These open divisions between catholics and tenant-righters presented a real threat to the electoral prospects of the Liberals in Ulster, and although they did not lead to a permanent breach at this time — the catholics, as we have seen, supported the Liberal Lea in the Donegal by-election of December 1879 — they clearly weakened the tenant-right movement. The most significant developments in fact during the months preceding the general election of 1880 were in areas where earlier tenant-right activity had had little impact — in south Armagh, where the Camlough Tenant-Right Association was formed in late 1879, and in Fermanagh, where the Fermanagh Tenant-Right Society was formed early in 1880.[109] Both these, however, owed their formation more to landlord failures on relief and rents and to the inspiration provided by the Land League activity in the south than to the example of the tenant-right associations in the north. And elsewhere, in the traditional tenant-right areas, the tenant-right bodies, with the possible exception of those in Antrim, were not markedly better organised in 1880 than they had been in 1874.

Nevertheless, the land question had by this time a momentum of its own and this, together with the depression, the rent campaign, and the Land League activity in the south, ensured that land would be the paramount issue in this election, so that the tenant-right Liberals were enabled to win unprecedented successes in the Ulster counties almost in spite of themselves. The *Coleraine Chronicle*, for example, expected a Tory collapse in the election but, it admitted,

> it cannot be said that the Liberals have been very active in promoting this result. Their attitude during the past two years has been more observant than aggressive ... In fact, Conservatism is on the eve of losing Ulster, not so much, perhaps, through the rapid growth of liberal ideas, as through Tory blindness, indifference, and folly.[110]

In the south the election was as much a conflict between Parnellites and anti-Parnellites as between home rulers and anti-home rulers, and was important mainly as a stage in the rise of Parnell.[111] In the north it marked the climax of the Ulster Liberal revival. Unprepared as the Ulster Liberals were for the election, interest in the land question and the absence of rivals for the catholic vote enabled them to mount and successfully carry a challenge to the Conservatives which surpassed all their previous efforts. Nineteen Liberal candidates went forward in fifteen constituencies, as against the previous maximum of fourteen candidates in twelve constituencies in 1874. Liberal activity on this scale had never before been seen in Ulster and, as it happened, it was never to be repeated. This was the last election, says MacKnight, 'in which the catholics were mostly united with the protestant Liberals'.[112] The home rule party, preoccupied with its own internal divisions in the south and still without a national organisation, was in no position to make any serious attempt to capture constituencies in the north. The result was that home rule candidates went forward only in Cavan, where Biggar and Fay, standing on a programme of home rule, land reform and denominational education, easily retained the seats they had won in 1874.[113] Elsewhere in the province the election was fought along traditional party lines.

Initially the Conservative press tried to make foreign policy and home rule the central issues in the election. But, as the *Belfast News Letter* later admitted, foreign policy did not 'influence the result of a single election' in Ulster,[114] while home rule never really became a live issue in the contest. The key question, the question on which it was widely and correctly assumed that the election would turn, was the land question and practically all the candidates made this the principal issue in their addresses and speeches.[115] The great majority of Liberals declared in favour of fixity of tenure at fair rents with the right of free sale, and virtually all of them wanted an extension of the facilities for tenant purchase, a number specifically looking to the establishment of a peasant proprietary as 'the ultimate solution of the Irish land question'. Alone of the Liberals, Samuel Black in Antrim, himself a tenant farmer, made a specific demand for a general reduction of rents.

Conservative candidates were equally anxious to meet the demands of the tenants. Whereas in 1874 they had been forced to adjust their position during the course of the campaign, they were now from the beginning committed to a more definite settlement of the tenant-right question. Every single Tory candidate in the counties accepted the need for further land reform and a greater protection of tenant interests, though some of the addresses were stated in fairly general terms. A number supported the removal of all doubts as to leasehold tenant-right. The majority, however, were prepared to go well beyond this, some favouring an extension of the facilities for purchase, others taking their stand on Macartney's bill which had recently passed the commons,[116] and several coming out as strongly in favour of the legalisation of the full custom of tenant-right as any of the Liberal candidates.[117] Conservative candidates in the boroughs obviously did not feel compelled to show the same interest in the land question. Land was discussed in these contests, but it clearly was not as important an issue in the boroughs, where the debate extended over a much wider range of topics and where the Conservatives won some early successes.[118]

In fact, the Conservatives made nearly a clean sweep in the boroughs, retaining the seven seats they already held and recapturing Carrickfergus, Newry and Coleraine — three of the four seats which had gone against them in 1874. In Dungannon, the one borough seat held by the Liberals, Thomas Dickson was re-elected with a reduced majority in a slightly higher poll.[119] Greater Conservative attention to registration and organisation had something to do with these successes,[120] but this manifestly was not the only reason. The truth was that the presbyterian middle classes in the boroughs were a good deal less enthusiastic in the cause of Liberalism and tenant-right in 1880 than they had been in 1874. The Liberal agent in Co. Down, for example, was informed that in Downpatrick 'our presbyterian and dissenting friends deserted us wholesale in the booths'.[121] It was the same in Derry, Coleraine, Dungannon — where Thomas Dickson was reported to have received hardly a dozen presbyterian votes[122] — Belfast and Newry.

Local Conservatives over the past six years had, in fact, shown particular sensitivity to presbyterian susceptibilities. Sir Henry Hervey Bruce in Coleraine — not normally known for his generosity of spirit — had become 'most attentive' to presbyterian interests after his defeat in 1874, and since then had granted a number of free sites for presbyterian churches and manses, subscribed to presbyterian charities, and exhibited great interest in presbyterian schools.[123] In the predominantly presbyterian town of Carrickfergus the Conservative, Thomas Greer, had similarly been cultivating support, showing liberality to local charities to the extent that a petition was lodged against his return on the grounds of bribery.[124] In parliament the Conservative MPs for Belfast and Derry City — both presbyterians — had strongly supported the presbyterian stand on non-denominational education.[125] There was also growing concern among sections of the presbyterian middle classes at the developments in the south and west. Many middle-class businessmen were only too aware of the implications of the Land League agitation for debts other than rents and for property other than landed property, and Conservative candidates played on these fears, offering a moderate settlement of the land question along the lines of Macartney's bill on the one hand, and warning against the Land League and the dangers of home rule on the other.[126] What the swing in the borough vote reflected was the abandonment of Liberalism by some of its presbyterian middle-class supporters at the very time it was enjoying its greatest success.

This success came almost entirely in the counties. Twelve Liberal candidates went forward in eight counties — the exception was Cavan — and of these eight were returned, a gain of five seats, all of them at the expense of the Tories. They took both seats in Donegal, Derry and Monaghan, and single seats in Tyrone and Armagh. The big disappointments were in Antrim and Down, both strong tenant-right counties with substantial presbyterian electorates, and counties where, outside of Derry, the Liberals had done best in 1874.[127] Yet for all the tenant-right activity and for all the resolutions in favour of returning tenant-right representatives to parliament, these two counties were from the Liberal or tenant-right point of view ill-prepared for an election.[128] In Down, for example, it was admitted by both sides that Crawford, who lost by only twenty votes, would have had a majority had there been a sufficient number of cars to bring his supporters to the poll.[129] The Conservatives, on the other hand, were well organised in these constituencies, perhaps precisely because their opponents had done so well in them in 1874.[130] Nevertheless, the Liberals might still have taken two of the four seats had it not been for the influence of the Belfast borough electors (in Antrim, where the Conservative majority was under 150 votes, this meant a clear gain of 250 votes for the Conservatives[131]), doubts about the ballot (sedulously spread by the Tory agents and press[132]), and some insidious intimidation (an obtrusively heavy landlord presence at the polling booths[133]).

All things considered, the Tories were fortunate to come out of the election as well as they did, suffering a net loss of only two seats. But the really significant developments had taken place in the counties, and there was no hiding the seriousness of the Tory defeat here — five seats lost and two narrowly saved, one (in Antrim) by less than 150 votes, the other (in Down) by a mere twenty-vote margin. Tory control of the counties — virtually complete in 1868 and only partially shaken in 1874 — was now shattered, with the Tories returning only eight of the eighteen county representatives as against seventeen in 1868 and thirteen in 1874. The Liberal tenant-right party, on the other hand, had triumphantly increased its representation in the counties from three to eight members.

The Conservatives initially put their losses down to poor organisation — the only two counties where proper electoral arrangements had been made were Antrim and Down — and certainly the Liberal successes in, for example, Armagh and Tyrone owed a good deal to Tory divisions and mismanagement.[134] But the Liberals were no better organised, and, indeed, had they been as well organised in Down and Antrim they would surely have taken at least a seat in each county. The Conservative collapse in the counties, in fact, was the result neither of Liberal effort nor of inadequate Conservative organisation. The reasons were more fundamental. The agricultural depression and rural distress of 1879–80 had exerted renewed pressure on the old community of interests between landlords and tenants in Ulster, and generally exacerbated anti-landlord feeling.[135] Tenant expectations of reform, moreover, had been roused by the Land League campaign in the south[136] so that with greater confidence in the ballot (despite the efforts of the Tory press) tenants were more inclined to take an independent line in the election. And despite the more advanced position taken by the majority of Tory candidates on the land question — basically they took their stand on Macartney's bill which, however, gave no security whatsoever against arbitrary increases of rent — they were still outbid by the Liberals with their support for the 3Fs and arbitration of rents and their more definite commitment to the creation of a peasant proprietary.

Moreover, the Tories were faced with the problem of reconciling their support for land reform with their political allegiance to a government and a party which had stubbornly resisted every single proposal for reform over the previous six years. Tory denials that the government was opposed to tenant-right and claims that it was committed to removing the imperfections of the act of 1870 — supported by a widely publicised letter to this effect from Sir Stafford Northcote to Lord Castlereagh — were simply unconvincing in view of the record of the government and the indiscreet statements of both Beaconsfield and Lowther.[137] And the fact that the government had allowed Macartney's bill to pass its second reading without a division less than a week before the dissolution of parliament — after having defeated the same bill in the previous year — was generally seen for what it was, viz. an electioneering ploy. At any rate, by the time polling started in the Ulster counties, Ulster Tory claims that they would be in a better position to influence the government were no longer tenable, for it was evident by that stage that the Liberals were going to have a clear majority in Britain, and this in itself may have influenced the county contests in the province.[138]

The election in the counties, in short, was decided on the question of tenant-right. The Ulster Tories had for some time recognised the importance of this question and were prepared to do something about it. But they laboured under the handicap of being attached to a party the bulk of whose members were more concerned about the danger of ideas crossing the channel, and whose leaders were apparently insensitive to the special problems of their followers in the north of Ireland. Many Ulster Conservatives attributed their losses to the obduracy of the government in the matter of land reform.[139] Thus they emerged from the election not only more anxious than ever to settle the land question on a permanent basis, but also alienated to some extent from their party colleagues in England, and quite determined to look to their own interests and, if need be, to act independently in the matter of land legislation.

8

# The Land League in Ulster

The results of the Irish elections of April 1880, Michael Davitt claimed, 'wrote the political doom of Irish landlordism'.[1] At the end of April, a national land conference in Dublin committed the Land League to a policy of compulsory land purchase with the introduction, as an interim measure, of a bill suspending for two years both the eviction of tenants of holdings valued at £10 and under and the landlords' power of recovering a higher rent than the poor law valuation from any tenant whatsoever. And in May, the election of Parnell as chairman of the Irish parliamentary party brought under his leadership both wings of the national movement.[2] These events marked the beginning of a new phase in the land agitation in Ireland.

But although the election of a Liberal government created expectations of reform in Ulster, the province remained for a time relatively unaffected by the developments in the south. The northern tenant-right press unequivocally rejected the programme drawn up at the national conference as unrealistic and damaging to the whole prospect of reform:

> It is foolish to expect changes of revolutionary magnitude, and therefore we regret the disposition of the Land League of the south to pursue an independent and most injudicious course in demanding the compulsory expropriation of Irish landlordism ... There can be no settlement of the land question that does not firstly consult the

real interests of both parties ... [It would be] foolish to ignore the fact that the great majority of the 600,000 tenant occupiers of Ireland must still hold under landlords.[3]

The demand in the north — as clearly evidenced by a fixity of tenure bill introduced by the Ulster Liberal members in June[4] — was still for the three Fs and a gradual extension of the Bright clauses, and the northern tenant-righters were anxious at this stage not to embarrass the government which, they believed, could be relied on to introduce a measure along these lines.[5] Confidence in the government's intentions was boosted by the appointment of the Bessborough commission in July, and the northern tenant-right press, while critical of the composition of the commission,[6] condemned Land League advice against giving evidence as 'suicidal folly', and urged the tenants to take full advantage of the inquiry: 'The scope and extent of the bill dealing with the amendment of the land act', advised Thomas Dickson, 'will depend altogether upon the evidence submitted to the commission'.[7] Thus the main efforts of the tenant-right associations during the late summer and early autumn months were directed towards preparing evidence for the Bessborough commission, and such tenant-right meetings as were held at this time were held almost exclusively for this purpose.[8] Apart from this work, there was practically no tenant-right activity in the province, the Antrim Central Tenant-Right Association, for example, taking a deliberate decision in October not to hold any public meetings until Gladstone's bill had been introduced. 'The tenant-right party', the *Coleraine Chronicle* complacently reported in mid-October, 'are at rest. Their work, in the meantime, has been done'; having stated their case before the land commission, the *Chronicle* continued, they could 'await the result with confidence'.[9]

At this stage, in fact, there seemed little likelihood that the rural peace in Ulster would be seriously disturbed. Early forecasts of a bountiful harvest were to a large extent vindicated by the results. The good season and the introduction of Champion seeds resulted in a bumper potato crop in particular. But virtually every crop — with the exception of hay — was up not only on 1879, but on the average yield of 1871-6, as illustrated by Table 8.1.

Table 8.1. Percentage difference between the average yield in
Ulster for the years 1871–76 and the yield in 1880[10]

| CROP | WHEAT | OATS | BARLEY | POTATOES | TURNIPS | FLAX | HAY |
|---|---|---|---|---|---|---|---|
| % difference | +7.9 | +5.5 | +5.9 | +11.8 | 0.0 | +0.4 | −5.0 |

Livestock also did well, with prices recovering and young store cattle selling at a better price than any year since 1840 with the exception of 1876.[11] 'Altogether', concluded the *News Letter*, 'the harvest of 1880 must be looked upon as one of the most abundant that has been in Ireland for at least a full generation past'.[12]

Such a conclusion, however, while it reflected and influenced the views of many landlords, rather overstated the extent of recovery in Ulster in 1880. If livestock prices and the prices of livestock products revived, the numbers of cattle, sheep and pigs in Ulster had all declined quite markedly during the poor seasons from 1877: cattle and sheep by 10 per cent and 12 per cent respectively; pigs more dramatically by over 50 per cent.[13] The higher crop yields also were to some extent balanced by lower prices — all tillage prices were down on the 1879 figures and continued to fall during the 1880s[14] — and by a decrease in the total acreage under crops, which resulted in total crop production being generally lower than, for example, that of 1878.[15] Moreover, the improvements of 1880 were neither universal not uniformly felt throughout the province. Heavy rains in July and August had caused serious flooding about Lough Erne and Lough Neagh and had done considerable damage to crops in some areas, while not all small farmers had been able to afford or take advantage of the new Champion seed potatoes.[16] In some counties crops did not come up to the average of 1871–76, and the figures in Table 8.2 suggest that while one might legitimately talk about agricultural recovery in counties such as Down, Derry and Antrim, or even Donegal, the concept was a good deal less tenable in Cavan, Fermanagh and Monaghan.

Table 8.2. Percentage difference between the average yield for counties
in Ulster for the years 1871–6 and the yield in 1880[17]

| | WHEAT | OATS | BARLEY | POTATOES | TURNIPS | FLAX | HAY |
|---|---|---|---|---|---|---|---|
| Antrim | –0.7 | +1.2 | +5.0 | +31.4 | +6.1 | –1.4 | 0.0 |
| Armagh | 0.0 | +2.4 | –4.0 | +12.1 | –6.9 | +8.2 | 0.0 |
| Cavan | –14.4 | 0.0 | –22.4 | –22.6 | –12.5 | –2.0 | +5.0 |
| Donegal | +6.5 | +10.3 | +6.4 | +14.3 | –2.6 | +10.7 | +16.7 |
| Down | +15.4 | +14.6 | +13.2 | +33.3 | +13.0 | +7.4 | –11.1 |
| Fermanagh | –1.3 | –9.9 | –3.3 | –16.7 | –3.1 | –17.8 | –5.0 |
| L'derry | –5.5 | +14.0 | +16.5 | +32.4 | 0.0 | –2.5 | –9.5 |
| Monaghan | +2.2 | –3.8 | –11.9 | –13.3 | –10.3 | +1.7 | –5.3 |
| Tyrone | –0.7 | +1.6 | –12.7 | 0.0 | –2.9 | –6.7 | –4.8 |

Overall, the evidence is that while there was a general improvement from 1879, the harvest of 1880 was hardly such as would compensate for the losses of the previous seasons. 'The calculation is not far wrong', observed the *Ballymoney Free Press*, 'that it would take three prosperous years to restore Ireland to the condition it enjoyed in 1876.'[18]

The truth was that despite the relatively good harvest of 1880 and the low-key activity of the tenant-right movement, there was a good deal of underlying unease among the tenants themselves. They believed in particular that rents, which had clearly emerged by this stage as the most crucial issue, required immediate and permanent adjustment. Their view was that because of 'the successive losses in crops' and the decrease in the number of livestock, 'a strong case exists for the revision of rents all over Ireland'.[19] Small farmers in particular were faced with immediate problems of debts and arrears. The precariousness of their position was explained in a confidential report by the county inspector of Armagh:

I do not apprehend distress in the coming winter from any failure in the harvest or agricultural depression, but a rigid enforcement of the payment of debts to banks, shopkeepers, etc., would plunge the agricultural classes into actual distress, for, as a rule, if the entire produce of the land were sold, the proceeds, at the present very low prices, would fall short of the debts. These remarks more especially apply to farmers holding from eight to twelve acres, who in many cases have no stock or anything to depend on but cereals, flax, etc.[20]

There was, in fact, no prospect of such tenants redeeming the arrears of rent which had been widely incurred in 1879–80, and one resident magistrate in Cavan categorically stated that 'arrears of rent will in most cases not be paid', while the county inspector of Monaghan thought that while 'tenants are apparently able to pay the present rent ... they will not be able to pay it and the arrears'.[21] In Tyrone it was claimed that small farmers were not even 'able to pay their present rents'.[22] In these circumstances tenants were clearly going to be looking for abatements, and with many landlords — often under great financial pressure themselves — seeing only what was generally regarded as an abundant harvest and agricultural recovery, the stage was set for open confrontation.

Political developments, too, were working towards this end. In July the Conservative peers defeated a government bill to limit costs in defending actions for ejectment in Ireland.[23] More controversially and more seriously, the lords in August — this time with the assistance of a majority of the Liberal peers — rejected the compensation for disturbance bill, which provided for compensation for tenants evicted for non-payment of rent from holdings of £30 or under in certain scheduled districts, if they could prove that their inability to pay rent was a result of the failure of crops over the previous two seasons. This bill, which was a purely temporary measure, affected only two counties in Ulster — Cavan and Donegal — but its defeat had repercussions throughout the province. If expectations of reform had been raised by the election of Gladstone and the appointment of the Bessborough commission and by the Land League campaign in the south, fears were now created that government forces on their own might not be sufficiently powerful to see the government measure through both houses of parliament.[24]

Under these circumstances, the tenant-right strategy of quiescently awaiting the government proposals seemed increasingly inappropriate both to the immediate economic needs of the tenants and to the long-term prospects of reform. A growing number of tenants began therefore to take spontaneous action in the matter of rents,[25] and increasingly too tended to look for leadership and organisation to the Land League, which now began to move into the vacuum left by the tenant-right movement in the north. 'Tis hard to blame the tenant farmers for joining the league', observed Bishop Donnelly of Clogher, 'They have many and heavy grievances and the league is the only organisation which offers to give them substantial protection.'[26]

THE DEVELOPMENT OF THE LEAGUE

Although a Land League meeting had been held at Belcoo in Fermanagh as early as December 1879, the league had made no direct impact on Ulster up to the end of the summer of 1880. A small number of locally organised meetings had been held — as, for example, at Ederney in Fermanagh in March, at Carndonagh in Donegal where a branch of the league had been established in July, and at Sessiagh in Monaghan in August[27] — but there had been no general league activity. It was only when the league campaign in the south reached a new level of intensity in September — following the rejection of the compensation bill and the return of the Parnellite MPs to Ireland at the close of the parliamentary session[28] — that the movement spilled over into the north. The league leaders in their efforts to make the agitation a truly national one were not unaware of the importance of the northern counties; as Joseph Biggar told supporters in Dungannon, their meeting was important because the common belief in England was that 'Ulster was opposed to the principles of the Land League ... and the voice of that large meeting would have a far greater influence than a meeting of the same size held in one of the other three provinces of Ireland'.[29] Hence Dillon at Buncrana in October announced the league's intention of establishing branches in every county in Ulster.[30]

A major demonstration was held at Ballyshannon at the end of

September, and this was followed by several meetings in October, the most important being a demonstration of several thousand at Killeavy in Armagh.[31] But although a number of branches were established in different counties, the extent of league influence at the end of October was still extremely limited.[32] The campaign really only started in earnest in November, with prominent league spokesmen addressing meetings in every part of the province. A major demonstration at Dungannon at the beginning of the month — the first in Tyrone[33] — was followed by meetings at Cookstown and Cavan, and at Clonmany and Ballyshannon in Donegal, and then at Belleek in Fermanagh where Parnell formally announced the opening of the campaign in the north.[34]

The movement spread rapidly over the next two months and continued unabated in the new year, with major rallies being held and branches established in every county in the province.[35] By the end of 1880 the Conservative press, which in October had been confidently predicting that the league would secure 'no footing in the loyal north', was admitting that it was 'extending its seditious influence into many parts which loyal subjects considered impregnable'.[36] There were meetings at Blacklion and Belturbet in Cavan in November, and at Scotstown and Carrickmacross in Monaghan in December and January, with branches being established at — among other places — Drumalane, Bawnboy and Kill in Cavan and Aghabog, Killevan, Shantonagh, Errigal Trough and Monaghan town. In Fermanagh there were meetings at Enniskillen in November, at Enniskillen, Derrygonnelly, Ederney and at Aghalane outside Brookeborough in December, at Tempo, Clabby, Lisnaskea and Florencecourt in January and February of 1881; by March 1881 it was being conservatively estimated that there were at least twenty league branches in the county.[37]

Progress in Tyrone was equally rapid, with meetings at Pomeroy, Coalisland, Dromore, Clogher, Donaghmore, Beragh, and Gortin, and branches established in Dungannon, Aughnacloy, Galbally, Dromore, and Greencastle. Donegal and Derry were both caught up in the movement; meetings were held at Milford, Ballybofey, Gortahork, Carndonagh, Buncrana, Dunfanaghy and Derrybeg in Donegal and at Gulladuff, Maghera, Draperstown, Ballinascreen and

Magherafelt in Derry, with a large number of branches formed in each county.[38] In Armagh there were meetings at Belleek, Keady, Crossmaglen and Forkhill with branches established at Killeavy, Cullyhanna, Mullabawn, Drominlee and Keady. Even Antrim and Down were affected, with meetings at Ballycastle, Loughguile and Toomebridge in Antrim, and at Mayobridge, Castlewellan, Rostrevor, Hilltown, Newry, Saintfield and Downpatrick in Down, and branches at Toomebridge, Loughguile, the Glens of Antrim, Glenravel and Castlejordan in Antrim and at Mayobridge, Castlewellan, Newry, Rostrevor and Newcastle in Down.[39]

This list of meetings and branches is not of course exhaustive, but it does give a broad indication of the intensity of league activity, the rapidity of its progress, and the general distribution of support. As a rule the league was strongest in the south-west of the province where Cavan, Monaghan and especially Fermanagh were virtually overrun,[40] and weakest in the north-east where, for example, Antrim was barely penetrated, a pattern of distribution which, it might be noted, was practically the inverse of that of the tenant-right movement. Whereas the main centres of tenant-right activity had been Antrim, north Derry (especially around Derry, Claudy, Eglinton, Limavady and Coleraine), north Down (with important societies at Newtownards, Bangor, Saintfield, Downpatrick and Banbridge), north Armagh (at Portadown, Armagh and Tandragee), east Donegal (especially at Letterkenny and Castlefin) and east Tyrone (where Cookstown was the hub of activity), the league with one or two exceptions never became strongly established in any of these areas.[41] Even in Monaghan, the league had more difficulty establishing itself in the south, where the Farney Tenants' Defence Association was in existence, than in the rest of the county.[42]

In Co. Down, while at least one meeting was held at Saintfield — where it met Orange opposition[43] — and while there was some league activity about Downpatrick, league influence was largely confined to the southern part of the county, more particularly to the areas around Newry, Mayobridge and Castlewellan. This pattern was repeated in Armagh with a fairly substantial league presence as one moved west from Newry, but with the northern half of the county

— above Keady — scarcely affected. League activity was more scattered in Tyrone — 'Land League meetings', said the *Ulster Examiner* at the beginning of 1881, 'have been held in almost every part of it' — but it met resistance in Cookstown and Tullyhogue, and it never took root in this north-eastern part of the county in the way that it did in the south and west.[44] In Derry the main centres of league activity were around Derry itself and in the south-eastern corner of the county in and around Maghera, Draperstown, Magherafelt and the Loup. The league was also widely supported in north and west Donegal — the Inishowen peninsula, for example, was extensively organised in early November before the campaign had got under way in most other northern counties[45] — but not on the east side of the county which remained largely immune to league influence.

Many of these areas in which the league was most strongly entrenched — as, for example, Gweedore, Inishowen, Belleek and west Fermanagh, Glangevlin in Cavan, south Armagh, Castlewellan in Down, even the Glens of Antrim — were areas in which there had been acute distress in 1879–80 and in which tenants were still faced with great economic uncertainty in 1880–1, frequently areas where landlords had by their apparent neglect of their traditional responsibilities in 1879–80 lost a good deal of their social credit,[46] and where, as Father McFadden of Gweedore told Somerset Ward, 'before it [the league] was formed the people did not know their power'.[47]

More generally, however, the areas in which the Land League became most firmly established in Ulster tended to be predominantly catholic areas, and this is reflected to some extent by the degree of clerical involvement, with priests chairing and addressing meetings and frequently acting as organisers and presidents of local branches.[48] Some, such as Father McCann, parish priest of Mullabawn, and, more notably, Bishop Donnelly of Clogher held back, having serious reservations about league methods and fearing the movement's subversive and revolutionary implications. But few dared to oppose it openly. Donnelly, for example, while holding himself aloof and while in private avowedly hostile, refused to take a stand against it: 'I would probably fail in any open effort to keep out the league', he explained to Hugh Montgomery, 'and I don't see my way with such absolute clearness as would call for decided action'.[49] But the clergy were, in the main, ardent and often active supporters, many of them like Bishop Dorrian sharing a joint concern for the welfare of their people and the future of their church. 'There is nothing', averred Dorrian, 'against the laws of God or man in this agitation — but the contrary.'[50] He viewed it rather as 'a legal and constitutional effort within the moral laws to remedy a great social evil, [and] rescue from misery and starvation thousands of our people'; and, he warned, 'for the priests to refuse sympathy with the people would be the ruin of religion'.[51]

If, however, support in Ulster was predominantly catholic, protestants also were won over in considerable numbers. The league leaders, in fact, made a deliberate and calculated bid for protestant support, making studiedly moderate speeches, adapting their campaign to northern conditions, and presenting the league as a constitutional, loyal and non-violent organisation working within the bounds of law. 'The plan of the Land League', one resident magistrate informed Dublin Castle, 'is evidently to win Ulster by moderate language and by abstaining from all breaches of the peace.'[52] League spokesmen denied that the movement was responsible for the spread of agrarian crime: in fact, quite the reverse — it 'had shown the people a legitimate way of redressing their wrongs'.[53]   And league supporters were repeatedly exhorted to abhor all acts of violence: 'the man who commits a crime', the president of the Falcarragh branch told a meeting at Dunfanaghy, 'is in the pay of the enemy'.[54] 'They were not there', said Jeremiah Jordan at Scotstown in December, 'to speak sedition against the queen, to wage war against the laws, or to fight against the constitution. (No, no)'[55] The stated purpose of the league meeting at Enniskillen in March 1881 was 'to petition her majesty the Queen and both houses of parliament ... in reference to the Irish land question'.[56] At the Holywell meeting 'three cheers for the queen' were called for and followed by 'loud and repeated cheering'.[57]   The meeting at Scotstown — much to the astonishment of the police reporter — was terminated with 'three cheers for the Royal Irish

Constabulary'.[58]

Home rule was, of course, discreetly kept in the background, and there was, indeed, very little criticism of the government, while frequent tributes were paid to Gladstone and John Bright; one speaker at Saintfield declared — and there were no voices of dissent — 'that that meeting had unbounded confidence in the greatest of uncrowned monarchs, the People's William — William Ewart Gladstone — (cheers) — and that they had great confidence in the tribune of the people, John Bright — (cheers)'.[59] Speeches critical of the government were sometimes made and home rule sentiments were occasionally expressed; but these were unusual.[60] The purpose of the meetings, it was generally conveyed, was not to attack or embarrass the government, but rather to strengthen its hand in settling the question. 'They were there', said Harold Rylett at Downpatrick, 'to assist the government to a proper solution of this great land question.'[61] Hugh Montgomery wrote to Forster that Jeremiah Jordan, an Enniskillen methodist businessman from a farming background whom Montgomery held largely responsible for the league's success with protestant tenants in Fermanagh, had from the beginning taken 'the line of persuading them that the Land League was a loyal and legal organisation and that its action was calculated to support the government in passing a good land bill'.[62] And in seeking a settlement of the question, league speakers were at pains to point out, 'the league did not recommend confiscation in any form'; even the London companies were to be treated in a 'just and equitable manner'.[63] It was hardly surprising that protestants who attended the league meeting at Sessiagh in August 'out of curiosity' were reported to have come away 'impressed by the moderation of the league's demands'.[64]

Above all, of course, the message was that the league was non-sectarian. Parnell commenced his speech at Belleek by informing his listeners that he was a protestant and a member of the synod of the Church of Ireland: 'This meeting', he continued, 'has been convened to declare that the land movement is not a sectarian movement, and that upon this platform of the land for the people all creeds and classes of Irishman may unite.'[65] Tenant farmers were urged 'not to be led away by party cries. It was not a party question', 'not a question of religion, but a question affecting the entire tenantry of Ireland'.[66] Emphasis was placed on the joint interests and common grievances of catholic and protestant tenants; landlords, the meetings were reminded, 'rack-rented the protestant as well as the catholic ... and confiscated his improvements as well as those of the catholic'.[67] At league meetings a prominent role was given to protestant speakers, who frequently reassured their co-religionists that they had nothing to fear from the movement. 'There was nothing in the agitation', Jeremiah Jordan told the Scotstown meeting, 'inimical to protestantism and Orangeism.'[68]

These attempts to assuage protestant fears evidently met with some success. Reports from all over the province showed that protestants as well as catholics were attending league meetings in significant numbers. James O'Kelly, MP for Roscommon, claimed in December that the league had been given 'a cordial and warm welcome' in every county in Ulster and had been supported 'by Orangemen, protestants, presbyterians and catholics'.[69] 'Men who voted for the conservatives last April', Sir Thomas Bateson told Salisbury at the end of December, 'are now openly fraternising with democrats whom six weeks ago they would not have touched with a long pole and the wave of communism has spread like wildfire.'[70] In Fermanagh in particular — where Jeremiah Jordan was using his not inconsiderable influence among the protestant dissenters[71] — the league was taken up by both protestants and catholics.[72] At the Derrygonnelly meeting, for example, protestants were reported to have 'outnumbered catholics two to one'.[73] 'Most of the presbyterians, the younger methodists, and I may say all the Romanists', the rector of Fivemiletown informed Hugh Montgomery, 'go in the "whole length of the unclean animal" with the Land League.'[74]

Even a number of Orangemen were won over, not only attending but helping in some instances to organise meetings and appearing as speakers. The two chief organisers of a league meeting held outside Brookeborough in December, for example, were both masters of Orange lodges.[75] Indeed, the number of Orangemen who supported the league in Fermanagh was sufficiently alarming for the Grand Orange Lodge to call a special emergency meeting in December to consider the problem, subsequently expelling a number of their brethren who had become members of the league and cancelling the warrants of two lodges because of league activity by their members.[76] At a league meeting at Kinnego in Armagh, chaired by the district master of the Kinnego Orange Lodge, Michael Davitt expressed his pleasure at speaking 'in an almost exclusively Orange district and to a meeting organised by and in the most part composed of sturdy Orange tenant farmers'.[77] Orangemen who attended a league rally at Mayobridge in Down were reported to have found themselves in sympathy with much of what was said.[78] 'He was an Orange tenant farmer', said one Orangeman at a league meeting in Dungannon, 'but he believed that tenant-right was as good for the Orange farmer as it was for the catholic farmer (cheers) ... There was no religion in the matter; it was simply a question as to whether they were to exist or not (cheers).'[79] And a number of Orangemen, even when they did not go as far as to support the league, refused to take action against it. An Orange counter-demonstration at Scotstown in Monaghan, for example, had to be abandoned because of lack of support, while a plan to send a contingent of Orangemen from Tullyhogue to help Captain Boycott was defeated by the district master, who declared that 'they would never join those forcing high rents on people in Mayo, as they required to have their own rents reduced'.[80]

Too much can, of course, be made of these examples of Orange and protestant support. In no other county in Ulster was there evidence of the same degree of protestant support for the league as there was in Fermanagh. In Antrim, for example, the secretary of the Glenravel branch of the league in his attempts to recruit members found 'protestants and presbyterians very cool'.[81] Certainly the Orangemen as a body were still very much on the side of the landlords and quite obviously the majority of protestants held themselves aloof from the league, if they did not actually oppose it.[82] But clearly a substantial number of northern protestant farmers were prepared to subordinate, at least temporarily, their basic suspicions of Parnell — fanned by both the Liberal and Conservative press in Ulster — to the more immediate opportunities offered for an advancement of their interests by a movement which promised to do more for them than any of the established organisations in the north. The success of the league in securing reductions of rent in the south and west and in combating eviction — frequent references to both of which were made by league spokesmen — made a strong impression on tenants in a province where landlords were showing increasing intransigence in the matter of rent reductions and making increasing use of the full resources of the law in their efforts to secure rent payments. Moreover, tenants were convinced, especially after the rejection of the compensation bill, that concessions would only be won by agitation — agitation to strengthen rather than to embarrass the government — and that the higher they pitched their demands the more they were likely to get.[83] What the Land League offered to all tenants was a degree of protection against the adversities of the time, an opportunity to lend support to the demand for radical land legislation and, above all, an instrument with which to pressurise landlords into remissions of rent.

## LEAGUE TACTICS, AGRARIAN CRIME AND RENTS

One effect of Land League activity in Ulster was to lead to a general escalation of tenant excitement, expectations and demands. 'You have no idea of the state of this country', James Crossle wrote to Sir William Verner's London solicitor in December. 'It is much worse than open rebellion, and the excitement increasing every day. The people are looking forward to the meeting of parliament to fulfil their wildest wishes.'[84] Hugh Montgomery's agent claimed that the tenants were 'all full of expectations of plunder', while Finlay Dun, travelling through Donegal, Derry and Tyrone, found tenants in 'a state of excitement and expectancy':

> Rents are badly paid, arrears accumulate, some who have the money do not pay it. Landlords and estate agents seldom stir from home after sundown or unarmed. Even on many good estates the tenants fall into the general state of idleness and unrest ... The land bill is anxiously looked for. The small farmer appears to anticipate from it not only the '3 Fs', but all possible and impossible boons. Even the better class of tenants are delaying many arrangements to see what turns up.[85]

Even Antrim and Down, Lord Cairns informed Beaconsfield, were affected by 'a restless uneasy spirit'.[86]

Inevitably, in the circumstances, there was a dramatic increase in the number of agrarian outrages — from an average of eleven for each of the first ten months of 1880 to forty-one in November, 109 in December and forty-six in January 1881.[87] Agrarian crime, however, was not necessarily either a concomitant or a corollary of league activity, and in many areas where the league was firmly established few outrages took place. Fermanagh, for example, where the league had a particularly strong presence, had the lowest number of agrarian offences of any county in Ulster during the months of most intense league activity;[88] 'no serious agrarian offence', wrote one resident magistrate in Fermanagh in April, 'has been committed in the locality since the introduction of the league'.[89] The league in fact, as we have seen, was anxious to dissociate itself from violence in Ulster, and league speakers actively discouraged it. The advice of the league organiser P.J. Sheridan at Bawnboy at the end of October 1880 was typical of the line adopted by most league spokesmen: 'I would exhort you to keep within the lines of the law, no such thing as burning hay or straw, or houghing, or anything else repugnant to civilised humanity'.[90]

Rather the main league weapon against those who acted contrary to league and tenant interests was the boycott, and this was widely and repeatedly advocated at league meetings throughout the province.[91] League supporters of course frequently went beyond this, and league speakers occasionally used language which could scarcely be described as temperate and which, whether intentionally or not, was almost certainly a direct incitement to violence and outrage.[92] But these were the exceptions, and the increase in the number of agrarian offences in Ulster reflected the heightened tension and feeling in the province rather than the direct influence of the league. Agrarian outrage represented not an extension of but rather the failure of, or at least frustration with, the official policy of social ostracism — its failure to stay evictions or prevent land-grabbing or maintain a united front on rents — and the revival of a more traditional weapon of rural social welfare.[93] Serious outrages, when they did occur, occurred almost always as a result of evictions or land-grabbing or strike-breaking, whereas the purpose of the league campaign was to prevent these things from happening.

At any rate, agrarian outrage, despite the widely publicised complaints of landlords and despite the increase in number, was never a really formidable problem in Ulster. There were cases of assault, of incendiarism, and of damage to property, but the vast majority of reported offences were cases of intimidation, most them threatening letters or notices; of a total of 195 agrarian offences reported in the province from the beginning of November 1880 to the end of January 1881, 133 were of intimidation by letter or notice, and eighteen of other forms of intimidation.[94] 'As a matter of fact', the *Coleraine Chronicle* claimed in February, 'Ulster has been almost free from agrarian crime. It is absurd to attach importance to threatening letters, as there is a general impression that many of them are written in a spirit of fun.'[95] A peculiar, even perverse, sense of humour perhaps, but the general point that most such letters were not to be taken too seriously is probably correct. This is not, however, to say that there was no intimidation in Ulster. Clearly these letters and notices reflected a wide and pervasive system of social pressure which few dared ignore; but equally clearly the number of serious agrarian outrages in the province was limited.

A large majority of such outrages as did occur arose out of attempts to enforce rent demands, but an energetic campaign was also conducted against evictions and land-grabbing. There were a number of instances of bailiffs and process servers being assaulted, and of tenants physically resisting eviction and sometimes reoccupying the holdings.[96] Two bailiffs serving processes for rent on the estate of Thomas Hope in Tyrone, for example, were surrounded by a large crowd, some with blackened faces and some armed, and were forced to give up the processes, go on their knees and swear 'they would not return again'.[97] A bailiff was shot dead near Churchill in Armagh while executing a decree for non-payment of rent, and another near Omagh while serving processes on a number of tenants.[98] In Glangevlin in Co. Cavan, a process server for Lord Annesley accompanied by a bailiff was met by a crowd of some hundreds organised by the Land League, and had to take refuge in Annesley's shooting-lodge from which the two of them were eventually extricated by a force of police.[99] Such tactics made evictions and process serving extremely difficult, and many landlords were clearly deterred from carrying out as extensive a policy in the matter of ejectments or decrees for rent as they would have liked; as James Crossle explained at the end of 1880:

> There are a dozen of the largest land agents in this county [Tyrone] present at this assizes, and they all complain they are getting very little rent. They have not and will not take legal proceedings for some time. If ejectments are executed no one will take the land. If decrees for rent are executed by the sheriff no one will or dare buy the crops.[100]

Land-grabbing in particular was vehemently denounced at virtually every league meeting in the province, and obviously — as testified by Crossle's statement — with some effect. Land-grabbers were 'the worst enemies' of the tenants, 'the curse of Ireland', 'accursed vipers — a bane to any society and a bane to Ireland'.[101] Yet land-grabbing, largely because of tenant-right, was never as serious a problem for tenants in Ulster as for tenants in the south (tenants in Ulster, even if evicted for non-payment of rent, were still entitled to compensation for their tenant-right), and there were in fact comparatively few outrages against it.[102]

The main priority in the north was rents, and the vast majority of agrarian offences in the province — 103 out of the 150 offences reported to the police in the last two months of 1880[103] — were directly related to this question. Pending a final settlement of the land question, the principal objective of league policy — in accordance with the resolutions agreed at the national conference in April — was to bring rents down to the government valuation, and tenants were urged to offer this as a body to the landlord or agent and if he 'refused to take what they offered him, say "good morning, sir" and leave him'.[104] If tenants acted together and maintained a united front, they were told, 'the landlords must give way and you must succeed in your conflict with them'.[105] Tenants who supported the league line were assured of league support,[106] but those who broke ranks were subjected to an intensive campaign of intimidation and boycott. Notices warning tenants not to pay their rents until they got a reduction were posted in most league areas; in several instances armed parties visited tenants to reinforce the warning, while shots were fired into the houses of tenants who were suspected of either having paid or being about to pay; and landlords and agents received letters threatening them with 'the same fate as Lord Leitrim' if they did not make concessions.[107]

Clearly the effect of this campaign — and indeed part of its purpose[108] — was to make it exceedingly difficult for landlords to collect rents, but the league spokesmen denied that they were advocating a 'no rent' policy;[109] and when such a policy was openly recommended by one league organiser at Sessiagh, exception was taken to it and it was immediately repudiated by the remainder of those on the platform.[110] Rather league policy was for rents to be reduced to government valuation level, and this was the line initially adopted at early league meetings in Ulster and the demand made by league supporters on a number of northern estates.[111] But Griffith's valuation was higher in the north, where it had been carried out a later date, and not all northern tenants were satisfied with a reduction of rents to this level.[112] As early as May 1880 the *Coleraine Chronicle* had argued that 'Griffith's valuation has ceased to be a reliable standard', and from late November the demand at league meetings in Ulster was for a settlement at a figure below Griffith's which, it was claimed, 'included the invested capital and industry of the tenant'.[113] 'They might consider Griffith's valuation a fair rent in Munster or Leinster or Connaught', said Michael Davitt at Downpatrick, 'but he maintained that in Ulster Griffith's valuation was a rack-rent — (hear, hear) — and the sturdy tenant farmers of the north of Ireland should set their faces against any such basis for the so-called fair rent.'[114] What was required, the Downpatrick meeting resolved, was a new valuation.

Thus tenants on many estates in the north sought reductions to a figure below — and sometimes substantially below — Griffith's, and were encouraged by their local league branches to do so. Tenants on the Jonesborough estate of Thomas Hamilton Jones JP in

Armagh, acting on the advice of the secretary of the Newry branch of the league, rejected an offer of a 10 per cent abatement, holding out instead for 10 per cent under Griffith.[115] The demand on the Conolly estate in Donegal was for 20 per cent, on the Johnston estate outside Ballyshannon 25 per cent, and on the Dunville and Bruce estates in Armagh and Tyrone 50 per cent.[116] The Marquis of Ely's tenantry in Fermanagh demanded an allowance of 33 per cent in accordance with a general resolution passed at an amalgamated meeting of the Boho, Belleek, Derrygonnelly, Garrison and Kilcoo branches of the league calling on all tenants not to pay rents unless they got a reduction of 6s 8d in the pound.[117] In Donegal, league pressure forced the Marquis Conyngham to make an abatement of 33 per cent.[118] Tenants on the Hill estate in Gweedore wanted 'the mountains returned to them and the rents reduced to what they were forty years ago'; an offer of 10 per cent was rejected, but Father McFadden, their spokesman, believed he could induce them to accept 25 per cent.[119]

One of the complaints of the Gweedore tenantry was that Hill 'had contributed nothing to relieve their distress', and it has been suggested in a study of several estates in mid-Ulster that the league 'tended to direct its campaign against landlords who were absentees, had not given abatements, or had raised rents in the late 1870s'.[120] Assuredly, estates such as those of Charlemont in Armagh and Tyrone, the Annesley estates in Down and Cavan, Lord Enniskillen's estate in Fermanagh, and the Archdale estates in Fermanagh were the subject of special attention by the league. But few estates in these areas were totally unaffected by league influence; even tenants on the estate of a popular landlord such as Hugh Montgomery 'mostly holding at and under the government valuation, refused to pay any rent unless they got 4s in the pound abatement', and several tenants who did pay 'refused to take receipts for fear they should be found out and made to suffer'.[121] 'It is now quite clear', Montgomery wrote to Gladstone's secretary at the end of November 1880, 'that the best liked landlords are not safe from the results of the teaching of these clever rascals, who persuade the tenants that every penny of rent we ever got was robbery.'[122]

It was not, however, only league areas which were affected. The excitement stimulated by league activities and by the rising expectations of reform proved very infectious, and the campaign for rent abatements spread to every part of the province with a much greater intensity and determination than in 1879–80. 'A few weeks since the Land League invaded Ulster', Sir Thomas Bateson complained to Salisbury, 'up to that moment rents were well and cheerfully paid, without a murmur — now all is changed ... The demand is 25, 30, and in some cases 50 per cent permanent reduction of rents on the plea of low prices caused by American importations.'[123] Where tenants had been looking for a temporary abatement of 10 per cent in the previous year, said the *Coleraine Chronicle*, they were now looking for permanent reductions greatly in excess of this.[124] Sir Thomas Bateson's tenants, satisfied with a 10 per cent remission in 1879–80, now wanted 25 per cent remitted. Similar demands were made on the Hilltown estate of the Marquis of Downshire, on the Keown-Boyd estate at Mealough, Co. Down, and on the Narrow-water estate of Major Hall. Tenants on the Hill-Trevor estate in Down demanded 30 per cent, those on the Irish Society's Culmore estate in Derry and on the Lurgan and Manchester estates in Armagh 50 per cent. Sir Richard Wallace's tenants wanted an abatement of 50 per cent on the year's rents and a permanent reduction of 25 per cent for the future.[125]

On many estates tenants made a point — indeed a virtue — of disavowing 'all sympathy with the disloyal and communistic doctrines of Mr Parnell and his party'.[126] Their case was that in view of bad harvests, low prices, and foreign competition, it was impossible for them to meet their existing obligations without subjecting themselves and their families 'to very great privation in the matter of food, clothing and education'.[127] But, whereas in the previous season refusals to pay rent had been unusual and tenants had generally been content to make respectful appeals to the goodwill of landlords, they were now much less deferential and much more inclined to withhold rents until abatements were made. And they were determined, as one tenant on the Wallace estate put it, to seek justice 'not in the attitude of hat-in-hand servility and cringing obsequiousness, but in the tone and language of manly and respectful independence'.[128]

'Manly and respectful independence' was not necessarily a prerogative of those with economic standing, but it was more easily practised by large than by small farmers, and it was the large farmers who took the lead in much of the rent agitation. The memorial for a 50 per cent abatement on the Lurgan estate was presented by a deputation 'comprising the most prominent farmers on his lordship's estates'. 'All the large farmers either personally attended or were represented' at a meeting called to present a memorial for a reduction of rent on Lord Massereene's Connor estate outside Ballymena, and the meeting of tenants on Sir Richard Wallace's estate was 'got up by the most respectable and largest farmers on the estate'.[129] In mid-Ulster also, the larger tenants played a prominent role and at least one agent held them responsible for the agitation: 'Another thing is that for the agitation in this country I blame the large farmers. They have taken a leading part in it and who could blame the poor for following their bad example.'[130]

The interest of large tenants in rent abatements is of course self-evident. But 'the game', as James Crossle observed, was also 'tempting' for small tenants. For many of these the plea made in rent memorials that they could not meet their present obligations was all too literally true; 'I fear', said Crossle, 'there are a good many who cannot pay at all, no matter how willing'.[131] For those who could pay, concessions of any kind were invaluable. And there was for all — if they could hang on to their holdings — the prospect of future reform with whatever benefits that might bring; as Father McFadden told the Gweedore tenants, 'the new land bill may do great things for the tenants — he was in great hope it would contain a clause remitting arrears'.[132] The majority of Ulster tenants may not have had the same enthusiasm for the Land League as the Gweedore tenants, but they, no less than the latter, were anxious to secure whatever concessions were going. Thus tenants throughout the province, whether in sympathy with the league or not, joined in the scramble for rent allowances and looked forward with mounting expectations to the coming legislation of the Liberal government. 'They have not got so far as to wish to abolish landlords yet', Lord de Ros wrote to Beaconsfield, 'but the sugarplum [of] continuing reduction of rents, fixity of tenure and free sale, so insidiously offered, is being greedily swallowed.'[133]

The growing restlessness of the northern tenants eventually forced the tenant-right movement to abandon the policy of near-passivity it had adopted in the late summer of 1880.[134] In November meetings were organised by the Newtownbreda Tenant Farmers' Association at Ballylesson and by the Lisburn Tenant-Right Association outside Moira; a new county Liberal registration and land law reform association was launched in Armagh, and steps were taken to reactivate the Cookstown Tenant-right Association; and major tenant-right demonstrations were held at Monaghan and at Tullyhogue near Cookstown. In December there were tenant-right meetings at Carrickmacross, Drumillar (near Scarva), Lurgan, Tandragee, Moneymore, Loughgall, Ballywalter, Millisle, Bangor, Toomebridge, Comber and Kilrea, while at the end of the month the Antrim Central Tenant-Right Association was finally spurred into action and laid plans for a series of public meetings in the new year.[135]

These meetings were primarily land reform rather than rent meetings as such. In deference to the current preoccupation with rents, demands were made at a number of them for reductions of rent to the level of Griffith's valuation and sometimes to a level below this.[136] But the main purpose of the meetings was to support the demand for land reform, and to stiffen the resolve of the government to carry worthwhile legislation against the expected opposition not only of the Tories but of many of their own supporters.[137] Expressions of confidence in Gladstone and his administration were made at virtually all these meetings and, significantly, the local Liberal MPs played a more prominent part in this agitation than at any previous stage of the tenant-right campaign. The reforms demanded were basically the same reforms on which the Ulster Liberals had fought the election of 1880 and which the tenant-right movement had been advocating for the previous ten years, viz. the 3Fs with an extension of the facilities for tenant purchase.

There was, however, a new urgency about the demand — it was, said Hugh Montgomery, 'a hundredfold as loud and determined' as it had been in the 1870s[138] — and there was a unanimity that had not always previously obtained in Liberal and tenant-right circles; nothing less than the 3Fs, the Ulster Liberals told Forster, would 'keep their constituents from joining the Land League'.[139] There were, moreover, some significant changes in emphasis; where priority had earlier — indeed up to October 1880 — been given to the demand for the 3Fs with peasant proprietorship seen as a subordinate and distant objective, by December the order of resolutions at tenant-right meetings was being reversed, with tenant purchase on full loans provided by the state being advocated as 'the true, real and only permanent solution of the land question'.[140] But, if the tenant-right societies came out more decidedly in favour of peasant proprietorship, their demand stopped short of compulsory purchase: 'We don't want to compel landlords to sell out against their will, we only want the government when an estate is in the market to pass a measure giving the tenants the first chance of purchasing'.[141] Peasant proprietorship was still seen essentially as a long-term policy carried out on a voluntary basis, except in the case of the London companies whose estates, not being private, could, it was claimed, 'be bought out if necessary by the government in a compulsory manner without any violation of the rights of private property'.[142]

It has been suggested that there was during this period 'tacit co-operation' between the tenant-right movement and the Land League, and that their aims were similar.[143] This is true to a point. In many respects, as we have seen, the Land League was a different organisation in the north, more constitutional in its approach, temperate in its language, and at times even supportive of the government. It was not always easy to define the exact boundary between the programmes being advocated at tenant-right and Land League meetings in Ulster,[144] and at least some people found the aims of the two movements sufficiently compatible for them to be able to share the two platforms;[145] some tenant-righters were clearly not unaware that the activity and the demands of the Land League could help bring about a solution on the lines advocated by the tenant-right associations; and, on occasion, speakers at league meetings indicated a willingness to accept the 3Fs as an interim measure of reform. The views expressed by John Pinkerton at a league meeting at Loughguile, for example, were indistinguishable from those being voiced by tenant-right leaders throughout the province:

> In conclusion, allow me to say if we refuse, as an instalment of justice,
> a moderate land bill, but oppose, through pique, a measure of
> protection, we are false to those interests we are here to advocate, and
> by a captious opposition we paralyse the hands of the only men, who,
> as members of the English cabinet, ever made an effort to redress the
> wrongs of our country.[146]

But instances both of platform sharing and of league speakers
giving even tacit approval to the tenant-right programme were the
exception, not the rule. The fact was that there were vital and
fundamental differences between the two movements. The Land
League, for all its attempts to keep home rule in the background,
was a movement with strong political overtones and ulterior political
objectives, which in themselves precluded any close co-operation
with the Liberal and tenant-right movement in Ulster. This point was
frequently made by the tenant-right press:

> The president of the Land League, it must be remembered by the
> Ulster tenant farmers, according to his own avowals, only takes up
> this land question as a means to an end. The agitation will, he has
> declared, be valueless in his eyes, if, beyond the expropriation of the
> Irish landlords, he may not see the expropriation of the British
> government in this country, or, in other words, the establishment of
> a so-called national independence, which could only mean the lawless
> dictation of himself and his agrarian followers on the ruins of all
> property, and we may say even all civilization.[147]

Even on the land question itself the tactics and policies of the two
organisations were widely divergent. While demands were made at
tenant-right meetings for reductions of rent, tenants were also urged
— as, for example, by the secretary of the County Down Farmers'
Association — not to 'repudiate existing obligations',[148] and tenant-
right speakers denied that they were in any way ill-disposed towards
the landlords; 'we have', said the chairman of the Bangor meeting,
'no quarrel with landlords as a class (hear, hear)'.[149] The tenant-right
campaign, in fact, was never a crusade against rents and landlordism

in the way that that of the Land League was, and the league tactics of the boycott and the rent strike were abhorred by the tenant-right leaders, who specifically dissociated themselves from the league.[150]

Moreover, while league speakers on rare occasions suggested that half a loaf in the form of the 3Fs might be better than no bread, Parnell at Belleek and the league as an organisation totally and absolutely repudiated this policy as a settlement of the question. Jeremiah Jordan told the meeting at Scotstown that 'the subject of the 3Fs was worn out, and was now comparatively useless'.[151] Michael Davitt held that 'though such a measure might have been accepted a few years ago, it was now an antiquated proposal buried beneath the advancing strides of the Irish democracy'. Davitt denied that any tribunal appointed by the government could even define what a fair rent should be, while Joseph Biggar claimed they would 'give rise to endless litigation'.[152] Even John Pinkerton, who was prepared to accept a compromise measure, declared that

> he had very little sympathy with the lukewarm resolutions moved lately at meetings under the auspices of the tenant-right associations. It [the programme of the 3Fs] was a sort of Holloway's pill supposed to cure all the diseases of the land question ... He believed that the tenant should have the option of purchasing his holding not merely when the landlord wanted to sell, but when the tenant wanted to buy.[153]

What the Land League stood for — and there was no ambiguity about league objectives in this respect — was the forcible expropriation of Irish landlords, which the tenant-right associations rejected as revolutionary and impractical. The *Ballymoney Free Press* thought that 'the proposed expropriation of the landlords would make the last condition of Ireland worse than the first', the *Weekly Northern Whig* that it would be 'a huge wrong ... and a national disaster'.[154] And the Rev. Archibald Robinson, one of the leading tenant-right campaigners in the north, warned that to demand from the government 'the abolition of landlordism, the expulsion or expropriation of the landlords, even though their pecuniary interests should be purchased, is in my opinion not only wildly utopian, but injurious to the case of the tenants'.[155] The programme of the tenant-right movement, said the *Coleraine Chronicle*, was 'more suited to northern aspirations'.[156]

This was then the basic and fundamental difference between the two movements: one wanted the extirpation of Irish landlordism, the other supported the concept of partnership in the soil. As Thomas Dickson explained at the height of the agitation:

> There are two propositions now before the country for the settlement of the land question. One party proposes that landlords should be abolished by the government taking compulsorily all the property, and giving it to the occupiers at twenty years' purchase on Griffith's valuation. Now, I appeal to the common sense of the County Down men I see before me, if they think that any government would propose such a measure, or that any House of Commons could pass a bill forcibly expropriating the landlords and requiring security on an advance from the state of 250 millions? I have all my life aimed at being practical, and I will never ask the tenant farmers to follow a will o' the wisp or create expectations utterly impossible of being realised. The Ulster tenant-right party ... advocate the 3Fs and the creation of a peasant proprietary by making the tenants the owners of every acre of land offered for sale.[157]

The Land League may have galvanised the tenant-right associations into action, forced them to give more prominence to tenant purchase at their meetings, and made their demand for tenant-right more strident and more urgent, but there never was and never could be any coalescence between the two movements.

## 9
# The Response to the Land Agitation

THE ANTI-LAND LEAGUE CAMPAIGN

Irish landlords were slow to react to the land agitation. An Irish
Land Committee had been formed in November 1879 for the
purpose of collecting and presenting evidence to the royal commission
on agricultural distress, and this continued in existence for the next
two years publishing pamphlets and generally arguing the landlords'
case.[1] But this was essentially a southern organisation, representing
the views of southern rather than northern landlords between whom
clear differences of opinion were beginning to emerge at this time.[2]
At any rate, apart from the work of this committee, there was up to
October 1880 little public response to the land agitation from any
section of the Irish landowning class, except for occasional letters to
the press and frequent appeals to the government to suppress the
agitation and introduce coercion.[3] Public opposition to the league, it
was believed, could only be undertaken at 'very great personal risk'.[4]

Northern landowners were of course in a better position to
campaign openly against the league, and once it started to spill over
into Ulster they finally began to bestir themselves and a more
substantive opposition emerged. At the end of October a large
demonstration organised by the constitutional associations of Down
and Antrim was held in the Ulster Hall, and this was followed in
early November by anti-league meetings in Dungannon and

Downpatrick.[5] The purpose of the meetings was to protest against the Land League — whose aims, it was contended, were almost precisely the same as those of 'the Fenian Brotherhood'[6] — and to urge the government to take immediate steps to restore law and order. Further meetings were held in December, but leading northern landlords were still at this stage displaying a curious reluctance to come out and campaign openly against the league. The Conservative press commented on the apparent complacency of Ulster landlords, claiming that they seemed to be 'as indifferent to their own interests as their enemies are active and earnest in their endeavours to annihilate them'.[7] It was not, however, that the landlords were indifferent to what was happening throughout the country. They were deterred rather by the evident disquiet on their own estates and by the ambivalent attitude of their own tenantry towards the agitation: 'In connection with this league business', the Rev. D.C. Abbott said in reply to Hugh Montgomery's proposal for an anti-league meeting at Enniskillen, 'I fear such a meeting as you name for Enniskillen would only show our weakness'.[8]

In fact, the most vigorous opposition to the league in Ulster came not from the landlords, but from the Orange order, and the dominance of the anti-league movement by the Orangemen and the irresponsible and embarrassing extremism of some of the latter may, in itself, help explain the early reluctance of many landlords to become involved in what rapidly developed into a policy of sectarian confrontation. There was, also, the openly hostile attitude of many of the Orange speakers to the landed classes, who had during the previous years tended to neglect the order.[9] However, the exigencies of the situation now forced the landlords into a closer alliance with the Orangemen. In the face of the rapid and apparently uncheckable progress of the league in Ulster, the Orange institution was increasingly seen as the only 'organisation capable of dealing with the condition of anarchy and rebellion'.[10] Even landlords who were not prepared to join its ranks themselves fully realised its usefulness as a weapon against the league.[11]

There was also the consideration that, left to their own devices, there was no telling where the Orangemen's increasing and increasingly radical interest in the land question might lead them.[12] Whereas at the Twelfth meetings in July hardly a single resolution had been passed on the land question,[13] by the end of October Orangemen were showing as keen an interest in reform as anyone else; and Orange leaders such as Thomas Peel of Armagh and the Rev. Stewart Ross of Belfast were claiming that rents were too high, that landlords were destroying tenant-right, and that further legislation was necessary to protect tenant interests.[14] Apart from the danger of the Orangemen actually joining the agitation — and this, as we have seen, was a real possibility — the anti-rent and anti-landlord statements of loyalists such as Peel, Ross and Whaley were potentially more damaging to the landlord cause and to landlord–tenant relations in Ulster than the activity of the Land League itself.[15] It was clear, in fact, that the landlords could not secure the full support of the northern protestant tenantry against the league without the assistance of the Orangemen. At the very least, Orangeism could be used to drive a wedge between the protestant farmers and the supporters of the league, perhaps even to undermine support for the tenant-right movement.[16] 'The dodge of sectarian fear etc. is not yet used out', wrote the Rev. Abbott to Montgomery, 'and I fear it is the only one to charm with in the north.'[17]

The result of all these considerations was that the propertied classes began to identify more closely with the Orangemen, and the institution itself began to assume a new importance in Ulster Tory politics — reflected and cemented by the *ex officio* appointment of the county and city grand masters as vice-presidents of the new Ulster Constitutional Union formed in December 1880 — and in the immediate crisis of 1880–1 became the main channel of northern protestant and landed opposition to the Land League. From October Orange demonstrations and counter-demonstrations began to be held in different parts of Ulster, with the campaign intensifying from November as Land League activity in the province increased. At the beginning of November, a specially convened meeting of the Grand Orange Lodge of Ireland issued an address condemning the league campaign as a conspiracy against property, protestantism and the union, deploring the failure of the government to protect lives and property, and pledging the institution to counteract by every means in its power the league's 'pernicious and communistic doctrines'.[18] These resolutions were repeated at Orange meetings throughout Ulster, and the government was warned — as was almost normal in such circumstances — that if it did not act to suppress the league, the Orangemen themselves would have to take action.[19] Orange members were advised to hold themselves in a state of readiness, Orange masters to organise and arm their men. The Fermanagh County Grand Lodge, for example, appointed a committee to arrange for the procuring and distribution of arms, while in December the Orange Emergency Committee instructed district masters that it was their duty to see that all the brethren in their districts were provided with suitable arms to defend the loyal population.[20]

At the same time, in a transparent attempt to pressurise the authorities into proclaiming Land League meetings and thus halting the progress of the league, the Orangemen began to hold a series of counter-demonstrations.[21] These were organised against league meetings at Mayobridge and Saintfield in Down, at Derrygonnelly and Brookeborough in Fermanagh, at Dungannon and Dromore in Tyrone, at Scotstown in Monaghan and at other centres. But although the league meeting at Brookeborough was proclaimed, the tactic generally was not successful. Not all the counter-demonstrations elicited the kind of loyalist response the Orange leaders had hoped for, those at Scotstown and Derrygonnelly, for example, having to be abandoned for lack of support.[22] And the Castle authorities — bombarded by league complaints about the hostility and bias of northern landed magistrates, and by league demands for protection against Orange attacks[23] — apparently accepted the view that the banning of the league meetings was counter-productive, and generally provided the necessary troop and police protection.[24]

What the counter-demonstrations did, however, was to raise the level of sectarian feeling in the province, and this was clearly part of their purpose. The main Orange strategy in the north was to identify the land agitation with sectarianism and home rule, and the Orange campaign was presented deliberately and unashamedly in these terms. Not many Orange leaders had the same unbounded confidence in the credulity of their followers as the Rev. Stewart Ross, who not only made the government party to the Land League conspiracy against protestantism, but told an Orange meeting in Belfast that 'he solemnly believed that Gladstone was a Jesuit in disguise'.[25] But speaker after speaker at Orange meetings insisted that the real purpose of the league was to uproot protestantism, sever the connection with England, and 'establish Rome rule in Ireland'.[26]

In these attempts to arouse sectarian feeling, frequent references were made to the difficulties faced by protestant landlords in the south and west of the country. The Boycott affair in Co. Mayo towards the end of 1880 was particularly important in this respect. Boycott's case was not exactly typical — he was not himself a landlord and his troubles were at least partly self-inflicted[27] — but it seemed to symbolise the plight of southern protestant landowners, and it was skilfully exploited by the northern Conservative press to arouse anti-league feeling and by the Conservative press in Ireland and Britain generally to underline the lawlessness in the south and the need for coercive legislation. Protestant landowners — like all landowners in the south — were obviously in an exposed and vulnerable position, and Orange speakers in the north made great capital out of this. Resolutions expressing sympathy with their co-religionists in the south were adopted at virtually every Orange meeting and, apart from the expedition of fifty labourers from Monaghan and Cavan to relieve Boycott,[28] Ulstermen subscribed also in terms of men and money to the activities of the Orange Emergency Committee and the Property Defence Association, two landlord protection agencies set up in December 1880.

These two organisations — the first established by the Grand Orange Lodge, the second formed at a meeting of landlords and agents in Dublin — tried in a variety of ways to combat the aims and frustrate the tactics of the league: men were supplied to serve writs where local process-servers had been intimidated; officials and representatives of the committees attended execution sales — i.e. sales of farms and other property seized for rent — thus preventing such proceedings being rendered abortive by league boycotting; armed caretakers — often retired policemen or ex-soldiers — were hired to occupy holdings from which tenants had been evicted; arms were supplied to loyalists in the south, and instructions issued to district masters on steps they should take to meet the league threat; and labourers — nearly always from Ulster — were provided for boycotted landlords so that during the spring and summer of 1881 the emergency committee had over 300 men, all northerners, working boycotted estates and farms in nineteen counties in Ireland.[29]

There were a number of instances of emergency committee activity in the north as, for example, in Monaghan, where the 'emergency men' under the leadership of Colonel Jesse Lloyd, Lord Rossmore's agent, successfully carried out a number of sales, procured labour for a number of boycotted landlords and tenants, and on one occasion brought in scutchers from Portadown to carry out work for a boycotted mill-owner in Scotstown.[30] But the work of these Dublin-based organisations had greater relevance to the southern provinces, and, although one or two local defence committees were formed in Ulster,[31] the Ulstermen generally were content to rely mainly on the strength of the Orange order to resist league influence in the north.

Nevertheless, in spite of the apparent vigour of the Orange opposition in Ulster, the land agitation, or more particularly protestant support for the agitation, was giving northern landlords growing cause for concern. Apart from those who actually joined the league, protestant and Orange tenants in general were showing a good deal less than enthusiasm for the anti-league campaign. Tenant farmers were conspicuous by their absence from an anti-league meeting at Downpatrick, and, as already noted, counter-demonstrations at Scotstown and Derrygonnelly had to be abandoned because of lack of support; those who did attend at Scotstown belonged, according to the local police report, to 'a lower status in society'.[32] Other counter-demonstrations had to be reinforced by Orangemen from Belfast and other towns.[33]

Tenant-right meetings too were evidently getting increasing support from Orange tenants[34] — Orangemen were appearing with greater frequency as speakers — and although one or two tenant-right meetings had earlier been obstructed by the Orangemen, though mainly by Orange artisans and labourers rather than by tenants,[35] this tactic had clearly been abandoned by the beginning of 1881. At a meeting of the Moneymore District Orange Lodge at the beginning of January, a motion of censure against Brother James Reid, the district master elect, for having attended a tenant-right meeting was withdrawn after Reid successfully — and to the obvious satisfaction of the majority of those present — defended the right of Orangemen to attend such meetings. And Orange opposition to a tenant-right meeting in Coleraine was abandoned after the resolutions — embracing the 3Fs — were published.[36] Shortly afterwards the Coleraine District Orange Lodge decided to prohibit discussion of the subject at lodge meetings: 'The land question should not come into our lodges. There is very far from unanimity of opinion between our brethren on this subject, and therefore we should not discuss it in our meetings.'[37] Orange tenants had clearly a deep interest in land reform, and an increasing number of them were prepared to argue that support for tenant-right was in no way incompatible with the defence of protestantism and the union.

Orange leaders and landed Tories were not unaware of these divisions in Orange and protestant ranks, nor of the strains being imposed on the loyalty of their followers by the issue. Sectarian confrontation politics on their own were manifestly not sufficient to prevent the land agitation from engulfing the north, and northern landlords were forced into a situation in which they either had to bow to tenant demands or else run the risk of losing their political and social influence.[38] Under the circumstances, they had no alternative but to take up the land question and demand an early and equitable settlement. General and sometimes ambiguous statements in support of reform — as, for example at Lurgan, Portadown, Stewartstown and the Ulster Hall in early November[39] — soon gave way to specific declarations and resolutions in favour of the 3Fs with increased facilities for tenant purchase. A detailed set of resolutions embracing the 3Fs was adopted by the Monaghan Grand Lodge in December, and similar resolutions were subsequently passed in one form or another at Orange meetings in Portadown, Newtownards, Ballymena, Armagh and other centres, with the *News Letter* urging landlords to support the new development so as to 'keep loyal men ... from becoming the prey of the tenant leaguers or land leaguers, or any other leaguers'.[40]

Northern landlords found it less difficult to accept these proposals than their counterparts in the south, mainly because they believed that legislation along these lines would not materially affect existing practices on their own estates. The 3Fs, they claimed, were common practice on the Conservative estates in Ulster, and they 'could not see why the Conservative landlords should object to a law to compel those who acted otherwise (if there were any) to act in the same manner as they had been doing'.[41] Many landlords felt that it had now come to the point where it was essential to have some statutory control on those landlords who by their behaviour were discrediting the whole class. Clearly it was in the interests of all landlords as well as tenants to impose some restraint on this minority, to accept some measure of reform which would control their excesses and thus remove what many landlords believed was one of the main sources of friction between landlords and tenants in Ulster. The only reservations were about unlimited freedom of sale which, it was contended, would be injurious to landlords and tenants alike;[42] more, if absolute freedom of sale was introduced and the landlord's veto over the incoming tenant completely abolished, 'there was not', Andrew Murray-Ker, a leading Co. Monaghan landowner, told an Orange rally at Monaghan, 'a protestant at that meeting who would be in the country five years hence'.[43] But, subject to landlords having a voice in the selection of incoming tenants, northern Orangemen and landlords had by early 1881 come out firmly in favour of legislation on the basis of the 3Fs.

RENT ABATEMENTS AND EVICTIONS

If landlords increasingly looked to the government to bring about a final settlement of the land question by legislation, they had in the meantime to deal with the rent demands and tenant disaffection on their own estates. As we have seen, landowners were faced in 1880–81 with a rent agitation more intense and more demanding than anything they had experienced in the previous season. Agricultural recovery in the province was uneven and incomplete, and at least some landlords were prepared to accept that tenants, many of them still burdened by debts and arrears, could not yet resume their full rental obligations. Lord Rathdonnell, for example, offered an unsolicited abatement of 50 per cent on the gale of rent due on 1 November, Sir William Johnston D.L. gratuitously gave a year's receipt for the six month's rent collected in November, and Lord Lurgan offered a 10 per cent remission; 'the crops are unusually abundant', explained John Hancock, Lurgan's agent, 'but the prices are low, the staple trade of our province is in a depressed state, and a considerable amount of money is due by many of you [the tenants] to shopkeepers and loan fund proprietors'.[44]

But landlords too had their debts. Many estates had fixed charges to meet, and with the accumulation of arrears over the previous seasons, landlord income had been seriously reduced. When the tenants on the Loughry estate in Tyrone peremptorily demanded an abatement of 25 per cent, their landlord told them truthfully that 'he had not that much of the rental to live on'.[45] Small landowners were particularly badly hit by the depression, but all estates were affected to some degree. 'I am sorry you cannot understand how distressed I am for money', the Earl of Charlemont wrote to his agent, 'Half the diamonds are in pawn and my lady would not sell or pawn to save me or herself.'[46] In reply to a memorandum from his agent about annual subscriptions to local charities, Lord Annesley, whose tenantry were £3,000 in arrear and whose office account was already overdrawn by nearly £2,000, asked, 'will you tell me where it [the money] is to come from?'. He had already, he added, reduced his personal expenditure to 'as nearly nil as I can make it' and would not 'spend one shilling I can possibly avoid while I am in debt ... My rents have not been paid and till they are I must perforce cease all subscriptions'.[47] 'I regret to say I cannot possibly remit to you any money at present,' James Crossle wrote to the impecunious Sir William Verner. 'We have only £600 in [the] bank and the outgoings up to 1st August next will be over £1,970 independent of the expenses at Churchill [Verner's Armagh estate].'[48] The arrears on the Verner estates were running at this stage at over £2,000 out of a total rent of about £12,000, and yet Crossle claimed that there were 'less arrears upon Sir William's property than upon any other of the same size in the counties of Tyrone, Armagh or Monaghan'.[49]

Crossle finally had to resort to raising a loan to meet the estate debts, and even here he ran into difficulty: 'I have this morning had a refusal from the *third* bank I have applied to. It appears the directors of all banks decline to lend money to Irish landlords at present.'[50] Other owners experienced the same problem. Hugh Montgomery's London solicitor, for example, found it next to impossible to raise a £3,000 loan for him in London: 'The difficulty now is where else to look for the money for there is no denying the fact that a very serious distrust exists as to the security of land in Ireland'.[51] Indeed, some of the major institutional lenders not only refused to give additional credit on Irish land, but began from 1880 to call in loans or ask for the provision of alternative English security.[52]

In such circumstances many landlords simply could not afford to show the same generosity or forbearance as in the previous year. Their view was that agriculture had recovered and there was no longer the same need to make special allowances. 'While always anxious to see a fair and generous allowance made in bad years by landlords to their tenants', Ellison Macartney, MP for Tyrone, wrote to a tenant meeting at Tullyhogue, 'I find no justification for such a demand this year after one of the most abundant harvests ever known in Ireland.'[53] Hugh Montgomery's agent James Pomeroy believed that the tenants had the money, and attributed their rent demands and refusals to pay not to tenant difficulties, but rather to the agitation and the generally disturbed condition of the country.[54] James Crossle also held this view, while the sub-inspector of Ballyshannon district reported that landlords in his area had been paid 'comparatively little of their rents ... although I feel perfectly satisfied the tenantry generally are in a position to discharge their liabilities'.[55]

Nevertheless, many landlords, anxious to avert rent strikes and obviate league influence and sometimes, too, quite desperate for money, were prepared to make concessions: 'it seems the small owners cannot forego getting what they can', it was explained, 'while the large estates — Caledon, Ranfurly, etc. — are told they must give a general reduction or the best tenants will go over to the league'.[56] And once some landlords made abatements, it was more difficult for others to resist the demand. Charlemont complained about the 'annoying accounts of the various reductions of rent', and held 'that fellow Hancock' — who had as early as October offered a 10 per cent remission to the Lurgan tenants — responsible 'for all the mischief in Armagh'.[57] James Pomeroy believed that there was no real case for rent allowances on Montgomery's estate, but was 'inclined to think that as Captain Archdale has promised an abatement ... something of the kind must now be done'. Montgomery acted promptly on this advice and offered an abatement of 10–20 per cent to his tenants before they actually submitted any petition.[58]

A number of landlords acted as Montgomery did and tried to pre-empt tenant demands by offering unsolicited abatements — generally from 5 to 15 per cent — to their tenants before petitions had been prepared. This was clearly what Lord Lurgan was trying to do in Armagh, and other landlords such as A.C. Innes of the Dromantine estate in Down, J.G. Richardson of Bessbrook, Major Stewart Blacker of Carrickblacker, T.R. Cope of the Mountnorris estate in Armagh and many others adopted the same tactic.[59] In many instances these offers were rejected by the tenants as inadequate, and the settlement of rents both in these cases and where tenant memorials were presented was often a compromise between what the tenants sought and what landlords were prepared to give. In some cases, however, as on W.F. Littledale's Deburren estate outside Newry and on the Mooney estate outside Castlewellan, landlords were forced to meet nearly the full demands of the tenants.[60]

Landlords generally, in fact, had much greater difficulty getting rents in 1880–81 than in 1879–80. But, on the whole, their tactics of making pre-emptive offers and of compromise — backed up frequently by the extensive use of ejectment processes — were not unsuccessful. Landlord offers frequently succeeded in undermining tenant unity — satisfying 'the respectable tenants'[61] — and rent strikes were, generally speaking, never nearly as effective in Ulster as they were in the south. On the Lurgan estates in Armagh, for example, where the tenants demanded a 50 per cent reduction, Lurgan's early offer of 10 per cent had the effect of splitting their ranks so that resistance on the estate eventually broke down; and on the Verner estates tenants gradually abandoned their stand for abatements ranging from 25 to 50 per cent and accepted the 15 per cent offered by Crossle.[62] There was, at any rate, an underlying tension between catholic and protestant tenants on some estates, which in itself frequently prevented rent action by tenants from being as effective as it might otherwise have been. At a meeting of Ranfurly tenants in Dungannon, resolutions in favour of paying no rent and boycotting those who did so displeased the protestant tenants that the majority of them left the room; unity was only restored when the meeting was reconvened and these resolutions withdrawn in favour of a straightforward petition for a rent reduction.[63]

Ranfurly, however, was one of a large number of landlords who flatly refused to make any concessions whatsoever to their tenants, even where memorials were accompanied — as they often were — by expressions of loyalty and disavowals of all sympathy for the Land League.[64] Ranfurly was prepared to accept that some tenants might have been hard hit by the deficiency in the flax crop, and he was therefore prepared to look at individual cases. But generally his view was that the harvest was abundant and that prices compared favourably with, for example, 1852, while rents had not increased in anything like the same proportion; the unrest on the estate, he concluded, was more a result of the importation of foreign and revolutionary ideas than of foreign produce.[65] Sir Victor Brooke took the same line as Ranfurly, viz. that individual tenants might require assistance, but that there was no case for a general reduction of rents, while the Earl of Charlemont's view was that not having given any reduction in the previous year, he saw less need to do so now.[66]

Ranfurly's, Brooke's and Charlemont's estates were in league areas. Landlords in non-league areas, especially in Antrim and north Down, were, if anything, even more intransigent in this matter of rent allowances. Sir Richard Wallace regretted the losses sustained by some of his tenants, but claimed that fears regarding American competition were exaggerated, that cattle prices were higher than they had been for some years past, and that his rents were 'less than Griffith's valuation for the land alone'.[67] Hunt Chambre, Lord Massereene's agent, referred to the high prices recently given for tenant-right on the Connor estate, claimed that the average rent per acre did not exceed ten shillings, and attributed the agitation for an abatement to a small minority on the estate.[68] Sir Thomas Bateson believed his rents were already low and considered that the good harvest had rendered a reduction quite unnecessary.[69] In short, if tenants generally were more demanding in 1880–81, the landlords for their part were a lot less sympathetic and much more inclined to take a firmer stand against tenant demands than they had in the previous year.

It was this hardening of landlord attitudes which more than anything else accounted for the great increase in the number of evictions in Ulster during this period. Landlords had already been making extensive use of ejectment processes to pressurise tenants into paying rents and arrears, and the number of civil bill ejectments entered for non-payment of rent in Ulster increased from 2,784 in 1879 to 3,161 in 1880 to 4,187 in 1881.[70] The vast majority of these were never executed, but Table 9.1 shows the dramatic rise in evictions during these years — from an annual average of 121 in 1870–78 to ten times that figure in 1881. More surprisingly, the rate of increase was greater in Ulster than elsewhere in the country, so that by 1881, Ulster, traditionally the province with fewest evictions, had the greatest number of evictions of all the provinces and, indeed, during the first three months of 1881 had more evictions than the other three provinces put together.[71]

Table 9.1. Evictions in each province of Ireland
in each year 1879–83[72]

| | ULSTER | ULSTER'S EVICTIONS AS % OF TOTAL | LEINSTER | CONNACHT | MUNSTER | IRELAND |
|---|---|---|---|---|---|---|
| ANNUAL AVERAGE 1870–8 | 121 | 19.4 | 147 | 201 | 155 | 624 |
| 1879 | 172 | 13.9 | 354 | 313 | 399 | 1,238 |
| 1880 | 497 | 23.6 | 484 | 387 | 742 | 2,110 |
| 1881 | 1,219 | 35.7 | 692 | 784 | 720 | 3,415 |
| 1882 | 1,176 | 22.6 | 1,091 | 1,457 | 1,477 | 5,201 |
| 1883 | 689 | 18.9 | 666 | 981 | 1,307 | 3,643 |

This greater increase in evictions in Ulster can be attributed at least partly to the relative weakness of the Land League in the north. As Forster reported to Gladstone in November 1880, 'there are very few [evictions] now — out of Ulster — the landlords fear to evict. Parnell is quite right ... in saying that the league has stopped evictions — though he ought to have said — the league and its attendant outrages.'[73] In Ulster itself the number of evictions dropped sharply in the last months of 1880 — from 191 in the third quarter of the year to fifty-five in the last quarter — as the Land League established its influence in different parts of the province. Many landlords were clearly afraid at this stage of driving the tenantry into open agitation. James Crossle, for example, was reluctant to execute ejectment decrees on the Verner estates 'for fear of raising the tenants into combination'.[74] Many landlords and agents, like Crossle, were hoping that rents and arrears would be largely paid in December and January once tenants realised the value of their crops.[75] But when this did not happen landlords were, for the reasons mentioned above, more inclined to use — and under the protection of the new coercion act passed in February could more confidently use — the full force of the law against recalcitrant tenants. Thus evictions increased again in the first quarter of 1881 — especially from February — reaching a peak in the three months from April to June 1881.[76] They continued at a high level during the remainder of 1881 and for most of 1882, and only in 1883 did the provincial pattern revert to what it had been prior to 1879.

An analysis of the evictions carried out in the first three months of 1881 — based on a confidential return made to Forster[77] — shows plainly that the vast majority (85.5 per cent) were for non-payment of rent. Moreover, whereas it had been alleged that the evictions in 1879 and early 1880 had largely been the work of parvenu landlords,[78] this return demonstrates quite clearly that the policy was now being more widely employed by the larger landowners; of the total number of evictions listed in the return for this three-month period, some 66 per cent were carried out by owners of 1,000 acres and more. One can perhaps make too much of this, and certainly it is not being suggested that all large proprietors or even a majority were resorting at this stage to a policy of wholesale eviction. In some counties the figures were inflated by the actions of a small minority of landlords; the Earl of Leitrim, for example, was responsible for seventeen of the twenty-five evictions in Donegal during these three months, R.J. McGeough for eighteen of the thirty-six carried out in Armagh — in other words, these two landlords between them accounted for a fifth of the total evictions in Ulster during the period covered by this return.[79]

But even allowing that the majority of landlords were still reluctant to evict and did so only as a last resort, and allowing too for the higher rate of readmission in Ulster,[80] there is no denying the fact that landlords in general — faced with a backlog of arrears, hard-pressed for money themselves, afraid that the coming legislation might deprive them of whatever powers they had for the recovery of arrears,[81] and often, too, resentful at what they considered the ingratitude of their tenants[82] — were no longer prepared to show the same indulgence to tenants, especially when they believed that the latter were deliberately and needlessly withholding payment. 'My intention', Annesley instructed his agent, 'is that if these tenants are able to pay, and refuse to do so, then that the law should be put into force against them.'[83]

In theory, Ulster landlords were in a better position to evict tenants than landlords in most of the south in the sense that they could afterwards recover their arrears by the sale of tenant-right, and this may help to explain the more rapid increase in evictions in Ulster than elsewhere in 1879–80.[84] In practice, however, the tradition on the larger estates in Ulster was for landlords and agents to avoid eviction as far as was possible by persuading tenants in arrears to sell out.[85] This had the double advantage of securing landlords their arrears and at the same time averting open conflict, and the advisability of such a policy was of course reinforced by the activity of the Land League in the province towards the end of 1880.[86] But the problem by 1881 was that in the depressed market for tenant-right an increasing number of tenants either could not or would not voluntarily sell their holdings, so that landlords and agents could no longer pursue this tactic with the same degree of success. 'Why is it', Annesley querulously asked his agent, 'that heretofore you have told me you always got the rent by selling the tenant-right and never had an eviction, and cannot do so now?'[87] William Shaw, Annesley's agent, no doubt replied along the same lines as James Crossle's son to Sir William Verner's solicitors in London: 'We are doing all in our power to get them [arrears of rent] in, but in many instances where tenants are most anxious to dispose of their farms, purchasers cannot be obtained'.[88]

Crossle was a compassionate though diligent agent on an estate where, by and large, the bulk of the rents had been paid up to November 1880, and yet he was eventually forced by pecuniary pressures to carry out a number of evictions. Other landlords, under even greater pressure, were still looking for the previous May's rents.[89] In such circumstances the increase in evictions was scarcely surprising. But even at their height evictions were still limited, and certainly there was never any total or near total breakdown of landlord–tenant relations in Ulster. Rather the agitation and the problems of collecting rents added to the conviction of Ulster landlords that a final settlement of the land question was urgently required if their position was to be maintained and something approaching normality was to be restored in Ulster. By 1881, in fact, the various parties and interests in Ulster — Conservatives and Liberals, landlords and tenants — were agreed not only on the need for further land reform, but also that such reform should be along lines of the 3Fs with an extension of the existing facilities for tenant purchase. This unity of opinion in Ulster was to have an important, in some respects a crucial, influence on the course of events at Westminster.

LAND REFORM

Gladstone, when he came into office in April 1880, was curiously ignorant of the seriousness of the situation in Ireland, and when it was forced on his attention he acted only hesitantly and reluctantly, hoping for a time that a good harvest would solve the problem and believing that the demand for land reform could be met 'simply by adapting and invigorating his old act.'[90] It was, in fact, W.E. Forster, the new Irish chief secretary, who took the initiative in meeting the crisis and who was the principal architect of Liberal policy in Ireland during these two years. Forster was convinced that 'the land question [was] the Irish question on which all else hinges', and it was he who was responsible both for the abortive compensation for disturbance bill and for the appointment of the Bessborough commission in the summer of 1880.[91] From an early stage he believed not only that land reform was necessary but that it 'must be strong and comprehensive'; 'we had better do nothing', he advised, 'than tinker'.[92] 'No bill will be a settlement of the question', he told Gladstone, 'will in fact do anything but harm which does not meet the popular demand for what is called the 3Fs — viz. fixity of tenure at a fair rent and with a free sale.'[93]

By this stage it was being increasingly widely recognised that fundamental concessions would have to be made to the Irish tenants. Forster's recommendations were supported by a series of resolutions passed by the Land Tenure Reform Committee (a cross-party group which had been set up in the previous year to study the whole question of Irish land tenure) and also by the Bessborough report and by the preliminary report of the Richmond commission (appointed in August 1879 to investigate agricultural conditions in Britain and Ireland). Four of the five members of the Bessborough commission signed the main report in favour of the 3Fs, and while the majority of the members of the Richmond commission specifically rejected these as a solution to the problem (advocating instead resettlement, emigration and public works), a minority report drafted by Lord Carlingford, an Irish landlord and former chief secretary for Ireland, and signed by six of the nineteen members of the commission, came out strongly in their favour.[94]

Gladstone, however, remained unconvinced. In December he was still hoping for something a good deal less than the 3Fs, and as late as January — after the Bessborough commission had reported — he spoke strongly in private against fixity of tenure and fair rents, 'saying that both were a robbery of the landlord'.[95] The weight of opinion was such, however, that Gladstone had to move his ground, but he came round only slowly to accepting the need for a radical measure, especially one which included fixity of tenure.[96] Forster was the leading member of the cabinet in bringing about this conversion and he made extensive use of Ulster opinion in doing so. At the beginning of November he warned Gladstone that 'no Ulster Liberal has a chance of return who does not pledge himself to it [the programme of the 3Fs] and even the Orangemen cry out for a strong measure at their excited meetings'.[97] In December, he passed on to Gladstone a memorial submitted to himself by the Ulster Liberal members demanding 'a substantive measure' of reform in the form of the 3Fs and 'not a mere amendment of the land act of 1870'; 'they tell me', said Forster, 'that nothing short of this will keep their constituents from joining the Land League'.[98] Forster forwarded another memorial in favour of the 3Fs to Gladstone in January, this time signed by 22,000 protestant tenants, none of them in any way connected with the Land League and many of them Orangemen.[99]

In the same month a deputation of Irish — mainly Ulster — Liberal MPs met the prime minister himself and impressed on him the importance of including the 3Fs and increased facilities for purchase in his bill.[100] It was not only, as the tenant-right press in Ulster pointed out, that 'a weak measure would be fatal to the Ulster party' or, as the *Daily News* argued, that the Liberal party owed a 'special obligation' to the Ulster Liberals;[101] it was rather that the Ulster demand was seen as the absolute minimum required to settle the question and sever the 'bond of discontent between Ulster and the rest of Ireland', perhaps even to keep Ulster outside the nationalist movement.[102] The importance of satisfying opinion in the northern province was strongly emphasised by George Shaw-Lefevre, one of the leading self-proclaimed Liberal experts on Ireland and Irish land tenure, in a memorandum specially prepared for the cabinet at Gladstone's request:

> I believe that these principles represent the almost unanimous opinion of all parties in Ulster at the present time, and are what they understand by the 'three Fs', viz. fixity of tenure, fair rents and free sale. Nothing less than this would, I think, satisfy them, and no scheme of land reform would have the faintest chance of acceptance in Ireland which has not the approval of the Ulster people. They form the main motive power of any reform; without them nothing can be done; with them much, I believe, can be done.[103]

By early 1881, in fact, it had been made clear to Gladstone that any reform which fell short of the 3Fs would fail to satisfy the Ulster tenants, and that any reform which failed to satisfy Ulster would *a fortiori* fail to satisfy Ireland as a whole. The only possible alternative was a substantial measure of peasant proprietorship, which the Liberals' deep-rooted aversion to public expenditure effectively precluded them from adopting and on which they occupied a position less advanced even than that of the British Tories.[104] For Gladstone and other Liberals local self-government reform was an essential prerequisite for state support for tenant purchase; only then would local institutions be established which could accept responsibility for the loans and give the state the necessary security.[105] In the meantime, the Liberals saw tenant purchase as having only limited application in Ireland.

Thus Gladstone reluctantly, and only after a long campaign of persuasion on Forster's part, introduced in April 1881 a bill that he had 'never expected to propose when he took office in April 1880'.[106] It was a bill which effectively conceded the main demands of the northern tenant-right movement — the 3Fs along with a moderate extension of the facilities for tenant purchase — and one which caused immense disquiet in British Liberal as well as Conservative circles.[107] The most immediate threat to the bill, however, came from the Conservatives, and the most immediate question at the time was whether it would be accepted by them, or whether they would use their control of the lords either to defeat it in the way that they had defeated the compensation bill or to emasculate it to the point where it would be unacceptable to the Irish tenants.

Northern landlords were, as we have seen, increasingly anxious to have the question settled. Many of them were convinced even before 1880 of the need for further legislation, and the events of 1880–81 — the Conservative losses in the election, the activity of the Land League, and the northern protestant and Orange support for the league and more generally and vociferously for reform — reconciled them to accepting a much more radical measure of reform than they would ever have contemplated in the 1870s. Their view was that nothing short of the 3Fs would settle the question, that tenants on the Conservative estates in Ulster already enjoyed the substance of these demands, and that legislation along these lines would merely give legal sanction to existing practices. Their attitude was well summed up by Ellison Macartney, the MP for Tyrone:

> Such a measure would not materially affect the system at present adopted on the largest and best managed estates in Ulster. I do not think that anything short of it will allay the ferment which the Land League agitation has raised.[108]

Macartney and other landed representatives were encouraged in this belief by government spokesmen, who presented the land bill to parliament as a measure designed mainly to curb the excesses of a minority of landlords — generally, according to Gladstone, the smaller landlords — and not calculated to inflict any injury or loss upon the great majority of landowners who had, said Gladstone in introducing the bill, 'stood their trial and ... [had] as a rule, been acquitted'.[109] Where there was harmony between landlords and tenants, and especially where landlords had already conceded the 3Fs, the bill, it was contended, would have practically no operation at all; 'in fact, all that would probably happen', claimed Hugh Law, the Irish attorney-general, 'would be that a certain number of rack-rented tenants would get their rents reduced and have a limited fixity of tenure. The government ... did not admit that there would be any loss to the landlord, except the loss of a power which he ought not to exercise.'[110] Carlingford, in moving the second reading in the lords, claimed that the main effect of the bill would be to place southern landlords like himself 'very much in the position in which the Ulster landlords are now'. He also maintained — and so too did John Bright and others — that the bill would cause 'the landlord no money loss whatever ... except in those cases in which a certain number of landlords may have imposed upon their tenants excessive and inequitable rents, which they are probably vainly trying to recover'.[111] Forster repudiated the suggestion that there would be 'a great rush into court' and argued — and this was an argument which had increasing appeal to Irish landlords — that landlords would benefit from the improved facilities for purchase which would, he maintained, help end the stagnation in the Irish land market.[112]

These assurances were not given only to discourage opposition to the bill; they were genuine convictions held by government ministers. Forster had earlier assured the cabinet that the 'actual position [of the majority of landlords] would not be changed'.[113] The fact was that neither the government nor anyone else really expected the act to have the effects it eventually had. Certainly the belief that rents on most of the larger estates would not be seriously affected by the act was shared by members of all parties in Ireland, though clearly not by the tenants. Parnell, for example, was voicing a widely held opinion when he declared that the act would 'practically speaking ... affect but a very small proportion of the rents in Ireland. It would leave the great majority of them untouched.'[114] This was the view especially of the majority of the leading proprietors in the north who had always maintained that their rents were moderately set. The Liberal landlord Hugh Montgomery deplored the fact that 'thoughtless persons should have prepared disappointment for many tenant-farmers by leading them to expect reductions of rent such as neither landlords nor legislation can possibly give them', while the *News Letter* observed that 'people must be extremely credulous if they fancy that the result of the new law will be a general reduction of rents'.[115] In fact, Ulster landlords did not expect the act to bring about any radical change in landlord–tenant relations in Ulster in the matter of rents or anything else: 'We are confident that Ulster will not give very much employment to the land court, and that as regards most of the large properties little or no change will be perceptible'.[116]

The Ulster Tories did not of course give an unqualified welcome to the bill. It was, they thought, complex and involved, 'in many respects an unjust measure as regards the landlords of Ireland ... especially the landlords of the south and west'.[117] But they wanted the bill to pass, and thirteen of the eighteen Ulster Tory MPs voted for the second reading with only one — Cole of Enniskillen — opposing.[118] If, however, they supported the second reading, they were also anxious to have the bill amended and simplified in committee. They were particularly concerned about the rent-fixing clause — 'so far as Ulster is concerned, it is beyond all doubt the cardinal section of the bill'[119] — about the constitution of the new court and the powers being given to the assistant commissioners, and about the fact that the court was closed to the landlord except with the consent of the tenant.[120]

Generally, they were anxious to safeguard landlord interests and limit the application of the bill, especially in the south — i.e. in the non-tenant-right provinces — where it represented a much more serious encroachment on landlord interests than it did in Ulster. Their policy was essentially one of supporting the legalisation of existing practices whether north or south and of resisting innovations which they believed to be contrary to landlord interests. But even in the latter case they were reluctant to push their resistance to the point where it would either delay or jeopardise the bill. Thus, despite their reservations about the bill and despite supporting a series of amendments against the government during the committee stage, their tactics were never wilfully obstructive, and they gave a steady support to the measure at its most crucial stages and in all its leading provisions. Their importance, however, lay less in the votes they registered than in the debilitating influence they had on the opposition of other sections of the Tory party to the bill.

The main Irish opponents of the bill were the Conservatives in the south. Of the seven Tory MPs returned for southern constituencies, six voted against the second reading, and this opposition continued during the committee stage and later in the House of Lords where southern interests were more strongly represented. The southern landlords were not totally opposed to reform. Although the Irish Land Committee had publicly adopted a hardline attitude, deprecating in particular all proposals for the 3Fs,[121] Irish landlords were, as Cairns informed Beaconsfield in December, prepared 'to accept any bill, not altogether unreasonable, rather than let the relations of landlord and tenant continue as they are'.[122] However, the bill introduced by Gladstone went well beyond what they had been prepared to accept. For them it was a much more radical break with past practices than it was for the Ulster landlords, a much more serious infraction of proprietorial rights, transferring, as they saw it, the property of the landlord to the tenant 'without giving the former a single farthing of compensation'.[123] It was, they claimed, 'a measure of confiscation, pure and simple', which would 'materially lower rents', 'lead to a large diminution in the value of every estate in Ireland', and convert landlords into 'mere rent-chargers — bailiffs for the recovery of rents and nothing more'.[124]

Southern landlords had a great deal more to lose than those in the north,[125] and many of them felt that their position had been compromised by the northern Conservatives who, because of their greater numbers, tended to be regarded in the commons as the main representatives of Irish Conservative opinion.[126] In the months preceding the introduction of the bill, while the predominantly southern Irish Land Committee was issuing pamphlets defending the landlords' position and opposing all proposals for change, the northern Conservatives and Orangemen were lending their weight to the campaign for reform, creating the impression, as the Earl of Donoughmore complained to Beaconsfield, 'that there is a pretty general consensus of opinion in Ireland for reform in the direction of the 3Fs'; 'this', he assured the Conservative leader, 'is certainly not the case'.[127] These divisions continued after the details of the bill were announced, with Colonel A.L. Tottenham, the Tory MP for Co.

Leitrim, bitterly accusing the Ulster landlords of being 'unable to look beyond their own selfish interests'.[128]

But, fiercely critical of the bill as they were, the southern Conservatives quickly realised, once the terms had been announced and especially after it had passed its second reading with northern Conservative support, that no more moderate bill would ever again be accepted by the Irish tenants. Thereafter, while still openly opposing the bill, they directed their main efforts to securing its amendment and, in particular, to arguing a case for both compensation and greater opportunities for the sale of estates.[129] In the final analysis, the southern Conservatives were more fearful of the consequences of defeating the bill than of it being passed. As the Marquis of Lansdowne, one of the most vehement critics of the bill, warned the lords:

> Its rejection would be the signal for the recrudescence of the conflict already raging there [in Ireland]; during the coming autumn and winter we should have to deal with anarchy and terrorism worse than those which have already made Ireland a bye-word ... These conditions could only have one result — they would lead to a renewal of the proposals now made to us in a probably more extreme and violent shape.[130]

The most determined opposition to the bill came from the English Conservatives, who regarded it as a threat not only to Irish landed property but to property rights in general. Despite earlier — and in some quarters of the party continuing — opposition to tenant purchase, the Tories had come round to the view that a moderate extension of the purchase clauses of the act of 1870 might provide the main solution to the problem, and the heads of such a bill had been drawn up and circulated in the cabinet before they left office in 1880.[131] But they were determined to resist any proposals which threatened in any way the fundamental rights of property. Hence they had, with the full support of the Irish Conservatives, vigorously opposed and finally rejected (through their control of the House of Lords) the compensation for disturbance bill of 1880, Beaconsfield seeing this 'as not merely an Irish measure but as the opening of a great attack on the land'.[132] The land bill of 1881 was regarded as a greater danger still. Northcote expressed the fear that they were 'being silently but rapidly drawn into the jaws of a whirlpool, which will engulf English as well as Irish landed property, and may probably not be satisfied with landed property alone'.[133] The Conservatives, in fact, wanted to defeat the bill for English rather than Irish reasons, and the English agricultural and property journal *Land* correctly identified the main threat to the bill as the 'English predilection for free contract and territorial privilege'.[134]

But in order to defeat the bill the Conservative leaders needed the full support of the Irish landlords. In the months leading up to its introduction they were anxious to prevent 'any appearance of disunion' and to discourage proposals being made on the Conservative side which, they feared, 'would simply be taken [by the government] as a point of departure'.[135] This whole strategy, however, was sabotaged by Ulster's support for the 3Fs. As Salisbury wrote to Beaconsfield:

> Ulster has surrendered to the three 3Fs and with Ulster doubtless will go Gibson, Cairns and Richmond — and a good number of our peers ... Bad for us, and bad for them! They have sacrificed every vestige of principle on which they can fight for proprietary rights: and we are left with the choice of giving in, or else of being *Hibernis Hiberniores*.[136]

The Ulstermen had, Beaconsfield agreed, 'sold the pass', and (as Beaconsfield and Salisbury expected and as Northcote predicted) the tactics of the Ulster party continued to vitiate Conservative opposition 'not only in the first division but throughout the conduct of the bill'.[137]

The Conservative party had, of course, the power to stop the bill in the House of Lords, but with the Conservative ranks divided there could be no question of rejecting it outright as had been done with the compensation bill. The English Conservatives could not take it on themselves to defeat a measure which, whatever its implications for landed property in Britain, was of most direct concern to Ireland and which all parties in Ireland now wanted to see passed. Salisbury, for reasons of his own — which had more to do at this stage with the leadership of the Conservative party than with the interests of Irish landlords — still wanted to provoke a confrontation between the two houses of parliament by insisting on a number of drastic amendments. But the other Conservative peers were increasingly uneasy and anxious for an arrangement with the government, especially after Gibson, who had been closely consulted by the party leaders throughout the crisis, 'strongly and plainly' told them at a private meeting on 13 August that 'the loss of the bill would by almost every rational man in Ireland be regarded as unmixed calamity'; 'it would', he warned, 'lead to a saturnalia of outrage'.[138] The Irish Land Committee, which had earlier encouraged and advised Salisbury on his amendments, also informed him at this time that they saw 'no advantage in further disputing the provisions of the bill'.[139] In these circumstances, therefore, Salisbury agreed to a compromise so that the bill finally went through in a shape not vastly different from that originally introduced by Gladstone. Sir Stafford Northcote, looking back on the events of the previous months, placed responsibility for the Conservative failure to defeat the bill squarely on the shoulders of the Ulster Conservatives, maintaining that it was impossible for his party to take decisive action against it 'in the face of their determination to pass the measure'.[140]

10
# The Land Act of 1881

Complex, confused and confusing though the land act of 1881 was, it contained in substance the three major principles for which the Ulster Liberals and tenant-righters had so long contended.[1]

The act empowered the tenant to sell his tenancy for the best price he could get subject to certain statutory conditions. These were that — the sale was to one person only except with the landlord's consent; the landlord was to have the option of buying in the tenancy at an agreed price or in the case of disagreement at a valuation settled by the court; the landlord could refuse to accept the purchaser on reasonable grounds, any dispute arising therefrom being left to the decision of the court; and the landlord was to recover from the purchase money any debts or arrears of rent or otherwise. Ulster tenants had the option of selling under this section of the act or according to the Ulster custom, but all tenants who exercised their right of sale — under either this section or the Ulster custom — were not entitled to compensation for disturbance or improvements, nor could tenants who received compensation for these afterwards sell their interest in their holdings.[2]

Fair rents were to be secured by the establishment of a judicial tribunal which, on application by the tenant or by the landlord or by the two jointly, would fix rents, which would stand for a period of fifteen years and would then become subject to revision by the tribunal.

Applications to fix rents could be made to either the county courts or the newly constituted land commission. No definition of a fair rent was attempted by the act, although it was stipulated — by the so-called Healy clause[3] — that no rent should be made payable in respect of any improvements carried out by the tenant or his predecessors in title. An an alternative to applying to the court to settle the rent, rents could be fixed outside the court by agreement between the landlord and the tenant and then registered with the court, again remaining valid for fifteen years. Where a tenant was faced with a demand for an increase in rent he could, instead of applying to the tribunal to have the rent fixed, either sell his tenancy, recovering from the landlord the amount by which the selling value was deemed by the court to have been depreciated by the demanded increase, or, if he refused to sell his tenancy and was evicted, claim compensation for disturbance.

Fixity of tenure was also conceded provided the tenant complied with certain conditions. These were that he paid his rent at the appointed time, that he did not subdivide or sublet without the consent of the landlord or cause persistent waste and dilapidation, and that he permitted the landlord entry to the holding to quarry, mine, make roads and drains, cut timber and turf, and hunt game. Some modest encouragement was also given to tenant purchase. Whereas the act of 1870 had authorised the Board of Works to advance up to two-thirds of the purchase money, this act allowed the land commission to advance three-quarters of the money which was to be repaid on the same terms as in 1870, i.e. at 5 per cent interest over thirty-five years. But purchase was clearly not seen by Gladstone as having a major part to play in the settlement of the question, and in the event only 731 tenants purchased under these provisions.[4] Other clauses authorised the advance of loans for reclamation, tenant improvements and emigration, but these were all equally ineffective.

These then were the main terms of the act. It has sometimes been assumed that its provisions entirely superseded the tenant-right custom, but this was not the case. Tenant-right continued to be sold after 1881, and tenants holding under the custom continued to enjoy advantages over and above those conceded to all tenants by the act.

First, holdings sold under the Ulster custom were not subject, as were other holdings, to the right of pre-emption by the landlord at a price fixed by the court; rather the landlord had to pay the full market value unless the custom on the particular estate provided otherwise. Again, whereas a tenant who was obliged to quit his holding during the statutory term in consequence of a breach of any of the conditions laid down by the act forfeited his right to compensation for disturbance, a tenant holding under the Ulster custom was entitled to full benefit of custom notwithstanding the breach of statutory conditions.[5] Later, too, when the *Adams v. Dunseath* case in 1882 virtually nullified the Healy clause as far as ordinary tenants were concerned, tenants holding under the Ulster custom were specifically exempted from the ruling.[6]

If, however, Ulster tenants still had special advantages under the act, some tenants — for example, leaseholders, 'future' tenants (i.e. holders of tenancies created after 1 January 1883), tenants of demesne lands and townparks, and tenants of grazing farms let at £50 and over — were excluded altogether from its benefits. Of these the most important numerically were the leaseholders, numbering some 135,000.[7] A clause was included which enabled the court on application by the tenant to set aside any lease which the landlord had unfairly imposed since 1870, but this proved to be practically a dead letter; only 138 leases in the whole of Ireland were revoked under it and only two of these were in Ulster.[8] In fact this was only one of many such clauses in an act which turned out to all intents and purposes to be primarily and almost entirely an act for fixing rents.

THE WORKING OF THE ACT

In contrast to its equivocal reception in the south, the land act of 1881 was extremely well received in Ulster. The original bill had been welcomed by the northern tenant-right movement in April as 'a great and statesmanlike measure', 'the greatest of all his [Gladstone's] great achievements'; it required some amendment in its details, of course, but the general feeling was that 'taking it all in all, it is the best measure which has yet been submitted to the British legislature on the Irish land question'.[9] There was some disappointment when Gladstone abandoned his attempt to include a definition of a fair rent in the bill,[10] but against this there was the positive gain of the Healy clause which specifically protected tenant improvements. Northern opinion was also roused to fever pitch by the attempts of the lords to emasculate the bill, but the bill when it was finally passed was universally regarded by the Ulster tenants as a major, in some respects even an unexpected, boon. 'I confess', wrote the secretary of one tenant-right association, 'that I never expected to get from any parliament so good a measure. It does give us all honest and practical Ulster men have ever asked for. It does give us, in fact if not in form, the three Fs.'[11]

If the landed Conservatives expected the act to be largely inoperative in Ulster, they were to be quickly and sadly disillusioned. Such indeed was the response that Davitt, William O'Brien and other nationalist politicians bitterly accused the northern tenants of defeating Parnell's policy of testing the act by rushing into the courts: 'That hardfisted body of men having done nothing themselves to win the act, thought of nothing but turning it to their own immediate use and repudiating any solidarity with the southern and western rebels to whom they really owed it'.[12] Certainly, once the bill became law, the Ulster tenants and tenant-right associations immediately began preparing to take advantage of it, and at the end of October — some four weeks after the court had opened — the *News Letter* remarked that 'the tenants are flocking into the land law court with a vengeance'; 'the process, in fact, of instituting a proceeding in the court "to fix a fair rent", as it is called, is so simple and so economical that every tenant is induced to try his chance'.[13]

The usual practice was for tenants on an estate or part of an estate to act together,[14] first of all approaching the landlord for a reduction and, if this was refused, contributing to a central fund and employing a solicitor to act on their behalf; the tenants on the Broadisland estate of George McAuliffe, for example, met as soon as the land court began to receive applications, memorialised their landlord for 'a substantial and permanent reduction' of rent and, when this was refused, decided to go into court as a body, each tenant paying six pence in the pound on his poor law valuation towards the legal expenses.[15] On other estates individual tenants or small numbers of tenants went forward in what were in effect, if not always in intention, test cases which were closely watched by landlords and tenants alike.[16] Often, where some originating notices had been served on an estate, the majority of tenants either voluntarily held back or were persuaded to hold back to see if the first judicial decisions provided a satisfactory basis for agreement. Towards the end of November, for example, only sixteen notices to fix rent had been served on Hugh Montgomery's estates: 'the rest of those who think they should get reductions (and I fear there are many)', wrote Montgomery, 'have agreed to wait six months or so on the chance of my being able to make them an acceptable offer when the commissioners have, by settling cases we know about, shown us what they mean by *a fair rent*'.[17] The huge majority of tenants were not in fact so foolish as to rush headlong into court until they were convinced that they had something to gain, and advice to tenants to test the act whether it came from Parnell or anyone else was really superfluous. 'All the tenants in Ireland are anxiously watching the proceedings in the new court', James Crossle informed Verner in October, 'and if there is anything to be gained they will *all* take advantage of it.'[18]

In the event, the first cases in Ulster resulted in reductions of 28–30 per cent and precipitated a spate of applications to the court.[19] By the end of December 62,331 originating notices had been received by the land commission, and 29,392 of these had come from Ulster (though it should be noted in relation to Davitt's criticism that a proportionately higher number had been served in Connacht),[20] while rents were being reduced on average by over 20 per cent and in exceptional cases by as much as 40 and 50 per cent and sometimes more.[21]

The Ulster landlords were naturally perturbed by these developments, but their response varied. Some, such as Sir William Lenox-Conyngham of Springhill in Derry, J. Leslie Beers of Coleraine, the Drapers' Company and the trustees of the Londonderry estate at Cloughmills, quickly arrived at amicable settlements with their tenants out of court.[22] In one or two instances landlords actually welcomed the prospect of rents being fixed by an independent body; the view of the Musgrave brothers, owners of the Kilcar and Glencolumbkille estates in Donegal, was that the land court relieved them 'from what we have always felt to be an invidious and disagreeable duty', while the Earl of Charlemont looked forward to having his rents raised under the new arrangements.[23] John Hamilton of St Ernan's estate in Donegal, believing that his rents were already low, refused to make any voluntary reduction, but philosophically accepted both that his tenants would use the land court and that the court would reduce his rents.[24] The majority of landlords, however, including many who had earlier been confident that they could stand over their rents and had therefore initially rejected tenant petitions, were increasingly anxious for a settlement out of court. But with tenant expectations raised by the early judicial decisions, such settlements were not easily arrived at.[25] James Crossle, for example, was prepared to offer tenants on Verner's Monaghan and Tyrone estates 20 and 15 per cent respectively, but found them determined to hold out for their original demands of 25 and 20 per cent. As it happened, agreements were reached on the Verner estates only after a number of holdings had had their rents fixed in court (the settlement conceded nearly the full amount demanded by the tenants), and this was the experience on other estates as well.[26]

Frequently landlords appealed these decisions not merely because they thought they were unfair (though they generally believed they were), but more because of their bearing on other rents and, as Annesley put it, 'in order to have an effect on other tenants'.[27] Crossle, reeling from the shock of the first judgments on the Verner estate in Tyrone, reluctantly decided to appeal: 'We have lodged appeals in all the late cases but three. The decisions are monstrous and if we could change some of them it would help to bring about a settlement with the others.'[28] Few were in any doubt as to the significance of the first appeal on Sir Richard Wallace's estate; it was, said the *News Letter*, 'considered generally to be a test case on the Lisburn estate, upon which there are 4,000 tenants'.[29] And the success which Wallace had in the case in virtually halving the reduction made by the sub-commissioners — from 19 per cent and 11 per cent — clearly made the exercise well worthwhile from his point of view.

But appeals generally were expensive — especially from September 1882 when it was decided that the full costs would have to be borne by the unsuccessful appellant — and the results disappointing. In the huge majority of cases the chief commissioners confirmed the rents fixed by the sub-commissioners, and where rents were changed the changes were minimal. To take one example: of eighty-two decisions appealed in Co. Down up to April 1882 (out of a total of 419 decisions given) the judicial rents fixed by the sub-commissioners were affirmed in seventy-five cases, and the total increase in the remaining seven cases represented an increase of 1 per cent on the gross judicial rent appealed from.[30] Landlords continued to appeal decisions — and more in Ulster than in the rest of the country[31] — but generally the rents fixed by the sub-commissions stood the test, and the proportion of judicial decisions appealed dropped from 38 per cent in 1881–2 to 27.5 per cent in 1882–3.[32]

In fact, landlords were best advised to avoid the courts altogether. Apart from the fact that litigation was damaging to landlord–tenant relations — still not an unimportant consideration from the point of view of most of the larger landlords[33] — it could also be extremely expensive. The Cairns committee — a House of Lords committee appointed in 1882 to investigate the administration of the act — estimated that the cost of each case to the landlord was between £10 and £15, and where an estate was divided into small tenancies the costs for the landlord could clearly amount to a very large, perhaps a prohibitive, sum.[34] Anyway, settlements out of court were on average lower (see Table 10.3), although this was at least partly because agreements were most likely to be reached on estates where landlord–tenant relations were good and rents moderate. And attempts to settle by agreement were not by any means unsuccessful. One useful lever which landlords had in this respect was the tremendous delay in court proceedings — bitterly complained about by tenants and tenant associations — and in the first year of the act's operation 4,060 agreements to fix fair rents were made in Ulster as against 4,883 cases settled by the sub-commissions (see Table 10.1).

Once the general level of judicial rents had been established and once more cases had been decided on particular estates, it was easier for both sides to come to an arrangement so that the number of rents fixed out of court increased dramatically in 1882–3, and continued to be the single most important method of settling judicial rents in succeeding years, as Table 10.1 illustrates.

Table 10.1. The number of originating notices to fix fair rents, the number of judicial rents fixed by the sub-commissioners and the number fixed by agreement in Ulster each year
August 1881–August 1885[35]

|  | 1881–2 | 1882–3 | 1883–4 | 1884–5 |
| --- | --- | --- | --- | --- |
| Originating notices | 32,485 | 5,994 | 7,010 | 2,156 |
| Sub-commission decisions | 4,883 | 13,762 | 12,393 | 2,809 |
| Agreements | 4,060 | 19,733 | 13,346 | 6,720 |

By August 1885, over 43,000 rents had been fixed in Ulster by agreement between landlord and tenant as against some 33,000 by the sub-commissioners. The fact that 56 per cent of the total number of agreements lodged with the land commission during this four-year period were from Ulster, whereas only 44 per cent of the total number of rents fixed by the land tribunals during the same period were in the northern province, suggests that Ulster landlords were much more successful in arriving at out of court settlements with their tenants than landlords in the three southern provinces.

Nevertheless, Ulster tenants continued for a time at any rate to serve originating notices in their thousands and continued too, despite the blandishments of the landlords and the Tory press,[36] to make extensive use of the rent fixing tribunals. As well as the rents fixed by the sub-commissions and by agreement, a limited number were also fixed by the civil bill courts and from May 1882 by valuers specially appointed by the land commission upon application by landlords and tenants. By August 1885, 48 per cent of all occupiers of holdings of five acres and over had had judicial rents fixed under the act as compared with 36 per cent of all occupiers of over five acres in

Ireland as a whole. Clearly Ulster tenants did make greater use of the act than those in the rest of the country. Perhaps surprisingly — and significantly, considering the criticisms of the sub-commissioners' decisions — the largest percentage reductions were those given by the civil bill courts as shown in Table 10.2, which summarises the operation of the act in Ulster.

Table 10.2. Judicial rents fixed in Ulster under the 1881
land act, August 1881–August 1885[37]

| | NO. OF CASES | TENEMENT VALUATION | FORMER RENT | JUDICIAL RENT | % REDUCTION |
|---|---|---|---|---|---|
| Sub-commissions | 33,848 | 470,267 | 568,080 | 450,381 | 20.7 |
| Civil bill courts | 1,561 | 18,621 | 23,928 | 18,762 | 21.6 |
| Agreements | 43,858 | 599,905 | 634,091 | 529,798 | 16.4 |
| Appointed valuers | 137 | 1,484 | 1,623 | 1,550 | 4.5 |

Over the same period, rents were reduced on average by 18.5 per cent — the average for Ireland was 18.2 per cent — the largest reductions coming in the first year of the act's operation as shown in Table 10.3.

Table 10.3. Average annual percentage rent reductions made in
Ulster under the 1881 land act, August 1881–August 1885.[38]

| | SUB-COMMISSIONS | AGREEMENTS | CIVIL BILL COURTS |
|---|---|---|---|
| 1881–2 | 22.6 | 18.0 | 22.8 |
| 1882–3 | 20.8 | 17.5 | 20.5 |
| 1883–4 | 20.3 | 15.5 | 22.1 |
| 1884–5 | 16.8 | 13.9 | 19.4 |

It had been suggested that elsewhere the decisions of the sub-commissioners were determined to a large extent by 'the varying intensity of the agrarian agitation', and that this explains the higher percentage reductions in 1881 and 1882.[39] But this was scarcely the case in Ulster, where much of the agitation died down after the act was passed and where the reductions were greater than those in the south. No doubt the decisions of 1881–2 were influenced to some extent by tenant expectations and local pressures, while those of 1883–5 reflected the gradual improvement in agricultural conditions. But the downward trend in the figures is also explained by the fact that it was generally those tenants with the most acute grievances who first took advantage of the act. 'We must not jump too hastily to conclusions about the sub-commissioners', Forster advised Hartington at the end of November, 'No cases were *selected* by the Commissioners, up to now they have been taken in the order of application, but naturally the hard cases were the first applications. So far as I can learn the justice of the actual decisions has been more impugned at a distance than in the locality.'[40] Generally, in fact, it was the smaller and more oppressive landlords — many of whom, the *Northern Whig* maintained, had purchased their estates in the landed estates court — who were early forced into court, with the larger estates, up to 1882 at any rate, 'almost untouched by the measure'.[41]

Where such cases did come before the tribunals, the reductions were frequently well below the average. The average reduction made by the sub-commissioners on Sir Thomas Bateson's Co. Down estate and on the Earl of Enniskillen's estate at Clones, Co. Monaghan was under 10 per cent, on the Massereene and O'Neill estates in Antrim under 15 per cent, on the Abercorn estate in Tyrone 12 per cent, and on the Londonderry estate in Fermanagh 9 per cent.[42] The Co. Down sub-commission set judicial rents in a number of cases from the estates of the Earl of Antrim, John Mulholland MP, Lord Bangor, R.P. Maxwell DL and R.E. Ward DL at levels 'not very much below the old rents'.[43] There were exceptions of course — Sir Hervey Bruce, for example, had his rents reduced by over 28 per cent, the Earl of Arran by 30 per cent and Lord Gosford by 23 per cent[44] — but, generally, the hearings in the first year or so of the act's operation confirmed the common belief that the smaller landlords and the purchasers in the landed estates court had been more exacting in their relations with their tenantry,[45] and the older landlords generally emerged from the courts with more of their credit and more of their rental intact.

Nevertheless, the early decisions of the sub-commissioners came as a great shock to all landlords. They had, they claimed, been hoodwinked by government spokesmen who had presented the land bill to parliament 'as a measure designed to apply only to a small section of Irish proprietors and not ... to the great majority of the landlords against whom no charge of exacting, harsh or excessive rents was attempted to be advanced'.[46] Yet all estates, they argued, were being subjected to sweeping and confiscatory reductions of rent on the basis of cursory surveys by sub-commissioners, 'the majority of whom have no practical acquaintance with the value of land and ... [whose] only qualification seems to be a downright hostility to the landed interest, and the most glaring partiality towards the tenants'.[47] A landlord conference held in Dublin in January and well attended by northern representatives fiercely denounced the administration of the act, although they went to some pains to point out that they were not opposed to the act itself.[48] Their main objections were that the act was being administered otherwise than the government had led them to expect, that decisions were being given on the basis of no apparent rule or principle, that 'despotic power over the whole landed property of Ireland' had been handed over to tribunals of 'untrained, underpaid men', and that these tribunals were indiscriminately reducing rents which in many cases had not been raised for twenty or thirty years or more.[49] This campaign of abuse against the sub-commissioners was vigorously carried on in private correspondence, in the press and in parliament, and culminated in the appointment of a select committee by the House of Lords (the Cairns committee) to investigate the administration of the act. The purpose of the campaign was plainly twofold: first, to influence if not to intimidate the sub-commissioners; and second, to lay the foundation for a claim to compensation.[50]

Yet much of the criticism was unfounded, and the case for compensation was unconvincing to politicians in England where the *Mark Lane Express*, on the basis of returns from sixteen different counties, estimated that the rents of new lettings were 30 per cent down on what they had been a decade before.[51] 'It seems too much forgotten', said the English agricultural journal *Land*, 'that even in England, where there has been no Land League agitation, from the sheer force of circumstances a reduction of rental, not so very different, has had to be very largely submitted to by landlords.'[52] The reductions in Ireland, in fact, were not nearly as outrageous as the landowners claimed. Charles Russell told the House of Commons that 'he was not aware of one single instance in which rent had been reduced in which the landlord had been able to produce any witnesses to justify the existing rents'.[53] In a number of cases — as, for example, in seventeen cases on the estate of John McEldowney near Ballycastle and in fifteen cases on the estate of Colonel Hannay outside Bushmills — no defence at all was put up by the landlords.[54] Giving decisions in thirty-six such cases from several estates around Portadown, in most of which it was admitted that a valuation had been made on the landlord's behalf, the chairman of the Armagh sub-commission stated that the obvious inference was that 'had the valuator been produced as a witness his testimony would have proved adverse to his employer's case'.[55]

In other cases, the landlords' valuers gave estimates which admitted the excessive nature of existing rents and which at times were not markedly different from the judicial rents fixed by the tribunal. In several cases on the estate of Margaret McCaw outside Portadown, where the sub-commissioners reduced the rents by 25.2 per cent, the landlady's own valuer's estimate of a fair rent on the estate was 22.7 per cent under the existing rent.[56] A valuer produced on behalf of the Biggar estate in Antrim — where the rents were reduced by 39 per cent — admitted that he could not defend the existing rents and suggested that they should be reduced by 16 per cent.[57] On the Biggar estate and many others, which were reported at this time in the press, rents had clearly been screwed up since their purchase in the landed estates court. On Major George Gray's estate in Antrim, where rents had been increased by 84 per cent since the time of purchase in 1850, the agent admitted that no money had ever been expended by the landlord on the estate and that it was only their income from handloom weaving which enabled the tenants to pay their rents.[58] On the Tyrone estate of Mrs Catherine Stewart, whose rents had been increased by about 20 per cent in 1874 (reduced by 20.5 per cent by the sub-commissioners), the valuer on the basis of whose valuation the increase had been made admitted that it had included tenant improvements.[59]

Numerous other such examples can be given, but the point is that the sub-commissioners did not act as recklessly or as unjustly as the landlords claimed, or as some historians would have us believe. Thomas Baldwin, an assistant commissioner with the Richmond commission, who had been extremely sceptical of tenant complaints up to 1881, told the Cairns committee that he was surprised by the amount of rack-renting he encountered as a sub-commissioner under the land act, while the *Northern Whig* observed in February 1882 that the tribunals had shown that rack-renting existed in Ulster 'to an extent never suspected by the most earnest and best informed advocates of the cause of the tenant farmers'.[60] Contrary to what the landlords claimed, many of the most sweeping reductions of rent were well-founded. Hugh Montgomery was critical of some of the decisions of the sub-commissioners, but thought that 'on the whole the confiscatory nature of their proceedings has been grossly exaggerated. The only cases settled yet about which I know anything ... do not strike me as unreasonable.'[61] Lord Waveney likewise maintained that the early decisions in Antrim were justified, while James Richardson told the House of Commons that 'he had taken considerable pains to visit many farms in Down, Armagh and Antrim, and he had been accompanied by a landstewart of great experience, and they were driven to the conclusion that where there had been a considerable reduction of rent it was perfectly justifiable'.[62] Even the Tory *Coleraine Constitution*, after persistently attacking the sub-commissioners for the better part of a year, admitted at the end of 1882 that 'in the majority of cases' they were discharging 'a difficult and embarrassing duty ... with impartiality', while *Land,* another early critic of the sub-commissioners, had by 1883 come round to the view that, allowing for certain vagaries in some of their decisions, 'the act has been carried into effect in a most satisfactory manner'.[63]

No doubt injustices were done to landlords and no doubt also to tenants, but the evidence was that the sub-commissions did their work in 'an honest, painstaking and skilful manner'.[64] Their decisions were, as we have seen, largely ratified by the chief commissioners whose integrity no one ventured to question, and were very much in line with those of the county chairmen who were generally reputed to be closely identified with the landed classes (see Table 10.3). The fact was that in a period of drastic deflation, with agricultural prices and tenant incomes in a process of near continuous decline, the land tribunals — and the other methods of fixing rents under the act — provided a mechanism by which landed income could be adjusted to the new economic circumstances in the way that it was being adjusted by market forces in England.[65] Although the act worked out in a way that Gladstone had never expected, he denied in 1883 that it had been in any way destructive of the property of Irish landlords:

> My belief is that we have been saving it ... and that the resulting reduction of rents has on the whole quite fairly corresponded with the general value of land at the present time, and with the tendency to excess of rent which has in many cases been incidental to the peculiar state of Ireland.[66]

Nevertheless, whether justified or not, the judicial decisions represented a reduction in gross income for many landlords of over 20 per cent and a reduction in net income — allowing for charges on estates — of considerably more than this. Land — for the majority of the larger owners at any rate — had rarely been seen as a purely economic investment, but this was a serious loss by any standards; for most it meant severe retrenchment and for some, coming as it did on top of the financial difficulties of the previous three years, it meant total ruin.[67] Moreover, landlords were faced at the same time with a serious deterioration in the capital value of their estates. The stagnation in the Irish land market was not a direct result of the land act — land sales and prices had fallen steeply since 1878 — but many landlords had hoped that the act, by settling tenant grievances and providing better facilities for tenant purchase, would result in an upturn in the market.[68] Not only did sales not pick up after 1881, but the judicial decisions clearly had a direct effect on the capital value of estates, depressing prices still further. Indeed, *Land* maintained that 'the depreciation in the selling value of land is altogether out of proportion to the reduction of rental'. *Land* attributed this to apprehension and uncertainty as to what would happen in the future: 'It is the sense of insecurity which is at the bottom of reluctance to buy. There has grown up a feeling that after so much has been conceded to agitation, more may be expected to follow, and that the man who has money had better do almost anything else with it than put it into Irish land.'[69]

No doubt there was a great deal of truth in this analysis of the situation, but there was another factor and that was that land had lost much of its social as well as its economic attractiveness for investors. What the land act had done was not only reduce landed income, but simultaneously carry the collapse of the old rural social structure a stage further by limiting landlord powers and removing much of the social influence that had gone with land ownership. Several witnesses complained to the Cairns committee in 1882 that the demeanour of tenants towards their landlords was altogether changed. The *Northern Whig* also claimed that the act had destroyed the landlords' social influence over the tenants in the same way that the ballot act had destroyed their political power, while James Shanks' biographer noted that it 'had given to the farmers a feeling of freedom and independence which they had never before enjoyed'; or, as Charles Russell put it, the act enabled the tenants 'to stand up like men before their landlords'.[70]

But if the attitude of the tenants toward their landlords changed, so too did that of the landlords towards their tenants. Landlords had already in 1880–1 been inclined to show less indulgence to tenants in the matters of abatements and arrears and now, with their powers curtailed by the land act and with their rental reduced by the sub-commissioners, they showed an even greater determination to stand on their remaining rights and exact all that was due to them. The instructions of the Earl of Annesley to his agent were both explicit and revealing:

> Your business is to fight my former tenants, but present enemies, by every means in your power, assisted by my lawyer ... I shall not be satisfied until legal steps have been taken against every defaulter on the Down estate, and in future this will be done as a mere matter of business, and a matter of course. The days of sentiment are in my opinion past.[71]

The situation was not quite as bad as Annesley painted it,[72] but clearly many landlords were deeply resentful of what they saw as base ingratitude and disloyalty on the part of their tenants who had rushed into the courts at the first opportunity. They were, therefore, less inclined to make the allowances they had in the past and more inclined to make early resort to legal proceedings against tenants in arrears. Not only were more proceedings taken in 1882 against tenants on the Verner estates than ever before — more, Crossle told Lady Verner, than 'during all my life time put together' — but they were taken at the March sessions rather than being delayed, as had been the normal practice on the estate, until the sessions in June.[73] The number of evictions on the estate was also unprecedented — a greater number, said Crossle, 'than during the last fifty years all put together' — and would indeed have been higher only the solicitors warned Crossle that such a policy 'would seriously injure the landlord in the pending trials in the land commission court'.[74]

The Verner estates were by no means exceptional in this respect. There were more evictions in Ulster in the twelve months following the opening of the land tribunals — from October 1881 to September 1882 — than in the previous twelve month period (1,308 as against 1,048), more indeed than in any single year since 1851.[75] Equally significantly, the percentage of readmissions both as caretakers and as tenants was down, from a combined total percentage of 66 per cent in the twelve months prior to the act to under 54 per cent in the twelve months after.[76] Although evictions dropped to a lower level in 1883, there were still four times as many as in 1879 and nearly six times as many as the annual average for 1870–8.[77]

Landlords were under greater financial pressure after 1881, and this helps to explain the more widespread use of legal action against defaulting tenants. But it was not only this. They also clearly believed that the 1881 act had relieved them of much of their social responsibility towards their tenants, and this was seen too in their withdrawal of various social contributions after the act was passed. Verner, for example, reduced his annual donations to orphan societies from £5 to £3 3s and totally cut off his subscriptions to schools outside his estate and to several other charities.[78] The factors which prompted these decisions were both economic and social. Sending a cheque for £2 for the teacher of Clonmaine school, Crossle instructed the Rev. James Towers to 'tell him this is the last donation he is to receive from Sir William Verner in consequence of the great reduction in his rents'.[79] And to the Rev. Thomas Stokes he wrote:

> I regret to say Sir William Verner has withdrawn his subscriptions from the Aughnacloy Fever Hospital ... I find now that he considers he has been so badly treated by his tenantry that he does not feel himself bound to continue subscriptions for their benefit. Now that they are so independent of their landlords, they may subscribe to their own charities.[80]

What landlords were doing after 1881 was not only practising retrenchment, but redefining their social role. Landownership in fact no longer had the same economic attractions nor the same social advantages, and conversely, from the landlords' point of view, no longer carried the same social responsibilities. Moreover, there was also and always the fear of further agitation and concessions or, as James Pomeroy put it, 'the certainty that nothing will be considered a final settlement which is really *most depressing*'.[81] Once it became clear, therefore, that compensation for landlord losses was not forthcoming,[82] a growing number of landlords began to feel that their best solution was to sell out, and landed spokesmen concentrated their efforts on securing greater facilities for tenant purchase. This, it was hoped, would have two effects. First, it would help to avert further agitation by increasing the number of tenant proprietors, thereby strengthening the whole institution of property.[83] And second, such a policy would, it was believed, relieve the deadlock in the Irish land market and allow the landlords a way out of their difficulties; or, as one cynical leader writer in England put it, 'there is "no market" and the British taxpayer is asked to pay for making one'.[84]

Thus one of the main resolutions passed at a meeting of Conservative landlords in Dublin in December 1881 urged the government to purchase at a fair price the properties of those landlords who wished to sell out, and this demand was reiterated during succeeding months by a number of leading Irish Conservative spokesmen.[85] Conservative support for tenant purchase was not new in itself — a number of Irish Tories had, as we have seen, argued for extended facilities during the land bill debates — but what was new was the growing consensus that the state should advance the whole of the purchase money to be repaid in yearly instalments lower than existing rents. This, it was increasingly believed, was what was needed to induce the tenants to purchase.[86]

These were the main recommendations put forward therefore in the first report of the lords' committee on the land act in April 1882.[87] A month earlier W.H. Smith, one of the Tory leaders in England, had given notice of a resolution to the same effect in the commons. Smith's action was supported by Salisbury and was clearly influenced as much by party expediency — it was in fact a scarcely disguised bid for Parnellite support — as by concern for the interests of Irish landlords,[88] but it marked the emergence of a new more constructive Conservative policy for Ireland, which led to the Ashbourne act of 1885 and which was eventually to culminate in the Wyndham act of 1903. Initially, however, the policy had a mixed reception among the members of Smith's own party and it was swiftly dropped after the Phoenix Park murders and the Kilmainham treaty.[89] But it re-emerged in 1883 when Lord George Hamilton, having consulted a number of leading Irish and Ulster landowners, put a similar proposal to the house which was accepted in principle by the government though not acted upon, and from this date land purchase virtually became the official Conservative remedy for the Irish land problem, and indeed for the Irish problem in general.[90]

TENANT DISSATISFACTION

If the landlords were unhappy about the administration of the land act, so too increasingly were the tenants, and analogous demands for a truly effective system of land purchase were being made by their spokesmen as well. Although the first decisions of the sub-commissioners in Ulster were generally 'regarded from the tenants' standpoint as satisfactory',[91] grievances soon began to emerge, and from December tenant meetings protesting against the administration of the act began to be held in different parts of the province. This renewed agitation was provoked at least partly by the landlord campaign against the rent tribunals, but the tenants also clearly believed that they themselves had genuine cause for complaint, though they continued to express approval of the act itself. One correspondent wrote in January 1882 that 'a deep and widely-spread spirit of dissatisfaction with the working of the land act pervades the entire north', while Charles Russell, making specific reference to the meetings in Ulster, warned Gladstone not 'to think that the administration of the act gives satisfaction. I believe that the tenant class are dissatisfied almost if not quite as much as the landlords.'[92]

Tenant criticisms focused mainly on two aspects of the act's administration. First, they complained that the sub-commissioners were not making sufficient allowance for tenant-right and tenant improvements, that the Healy clause was being ignored, and that the judicial rents were encroaching on the tenants' interests. The Route association, in a resolution typical of those being passed by tenant societies all over the province, stated their belief 'that the reductions of rent are not in complete conformity with the goodwill element of Ulster tenant-right and the Russell-Healy clause of the act'.[93] Thomas Dickson claimed — and this point was repeated time and time again by other tenant spokesmen — that the sub-commissioners were following too closely the government valuation (see Table 10.2), which not only included tenant improvements and buildings but was 20–25 per cent higher in Ulster than in the south and west.[94] Frequently it was pointed out that the sub-commissioners' reductions in Ireland were lower than those made by landlords in England, where the landlords carried out all the improvements themselves.[95]

Tenants were quick, too, to denounce the court of appeal's decision in the case of *Adams v. Dunseath* in February 1882, which appeared to nullify or at the very least seriously circumscribe the Healy clause by stating that the court in fixing a fair rent should take into account the length of time the tenant had 'enjoyed' the improvements made by him, and that the landlord was entitled to rent on the increased letting value of the land in so far as it was due to the qualities of the soil.[96] This judgment was held to be contrary to both the spirit of the act and the intentions of its authors,[97] but it did not in practice, as the Irish lord lieutenant Lord Spencer informed Gladstone in 1883, have any real influence on the later decisions of the courts.[98] It did not, at any rate, apply to holdings subject to the tenant-right custom (exemption from this was one of the additional privileges held by tenants under the Ulster custom after 1881).[99] Nevertheless, the decision caused a flurry of anxiety and alarm at the time — tenants were afraid that the sub-commissioners would be inadvertently influenced by the case — and added to the whole tenant chorus of censure against the administration of the act; as the chief commissioner Justice O'Hagan told Charles Russell, 'its mischief is less in any practical effect it has so far had than in the apprehension it has excited'.[100]

The second major tenant complaint about the administration of the act centred on the slow progress being made by the tribunals in fixing judicial rents. 'The great blot upon the act', Thomas Dickson told the commons, 'was the delay in its administration ... The great grievance to the tenants arose from the fact that during all the time they had to wait they were bound to pay what they called a rack-rent, and that the judicial rent did not date from the time of the originating notice.'[101] After three months' work the sub-commissioners had disposed of only 550 out of 70,000 cases, and the *News Letter* estimated that at their current rate of progress it would take them fifteen years to deal with all the applications.[102] At the beginning of March 1882, James Richardson pointed out to Forster that of nearly 5,000 originating notices in Armagh, only eighteen had been settled up to the end of January. In Derry only 100 out of 3,000 applications had been decided by April, only twenty-five out of 600 in the Route district by the end of February.[103] 'The machinery provided by the government for the administration of the act', concluded Samuel McElroy, 'is altogether inadequate to give relief in proper time to the rack-rented tenantry of Ireland.'[104]

Tenants also claimed that the landlords were deliberately multiplying appeals in order to frustrate the purpose of the act and force them into settlements outside the court — it was estimated that 60 per cent of the decisions in Ulster in the first three months of the act's operation were appealed — and that they were also taking advantage of the delay in fixing rents in order to get rid of tenants in arrears.[105] In these circumstances the tenants demanded two things: first, they wanted additional sub-commissioners appointed to relieve the deadlock in the courts; and second, they wanted the judicial rents made retrospective to the first gale day after the originating notice was served.[106]

The government was not unaware of the problems being created by the block in the courts nor of the mounting disquiet of the tenants.[107] In an attempt to relieve the pressure on the courts, four new sub-commissions were formed in April, bringing their total number to sixteen, and in May a new arrangement was introduced whereby the court could, upon application by the landlord and tenant, appoint special valuers to ascertain a fair rent which would then be filed in court.[108] Few tenants, however, took advantage of this new procedure — mainly because of their deep distrust of professional valuers[109] — and although the number of cases settled did rapidly increase with time, much of the backlog still remained.

It was partly in order to ease this situation and partly in order to meet landlord criticisms that the government decided in September to appoint new court valuers for an experimental period of three months; these would, it was hoped, both expedite the work of the land courts and give the landlords greater confidence in them, and thus diminish the number of appeals.[110] Their appointment, however, caused an outcry in Ulster. Professional valuers were almost by the nature of their occupation identified with the landlord interest, and resolutions condemning their appointment were passed at tenant meetings all across the province in an outburst of tenant activity which equalled anything the province had seen since 1868.[111] More alarmingly, tenants began to consider the advisability of withdrawing from the courts altogether until the valuers were dismissed.[112] In face of this new crisis, the government, clearly taken aback by the vehemence of the tenant protests, decided in November to discontinue the experiment — Gladstone, it emerged, had from the first been opposed to the appointments — so that court procedures after this date reverted to what they had been beforehand with the sub-commissioners fixing rents on the basis of their own surveys and the evidence submitted by both sides in the dispute.[113]

The government had earlier gone a good part of the way towards solving another problem which had been prejudicing the success of the act in parts of Ulster as well as (though not to the same extent as) in the south and west. This was the problem of arrears.[114] Two assumptions are commonly and erroneously made about arrears: first, that the question had little relevance to Ulster; and secondly, and more widely and fundamentally, that tenants in arrears were excluded from the provisions of the 1881 act. With regard to the first, while arrears may not have been nearly as serious a problem in Ulster as in Connacht, the level of arrears in the province was not far short of the combined total of Leinster and Munster (see Table 10.4). Donegal in particular was badly affected, more so indeed than any other county in Ireland with the exception of Mayo and Galway,[115] but no county in the north was free of arrears and some estates were seriously affected. At the beginning of May 1882 the rental on the Verner estates in Armagh and Tyrone was over £3,300 in arrears up to 1 November 1881 out of a total rental for these two estates of just under £10,000, and Crossle claimed that the great majority of other estates that he knew about were substantially worse off at that stage.[116] The prominence given to the question at tenant meetings in the province reflected its general importance, even if its settlement was not quite as vital to the success of the act there as in the south.

With regard to the second assumption, there was nothing in the act of 1881 which in itself precluded tenants in arrears from applying to the land courts to have judicial rents fixed.[117] Rather the problem was that tenants in arrears were so totally at the mercy of the landlords that they were afraid to apply to the courts in case the landlords took action against them; as Thomas Dickson explained in parliament, 'the very fact of the arrears prevents the tenant from applying to the land court, for he is threatened with a writ for arrears, and an eviction is sure to follow'.[118] Hans McMordie, a leading tenant-right solicitor, claimed that many of these tenants 'who had sought the protection of the courts had had ejectment decrees taken out against them'.[119]

Proceeding by ejectment for non-payment of rent was one method open to the landlord to get rid of a tenant in arrears. Under this procedure, however, the tenant had six months in which to redeem. Another swifter method, and one which was increasingly used at this time, was for the landlord to act under a writ of *fieri facias*, by which the tenant's interest could be sold out and after which the tenant had no right of redemption. Charles Russell told the commons that

> cases had been mentioned to him in which the landlords, having been served with originating notices, had resorted to a countermove by which what was called, in the language of the people, 'Dublin writs' came down to recover arrears. Does the House realise the effect of that? By proceeding in superior courts on a judgement of *fi.fa.* the landlord is entitled to sell out the tenant's interest and his effects. This spoliation goes on, and the new tenant coming in does not come under the protecting provisions of the act.[120]

The *Impartial Reporter* claimed that Fermanagh was 'being flooded with writs from the superior courts ... It is those tenants, who, owing a year's rent or over, have sought the intervention of the land court to fix a fair rent, who are being victimised in this fashion'.[121] The *Reporter* warned that the landlords were forcing a renewal of the agitation and would only have themselves to blame for the outcome.

This point was not lost on the Conservatives, many of whom, like the Liberals and nationalists, demanded that something be done to settle the question; Charles Lewis, for example, argued in the House of Commons that the act 'would prove a miserable failure' unless steps were taken to remedy the grievances arising from the existing arrears of rent.[122] The government had, in fact, included an arrears clause in the 1881 act which, on application by the landlord and tenant jointly, allowed arrears on holdings rated at £30 and under to be wiped out on payment by the tenant of one year's rent and the advance by the land commission of a sum not exceeding one year's rent or half the antecedent arrears.[123] However, the fact that the application depended on the assent of the landlord and that the land commission advance had to be repaid by the tenant rendered the clause almost totally inoperative. Thomas Dickson sent Gladstone the copy of a letter from a group of Tyrone farmers who had actually had their rents reduced by the land court, but who were still being evicted for arrears, the landlord refusing to join them in their application under this clause:

> We got our rents fixed December 8th ... but this does us no good as the landlord got writs and evicted us all out in January. We got the forms from Dublin for the arrears but the landlord would not sign his hand so the arrears clause is lost to the tenants. We put our interest in the farms up for sale, but no one would buy as the landlord told them not to buy until time of redemption would be past, and the landlord would then sell them himself.[124]

Finally in May 1882, following the Kilmainham agreement with Parnell, Gladstone introduced a bill providing for the settlement of arrears on holdings valued at £30 and under with the tenant paying one year's rent, the state another year's rent (or half the arrears up to one year's rent), and the rest of the debt being extinguished.[125] The immediate introduction of this bill, however, only tended to exacerbate the problems it was intended to solve. On the one hand, tenants, once they realised that there was a possibility that part of their debts would be cancelled, began to withhold rents.[126] On the other hand, some landlords redoubled their efforts either to secure arrears or to get rid of tenants in arrears before the bill was passed.[127] Once the bill became law, however, arrears ceased being both a major irritant to landlord–tenant relations and a major obstacle to the successful operation of the land act. Ulster tenants took immediate advantage of it (although many of the poorest found it impossible to raise even a year's rent, and were thus debarred from the benefits of the bill),[128] while landlords also benefited, recovering in many cases as much as half of arrears which otherwise would have been irretrievably lost.[129] Some 41,000 tenants — or more than 20 per cent of all occupiers of over one acre — had arrears amounting to over £560,000 extinguished under the act, while practically £240,000 was paid by the land commission to the landlords. Far from the act having no relevance to the province, 33 per cent of the applications made under it were in respect of holdings in Ulster, and almost a third of the money paid out under the scheme was paid to Ulster landlords. Only Connacht as a province benefited more, as Table 10.4 illustrates.

Table 10.4. Payments made under the arrears act and the amount of arrears cancelled[130]

|  | NO. OF HOLDINGS | ARREARS EXTINGUISHED (£) | LAND COMMISSION PAYMENTS TO LANDLORDS |
|---|---|---|---|
| Ulster | 41,134 | 561,392 | 239,125 |
| Leinster | 12,879 | 223,902 | 97,920 |
| Connacht | 52,883 | 634,332 | 273,716 |
| Munster | 18,994 | 341,198 | 156,823 |
| Ireland | 125,890 | 1,760,824 | 767,585 |

Once the arrears question was settled, the only other outstanding grievance which remained for northern tenants was the exclusion of leaseholders and holders of townparks from the benefits of the act. Nearly 20 per cent of all Ulster tenants held under lease ranging from a low of about 8 per cent of the tenants in Donegal to over 33 per cent of those in Antrim.[131] Yet the exclusion of leaseholders did not emerge immediately as a serious grievance in the north, and was scarcely mentioned at early tenant meetings called to consider the terms and administration of the act.[132] But as time went on, with yearly tenants receiving 20 per cent reductions of rent, leaseholders began to feel their exclusion more keenly, and the question began to figure more prominently at tenant meetings. Not surprisingly, it was the Antrim associations that took the lead. In February the Route association produced a revised set of rules which set out three main objectives, viz. the inclusion of leaseholders in the 1881 act, the extension of its provisions to occupiers of townparks, and the establishment of a peasant proprietary; and gradually from this time, and especially after grievances over arrears and the appointment of court valuers had been settled, other societies increasingly gave priority to this programme.[133]

The tenant argument with regard to leaseholders was that it was illogical to deny them the benefits of the act, for they were just as oppressively rented as yearly tenants and just as much at the mercy of the landlords. Charles Russell, for example, could 'see no sufficient ground, speaking generally, why the rent of a leaseholder should not be judically ascertained as well as that of a tenant from year to year', while Dr R.H. Todd maintained that 'in Ireland there was no such thing as free contract in a lease. There was only one side to the bargain, the landlord had it all his own way, and the tenant was completely at his mercy.'[134] The grievance about townparks was mainly that agricultural holdings were being unjustly defined as such because they were adjacent to villages 'which in England', it was claimed, 'would be called hamlets'.[135] The government, however, refused to make any concessions on these points. Spencer warned Gladstone that it would 'be most dangerous to open up the whole question of leases', while Edward Litton, one of the three land commissioners, advised that any change in the law in respect of the definition of townparks would be 'surrounded with excessive difficulties', and thought that 'in practice' at any rate there was 'no real grievance'.[136]

In short, while the act of 1881 had satisfied most of the demands of Ulster tenants, it had not given them all that they had hoped for. Certain grievances still remained. And with landlord denunciations of the judicial reductions of rent on the one hand and tenant dissatisfaction with their inadequacy on the other, there seemed precious little prospect of effecting a satisfactory compromise between the two interests. The land act, it was felt, had reached virtually the last point in the sphere of reconciliation on the basis of a joint partnership in the soil. Thus tenants as well as landlords increasingly thought in terms of tenant purchase as the final solution, and they were encouraged to do so both by the political manoeuvres of the Tory party at Westminster and by the adamant refusal of the government to countenance any further amendment of the existing system.[137] 'There does not appear to be a resting place for double ownership of the soil', observed the *Ballymoney Free Press* as early as December 1881. Other tenant papers agreed that 'finality' would not be reached 'until every farmer is the owner of his own farm'.[138] Some reservations were expressed by Liberal and tenant-right spokesmen about advancing the whole of the purchase money to tenants, others about the injustice of landlords being bought out at existing rents.[139] But generally and increasingly from 1882 northern Liberals and northern tenants, like many Tories and landlords, saw tenant proprietorship — but not as yet compulsory purchase — as the panacea not only for tenant problems, but for the general problems of the country:

> We require the establishment of a peasant and occupying proprietary in order to abolish those perpetual wars between landlords and tenants which disturb the peace of the empire ... in order to make our peasants thrifty, economical, industrious, comfortable, prosperous and law-abiding; in order to enlarge our class of shopkeepers; in order to increase the wealth, prosperity and happiness of the entire country.[140]

By 1883 in fact there was near unanimity in Ulster on the principles of the policy. All that still divided landlords and tenants in the province was the terms of purchase.

11

# The Eclipse of the Land Question
# and Liberal Collapse

The land act of 1881 did not, then, settle the land question. In the south its most immediate effect was not to end the agitation, which continued with unabated vigour, but rather to split the national movement, with moderate opinion — including the catholic hierarchy and the majority of the parliamentary party — favouring its acceptance and the Land League militants and their American allies demanding its rejection. At a major Land League conference in Dublin in September, Parnell produced the compromise formula of 'testing' the act, and then embarked on a series of deliberately provocative speeches, ostensibly intended to expose 'the hollowness of the act', in reality designed to placate the radical wing of the land movement by masking his qualified acceptance of it. Parnell's actions convinced the government that he was determined to sabotage the act and resulted in — if they did not positively invite — his arrest in October. In prison Parnell finally agreed to sign the famous 'no rent manifesto' which, as he could hardly have failed to have foreseen, led to the immediate suppression of the league.[1]

These events were watched with close interest in Ulster. But they had no palpable influence on developments in the province. There was never any danger of Ulster rejecting the act, or of the Land

League campaign being able to continue at the same level of intensity in the north once the act had been passed. Protestant support for the league — always conditional at any rate on the league pursuing a policy of moderation in Ulster — was immediately withdrawn, and such limited co-operation as there had been between the league and the tenant-right movement quickly came to an end, with the league branches in Ulster repudiating the act as 'utterly unsatisfactory' and the tenant-right associations welcoming it as a major boon.[2] When, for example, an attempt was made in Fermanagh, where the league had had considerable protestant support, to extend the campaign, the leading tenant-right paper warned that the Land League in the county had never gone beyond 'the old lines of tenant-right and ... Fermanagh will not advance any further'.[3] The league, in short, had reached the limits of its protestant support and had now no further attraction for the protestant tenant farmers nor for the tenant-right movement, which quickly began to distance itself from it.[4] And with the catholic hierarchy strongly advising tenants to take advantage of the act, catholic support too began to fall off, one Tyrone priest claiming in September that league support was now confined to the lower classes 'in the towns and mountainous districts'.[5]

The 'no-rent' manifesto and the government proclamation completed the collapse. The 'no-rent' manifesto was unanimously condemned by the tenant-right press as a 'reprehensible' and 'stupendous' piece of folly.[6] The catholic clergy also came out strongly against it. At a land convention in Cavan some days after the manifesto was issued, a resolution urging its adoption was vigorously repudiated by three priests who were present and was heavily defeated.[7] Many priests publicly denounced it from the pulpits and advised their parishioners 'not to pay any attention to such notices'.[8] Bishop Dorrian, who had always been sympathetic to the league, deprecated the executive's action and refused for a time to believe that Parnell had actually signed the manifesto.[9] In the circumstances, the tactic was a total failure in Ulster. No-rent placards were posted in various areas — for example, in Monaghan, Armagh and parts of Donegal — and attempts were made on various estates — for example, on the Earl of Erne's Boho estate, and on the Verner and Annesley estates — to get tenants to withhold rents, but with no great success;[10] as Montgomery's agent informed him, 'I don't think this Land League business seems to take any hold at all in these parts'.[11] Despite occasional meetings under the auspices of the Ladies' Land League and sporadic confrontations on a number of estates in 1882, the Land League in Ulster was to all intents and purposes dead by the end of 1881.

In truth, however, it was the land act and not the no-rent manifesto or the government proclamation which had killed it. Even before the Land League conference had met in September 1881, a by-election in Tyrone had shown that the league was already divided and in serious decline in the north. Thomas Dickson, the Liberal nominee, was, as T.P. O'Connor admitted, 'an excellent candidate' with impeccable tenant-right credentials and a record of opposition to coercion which was well calculated to appeal to the Land League vote in the constituency.[12] The Tory candidate was the Orangeman and former MP for Dungannon, Colonel Stuart Knox, who was handicapped both by his past hardline attitude to land reform and by his identification with the Ranfurly interest.[13] In these circumstances it seemed initially that Dickson would get the combined support of the presbyterian and catholic tenant farmers and be carried in on a wave of tenant gratitude for the act of 1881.[14]

Then towards the end of August Parnell issued a manifesto urging the Tyrone electors not to pledge themselves, rejecting Dickson as a 'supporter of the present coercion government', and stating that a Land League candidate would go forward. Within days the candidate was named as Harold Rylett, a unitarian minister from Moneyrea in Co. Down and one of the leading league figures in Ulster. Rylett promised in his address to support tenant ownership, grand jury reform, the extension of the franchise and — well down on the list — 'a large and generous measure of self-government'; but he came forward mainly in protest against the coercive policy of the government and with the clear intention of defeating Dickson rather than with any hope of winning the seat.[15]

Rylett's nomination came as a total shock not only to the Liberals but to the Tyrone Land League, many of whose members and branches had already committed themselves to supporting Dickson; indeed, Rylett himself had been party to an earlier circular to league branches giving qualified approval to Dickson's candidature. The result was that the Land League in the county was seriously split, several of the branches openly disapproving of Parnell's action and continuing to support Dickson.[16] The catholic clergy too were divided; not only did they dislike the prospect of supporting a unitarian minister and facilitating the return of Knox — whose campaign was blatantly sectarian[17] — but many of them also resented Parnell's dictatorial action in trying to impose a virtual stranger on the county. The clergy in Dromore did instruct their people to vote for Rylett, but the parish priests in Omagh and Cookstown came out strongly against him, and one clergyman estimated that only about four of the seventy or so priests in Tyrone supported the Parnellite candidate.[18]

In the event, Dickson was returned by a combination of catholic and presbyterian votes with Rylett coming bottom of the poll.[19] This result was widely seen — even by the league leaders — as a major rebuff to the league and led to much recrimination within the movement itself; 'the prestige of the league', thought Davitt, 'was much shaken in the north in consequence'.[20] Gladstone and other Liberal leaders welcomed Dickson's 'unexpected victory' as evidence of Parnell's waning influence, but Forster was a good deal less sanguine and warned Gladstone against such an interpretation.[21] The fact was that the league had done surprisingly well in an election against an exceptionally strong tenant-right candidate. Dickson had clearly benefited from the land act, polling a higher number of protestant votes than Litton had in 1880 and apparently getting the support of a number of Orangemen.[22] But Rylett had, it was generally agreed, polled half the catholic constituency in Tyrone, and this in spite of the opposition of the clergy and in spite of the confused circumstances of his nomination.

The election, in fact, marked an important stage in the disintegration of the catholic–Liberal alliance, demonstrating that a substantial and increasing number of catholic laity were no longer prepared to accept the clerical strategy of alliance with the Liberals as the only alternative to Toryism. This served as a warning to the clergy, who from 1881 gradually began to disengage from Liberal politics,[23] but it was only with the establishment of the National League in Ulster in 1882 that a really viable alternative to the Liberal alliance was provided and it was only then that 'the hitherto established patterns of Ulster politics' were finally broken.[24] The Tyrone by-election gave an indication of things to come, but in the meantime it was rightly seen as a statement of support for Gladstone and the land act and a rejection by the north of the Land League programme of the south.

The trends revealed in the Tyrone election were confirmed by another by-election, this time in Derry, before the end of the year. Again the contest between the Liberals and Conservatives was complicated by the nomination of a Land League candidate (Charles Dempsey, editor of the *Ulster Examiner*); it was complicated further by the publication of a letter from F.H. O'Donnell to *The Times* saying that he had been instructed to go to Derry and direct Parnell's followers to support Wilson, the Conservative candidate, on the basis that Conservative policy on land reform was practically identical with the platform of Parnell and the Land League, viz. peasant proprietorship and landlord compensation.[25] The *Ulster Examiner* of course repudiated this advice, but basically Dempsey's candidature was primarily intended to defeat A.M. Porter, the Liberal candidate, at any rate, and he eventually withdrew from the contest on the eve of the poll urging his supporters to vote against the nominee of the coercion government.[26] Not all catholics took this advice, however, and Porter was returned with the catholic vote dividing more or less as it had done in the election in Tyrone.[27]

What majority opinion had done in these two elections in Tyrone and Derry was to define its position in relation to the land question, and it was one of gratitude to the Liberals for the act of 1881 and of continuing adherence to the Liberal and tenant-right cause.[28] Tory expectations that the act would satisfy tenant demands and 'greatly conduce to the restoration of political landmarks'[29] had clearly been disappointed, and events over the next two years, both in Ireland and at Westminster, combined to prevent the act from being seen as a final settlement of the question and to maintain the divisions which had emerged in Ulster society during the previous decade.

In Ulster, dissatisfaction with the administration of the act led to a renewal of agitation from December, and this reached a new level of intensity in the early months of 1882 with the landlord conference in Dublin in January, the appointment of the lords' committee to inquire into the working of the act in February, the large number of landlord appeals against the sub-commissioners' decisions, and their more hardline attitude to tenants in arrears all being seen as part of a general landed conspiracy against the act. The tenant fear was that the landlords were determined to intimidate the sub-commissioners so as to defeat the purpose of the reform in the same way as they had, it was claimed, destroyed the act of 1870.[30] Thus tenant protest meetings were held in virtually every part of the province, new tenant associations were formed in different areas (for example at Ringsend, Kilrea, Ballycarry, Kilwaughter, Glenarm and other places), others which had been defunct were resurrected (most notably the Fermanagh Farmers' Association and the County Monaghan Tenants' Defence Association), and the membership of existing associations increased.[31] Tenant-right activity continued at a fairly high level during most of 1882, for just as tenant fears with regard to landlord intentions began to subside the agitation was given a renewed impulse by the appointment of court valuers in September.[32] It was only when these were withdrawn at the end of November that the excitement began to die down.

At Westminster, both main parties showed a disposition to use the land question for party advantage. It was the Conservatives who reopened the question in March 1882 with the notice of a motion from W.H. Smith in favour of extending the facilities for tenant purchase. Smith's motion, accompanied as it was by an almost simultaneous resolution from Sir John Hay against coercion, was plainly intended to embarrass the government and win Parnellite support, and prompted one independent journal to regret that the land settlement was 'once more in danger of being marred and spoilt by the manipulation of an immense question for merely party motives'.[33] The Kilmainham pact and the introduction of the arrears bill by the government were at least partly a response to this new Conservative initiative, which was immediately abandoned once details of the Kilmainham agreement became known.[34] The Conservatives, under Salisbury's guidance, saw the arrears bill mainly as an opportunity to force a dissolution and improve their position before the government turned its attention to parliamentary reform,[35] but eventually gave way under pressure from their Irish — especially their Ulster — supporters[36] and because by August their electoral prospects were no longer as promising as they had been at the beginning of the crisis.[37] In 1883 they made another attempt to outflank Gladstone by again taking up land purchase with Lord George Hamilton's resolution in the commons, while Gladstone for his part turned increasingly to local government reform as a necessary precondition for a final settlement of the land question along the same lines.[38]

All these developments served to keep the land question alive — those in Ireland by stimulating tenant fears with regard to the administration of the act, those at Westminster by arousing tenant expectations of further concessions. 'It is idle to expect the agricultural population to settle down into an acceptance of the land act', the land commissioners advised the government, 'while they are kept in daily expectation of advanced legislation.'[39] The result was that tenant-right activity continued in Ulster, with the tenant-right movement from 1882 focusing its attention more and more on the amendment of the 1881 act with a view to extending its benefits to leaseholders and holders of townparks and facilitating the creation of a tenant proprietary. These were the main objectives of the Ulster Land Committee, which was established in January 1883 in an attempt to co-ordinate tenant-right activity throughout the province.[40] This was the first provincial tenant-right organisation ever formed in Ulster, and it reflected the continuing importance of the land question some eighteen months after Gladstone's second land act had been passed. In some respects it marked the climax of tenant-right effort in the province, but it was never to have either the support or the influence its leaders had hoped.

The fact was that, in spite of the continuing demands for the amendment of the 1881 act, the most serious grievances of the tenants had been remedied and their main demands had been met by this stage. This is not to say that the land question had been finally settled or that it ceased to be important; complaints were still made that the protection given under the act was inadequate, that the judicial rents were too high, and that the sub-commissioners made too small an allowance for the interests and improvements of the tenants; and demands were still made for the inclusion of leaseholders and townpark holders in the benefits of the act, and later for judicial rents to be fixed for five instead of fifteen years and for the introduction of compulsory purchase.[41] And land was still the main issue in a by-election in Monaghan in June of 1883. But by this time tenant grievances were not nearly as oppressive and the land question was no longer as potent a source of division in northern society and northern politics. Apart from the exclusion of leaseholders from the 1881 act, disputes about land tenure had by and large been settled, and both landlords and tenants were now agreed on the principle of purchase as the ultimate solution to the land question itself. If anything, with the deadlock in the Irish land market, increased government aid for purchase was of more pressing importance to the landlords than it was to the tenants; as Thomas Dickson pointed out in 1884, 'the Irish tenant is under no pressure to buy. He has had his rent fixed, he sits secure against eviction or arbitrary increase of rent, and he will not purchase unless he can do so on reasonable terms'.[42]

This agreement on the land question and this relative tenant complacency clearly had important implications not only for the tenant-right movement, but for Ulster politics in general. By depriving tenant-right of much of its agitational and political force, it both undermined the dynamic of Liberal growth in the province and opened the way for 'the restoration of political landmarks' and 'the return to traditional allegiances' which the Tories had hoped for in 1881. What finally eclipsed the land question and led to the completion of this process was the so-called nationalist invasion of Ulster from 1883.

## THE NATIONAL LEAGUE IN ULSTER

Although Parnellite tactics had been defeated in the Tyrone and Derry by-elections at the end of 1881, the elections had revealed a sizeable support for Parnell's party and one which had an obvious potential for growth. But after the suppression of the Land League no immediate effort was made to develop this. The only leading nationalist figure who had any direct involvement in Ulster affairs during 1882 was Michael Davitt, who had always shown more sensitivity to northern protestant interests and taken a more active — though still only sporadic — interest in the province than other nationalist leaders, and who was regarded by some sections of northern opinion as something of a hero, if not a walking saint.[43] Davitt undertook a speaking tour of the province in November, but by this time the national movement was seriously split between those who supported and those who opposed his policy of land nationalisation, and his activities in Ulster were looked upon with great suspicion by many of his more conservative colleagues: 'I am sorry to hear you offer a platform to Davitt', Joseph Biggar wrote to a leading member of the Belfast branch of the National League, 'His nationalisation scheme is the dream of a lunatic.'[44] But if the right wing of the party distrusted Davitt's intentions in the north — and everywhere else — they themselves had largely ignored the province since the Tyrone election, and by and large continued to do so until well into 1883.

Nevertheless, the new National League, which was established in October 1882, began almost immediately after its inception, and with no particular efforts on the part of the league leaders, to develop in the north. This development took place generally in areas where the Land League had been strongly entrenched and usually under the same local officials, many of whom were clearly hoping to pick up the threads of the late agitation.[45] By the end of January 1883, there were forty-two branches in Ulster with a total membership of between four and five thousand, an average roughly of just over 100 members per branch.[46] Fourteen of these branches were in Cavan, six in each of Donegal and Derry, five in Tyrone, four in Down, and three in each of Armagh and Fermanagh; no branches had been established in Monaghan, and outside of that in Belfast there were none in Antrim.[47]

However, the number of branches does not in itself reflect the degree of support for the league. Perhaps surprisingly, the county with the largest membership was Armagh, whose three branches had a combined total of about 1,600 members or nearly 40 per cent of the total membership for the province (the Camlough branch alone had 1,000 members[48]), while the four branches in Down had between them only ninety-eight members. In some cases, in fact, the branches had been established and no more — the membership of several was in single figures — and with occasional exceptions such as those at Camlough and Crossmaglen in Armagh and Crossroads in Donegal there was clearly no great enthusiasm for the movement. In several areas, as for example at Dromore and Trillick in Tyrone, Swanlinbar in Cavan and in parts of Fermanagh, the organisation met strong resistance from the catholic clergy; the Carrivemaclone branch in Armagh, for example, fell through after being denounced from the altar by the local curate, who said that 'he was determined along with the parish priest to give it every opposition in that parish'.[49] And while clergy in other areas supported it — to the point of accepting offices in the branches at Camlough, Crossmaglen, Carrickmore, Virginia, Arney and other places — the movement generally was reported to be making very slow progress in the province, with only twelve additional branches established there in the six months up to the end of July 1883.[50]

The National League was, of course, essentially an electioneering organisation with a strictly constitutional purpose, and with no general election impending it was scarcely surprising that it did not elicit the same enthusiasm or have the same immediate impact as the Land League. Two developments, however, added to the significance of its presence in Ulster, and changed the whole complexion of northern politics from mid-1883: first, a by-election in Monaghan at the end of June followed by a more determined effort by the league leaders to win support in Ulster; and second, a rather frenetic counter-agitation got up by the Orange order against the league.

The Monaghan by-election of June 1883 may truly be said to mark a turning point in Ulster politics. No branches of the National League had as yet been established in Monaghan, but Parnell, once the vacancy occurred, immediately announced his intention of putting forward a nationalist candidate.[51] The candidate chosen was Tim Healy, sitting MP for the borough of Wexford and, though still only twenty-eight years of age, already a national figure. Healy had been responsible for the famous 'Healy clause' of the 1881 act, and his selection — confirmed by a convention at Castleblayney — was well calculated to appeal to the tenant vote in the constituency.[52] And during the campaign itself Healy's supporters concentrated mainly on the land issue, advocating also local government and franchise reform, but keeping home rule 'very discreetly in the background'.[53]

The Liberal candidate was Henry Pringle, a Clones butter merchant, who was actively supported by the Ulster Land Committee and campaigned mainly on its programme, advocating tenant proprietorship, the inclusion of leaseholders and townpark holders in the benefits of the 1881 act, more allowances by the sub-commissioners for tenant improvements, and local government reform.[54] The Conservatives, too, acknowledged the importance of the land question, bypassing the landed families for the first time in the history of the constituency and nominating John Monroe, a prominent QC, as their candidate. Monroe, whose meetings were frequently chaired by tenant farmers, supported tenant purchase and local government reform, appealed for protestant solidarity and opposed the extension of the franchise to 'large numbers who are unfitted to exercise it.'[55]

The result of the election was dramatic in its implications. Healy, strongly supported by leading members of the National League including Parnell himself, was returned at the head of the poll with a majority of ninety-one over the combined vote of his opponents. Pringle received only 270 votes, less than 5 per cent of the total cast.[56] The election in fact was a disaster for the Liberals. They had almost certainly lost some protestant votes — to Healy because of the land question, to Monroe because of the nationalist threat — but the obvious reason for their collapse in the constituency was the defection *en masse* of their catholic supporters. One of the features of the election, and a significant sign of the movement of catholic opinion, was the near solid support of the catholic clergy — up to this time firm supporters of Liberal pretensions in the county — for

Healy. 'Their chapels were converted into committee rooms and the priest did more effectual electioneering work than any paid canvasser could have done ... The catholic vote went ... as one man for Mr Healy.'[57] The Liberals denied that Monaghan was at all similar to other Ulster counties; but, even allowing for the higher number of catholic votes in this constituency than in most others in the province, the Monaghan by-election had graphically exposed the weakness of the Liberals once the catholics ceased to support them. Healy later claimed that 'the Monaghan victory marked the end of Liberalism in Ireland'.[58] This was not absolutely true even in electoral terms, for the Liberals went on to win a by-election in Antrim in 1885. But on any reading of the situation in 1883, the future for the Liberal party in Ulster looked extremely bleak.

The nationalists of course were euphoric, interpreting the result as a victory for nationalism and home rule. 'The contest was not fought ostensibly on nationalist principles', said one English journal, 'though now it has been won the organs of the party are ridiculing the idea that Mr Healy would have taken off his coat except to obtain a triumph for home rule.'[59] Healy, immediately after the contest, made clear the future intentions of the nationalists in Ulster, claiming that they would at the first opportunity take the other Monaghan seat and 'insist upon a share of power in counties like Donegal, Derry, Tyrone and Armagh'.[60] The Tories, too, realised the implications of Healy's success, but were not entirely displeased at the turn of events in Monaghan, welcoming the movement of protestant opinion in their direction: 'I believe that election', Monroe afterwards wrote to Salisbury, 'has already borne and will yet bear good fruit.'[61] From the Tory point of view Monroe's interpretation was not very wide of the mark. If the election was fought principally on the land question, the outcome helped to ensure that future conflicts would revolve around the question of home rule. In fact, it marked the beginning of a definite process of polarisation in Ulster, which was to continue over the next three years, and which was to lead to the effacement of the Ulster Liberal party as a political force and the subordination of the land question as a political issue.

Efforts were soon being made by the National League to extend its influence into different parts of the province, and from late August — after parliament had been prorogued — a series of public meetings addressed by leading members of the party were held in different areas, but especially in Tyrone, Fermanagh and south Derry. The purpose of the meetings was to stimulate support and establish constituency organisations in preparation for the next general election; Timothy Harrington, the secretary of the National League, later admitted that in the field of registration 'special attention' was paid to Ulster, and claimed that 270 of the 1,040 National League branches established by 1885 were in the northern province.[62] But, although the league was essentially a home rule organisation with 'national self-government' as its primary objective, priority in this campaign in Ulster — in its early stages at any rate — was given to the land question with only muted references to home rule. 'A noteworthy fact', it was reported to Dublin Castle at the end of 1883, 'is the absence of the usual home rule resolution (or in a "weakened" form) at these gatherings [in the north].'[63] The league leaders were anxious in fact not to antagonise the northern protestants: hence their concentration on land and hence also their more direct appeals for protestant support.[64] Michael Davitt and others, including Parnell himself, warned those attending and speaking at league meetings in Ulster to 'carefully avoid using any language which might be misconstrued as language unfriendly or in antagonism to the protestant religion of Ulster'.[65]

Attempts to woo protestant support, however, were almost totally unsuccessful. As has been correctly pointed out, the land question never had the political potential in this respect that some of the nationalist leaders believed,[66] and the 'nationalist invasion' of Ulster met with immediate and militant opposition from the Orange order. Politically quiescent during the 1870s, the order had, as we have seen, assumed a new prominence during the Land League crisis of 1880–1. Its growth had continued since then, stimulated partly by the continuing unrest in the country, partly by distrust of government intentions and government weakness as seen in the Kilmainham 'treaty'.[67] The order saw itself as 'virtually the only bulwark in the country ... against the forces of rebellion, anarchy and plunder'.[68]

Thus when the nationalists began their campaign in the north, it was the Orangemen — led by the landed classes who had acquired a new enthusiasm for the movement — who took the initiative in opposing them. The expedient adopted is explained by MacKnight: `Whenever a nationalist meeting from the south was announced in the north, a counter Orange demonstration was summoned to be held, on the same day, at the same hour, and in the same neighbourhood'.[69] These counter-demonstrations were, as Trevelyan told parliament, 'to a great extent demonstrations of bodies of armed men', and were accompanied by threats of armed resistance and on occasions by outbreaks of violence; and they were clearly intended not only to 'repel the Parnellite invasion' but mainly to force the government into banning all meetings.[70]

The first nationalist meetings — in Draperstown, Pomeroy, Strabane, Castlederg and Drumquin (all in September) — passed off uneventfully.[71] But meetings at Aughnacloy, Dungannon and Omagh in September and at Roslea in October were met by counter-demonstrations of Orangemen. In each case the authorities moved large forces of police into the areas concerned, and although shots were fired at Roslea serious collision between the two parties was averted. However, at the beginning of November, when Orangemen resisted an attempt by the lord mayor of Dublin to address a meeting in the Guildhall in Derry — this was not in fact a National League meeting at all — shots were again fired and this time two men were seriously wounded.[72] This incident, following on Roslea, prompted the authorities to take action, and when loyalists responded to a proposed nationalist meeting at Garrison in Fermanagh by calling another counter-demonstration, the government banned both meetings. Meetings at Newry, Cootehill, Blacklion, Castlewellan, and Park in Derry were likewise proclaimed. However, a league meeting and an Orange counter-demonstration were permitted at Dromore and again there were disturbances, culminating in the death of a young man.[73] This convinced the government — which initially had privately welcomed the expression of loyalist opinion in Ulster[74] — of the necessity of laying down firm regulations, and it was decided that in future counter-demonstrations only should be banned.

These events had far-reaching effects on the political situation in the north. On the loyalist side the Orange institution grew both in strength and in membership; Saunderson, for example, who had early recognised its potential, claimed in 1884 that 'the organisation had made more progress in the past three or four years than the most sanguine Orangeman would have thought possible'.[75] The landed classes, who had neglected it during the 1870s, now clearly saw it as the one organisation in which they could identify with the protestant rank and file, and through which they could re-establish their hold over the protestant tenantry and reverse the trends which had threatened their position over the previous decade and a half. 'If there was no such thing as an Orange society', said Lord Rossmore, urging the landlords to join, 'I don't think there would be anything at all to bring landlord and tenant together.'[76] Even Stafford Northcote — like other British Conservatives suspicious of the excesses of the Orangemen and generally anxious to distance himself from them — felt obliged on his visit to the province in the autumn of 1883 to acknowledge their importance.[77]

On the nationalist side there was mounting anger and resentment both at the Orange attempts to prevent and disrupt their meetings — the leaders of the Orange counter-demonstrations were usually members of the bench who were supposed to be responsible for the maintenance of order — and still more so at the government's surrender to Orange pressure. After the proclamation of a meeting in Newry, for example, it was reported that 'nothing could possibly exceed the bitterness which the proclamation of the nationalist meeting has created here'.[78] The paradox was that it was the provocative tactics of counter-demonstration and the Orange success in influencing government policy which gave the National League the very stimulus it needed in the north. The earlier meetings in September had elicited no great enthusiasm from northern catholics, and reports on the development of the league at this time were still that it was making only very slow progress.[79] But the Orange counter-demonstrations provoked great excitement, giving the National League movement a welcome shot in the arm at a time when it seemed to be flagging. The central branch issued a circular in January urging the county branches to make renewed efforts to expand their membership, and this was well responded to in Ulster. 'There is no doubt', the police reported in mid-1884, 'but that the league is extending its influence in portions of the northern counties ... especially in Tyrone.'[80]

LIBERAL DECLINE

The party which suffered most from these developments was the Liberals. With each demonstration and counter-demonstration, with each riot and disturbance, emotions were rising, attitudes were hardening, and politics — with the land question now nearly forgotten — were increasingly being seen in terms of Orange v. Green. Disturbances continued throughout 1884 and 1885. There were sectarian clashes in towns such as Enniskillen, Derry, Armagh and Dungannon, and riots in Lurgan and Portadown and on a more serious scale in Belfast. Attempts to dynamite the Tower of London, the House of Commons, and Westminster Hall at the beginning of 1885 added to the general excitement.[81] In these circumstances, the defection of catholics and protestants from the Liberal ranks was accelerated.

The parliamentary reform acts of 1884–5 exacerbated Liberal problems. The creation of single member divisions by the redistribution act of 1885 enabled catholics to return members of their choice for constituencies such as South Down, South Armagh and South Derry, all counties in which catholics were outnumbered by the protestant population, and in which under the old system the only alternative to the Tories had been the Liberals. The main Liberal fears, however, were attached to the franchise bill of 1884, and to some extent they were justified, not because the new voters were all, or even predominantly, agricultural labourers holding extreme opinions,[82] but rather because the creation of a wider electorate magnified both current developments in Ulster politics and already existing weaknesses in Liberal organisation. By introducing household suffrage, the act trebled the Ulster electorate — from 95,000 to nearly

265,000 — and made vigorous and efficient party organisation more essential than ever. Both the Conservatives and nationalists realised this, and both were active in registration work in the north. The Liberals, on the other hand, played little part in the revision courts. Timothy Harrington claimed in August 1885 that 'the Liberal party have left the field of registration this year, no agent being employed, and the battle of the franchise is between Conservatives and nationalists'.[83]

At any rate, the Liberals made little appeal to the new voters. There was no Chamberlain in Ulster to put forward an 'unauthorised programme', and Liberal policies in 1884–5 continued to reflect their dependence on the tenant farmers. Individual members complained about the neglect of the newly enfranchised classes,[84] but the party as a party was either unwilling or unable to make a radical and positive bid for their support. In the heightened emotions of this period, such a bid would hardly have been successful, but it said little for the vigour of the party that none was made. Organisational deficiencies and a certain social exclusiveness — the party prided itself on representing the 'most respectable classes' in the community [85]– put the Liberals at a serious disadvantage in the new electoral conditions created by the acts of 1884 and 1885.

But even before these reforms were passed the Liberals were in a process of irreversible decline. On the one hand, Parnell had already captured the catholic vote in the north. In 1884 when the Liberals failed to win a by-election in Down — where they had lost by only twenty votes in 1880 they were now defeated by 400 votes in a substantially smaller poll — MacKnight was complaining that 'the catholics ... were now for the most part nationalists'.[86] 'As far as we can ascertain', wrote Hugh Montgomery some months later, 'the Roman catholic voters in the country districts of Ulster are, with exceptions that one may count on one's fingers, all enrolled in the National League and the Roman catholic clergy are acting as Parnellite registration and electioneering agents.'[87] On the other hand, the protestants increasingly looked to the Conservative party and the Orange order to resist the nationalist challenge. Home rule did for the Ulster Tories what they had earlier hoped concessions on land would do: it re-established their identity of interests with the protestant tenant farmers and restored landed political hegemony in the counties. This process had already been facilitated both by the land legislation of 1881 and by Tory willingness to meet the tenants' remaining demands. The Ashbourne land purchase act of 1885, for example, advancing the whole of the purchase money to tenants to be repaid over forty-nine years at 4 per cent interest, was introduced by an Irish Conservative and passed by a Conservative government, and seemed to provide conclusive proof that the ultimate solution to the land question was as likely — perhaps more likely — to be undertaken by the Conservatives as by the Liberals. Criticisms were made of the terms of purchase, and demands for the compulsory sale of estates continued to be made at times over the next two decades. But the act was a success, and especially so in Ulster where agreements of sale were almost equal in number to those in the rest of the country.[88]

By 1885 in fact — indeed by 1883 — the land question, while still important, was no longer as vital an issue in northern politics. A conference of the Ulster Land Committee in Belfast in November 1885, for example, was attended by only fifty people.[89] The very success of the land act of 1881 had undermined support for the tenant-right movement, while the Tory concessions had deprived Liberalism of its distinctive appeal to the tenant farmers. 'The rural enthusiasm [in Ulster]', wrote W.S. Armour, 'was not so much for Liberalism as it was then a creed in Scotland as for tenant-right.'[90] Once the solution to the land tenure question was agreed upon, Liberalism for many of its adherents in Ulster almost ceased to have a *raison d'etre*. It is significant that the only election after 1881 in which the Liberals improved their position was in Antrim, where leaseholders, who had not benefited from the 1881 legislation, formed an unusually large proportion of the tenantry. In every other case they lost ground. Samuel McElroy explained the predicament of the party in 1885:

> In 1880 the Liberals had a good distinctive programme in the 3Fs. That programme was largely fulfilled by the land law act, and doubts are abroad about whether there is any difference between Conservatives

and Liberals on the land question. Lord Ashbourne's land purchase act has produced the impression that the Conservatives are as much in earnest as the Liberals in the effort to establish a peasant proprietary.[91]

Many Liberal supporters could no longer see any points of real difference between the two parties: 'Every point of importance upon which Liberals and Conservatives in Ulster have fought in years gone by,' wrote Hugh Montgomery, 'has been won by the Liberals ... no great question now divides Liberal from Conservative in Ireland.'[92] The disestablishment of the Irish church had already removed one major obstacle to protestant unity. The land legislation had gone some way towards removing another. And events from 1883 in both Ulster and Westminster — where the party manoeuvres for the Irish vote were, if anything, more alarming to northern protestants than the activities of the National League[93] — had consolidated protestant support behind the Conservative party, not because the Liberals were suspect in their support of the union, but rather because the Conservatives were traditionally more identified with it and by their willingness to articulate the religious fears of northern protestants seemed more prepared to go to any lengths to defend it.

The general election of 1885 revealed how far the situation in Ulster had changed from 1880.[94] The nationalists, already certain of the catholic vote, concentrated on land grievances in an attempt to win the support of the protestant tenant farmers. The land question also figured prominently in the addresses of the Liberal and Conservative candidates, but with virtual agreement between them on the issue — candidates on both sides were prepared to extend the benefits of the 1881 act to leaseholders and those of the 1885 act to tenants who had purchased under the terms of Gladstone's measures of 1870 and 1881 — it was no longer the decisive issue; if anything, in the contest for the protestant tenant vote the Conservatives had the edge, claiming credit for the Ashbourne act of 1885 and advocating fair trade as the real answer to the fall in agricultural prices.[95] The key question was home rule. 'Union with Great Britain', maintained the *News Letter*, 'is the question of the hour.' The *Whig* agreed, adding that 'in Ulster, at least, all other political considerations are secondary'.[96]

And on this issue the province divided almost equally between Tories and nationalists and along strict sectarian lines, with the Liberal party coming nowhere.

Organisationally unprepared, and with many Liberal supporters believing that the old party divisions were no longer relevant, the Liberals, who had already lost their catholic support, were in no condition to resist the claims of the Conservatives to be the exclusive representatives of loyalist opinion in Ulster. Of the thirteen Liberal candidates who went forward in the election, two (Wylie in Mid-Armagh and Gunning-Moore in East Tyrone) retired rather than split the anti-nationalist vote, while the remainder were convincingly beaten by the Tories. In one sense, with the catholics already firmly committed to Parnell, the real contest in 1885 was for the protestant vote. To capture this the Tories were prepared to intervene against the Liberals in former Liberal constituencies such as Tyrone and Derry, even at the risk of allowing the nationalists in. The Liberals, on the other hand, were not as steadfast in their allegiance to party interests. Although the Liberal leaders were deeply incensed by the electoral tactics of the Tories, the hostility of most of their supporters to the latter was never as strong as their fear of home rule. While their leaders advised against giving support to Tory candidates and argued that Liberals should stand 'in every constituency regardless of the consequences', the majority of rank and file members deemed it more important to defeat the Parnellites than to assert the claims of their own party against the Conservatives. Thus they voted Tory in constituencies such as Derry, North Tyrone, Mid-Armagh and others, and by doing so helped to vote their own party virtually out of existence. As a leading member of the Ulster Reform Club told James Bryce at the beginning of 1886:

> The Liberal party here has, for the time, disappeared as a factor in Ulster politics. While most of the leaders and the more intelligent followers remain true to the party, the great masses of the rank and file, especially in the rural districts have gone over to the Tories; or rather forgetting old differences in face of what they consider the common danger, the masses of the two parties have amalgamated as Unionists.[97]

If the Liberal rank and file had already coalesced with the Conservatives, events over the following months — with mounting evidence of Gladstone's intentions — led the majority of the Liberal leaders in the same direction, and at a joint meeting in the Ulster Hall in April the two parties agreed to co-operate in opposition to home rule, though deciding against amalgamation.[98] Tory electoral behaviour, episcopalian insensitivity to presbyterian status grievances, and the land question — mainly the question of compulsory purchase — over the next twenty years gave rise to occasional outbursts of Liberal independence, but by mid-1886 the Ulster Liberal party as a political force was to all intents and purposes dead.

The electoral pattern which had emerged in Ulster in 1885 was confirmed by the general election of July 1886 and by practically every election in the future. Not even Gladstone's offer of a massive — though hardly generous — scheme of land purchase to accompany home rule in 1886 could persuade northern protestant tenants to abandon their position.[99] Every issue in Ulster politics now and for the indefinite future was to be subordinated to the overriding question of the union. The land question had promised for a period of fifteen years to promote the development of a more conventional form of politics in Ulster, but this development was now aborted, and politics in the province set into a hard and permanent sectarian mould.

AFTER 1886

The land question did not cease to be important in Ulster after 1886, nor did agrarian radicalism disappear. After the partial recovery of agriculture in the early 1880s, depression set in once more in 1885–6 with a sharp fall in prices to levels even lower than in 1879. Complaints about the excessively high level of judicial rents and demands for abatements were made in all parts of the province, with the larger tenants, the main beneficiaries of the legislation of 1870 and 1881, again taking the lead.[100] And although the 'plan of campaign' — under which tenants offered what they considered to be a 'fair rent' to the landlord and withheld all rent until this was accepted — was adopted on only a limited number of estates in Ulster

— mainly in Donegal — it had a wider impact there than has generally been allowed. Northern landlords, clearly alarmed by the 'plan' and the prospects of renewed agitation, were forced to make rent concessions which, in many cases, they could ill-afford.[101] And, despite their general hostility to any further government interference between landlord and tenant, they were persuaded by the exigencies of the political situation to support a new Conservative land bill in 1887.[102] This measure — introduced at least partly in order to satisfy Liberal–unionist and protestant tenant opinion — provided for a revision of the judicial rents fixed before 1886 and for the admission of leaseholders to the benefits of the act of 1881. This latter concession met one of the main remaining tenant grievances in Ulster, while the further reduction in rents meant that tenants generally were able to escape the worst effects of the fall in the value of agricultural output, which was borne almost entirely by the landlords.[103]

However, neither the act of 1887 nor a further land purchase act in 1891 fully satisfied tenant demands. 'Much restlessness', Hugh Montgomery informed a correspondent in late 1892, 'still prevails among the bulk of the tenantry, protestant as well as catholic.'[104] Tenants continued to complain that in the settlement of judicial rents insufficient allowance was made for tenant improvements, and, later, that the administration of the appeals procedure by the land commission was working to the tenants' disadvantage and encouraging landlord appeals.[105] Landlords also, it was claimed, were making more determined efforts than ever to destroy tenant-right, refusing at times to recognise the purchasing tenant and often forcing tenants to sell under the act of 1881 — which gave landlords the right of pre-emption — rather than under the Ulster custom.[106] Moreover, certain categories of land — tenancies created since the passing of the 1881 act, land held by 'caretakers', townparks, demesne land, grazing land above £100 in value, and sub-let land — were still excluded from the rent-fixing clauses of the legislation.[107]

The main source of grievance, however, was that tenants paying judicial rents were paying on average between 20 and 25 per cent above what tenant purchasers under the acts of 1885 and 1891 — and, later, 1896 — were paying in annuities to the government.[108]

The problem was that most landlords were unwilling to sell at the prices offered under the land purchase legislation. And landlords in Ulster, where the Ulster custom provided greater security for rents and where rents were generally well paid, were showing more obduracy in this respect than their colleagues in the south and west, who were plainly in a more vulnerable position.[109] 'The purchase act of 1891', James Bryce reported to Gladstone, 'has not worked at all well in Ulster ... because the landlords, getting their rents well paid, stand out for exorbitant prices.'[110] In these circumstances there was a steadily growing demand for compulsory purchase. The paradox was that the Conservatives, in their efforts to pacify the country and ultimately safeguard landlord interests, were offering to tenants terms of purchase which actually fuelled the agitation for the compulsory expropriation of all landlords.

The conflict of interests between landlords and tenants resurfaced in 1894–5 after the immediate threat of home rule had passed, with the tenants under the leadership of T.W. Russell supporting the land reform proposals of John Morley. The Conservative land purchase act of 1896 — accepted only grudgingly by the Irish landlords — conceded the substance of Russell's demands by bringing sub-let land under the act of 1881, streamlining the rent assessment procedures, and extending the facilities for purchase.[111] This act temporarily quietened the agitation. But its effect on land sales in Ulster was less than dramatic. Landlords still refused to sell, and the demand for compulsory purchase continued to grow in strength. In the general election of 1900, candidates on all sides supported this policy, and immediately after the election Russell embarked on a fresh campaign, launching the Ulster Farmers and Labourers Union and Compulsory Purchase Association at a conference in the Ulster Hall, Belfast in June 1901.[112] The fact that this was attended by several thousand delegates reflected the continuing importance of the land question some twenty years after Gladstone's revolutionary measure of 1881.

The message was not lost on the landlords or the unionist leaders. Land was still manifestly a major threat to unionist unity, and the dangers of postponing a permanent settlement of the question were again graphically illustrated by the defeat of official unionist candidates by independent compulsory purchase candidates in by-elections in East Down and North Fermanagh — normally safe unionist constituencies — in 1902 and 1903 respectively.[113] It was against this background that the Wyndham land purchase act of 1903 was passed. Introduced by a Conservative government on the initiative of Irish unionist landlords, the act offered more generous terms than any previous purchase act for landlords and tenants alike; for tenants the period of repayment of loans was extended and the interest rate lowered; for landlords there was the incentive of a 12 per cent bonus on the selling price.[114]

In spite of these inducements, however, many northern landlords were still unwilling to sell, and proportionately less land was sold under Wyndham's act in Ulster than in the rest of Ireland.[115] The Russellite campaign for compulsory purchase continued, and it was only with the devolution crisis of 1904–5 — skilfully exploited by the Ulster unionist leaders — that the Russellite threat was finally defeated and unionist unity restored.[116] Russellite candidates contested nine seats in Ulster in the general election of January 1906 but, apart from Russell himself, only one — R.G. Glendinning in North Antrim — was returned.[117] Russell subsequently abandoned his campaign and took office under the Liberals in 1907. The land question was still not quite dead as a political issue — indeed it was only finally settled when the principle of compulsory sale was adopted in 1925 — but the time when it could radically alter the shape of Ulster politics was clearly well past.

# Conclusion

The landed classes continued in the post-Famine period to dominate the political and social life of Ulster. This domination was based at least partly on coercion, but only partly. In fact, the relationship between landlords and tenants was complex and reciprocal, more complex perhaps in Ulster than in the rest of the country. There was a close community of interests between the two classes in Ulster, more particularly between the landlords and their protestant tenants. What they shared was a common protestantism, a sense of apartness from the native catholic population, and a set of social values which above everything else helped to reinforce the fabric of rural society. Most tenants did not necessarily see any conflict — certainly not any political conflict — between their interests and those of the landlords, and they willingly deferred to the latter in both politics and social life. In return for this deference, tenants received social benevolence in a variety of forms, a benevolence which was often of vital importance to the smaller tenants, providing them with a social security they would not otherwise have had. The landed classes for their part took their political and social duties seriously, seeking through them mainly an enhancement of their prestige and standing in the local community.

The identification of interests between landlords and tenants, however, began to break down under the influence of post-Famine economic and social developments. The 1850s and 1860s were, largely as a result of an expanding market in Britain, years of rising agricultural prosperity in Ireland. The nature of the demand in Britain as well as a shortage of labour in Ireland encouraged during this period a move in Ireland from arable to livestock farming. Thus Irish farmers increasingly derived their income from livestock and livestock products, though in Ulster — with almost 80 per cent of the farms still under 30 acres — the predominant type of farming continued to be mixed. At the same time, the new market conditions encouraged throughout the country the consolidation of farms, and this was further stimulated in Ulster by the disappearance of handloom weaving, which in the past had enabled many small tenants to supplement an income from agriculture which on its own would scarcely have enabled them to survive. Thus both the decline in the number of holdings under fifteen acres and the increase in the number of those over fifteen acres were considerably greater in Ulster than in the rest of the country. What this meant was that the increasing agricultural prosperity of the province was being shared by a progressively smaller number of people; in other words, there was in Ulster during this period a striking increase in both productivity and *per capita* income.

Not everyone shared in the new prosperity or shared in it to the same degree. Generally speaking, the east — with superior natural conditions and a convenient and expanding market in Belfast as well as Britain — did better than the west; and larger farmers, who could normally adapt more easily to livestock farming, did better than small farmers, many of whom derived only a marginal advantage from the improved conditions of these decades. The larger tenants did, however, benefit, and by 1870 there were more of them. In other words, there had emerged in Ulster by this stage a larger, more prosperous rural bourgeoisie, who were obviously a great deal less in need of the kind of paternalistic assistance traditionally given by landlords to their tenants and dependants, and whose interests were clearly vastly different from those of the smaller tenants. Still prepared to defer to the superior social claims of the landed classes, their economic and social advancement made them anxious, if not yet determined, to exact some acknowledgement of their own position in society.

More important was the growing realisation of the insecurity not only of their new prosperity but of their tenant-right investment in the soil, which was variously estimated in the 1870s at figures ranging from £20 million to £40 million. Landlords had acquiesced in the development of this custom at the beginning of the century, but from the 1830s market conditions made them more and more anxious to curtail it, especially after the Devon commission in 1845 had drawn attention to the threat it posed to their property interests in the soil. Thus, while few landlords dared defy public opinion by openly attacking tenant-right, they increasingly tried to undermine and restrict it in more gradual ways.

From the tenants' point of view there were four main dangers to tenant-right — evictions, increased rents, estate rules, and the sale of estates in the landed estates court. Of these the least important in the sense of being the least likely to materialise was eviction. But while evictions may have been rare and may have affected mainly the smaller tenants, the widespread use of notices to quit meant that even more prosperous tenants were never allowed to forget the vulnerability of their position; crossing the landlord could have the same consequences for a larger as for a smaller tenant, as Peter Robinson, a tenant of 168 Cunningham acres on the estate of Sir Hervey Bruce, found to his cost in 1869.[1]

A more immediate threat to the tenant's interest, however, was his liability to have his rent increased at any time. Even if rents appeared on average moderate by the late 1860s, landlords still took a very high proportion of the value of agricultural output in view of what they put into agriculture themselves. Moreover, the level of rents was uneven, falling more heavily on some tenants than on others, and there were as well many cases of arbitrary, frequent and excessive increases of rent. What worried northern tenants in particular was the effect these had on the value of their tenant-right, the more so as landlords tended to take the opportunity of changes of tenancy to impose them. From the tenants' point of view it was essential, if the value of their tenant-right was to be maintained, for the landlords' power of raising rents to be controlled.

The introduction and development of estate rules, especially those which directly sought to limit the price of tenant-right, also clearly threatened the tenants' interest in the soil. There was in Ulster by the 1860s a general conviction that landlords were out to destroy the tenant-right custom, and once this took root, and once suspicions as to landlord intentions began to grow — whether or not they had any substance — the element of mutual trust on which the whole tenant-right custom was based began to diminish and social relations began to deteriorate.

However, what contributed more than anything else to the breakdown of the semi-feudal relationships of the past was the sale of land in the landed estates court. Some of the new purchasers were content to assume the traditional role of estate owners with all the responsibilities that went with it. But many looked on their purchases as commercial rather than political or social investments, and plainly felt less bound by the ties and obligations traditionally associated with land ownership.

In short, the whole basis of landlord–tenant relations was changing in Ulster. Just as tenants were for a variety of reasons and from a combination of causes tending to become more independent, so the landed classes were also gradually ceasing to perform those social and local functions which in the past had served to legitimise their superior role and status in society. In these circumstances, tenants were increasingly anxious to secure some kind of legislative protection for their interest in the land. It was largely fears for the future rather than the pressure of existing grievances which encouraged them to look for such protection. But the insecurity of their position and the value and vulnerability of their interest made them reluctant to antagonise their landlords by explicitly demanding or openly agitating for land reform. If the Ulster custom gave northern tenants a measure of security which those in other parts of the country did not have, it also paradoxically made them more dependent on the goodwill of the landlords; as James McKnight pointed out, tenant-right, while still unrecognised by law, was 'the great instrument of Ulster's political subjugation'.[2] Moreover, Ulster tenants were afraid that if legislation was introduced it could actually leave them worse off than they were. Tenants in the north had, in fact, less reason for agitation in the sense that their grievances were generally less acute than those of tenants in the south, and more reason for caution in the sense that they had a great deal more to lose. These considerations plus the fact that no organisation existed in Ulster through which tenant demands could be expressed meant that the land agitation was slower to start there than in the southern part of the country. Towards the end of 1869, however, with expectations of reform increasing, with a growing realisation of the dangers of silence, with a number of landlords already imposing agreements on their tenants in anticipation of Gladstone's bill, and with the organisation and leadership finally provided by a number of middle-class political activists, northern tenants joined in the agitation which had already started in the south so that within a matter of months a tenant-right movement of some importance had been established in the northern province.

The 1870 land act was, on the whole, well received in Ulster and in the first years of its operation enjoyed considerable success. Although landlord-tenant relations on many — especially the larger — estates remained largely unchanged, the act had, by placing these relations on a more strictly defined legal basis, provided a legal security for tenant-right which had not existed in the past and through this gave tenants a greater sense of independence. But, conversely, landlords themselves tended to stand more on their legal rights, and the act contributed to the weakening of the close identity of interests between landlords and tenants in Ulster which had already been taking place before 1870.

For the larger tenants, with their greater prosperity and self-reliance and their enhanced investment in tenant-right, the act represented a positive gain. For smaller tenants, with their greater economic dependence on the goodwill of the landlords, the new legal security was often an inadequate compensation for the withdrawal of the kind of social benefits they had had extended to them before 1870. Certainly the reluctance of Ulster landlords to make voluntary concessions to tenants in the depression of the late 1870s was not unrelated to the more legalistic view they were inclined to take of their relations with their tenantry after 1870. But even for the wealthier tenants the protection provided by the act soon proved to be less than complete. Doubts about leasehold tenant-right, the confiscation of tenant-right on townparks, the imposition of leases and agreements, the expense and uncertainties of litigation, and above all the failure of the act to control rents and the growing tendency of landlords to raise rents at the time of sale — all these created demands during the 1870s for amending legislation. Having 'shifted their moorings', having disturbed the mutual trust on which the tenant-right custom depended, having moved from the protection of the old semi-feudal system with its tacit and reciprocal understandings and responsibilities, it now became more essential than ever for tenants to secure full legal protection for their rights.

Tenant demands for this were articulated by the tenant-right movement, and tenant dissatisfaction and aspirations were increasingly channelled by this movement into electoral support for the Liberal party. Formed in 1869 to support the campaign for reform and express northern tenant demands, the tenant-right movement turned after 1870 to protecting tenant rights under the act. This legal and protective work continued during the remainder of the decade, but from 1872 as the defects of the act became more apparent the movement became more and more directly involved in political activity.

This was a development which was welcomed and encouraged by the leaders of the movement, many of whom were drawn from the commercial and professional classes of the towns. These classes had close social and commercial links with the tenant farmers and had themselves direct economic, social and political grievances against the landed classes. The presbyterian ministers and middle classes in particular resented the episcopalian dominance of social and political life in Ulster and their own exclusion from the whole system of government and patronage, and many of them were primarily interested in removing the status discrepancies between themselves and the episcopalians. Thus, if the tenants themselves rarely looked beyond their own immediate interests, there were others in the movement who saw it chiefly as a means of challenging the episcopalian and landed ascendancy in the province. Many of these were already involved in Liberal politics and supported tenant-right not only as an issue on which tenants could be weaned from their traditional allegiance to the Tory landlords, but as the one issue on which the Liberal party could unite its often conflicting components and divert attention away from other major divisive issues such as home rule and education, both of which threatened to deprive it of its catholic vote, its main source of support in the province. The need for a unifying issue such as tenant-right and the need for the party to stick to an anti-ascendancy programme were clearly demonstrated by the Derry by-election of 1872; and the potential of tenant-right both as a unifying issue and as a means of attracting tenant support — especially after the tenants had been given a new and greater political importance by the ballot act of 1872 — was fully revealed in the Tyrone by-election of the following year.

By 1874 the tenant-right movement had succeeded in making tenant-right the key issue in Ulster politics, and the general election of that year was fought mainly — indeed in the counties almost exclusively — on that question. In that election it enabled the Liberals for the first time to prise some of the county seats away from the Conservatives, and it continued during the remainder of the decade to be the determining factor in Ulster politics. It was on the basis of its support for tenant-right and its identification with the tenant-right movement that Liberalism continued to grow in strength during this period, so that by 1879 the indications were that the Conservative hold on the province had been seriously weakened.

The Ulster Conservatives themselves were not directly responsible for this. They had been quick to respond to the tenant-right threat both in 1874 and after, and by 1879 they had moved a good deal further in the direction of tenant demands and in support for land legislation than either their colleagues in Britain or those in the south of Ireland. Ulster landlords found it easier to support such legislation, for two reasons: first, what was being demanded by the tenant-right associations was already conceded by convention on the larger estates in Ulster; and second, with no serious racial or religious divisions between landlords and the majority of tenants in Ulster, Ulster landlords had sufficient faith in the traditional deference of their tenants to believe that landed political and social dominance would continue once the immediate cause of friction was removed. But the Ulster Tories were handicapped throughout this period by the attitude of the Tory leaders at Westminster, who not only refused to meet their demands for legislation, but continued to embarrass their followers in Ulster by their indiscriminate abuse both of the land act of 1870 and of tenant-right in general.

The development of Ulster politics between 1872 and 1878, then, was determined mainly by the land question. But that development reflected the fundamental changes which had taken place in Ulster society over the previous two decades: the gradual disintegration of traditional relationships in the counties, the emergence of an economically independent tenantry (many of them with social ambitions), the simultaneous emergence of a self-confident and more assertive presbyterian commercial and professional middle class in the towns, and the growing interdependence and emergence of common interests between these two (an alliance of interests which seemed likely to replace that between landlords and tenants in the counties). Landlord–tenant relations were already in a state of transition before 1870. But the tenant-right movement, the land act, and the ballot enabled the tenant-right leaders to direct tenant dissatisfaction and tenant aspirations into political channels and challenge the whole Tory landed hegemony; the result was that this was already under severe pressure in the province before the onset of the agricultural depression and the formation of the Land League in the south at the end of the 1870s. But for the majority of those who took part, this was essentially a movement with limited objectives. Ulster tenants were willing to use whatever instruments were at hand to achieve their own ends. Thus they supported the tenant-right movement and the Liberal party because it suited them to do so. And a number of them were equally prepared to make use of the Land League when it appeared in Ulster.

The agricultural depression of the late 1870s brought to a head many of the developments which had been taking place in Ulster during the previous decade. In many respects the depression had as far-reaching effects in Ulster as in the rest of the country, and certainly the distress in some parts of the north was every bit as serious as in any part of the south. Small farmers and labourers were particularly badly hit, and had it not been for the work of the various relief organisations many of them could scarcely have survived the winter of 1879–80. But all rural classes were affected. If the depression inflicted severe hardship on the smallholders and labourers, it also threatened to undermine the increasing prosperity of the larger farmers and — an additional and crucial factor in Ulster — to destroy the value of their tenant-right investment in the soil. It was primarily in order to protect these that the larger tenants took the lead in the agitation for rent abatements at this time, but they were readily joined by the smaller tenants, many of whom were already not only in arrears from previous seasons, but frequently under pressure from shopkeepers and loan banks for the repayment of debts, and some of whom could pay no rent at all. While many landlords responded generously to the demands of the situation, others refused — indeed in many instances were too impoverished — to make any allowances whatsoever, and the general feeling was that the landlords as a class had not done all that they might have done to meet tenant needs.

This feeling undoubtedly contributed to the more independent line taken by tenants in the general election of 1880. This election represented a major breakthrough in the Ulster counties by the Liberals, who increased the number of county seats in their control from three to eight and narrowly missed winning two others. These successes were based almost entirely on the tenant-right question, and came at a time when many of the urban middle-class supporters of the party were already beginning to realise and fear the implications of the land agitation in the south. But landed political predominance in the counties had now been plainly shattered, with the Tories, already labouring under the handicap of the Disraeli government's record on land reform, retaining control of only eight of the eighteen county seats as against seventeen in 1868 and thirteen in 1874. Clearly the traditional bonds of allegiance between the landlords and tenants — under pressure before 1870 — had been stretched to breaking point by the events of 1879–80, and such successes as were won in 1880 were won only by the readiness of the Tory landed candidates to concede the full demands of the tenants with regard to tenant-right.

The election added to the conviction of the landed Tories that there
would be no 'return to traditional allegiances' until the land question
was finally and permanently settled.

The election of Gladstone, the appointment of the Bessborough
commission, and the Land League campaign in the south led to
rising expectations of reform in Ulster which were, however, seriously
checked by the defeat of the compensation bill in the House of
Lords in August 1880. The fear was now created that the landed
interest in the lords would defeat whatever government proposals
were introduced. Added to this was the fact that the landlords, seeing
only the improved harvest of 1880 and frequently under great financial
pressure themselves, were adopting a more hardline attitude in the
matter of rents. The result was that the tenants — with the tenant-
right movement complacently awaiting the government proposals
and not at all inclined to lend its weight to demands for rent
abatements — turned increasingly to the Land League which, tailoring
its policy and tactics to suit northern conditions, began to spread
rapidly in Ulster, deriving its support mainly from the catholics, but
also to an extent which surprised and disconcerted the loyalist leaders
from protestant tenants as well. But the protestant support for the
league was essentially pragmatic; it was the potential of the league
for securing land reform and reducing rents that attracted northern
protestant tenants, not any desire for the extirpation of Irish
landlordism and certainly not any sympathy with the ulterior political
objectives of the league leaders. The main legislative demands of the
northern tenants continued to be articulated by the tenant-right
movement, which was eventually galvanised into action by the Land
League campaign, and once these demands were met by the act of
1881 protestant support for the league quickly fell off. The point
cannot be too strongly made that the support was a purely temporary
phenomenon and was neither the beginning of nor the basis for a
more permanent alliance between the different groups involved.

Nevertheless, it reflected at the time the degree to which the northern
tenants had become alienated from the landed classes, and it was of
course immensely alarming to the latter. They tried to counter it in
two ways. First, they looked increasingly to the Orange order as the

only organisation capable of meeting the league threat in the north and undermining protestant support for the league, and the revival of Orangeism and its re-identification with the landed classes — who had neglected it during the previous decades — were among the most significant of the consequences of the land war for Ulster. And secondly, they themselves accepted and positively supported a more radical settlement of the land question than they would ever have countenanced in the 1870s. It was not so much that they supported land reform because they put the preservation of their political ascendancy before economic self-interest (their tardy response to tenant requests for rent abatements in 1880, and their readiness to resort to the full force of the law in order to exact what was due to them showed that they were as keenly aware and as protective of their economic interests as anyone else); rather they believed and were, indeed, encouraged by government spokesmen to believe that the legalisation of the 3Fs would not radically alter the existing situation and current practices on their own estates. Thus they supported Gladstone's proposals and played a vital role in ensuring their safe passage through both houses of parliament.

However, if Ulster landlords looked to the act to restore landlord–tenant relations to what they had been before the emergence of the tenant-right question, they were to be sorely disappointed. The act worked out in a way that neither they nor anyone else had expected, and they themselves were party to the fierce attacks which the landed classes in general made on its administration from 1881. But they were never prepared to carry these attacks to the point of jeopardising the success of the measure. What the act had done, in fact, was to provide a mechanism by which rents could be adjusted to meet the new economic circumstances created by the opening up of the American west and the general world-wide decline in prices. Gladstone was right: he had saved the landed interest in Ireland, for only by such an adjustment could social order be restored and the country saved from more serious social dislocation.

As it operated, however, the act represented a serious economic loss to landlords in terms both of income and of the capital value of their estates. As a result of these factors and also the greater independence being shown by tenants, the landlords began after 1881 to redefine their social role, withdrawing more rapidly than they had in the 1870s the kind of social benevolence which had in the past legitimised their social and political pre-eminence. It can, indeed, be argued that landlord–tenant relations in Ulster, if measured by the number of evictions, actually reached their nadir in the months after rather than before the act was passed. The act finally ended the kind of semi-feudal relationships which had existed in Ulster up to and even after the Great Famine and which had begun to disintegrate with the new economic and social developments from the 1850s. By depriving landlords of much of what remained of their social and political influence, it also deprived land of many of its non-economic as well as its economic attractions, and encouraged many landlords to think in terms of selling out.

The tenants also were turning increasingly to purchase as the ultimate solution to the land question. Although welcoming the act of 1881 as a major boon, they too had their grievances after 1881. In particular there was dissatisfaction with the administration of the act and with the alleged failure of the sub-commissioners to make sufficient allowance for tenant-right and tenant improvements; there were also the problems still facing tenants in arrears; and there was the exclusion of leaseholders. The result was that tenant-right activity in the province continued after the act had been passed, reaching a peak indeed when the court valuers were appointed at the end of 1882. But although complaints about judicial rents and demands for the inclusion of leaseholders in the benefits of the act continued to be made after 1883, and although friction continued on many estates (especially from 1885 when a recurrence of depression forced many tenants to look for an abatement even of their judicial rents), the most pressing tenant grievances had been resolved and the major points of conflict between landlords and tenants over land tenure had been settled.

Not only had the immediate crisis in landlord–tenant relations passed: the single most important issue dividing the Liberals and Conservatives had been temporarily settled. The very success of the land legislation had deprived Ulster Liberals of much of their political capital. The land question had proved an effective rallying point for the opponents of the Tory and episcopalian landed ascendancy, but once the principle on which it could be settled was agreed upon, the forces that had mustered on that issue tended to dissipate, though many of their real grievances — often, as in the case of the presbyterian urban middle classes, not directly related to land at all — remained.[3] For many tenant farmers in particular, Liberalism had never meant more than the protection of their tenant-right and a curtailment of landlord power, and once these were achieved their enthusiasm for the cause rapidly waned.

What finally completed the collapse of the Liberal party, consolidated Ulster protestant support behind the Tory party, and restored the political hegemony of the landed classes was the nationalist campaign in Ulster from 1883. Protestant forces could more easily coalesce behind the Tory party because the land tenure question — the most potent source of division among protestants after the Irish church had been disestablished — had now largely been settled. And, if the land legislation had removed a major obstacle to protestant unity, it had at the same time neutralised the one area of common grievance between catholics and protestants on which the nationalists could ever conceivably have hoped to appeal to northern protestants; the leaders of the National League still gave priority to land in their campaign in Ulster, but tenant grievances there were no longer sufficiently oppressive for the nationalists to have any success in this respect. The political independence of the presbyterian tenant farmers did not, of course, disappear entirely. It resurfaced on different occasions during the next twenty years, but only when there was no immediate danger to the union and only in areas where unionist control was secure. Ulster politics were henceforth to be dominated by the two diametrically opposed ideologies of unionism and nationalism. There was no longer any place for Liberalism. All those developments which over the previous two decades had promised to make Ulster an increasingly Liberal province now came to an end. The Ulster Liberal was not quite an extinct species, but Ulster Liberalism as a political force was dead and gone. The defeat of Russellism in 1906 clearly reflected the established priorities of Ulster politics.

# APPENDIX I

Religious distribution of tenant farmers in Ulster in 1871 (per cent)

|  | CATHOLICS | EPISCOPALIANS | PRESBYTERIANS | METHODISTS AND OTHERS |
|---|---|---|---|---|
| Antrim | 21.62 | 11.00 | 62.91 | 4.46 |
| Armagh | 50.45 | 24.97 | 20.80 | 3.77 |
| Cavan | 78.97 | 15.41 | 4.55 | 1.07 |
| Donegal | 75.04 | 11.92 | 11.79 | 1.26 |
| Down | 32.97 | 11.80 | 51.68 | 3.55 |
| Fermanagh | 50.14 | 42.00 | 2.32 | 5.54 |
| Londonderry | 42.56 | 10.75 | 44.27 | 2.41 |
| Monaghan | 71.05 | 12.23 | 16.00 | 0.73 |
| Tyrone | 52.92 | 23.34 | 21.62 | 2.12 |
| Ulster | 52.68 | 17.08 | 27.42 | 2.64 |

*Source: Census of Ireland, 1871: Part 1, Area, Houses and Population ... Vol III. Province of Ulster* ... [C.964 — I to X], H.C., 1874, lxxiv, 1.

# APPENDIX II

Agricultural trends in Ulster 1847–76

Table 1. Acreage under crops and pasture in Ulster 1847–76

|      | CEREALS   | ROOT CROPS | FLAX    | MEADOW AND CLOVER | GRASS     |
|------|-----------|------------|---------|-------------------|-----------|
| 1847 | 1,116,511 | 216,601    | 53,701  | 263,149           |           |
| 1851 | 1,046,417 | 420,026    | 125,407 | 260,145           | 2,111,736 |
| 1861 | 942,804   | 494,172    | 143,206 | 372,801           | 2,092,366 |
| 1871 | 800,397   | 491,336    | 147,065 | 465,687           | 2,179,427 |
| 1876 | 738,761   | 464,386    | 129,051 | 470,025           | 2,258,614 |

Table 2. The number of livestock in Ulster 1847–76

|      | CATTLE    | SHEEP   | PIGS    |
|------|-----------|---------|---------|
| 1847 | 834,874   | 238,493 | 111,733 |
| 1851 | 940,993   | 253,133 | 246,831 |
| 1861 | 1,023,039 | 387,481 | 243,409 |
| 1871 | 1,161,088 | 542,101 | 421,464 |
| 1876 | 1,172,274 | 456,642 | 377,036 |

*Sources: The agricultural statistics of Ireland for the year 1871* [C.762], H.C. 1873, lxix, 375, pp. xlix, lxxx; *The agricultural statistics of Ireland for the year 1876* [C.1749], H.C. 1877, lxxxv, 529, pp. 30–31, 52; *The agricultural statistics of Ireland for the year 1881* [C.3332], H.C. 1881, lxxvi, 93, p. 53.

# APPENDIX III

Size distribution of farm holdings in Ulster above one acre, 1845–81

|      | 1–5 ACRES | 5–15 ACRES | 15–30 ACRES | 30+ ACRES | TOTAL   |
|------|-----------|------------|-------------|-----------|---------|
| 1845 | 53,149    | 115,463    | 56,150      | 28,206    | 252,968 |
| 1851 | 29,709    | 85,176     | 57,651      | 37,813    | 210,349 |
| 1861 | 28,458    | 82,053     | 57,660      | 39,494    | 207,635 |
| 1871 | 24,232    | 73,647     | 56,878      | 41,071    | 195,828 |
| 1881 | 21,971    | 68,362     | 55,227      | 42,510    | 188,070 |

P.M.A. Bourke has demonstrated the unreliability of the 1841 census figures of farm size, and the figures for 1845 have been adapted from returns provided by the poor law commissioners.[1] There are two main problems here. First, the returns were arranged by poor law union rather than by county, and the poor law union and county boundaries are not coterminous. Nevertheless, there is a very close match, and the figures have been corrected from the agricultural returns for 1848 which give the number of holdings in each poor law union according to county.[2] The second major problem is that the poor law commissioners used different categories of size from those in the census and agricultural returns. Bourke, in producing his revised figures for Ireland, used the mathematical device of accumulating to the different breaks in the 1845 returns (5, 10, 20, 50 acres) and fitting a curve, and this has been done here.[3] The results clearly have to be interpreted with discretion, but the figures for the lower categories — up to 15 acres — should be pretty near the mark. At the very least, they provide a useful basis for comparing the number of holdings before and after the Famine.

# APPENDIX IV

Statistics of cases in Ulster under the land act of 1870

Table 1. The number of cases under the act, 1870–78

|  | IRELAND | ULSTER | CASES IN ULSTER AS % OF TOTAL |
|---|---|---|---|
| 1870–1* | 526 | 287 | 54.6 |
| 1872 | 599 | 346 | 57.8 |
| 1873 | 726 | 382 | 52.6 |
| 1874 | 1,061 | 791 | 74.6 |
| 1875 | 929 | 630 | 67.8 |
| 1876 | 472 | 275 | 58.3 |
| 1877 | 598 | 317 | 53.0 |
| 1878 | 514 | 270 | 52.5 |
| TOTAL | 5,425 | 3,298 | 60.8 |

*This act was in operation for only a short period in 1870 and proceedings for that year have been included with those for 1871 in this and the other tables.

Table 2. The gross amount awarded as compensation under the act, 1870-78

| | IRELAND (£) | ULSTER (£) | AWARDS IN ULSTER AS % OF TOTAL | FOR ULSTER TENANT-RIGHT | % IN ULSTER FOR TENANT-RIGHT |
|---|---|---|---|---|---|
| 1870–1 | 13,664 | 9,956 | 73 | 4,558 | 46 |
| 1872 | 19,367 | 10,832 | 56 | 5,101* | 69* |
| 1873 | 19,638 | 8,448 | 43 | 2,122* | 28* |
| 1874 | 19,450 | 9,186 | 47 | 5,954 | 65 |
| 1875 | 21,184 | 11,672 | 55 | 6,221 | 53 |
| 1876 | 15,023 | 9,210 | 61 | 6,502 | 71 |
| 1877 | 15,401 | 8,877 | 58 | 5,152 | 58 |
| 1878 | 17,063 | 8,305 | 49 | 5,969 | 72 |
| TOTAL | 140,790 | 76,486 | 54 | 41,579 | 54 |

*Not all the compensation awarded in Ulster in these two years could be accurately classified. These are the amounts for tenant-right and the percentages of the compensation where classification was returned.

Table 3. The average value of the awards made under the act, 1870–78

|  | IRELAND (£) | ULSTER (£) |
|---|---|---|
| 1870–1 | 69 | 81 |
| 1872 | 95 | 93 |
| 1873 | 83 | 80 |
| 1874 | 87 | 101 |
| 1875 | 96 | 128 |
| 1876 | 86 | 97 |
| 1877 | 92 | 107 |
| 1877 | 98 | 106 |
| 1870–78 | 88 | 99 |

Table 4. The nature of the claims made in Ulster, 1870–6

| | 1870–1 | 1872 | 1873 | 1874 | 1875 | 1876 |
|---|---|---|---|---|---|---|
| Loss on quitting holding | 205 | 231 | 255 | 222 | 189 | 188 |
| Improvements | 218 | 268 | 272 | 228 | 200 | 183 |
| Ulster tenant-right | 182 | 240 | 257 | 724 | 578 | 217 |
| Incoming payments | 6 | 56 | 40 | 34 | 50 | 40 |
| Total number of cases | 287 | 346 | 382 | 791 | 630 | 275 |

*Sources: Judicial statistics (Ireland), 1871: Pt I. Police, criminal proceedings, prisons; Pt II. Common law, equity, civil and canon law* [C.674], H.C. 1872, lxv, 235, pp. 91–4, 236; *Criminal and judicial statistics (Ireland), 1872: Pt. I. Police, criminal proceedings, prisons: Pt. II. Common law, equity, and civil law* [C.851], H.C. 1873, lxx, 247, pp. 89–81, 228–9; *Criminal and judicial statistics ... 1873 ...* [C.1034], H.C. 1874, lxxi, 251, pp. 84–7, 228–9; *Criminal and judicial statistics ... 1874 ...* [C.1295], H.C. 1875, lxxxi, 259, pp. 79–81, 222–3; *Criminal and judicial statistics ... 1875 ...* [C.1563], H.C. 1876, lxxix, 273, pp. 76–9, 222–3; *Criminal and judicial statistics ... 1876 ...* [C.1822], H.C. 1877, lxxxvi, 261, pp. 78–80, 222–3; *Criminal and judicial statistics ... 1877 ...* [C.2152], H.C. 1878, lxxix, 265, pp. 78–81, 222–3; *Criminal and judicial statistics, 1878 ...* [C.2389], H.C. 1878–9, lxxvi, 279, pp. 69–72, 138–9.

# Notes

## Introduction

1 One important exception is W.E. Vaughan, *Landlords and tenants in mid-Victorian Ireland* (Oxford, 1994).

2 This was a view which was early propagated by nationalist politicians. See e.g. Michael Davitt, *The fall of feudalism in Ireland* (London and New York, 1904), p. 332; William O'Brien, *Recollections* (London, 1905), p. 322; T.M. Healy, *Letters and leaders of my day*, 2 vols (New York, 1929), i, 134.

3 See J. Mokyr, *Why Ireland starved: a quantitative and analytical history of the Irish economy, 1800–1850* (Repr., London, 1985), p. 275.

4 C. Kinealy, *This great calamity, the Irish famine 1845–52* (Dublin, 1994), p. 281; M.E. Daly, *The famine in Ireland* (Dundalk, 1986), pp. 62–3; Frank Wright, *Two lands on one soil: Ulster politics before home rule* (Dublin, 1996), pp. 121–2, 126.

5 *Returns from the court for the sale of incumbered estates in Ireland, up to the 1st day of April 1853* ... H.C. 1852–53 (390), xciv, 599, p. 1.

6 J. S. Donnelly Jr, 'Landlords and tenants', in *A new history of Ireland: Ireland under the union, 1801–70*, ed. W.E. Vaughan (Oxford, 1989), p. 332.

7 Kinealy, *This great calamity*, pp. 86–7; Wright, *Two lands on one soil*, pp. 105, 112–14. See also J. Grant, 'The Great Famine and the poor law in Ulster: the rate-in-aid issue of 1849', *I.H.S.*, xxvii (1990), pp. 31–33.

8 Kinealy, *This great calamity*, p. 283; Grant, 'The Great Famine and the poor law', p. 32.

9 Kinealy, *This great calamity*, p. 167; Wright, *Two lands on one soil*, pp. 107–9; G. Mawhinney and E. Dunlop (eds), *The autobiography of Thomas Witherow 1824–1890* (Draperstown, 1990), p. 71; J. Bardon, *A history of Ulster* (Belfast, 1992), p. 286.

10 Wright, *Two lands on one soil*, p. 107.

11 J.H. Whyte, *The independent Irish party, 1850–9* (Oxford, 1958), p. 7; B.A. Kennedy, 'The tenant-right agitation in Ulster, 1845–50', *Bulletin of the Irish Committee of Historical Sciences*, no. 34 (Nov. 1944), pp. 2–5.

12 Whyte, *The independent Irish party*, pp. 19–20, 85–9.

13 For this election, see *ibid.*, pp. 82–6; Wright, *Two lands on one soil*, pp. 201–7.

## Chapter 1

1 *Summary of the returns of owners of land in Ireland, showing with respect to each county, the number of owners below an acre, and in classes up to 100,000 and upwards* ... H.C. 1876 (442), lxxx, 35, pp. 16–21; *Return of the names of proprietors and the area and valuation of all properties in ... Ireland,* H.C. 1876 (412), lxxx, 395, pp. 97–178.

2 The most authoritative and valuable discussion of landed influence in Ireland is K.T. Hoppen, *Elections, politics and society in Ireland, 1832–1885* (Oxford, 1984), pp. 89–170.

3 For a brief outline of the structure of local government in Ireland see W.F. Bailey, *Local and centralised government in Ireland, a sketch of the existing systems* (London and Dublin, 1888). For a more recent account, see V. Crossman, *Local government in nineteenth century Ireland* (Belfast, 1994).

4   Election results and statistics are taken from B.M. Walker (ed.), *Parliamentary election results in Ireland, 1801–1922* (Dublin, 1978); and the local press.

5   Whyte, *The independent Irish party*, pp. 66–68; Hoppen, *Elections, politics and society*, pp. 147–50.

6   *C.C.*, 21 Aug. 1869.

7   Conyngham to Lord Francis Conyngham, 25 Sept. 1868, copy in *B.U.*, 29 Sept. 1868; John Hamilton, *Sixty years' experience as an Irish landlord* (London, 1894), p. 270.

8   Statement of F.R. Falkiner QC, *N.W.*, 21 Dec. 1872.

9   Quoted in *C.C.*, 14 Aug. 1869.

10  *Ibid.*, 30 Oct. 1869.

11  *Census of Ireland, 1871: Part 1, Area, houses, population ... Vol. iii Province of Ulster ...* [C964-I to X], H.C. 1874, lxxiv, I, p. 991; F.S.L. Lyons, *Culture and anarchy in Ireland 1890–1939* (Oxford, 1979), p. 139. See Appendix I for religious distribution of tenant farmers in Ulster.

12  B.M. Walker, *Ulster politics, the formative years 1868–86* (Belfast, 1989), p. 42.

13  *B.U.*, 23 May 1868; *C.C.*, 1 Jan., 14 May 1870, 23 Dec. 1871; *N.W.*, 9 Feb. 1870.

14  The local press is full of reports of such celebrations. See e.g. *B.N.L.*, 8 Oct. 1872; *N.W.*, 12 Feb. 1879.

15  H.S. Morrison, *Modern Ulster, its character, customs, politics and industries* (London, 1920), p. 32.

16  *N.W.*, 19, 28 Dec. 1872.

17  *Ibid.*, 19 Dec. 1872. See also Hertford to W. Stannus, 27 Dec. 1852, in B. Falk, *Old Q's daughter: the history of a strange family* (London, 1937), pp. 239–40.

18  See e.g. *Reports from poor law inspectors in Ireland as to the existing relations between landlord and tenant ...* [C.31], H.C. 1870, xiv, 37, p. 83.

19  Hoppen, *Elections, politics and society*, pp. 129–37; James Godkin, *The land war in Ireland* (London, 1870), pp. 313–4; Hugh Montgomery to Thompson, August 1879, Montgomery Mss. D1121/5. While most landlords made social donations of one kind or another, few ran the risk of bankrupting themselves through philanthropic effort. Sir William Verner's contributions, for example, amounted to just under 2 per cent of his rental. Verner Mss. D236/488/3, pp. 7, 12–3, 353, 369–71; 'Abstract estate account, 1879', D236/485.

20  Hamilton, *Sixty years' experience as an Irish landlord*, p. 374; G. Shaw-Lefevre, *English and Irish land questions, collected essays* (2nd edn, London, 1881), p. 136.

21  Hugh de F. Montgomery, 'The present aspect of the Irish land question', *Macmillan's Magazine*, xxxii (May, 1875), p. 39; J.S. Mill, *Chapters and speeches on the Irish land question* (London, 1870), p. 95.

22  *Report of her majesty's commissioners of inquiry into the working of the Landlord and Tenant (Ireland) Act, 1870, and the amending acts ...* [C.2779], H.C. 1881, xviii, 1 (hereafter cited as *Bessborough Commission*), Q.5973. See also *ibid.*, Q.6102–3; Hugh de F. Montgomery, *Irish land and Irish rights* (London, 1881), pp. 13–14; *Preliminary report of the assistant commissioners for Ireland* [C.2951], H.C. 1881, xvi, 841, pp. 5–6.

23  *B.N.L.*, 9 Feb. 1874.

24  *N.W.*, 28 Jan. 1874.

25  *C.C.*, 23 Dec. 1871.

26 Vane Londonderry to Earl of Beaconsfield, 15 August 1878, Disraeli Mss. B/XXI/V/37; *Armagh Guardian* 2 July 1886; Verner Mss. D236/488/5, pp. 137, 436–7.

27 Montgomery to Thompson, 28 January 1875. Montgomery Mss. D1121/4.

28 W.B. Gwynn, *Democracy and the cost of politics in Britain* (London, 1962), pp. 86–7.

29 *B.N.L.*, 25 Jan. 1872. Although Charles Russell was defeated in the Dundalk election of 1874, his legal fees for the year were double those of the previous year and his income showed a further substantial increase after his election to parliament in 1880. R Barry O'Brien, *The life of Lord Russell of Killowen* (London, n.d.) pp. 122, 208.

30 Lord Ernest Hamilton, *Forty years on* (London, n.d.), pp. 203, 222–4.

31 Lord A.E. Hill-Trevor to Beaconsfield, 20 April 1880, Disraeli Mss. C/1/B/138.

32 Lady Leslie to Earl of Iddesleigh, 2 Dec. 1885, Salisbury Mss. Ser. E; Lady Leslie to Salisbury, 24 June 1892, *ibid.* Y/2/L.

33 Sir Stafford Northcote to Salisbury, 2 Jan. 1882, Salisbury Mss. Ser. E.

34 Lewis to Duke of Abercorn, 13 Nov. 1886, *ibid.* D/28/8.

35 Adair to Gladstone, 17 Sept. 1869, 2 Dec. 1869, 26 Sept. 1870, Gladstone Mss. 44422, f. 38, 44423, f. 38, 44423, f. 259; 44428, f. 117; McClure to Gladstone 6 Feb. 1874, *ibid.* 44442, f. 172. Adair was raised to the peerage as Baron Waveney in 1873.

36 Knox to Disraeli, 16 Mar. 1874, Disraeli Mss. B/XIII/B/21 a, b.

37 Sir Thomas Bateson to M. Corry, 24 November 1874, *ibid.* B/XXI/J/83; Michael Hicks-Beach to Disraeli, 29 December 1875, *ibid.* B/XXI/J/94a; Marquis of Hamilton to M. Corry, 17 October 1876, *ibid.* B/XXI/J/98. Johnston himself wrote at least a dozen letters to Disraeli and Corry in 1874 and 1875 asking for an appointment. *Ibid.* B/XXI/J/81–104.

38 Ranfurly to Salisbury, 26 June 1895, Salisbury Mss./E; Duke of Abercorn to Salisbury, 26 Feb. 1896, *ibid.* Ranfurly was appointed to the governorship of New Zealand in 1897. Hill was not so successful.

39 William Harcourt to Lord Spencer, 11 June 1885, Harcourt Mss IVA/6/33; Dickson to James Bryce, 29 July 1892, Bryce Mss. U.B.5.

40 Belmore to Salisbury, 15 Jan. 1892, Salisbury Mss./E.

41 *B.N.L.*, 5, 7 June 1872.

42 *N.W.*, 21 Feb. 1874. See also R. Smyth to Gladstone, 21 Feb. 1874, Gladstone Mss. 44443, f. 7.

43 See Hoppen, *Elections, politics and society*, pp. 82–3.

44 See e.g. Rev. John Doherty PP to Lord O'Hagan, 7 May 1880, O'Hagan Mss. D2777ADD/47.

45 W.A. Dane to Lord Mayo, 5 Feb. 1868, enclosed with note from Mayo to Lord Abercorn, 5 Feb. 1868, Abercorn Mss. T2541/V.R. 85/38; Col. Taylor to Lord Abercorn, 5 Feb. 1868 enclosed with letter from Mayo to Abercorn, 5 Feb. 1868, *ibid.* T2541/V85/37.

46 Lord Claud Hamilton to Abercorn, 22 Jan. 1867, Abercorn Mss. T2541/V.R.128; Thomas W. Heygate to Abercorn, 24 Jan. 1867, *ibid.* T2541/V.R.135. The Hamiltons were assiduous in guarding their interests in north-east Ulster. See also Lord Claud Hamilton to Abercorn, 31

Dec. 1866, *ibid.* T2541/V.R.113; same to same, 28 Nov. 1868, 29 Nov. 1868, 2 Dec. 1868, *ibid.* T2541/V.R.299, 300, 311.

47 Dowse to O'Hagan, 27 April 1869, O'Hagan Mss. D2777, ADD/37. See also Thomas Dickson MP to O'Hagan, 31 July 1880, *ibid.* D2777, ADD/47.

48 *C.C.*, 30 April 1871. See also *ibid.* 18 June 1870. If county lieutenants were reluctant to nominate presbyterians for the bench, they seemed absolutely determined to prevent the appointment of catholics. For catholic difficulties in this respect see John Harbinson, Cookstown to O'Hagan, 11 April 1869, 4 Jan. 1881, 21 Mar. 1881, O'Hagan Mss. D2777, ADD/37, 50.

49 *N.W.*, 31 Aug. 1872. See also *ibid.*, 6, 9 Jan. 1874: 22 June, 10 Aug. 1880.

50 *Ibid.*, 19 April 1880.

51 For the agricultural depression of 1859–64, see J.S. Donnelly Jr, 'The Irish agricultural depression of 1859–64', *Irish economic and social history*, iii (1976), pp. 33–54.

52 G. Best, *Mid-Victorian Britain 1851–75* (revised edn, St Albans, Herts, 1973), pp. 111–19; J. Burnett, *Plenty and want, a social history of diet in England from 1815 to the present day* (Harmondsworth, 1968), pp. 123, 131.

53 Thomas Barrington, 'A review of Irish agricultural prices', *J.S.S.I.S.I.*, pt ci, xv (Oct. 1927), pp. 251–3.

54 *Census of Ireland, for the year 1841,* p. 364; *Census of Ireland, 1871: Part I. Area, houses and population ... vol. iii, province of Ulster ... Summary tables and indexes* [C.964-I to X], H.C. 1874, lxxiv, pt I, p. 991. The actual numbers had fallen from 281,576 in 1841 to 133,433 in 1871.

55 *Reports from poor law inspectors on the wages of agricultural labourers in Ireland* [C.35], H.C. 1870, 1, pp 3–5, 9, 18–19; *Reports on landlord–tenant relations*, p. 113. For the condition of agricultural labourers, see J.W. Boyle, 'A marginal figure: the Irish rural labourer', in S. Clarke and J.S. Donnelly Jr (eds), *Irish peasants; violence and political unrest, 1780–1914* (Manchester, 1983), pp. 311–337; D. Fitzpatrick, 'The disappearance of the Irish agricultural labourer, 1841–1912', *Irish Economic and Social History,* vii (1980).

56 A valuable survey of agriculture in Ulster during the nineteenth century is contained in L. Kennedy, 'The rural economy, 1820–1914', in L. Kennedy and P. Ollerenshaw (eds), *An economic history of Ulster, 1820–1939* (Manchester, 1985), pp. 1–61.

57 *The agricultural statistics of Ireland for the year 1871* [C.762], H.C. 1873, lxix, 375, p. xlix; *The agricultural statistics of Ireland for the year 1876* [C.1749], H.C. 1877, lxxxv, 529, pp. 30–31, 52. See Appendix II.

58 *Agric. Stats. for 1871*, p. lxxx; *The agricultural statistics of Ireland for the year 1881* [C.3332], H.C. 1881, lxxvi, 93, p. 53. See Appendix II.

59 *Returns of agricultural produce in Ireland in the year 1854.* [2017], H.C. 1856, liii, 1, p. xli; *Agric. Stats. for 1876*, p. 55.

60 J. O'Donovan, *The economic history of livestock in Ireland* (Cork, 1940), pp. 206–7.

61 J.N. Murphy, *Ireland, industrial, political and social* (London, 1870), p. 39; Letters of S.M. Shannon to *N.W.*, 5 May 1874 and *C.C.*, 19 Sept. 1874.

62 Florence Mary McDowell, *Other days around me* (Belfast, 1972), p. 127.

63 *B.N.L.*, 23 Feb. 1872.

64 See e.g. *B.U.*, 19 Sept. 1868.

65  *W.N.W.*, 11 Sept. 1869; *B.N.L.*, 2
    June 1874, 17 Aug. 1874; Godkin, *The
    land war in Ireland*, pp. 319, 350;
    Murphy, *Ireland, industrial, political and
    social*, pp. 187–9.

66  *Agric. Stats. for 1871,* pp. xiii, xx.

67  Godkin, *The land war in Ireland*, pp.
    349–50.

68  Murphy, *Ireland, industrial, political and
    social*, pp. 121–2; William O'Connor
    Morris, *Letters on the land question of
    Ireland* (London, 1870), pp. 252, 264.

69  See Appendix III.

70  *Agric. Stats. for 1861*, p. xiv; *Agric.
    Stats. for 1871*, p. xii; *Agric. Stats. for
    1881*, p. 9.

71  Mokyr, *Why Ireland starved*, p. 19.

72  Thomas W. Grimshaw, 'A statistical
    survey of Ireland, from 1840 to
    1888' *J.S.S.I.S.I.*, pt 1, lxviii, vol. ix
    (December, 1888) p. 343. See also P.
    Ollerenshaw, 'Industry 1820–1914',
    in Kennedy and Ollerenshaw (eds),
    *Economic history of Ulster*, pp. 73–5.

73  *Reports on landlord–tenant relations*, pp.
    109–10.

74  *Ibid.*, pp. 15, 144.

75  See W.E. Vaughan, 'Agricultural
    output, rents and wages in Ireland,
    1850–1880', in *Ireland and France 17th–
    20th centuries: towards a comparative
    study of rural history*, ed. L.M. Cullen
    and F. Furet (Paris, 1980), pp. 88–9.

76  James H. Tuke, *Irish distress and its
    remedies, a visit to Donegal and
    Connaught in the Spring of 1880* (4th
    edn, London, 1880) p. 91. Tuke was
    an English Quaker and banker
    whose experiences of relief work
    in Ireland went back to the Famine
    and who was widely regarded as an
    authority on the Irish land system.

77  See S.H. Cousens, 'Emigration and
    demographic change in Ireland,
    1851–1861', *Economic History Review*,

    xiv (1961), pp. 275–288; S.H.
    Cousens, 'The regional variations in
    population changes in Ireland,
    1861–81', *ibid.*, xvii (1964), pp. 301–
    321.

78  *Bessborough Commission*, Q.5407.

79  J.M. Mogey, *Rural Life in Northern
    Ireland* (London, 1947).

80  In 1881 there were 188,070 holdings
    of more than one acre in Ulster in
    the hands of 174,728 occupiers
    (*Agric. stats. for 1881*, pp. 8–9). The
    point is also worth making that
    while tenants of farms of over
    thirty acres made up less than 30
    per cent of the total Irish tenant
    population in 1871, they occupied
    some 76 per cent of the farming
    land. *Agric. stats. for 1871*, p. xiii.

81  See *N.W.*, 10 Feb. 1872. See also W.
    P. Coyne (ed.)., *Ireland, industrial and
    agricultural* (Dublin, 1902), p. 130;
    *N.W.*, 25 Aug. 1879.

82  'Irish farmers and joint stock bank
    deposits' in *Pall Mall Gazette*, repr. in
    *N.W.*, 12 Feb. 1880.

83  *N.W.*, 25 Aug. 1879.

84  As late as the 1850s there appears to
    have been a widespread distrust of
    banks especially among the smaller
    farmers, and there are many stories
    of tenants keeping considerable
    sums of money in the thatch of
    their cottages, in mattresses and
    other supposedly safe hiding places.
    See e.g. W.S. Trench, *Realities of Irish
    life* (London, 1868), pp. 198, 208.

85  *C.C.*, 11 Sept. 1869; O. Robinson,
    'The London Companies as
    progressive landlords in nineteenth
    century Ireland', *Economic History
    Review*, 2nd ser., xv, no. 1 (1962–3), p.
    117.

86  *Reports on landlord–tenant relations*, pp.
    15, 108–9, 143.

87 See e.g. *C.C.*, 15 Aug., 16 Oct. 1874.

88 *Census, 1841*, pp. 362–3; *Census of Ireland for the year 1851: Part vi, General report* [2134], H.C. 1856, xxxi, 1, p. 524; *Census of Ireland for the year 1861; Part v, General report* [3204–iv], H.C. 1863, lxi, 1, p. 366; *Census, 1871*, p. 970; *Census of Ireland, 1881: Part i: Area, houses etc, vol iii, province of Ulster* [C.3204-I to X], H.C. 1881, lxxviii, 1, pp. 967–8.

89 *N.W.*, 26 Feb. 1872.

90 See e.g. the sale of the household contents of a farm at Killough, County Down, *N.W.*, 6 Jan. 1874. For other examples of itemised lists of the contents of well-furnished farmhouses being offered for sale, see *ibid.*, 21 June, 20 Aug., 18 Sept. 1872, 27 Oct. 1875; *C.C.*, 3 April 1869, 21 June 1871, 10 Oct. 1874; *L. Journ.*, 13 Oct. 1869; *Ballymena Advertiser*, 6 Feb., 17 April 1875; *B.F.P.*, 30 Mar. 1876.

91 *Thirty-ninth report from the board of public works, Ireland: with the appendices, for the year 1870–1* [C 383], H.C. 1871, xvi, 307, p. 48.

92 Godkin, *The land war in Ireland*, p. 320; O'Connor Morris, *Letters on the land question*, p. 284.

93 *C. Const.*, 4 Oct. 1879.

94 *C.C.*, 21 Jan. 1871. For the activities of one trader in Coleraine during these years, see the autobiographical memoir of A.J.H. Moody, provision merchant, PRONI, T2901/4/1.

95 *B.N.L.*, 29 Aug. 1874; Florence Mary McDowell, *Roses and rainbows* (Belfast, 1972), pp. 43–51; Hoppen, *Elections, politics and society*, pp. 437–9.

96 *Thirty-ninth report from the board of public works*, p. 48.

97 *B.F.P.*, 24 June 1875.

98 Quoted in J.L. McCracken, 'The late nineteenth century', in Moody and

Beckett (eds), *Ulster since 1800, a social survey*, p. 52.

99 McDowell, *Roses and rainbows*, pp. 167–8.

100 *W.N.W.*, 9, 16, 23 Oct. 1869; *C.C.*, 12 Sept. 1874; McDowell, *op. cit.*, p. 192.

101 McDowell, *op. cit.*, p. 168.

102 Morrison, *Modern Ulster*, p. 49.

103 McDowell, *Roses and rainbows*, pp. 172–3. For the social divisions between farmers and labourers, see also Morrison, *op. cit.*, pp. 50–51; Lynn Doyle, *An Ulster childhood* (London, 1921), pp. 143–7.

104 *N.W.*, 23, 24 Nov. 1875, 3, 9, 10, 14 Dec. 1875; *Ballymena Advertiser*, 18 Sept., 25 Dec. 1875; *B.F.P.*, 16 Sept., 7, 28 Oct., 16, 23 Dec. 1875.

105 *N.W.*, 16 Aug., 13 Sept. 1875.

106 N. Atkinson, *Irish education, a history of educational institutions* (Dublin, 1969), pp. 94–9; J. Magee, 'Catholic education in Ireland 1800–1920', in *Aspects of Catholic education* (Belfast, 1971), pp. 19–24.

107 D.H. Akenson, *The Irish education experiment, the national system of education in the nineteenth century* (London, 1970), p. 275.

108 *Eighth report of the Commissioners of National Education in Ireland for the year 1841* [398], H.C., 1842, xxiii, 339, p. 48: *Eighteenth report ... 1851*, vol. ii [1583], H.C. 1852–3, xliii, 1, pp. 124–5: *Twenty-eighth report ... 1861* [3026], H.C. 1862, xx, 249, pp. 220–1: *Thirty-eighth report ... 1871* [C.599], H.C. 1872, xxiii, 253, p. 580: *Forty-eighth report ... 1881* [C.3234], H.C. 1882, xxiv, 77, p. 6: *Census of Ireland for the year 1851: Part iv, Report on ages and education* [2053], H.C. 1856, xxix, 1, p. xii: *Census of Ireland for the year 1861: Part ii, vol 1, Report and tables and ages and education* [3204-I], H.C. 1863; lvi, 1, p. 18: *Census,1881, pt 1*, p. 963.

109 *N.W.*, 7 Aug. 1872.

110 J.R.R. Adams, *The printed word and the common man: popular culture in Ulster 1700–1900* (Belfast, 1987), p. 161. This expansion of the press followed the repeal of the stamp and paper duties in 1855 and 1860 respectively, and both reflected and stimulated the increasing literacy and social and political awareness of the people.

111 *N.W.*, 14 Feb. 1870.

112 J. C. Rutherford, *An Ards farmer; or, an account of the life of James Shanks, Ballyfounder, Portaferry* (Belfast, 1913), p. 8.

113 During the last quarter of the nineteenth century in England an increasing number of elementary schools developed what were known as 'higher tops' to do more advanced work with those pupils who were anxious to stay on at school after passing through the final elementary grade.

114 *Census, 1881*, p. 1003.

115 McDowell, *Other days around me*, p. 41.

116 See e.g. Dr James McIvor, Rector of Newtownstewart to Bishop of Derry and Raphoe, 1856, commenting on the 'deplorable and increasing want' of 'intermediate' schools for the middle classes, quoted in J.A. McIvor, *Popular education in the Irish presbyterian church* (Dublin, 1969), p. 116.

117 Secondary schools in Belfast such as St Dominic's and the Belfast Ladies' Collegiate School (founded in 1869 and later becoming Victoria College) catered for boarders from all over the province. See M.W. Cunningham, 'Victoria College: the early years', *Pace*, x (1978–9), pp. 307.

118 *Report of the intermediate education board for Ireland for the year 1881* [C.3176], H.C., 1882, xxiv, 17, p. 2.

119 *Census, 1841*, pp xxxii, 358; *Census, 1881*, pp. 963, 965.

120 Tuke, *Irish distress and its remedies*, pp. 14, 26–9.

121 *Ibid.*, p. 8; see also Hamilton, *Sixty years' experience as an Irish landlord*, p. 412; Lord George Hill, *Facts from Gweedore* (repr., with introd. by E.E. Evans, Belfast, 1971, of 5th edn, 1887), p. 13.

122 *Census, 1841*, p. 364; *Census, 1881*, p. 972; There were also five times as many governesses in Ulster in 1881 as in 1851 — 1,565 and 300 respectively. *Census of Ireland for the year 1851, pt vi: general report* [2134], H.C., 1856, xxxi, 1, p. 527; *Census, 1881*, p. 982.

123 *C.C.*, 21 June 1873.

## Chapter 2

1 O'Connor Morris, *Letters on the land question*, p. 242. For an authoritative discussion of tenant-right during this period, see Vaughan, *Landlords and tenants*, pp. 67–102. See also B.L. Solow, *The land question and the Irish economy, 1870–1903* (Cambridge, MA, 1971), pp. 24–45.

2 Statement of James McKnight to *Bessborough Commission*, Q.4654, p. 173.

3 *Reports on landlord–tenant relations*, pp. 15, 108–9, 143.

4 O'Connor Morris, *op. cit.*, p. 265; Dun, *Landlords and tenants in Ireland*, pp. 106, 110.

5 *Reports on landlord–tenant relations*, p. 12; O'Connor Morris, *Letters on the land question*, p. 254; O. Robinson, 'The London companies and tenant-right in nineteenth century Ireland', *Agricultural History Review*, 18 (1970), pp. 54–63; Dun, *Landlords and tenants in Ireland*, pp. 116, 121, 128.

6 *Bessborough Commission*, Qs5558–9. See

also *Reports on landlord–tenant relations*, p. 13.

7   *B.N.L.*, 1 Feb. 1872; Verner Mss. D236/472; *Reports on landlord–tenant relations*, p. 101.

8   See Vaughan, *Landlords and tenants*, pp. 67–70.

9   'Memoranda on land bill', 8 March 1870, Gladstone Mss. 44425, f. 212.

10  *Reports on landlord–tenant relations*, p. 102.

11  *Report from the select committee of the house of lords on the Landlord and Tenant (Ireland) Act, 1870 …* H.C. 1872 (403), xi, 1, (hereafter cited as *Chelmsford Committee*), Q269. See also statement of Isaac Butt, *N.W.*, 21 Jan. 1870; *Devon Report*, p. 14.

12  *Chelmsford Committee*, Q269; Lyall, *Life of Dufferin*, p. 153; *B.N.L.*, 19 June 1874; Robinson, 'London companies and tenant-right', pp. 55, 59.

13  McKnight, 'Notes on Ulster custom', March 1870, Gladstone Mss. 44425, f. 208.

14  *Chelmsford Committee*, Q2319.

15  See below, pp. 44-47; Isaac Butt, *Land tenure in Ireland; a plea for the Celtic race* (3rd edn, London, 1866), p. 55.

16  Dun, *Landlords and tenants in Ireland*, p. 259; *Bessborough Report*, p. 10.

17  Lyall, *Life of Dufferin*, p. 153. See also speech of Samuel Smyth at a tenant meeting in Moira, *N.W.*, 11 July 1874.

18  See *Devon Report*, p. 14; Montgomery, 'The present aspect of the Irish land question', p. 40.

19  W.A. Maguire, *The Downshire estates in Ireland 1801–1845, the management of Irish landed estates in the early nineteenth century* (Oxford, 1972), pp. 144–5; W.H. Crawford, 'Landlord–tenant relations in Ulster, 1609–1820' *Irish Economic and Social History*, ii (1975),

pp. 17–20. This was the view also of Lord Dufferin and others. *N.W.*, 18 June 1870.

20  N.D. Palmer, *The Irish Land League crisis* (New Haven, CT, 1940), p. 46.

21  *Bessborough Commission*, Q40446.

22  Dun, *Landlords and tenants in Ireland*, pp. 101, 121; Robinson, 'The London Companies and tenant-right', p. 59.

23  *N.W.*, 22 Aug. 1874.

24  Godkin, *The land war in Ireland*, p. 328. See also *N.W.*, 18 Nov. 1872.

25  See below, p. 49.

26  See *Devon Report*, p. 15. The belief that the Ulster custom was responsible for the greater prosperity of Ulster is critically discussed in Solow, *Land Question*, pp. 30–32; Kennedy, 'The rural economy', pp. 40–41. See also Vaughan, *Landlords and tenants*, pp. 80–7.

27  *N.W.*, 24 April 1879.

28  Shaw-Lefevre, *English and Irish land questions*, p. 133.

29  *Report on landlord–tenant relations*, p. 103.

30  *N.W.*, 18 June 1870.

31  Montgomery, 'The present aspect of the land question', p. 39.

32  Dun, *Landlords and tenants in Ireland*, p. 108; *Bessborough Commission*, Qs5718–9.

33  *Reports on landlord–tenant relations*, p. 12; R.B. O'Brien, *The parliamentary history of the Irish land question from 1829 to 1869; and the origin and results of the Ulster custom* (London, 1880), pp. 174, 177–8; Butt, *Land tenure in Ireland*, p. 47.

34  *Bessborough Commission*, Qs4654, 6216–8.

35  Kennedy, 'The tenant-right agitation in Ulster', p. 2.

36 McKnight's statement to *Bessborough Commission*, p. 173; *N.W.*, 21 Jan. 1874.

37 *Bessborough Report*, p. 6.

38 Kennedy, 'The tenant-right agitation in Ulster', pp. 2–5; Whyte, *The independent Irish party*, pp. 6–8.

39 *N.W.*, 19 Jan., 9 Dec. 1870, 17 April 1875.

40 *Bessborough Commission*, Qs5516, 5867, 6439, passim.

41 *Reports on landlord–tenant relations*, pp. 14, 96–100, 139–40.

42 *Return by provinces and counties … of evictions which have come to the knowledge of the constabulary in each of the years from 1849 to 1880, inclusive*. H.C. 1881 (185), lxvii, 725, pp. 3–4.

43 Solow, *The land question*, pp. 56–7. On this basis readmissions during the 1870s work out much higher in proportion to evictions than readmissions during the previous fifteen years so that the estimate of one-third readmitted as caretakers may be a little high. At any rate, even where a tenant was readmitted as a caretaker he was deprived of his status as a tenant and was placed entirely at the mercy of the landlord.

44 This is based on the figures in the constabulary returns and makes no allowance for those readmitted as caretakers during the 1870s.

45 Dun, *Landlords and tenants in Ireland*, p. 124; Godkin, *The land war in Ireland*, p. 316; Earl of Annesley to William Shaw, 12 May 1881, Annesley Mss. D1854/6/8, p. 2; *Bessborough Commission*, Qs6057–8.

46 *N.W.*, 7 Feb. 1870.

47 *B.U.*, 29 July 1869.

48 *C.C.*, 25 Dec. 1869.

49 *N.W.*, 20 April 1870.

50 *Bessborough Report*, p. 59. See also Dun, *Landlords and tenants in Ireland*, pp. 258, 262.

51 O'Connor Morris, *Letters on the land question*, p. 274

52 *N.W.*, 22 Jan. 1874.

53 *Reports on landlord–tenant relations*, p. 140; *Bessborough Report*, p. 3. See also *Preliminary report from her majesty's commissioners on agriculture* [C.2778], H.C. 1881, xv, 1 (hereafter cited as *Richmond prelim. report* ), p. 20; Irish Land Committee, *The land question, Ireland no. iii, facts and figures* (London and Dublin, 1880), pp. 12–17.

54 Solow, *The land question*, p. 76.

55 Vaughan, *Landlords and tenants*, pp. 48–52; W.E. Vaughan, 'Landlord and tenant relations in Ireland between the famine and the land war, 1850–1878', in *Comparative aspects of Scottish and Irish economic and social history, 1600–1900*, ed. L.M. Cullen and T.C. Smout (Edinburgh, 1977), p. 216; Vaughan, 'Agricultural output, rents, and wages in Ireland', p. 85.

56 C. Ó Gráda, *Ireland before and after the famine, explorations in economic history, 1800–1925* (Manchester, 1988), pp. 68–9, 128–131; M.E. Turner, 'Towards an agricultural prices index for Ireland, 1850–1914', *Economic and Social Review*, xviii (1987), pp. 123–36. See also M.E. Turner, 'Output and productivity in Irish agriculture from the famine to the great war', *Ir. Econ. Soc. Hist.*, xvii (1990), pp. 62–78; W.E. Vaughan, 'Potatoes and agricultural output', *ibid.*, pp. 79–92. This debate centres more on the value of agricultural output — more particularly the value of the potato crop — than on the actual level of rents, and Turner's most recent estimates of output are not far removed from those of Vaughan. M. Turner, *After*

*the famine: Irish agriculture 1850–1914* (Cambridge, 1996), pp. 101–113.

57 *Reports on landlord–tenant relations*, p. 84; Irish Land Committee, *The land question, facts and figures*, pp. 29–36; Ó Gráda, *Ireland before and after the famine*, pp. 134–5; Robinson, 'The London companies and tenant-right', p. 59. For landlord investment in Ireland generally, see C. Ó Gráda, 'The investment behaviour of Irish landlords 1850–75; some preliminary findings', *Agricultural History Review*, 23 (1975), pp. 139–55.

58 *N.W.*, 3 Oct. 1874. See also *ibid.*, 22 Jan. 1874; *B.F.P.*, 27 Jan. 1870; *Ballymena Advertiser*, 18 Dec. 1875 and McKnight's statement to *Bessborough Commission*, p. 173 for similar sentiments.

59 *N.W.*, 22 Jan. 1874. See also *Richmond prelim report*, p. 20.

60 *Reports on landlord–tenant relations*, pp. 11, 96; *Richmond prelim. report*, p. 11. See also resolutions passed at tenants' meeting at Magherafelt in November 1869, *W.N.W.*, 6 Nov. 1869.

61 W.E. Vaughan, 'A study of landlord–tenant relations in Ireland between the famine and the land war, 1850–78' (PhD thesis, Trinity College, Dublin, 1973), pp. 47–65; *Bessborough Commission*, Qs5825–30.

62 *N.W.*, 14 Dec. 1875.

63 *Bessborough Commission*, Qs5074–5. See also evidence of Rev. Patrick McGeaney on behalf of Camlough Association, *ibid.*, Q5855.

64 *N.W.*, 22 Jan. 1874.

65 *Bessborough Commission*, Qs.4522, 4621–2, 5055, 5060, 5381–94, 6228–32, 6305, passim.

66 *Ibid.*, Q6202.

67 Montgomery, *Irish land and Irish rights*, pp. 37–8; *Bessborough Commission*,

Qs4447–63, 6049, 6387; *W.N.W.*, 14 Aug. 1875. See also *Reports on landlord–tenant relations*, p. 105.

68 See Montgomery, *Irish land and Irish rights*, p. 36–8.

69 See e.g. resolutions at tenant meeting at Toome, *C.C.*, 15 July 1871.

70 Robinson, 'London companies and tenant-right', p. 61; Dun, *Landlords and tenants in Ireland*, pp. 116–7; *C.C.*, 28 Dec. 1872; *Bessborough Commission*, Qs6406–12, 6432, 5726–36, 6301, 4626–9.

71 *Bessborough Commission*, Qs4983–4. See also *Reports on landlord–tenant relations*, p. 12; Godkin, *The land war in Ireland*, p. 327.

72 *Reports on landlord–tenant relations*, p. 142.

73 *Ibid.*, pp. 139, 142; O'Connor Morris, *Letters on the land question*, pp. 258, 265.

74 *Ibid.*, p. 268.

75 *Hansard*, 3, cxcix, 344–5 (15 Feb. 1870); *ibid.*, cc, 783–4 (28 Mar. 1870). See also *N.W.*, 3 Jan. 1870; Thomas MacKnight, *Ulster as it is*, 2 vols (London, 1896), i, 106–7.

76 The encumbered estates act of 1849 simplified land transfer procedures and empowered the new court to sell estates on application from either owners or those who had a legal claim on the estate. In 1858 the powers of the court were extended to unencumbered properties, and the judges and officers of the court were transferred to a new court called the landed estates court. For the establishment of the encumbered estates court, see P. G. Lane, 'The encumbered estates court, Ireland, 1848–9', *Economic and Social Review*, iii (1971–2), pp. 413–453.

77 Out of 8,550 purchasers up to 1858, only 324 came from outside Ireland and most of these purchased within the first year or two of the operation of the court. Percy Fitzgerald, *The Story of the incumbered estates court* (London, 1862), pp. 46–7.

78 *Returns of the total value of lands sold in the incumbered estates court and landed estates court, Ireland ...* H.C. 1870 (101), lvii, 302, p. 2; *Returns of the amount of purchase money realised by the sale of estates in the landed estates court (Ireland) each year, from 1870 to ... the 1st day of June 1880 ...* H.C. 1880 (303) lx, 377, p. 1.

79 *Ibid.*; *Return of the number of estates sold by the landed estates court during each of the last ten years ...* H.L. 1874 (228), xvi, 139, p. 1.

80 J.S. Donnelly Jr, *The land and the people of nineteenth-century Cork: the rural economy and the land question* (London, 1975), p. 131; Hoppen, *Elections, Politics and Society*, p. 106.

81 *B.U.*, 5 Mar. 1867; *N.W.*, 8 Dec. 1870; *L. Stand.*, 14 Dec. 1870; *Chelmsford Committee*, Q2122.

82 Godkin, *The land war in Ireland*, p. 10; Dun, *Landlords and tenants in Ireland*, p. 8.

83 A.G. Richey, *The Irish land laws* (2nd edn, London, 1881), p. 60; O'Connor Morris, *Letters on the land question*, p. 258; O'Brien, *Parliamentary history of the land question*, p. 86; Montgomery, *Irish land and Irish rights*, p. 5; Shaw-Lefevre, *English and Irish land questions*, pp. 147–8; Mill, *Chapters and speeches*, p. 115.

84 *Reports on landlord–tenant relations*, p. 38. See also *ibid.*, pp. 14–15, 96–7, 139–40, 142; *Bessborough Report*, p. 6.

85 Irish Land Committee, *The land question, facts and figures*, p. 37.

86 *Reports on landlord–tenant relations*, pp. 14–15, 96–7, 142.

87 Dun, *Landlords and tenants in Ireland*, pp. 172–4.

88 *N.W.*, 8 Jan. 1874, 12 April 1875.

89 *B.U.*, 3, 8 Jan. 1867, 5 Mar. 1867; *C.C.*, 31 Dec. 1881.

90 *N.W.*, 4 Feb. 1882.

91 *Ibid.*, 18 April 1870.

92 *Ibid.*, 16 Nov. 1882.

93 *Ibid.*, 3 June 1882.

94 Dun, *Landlords and tenants in Ireland*, p. 173.

95 *Bessborough Commission*, Qs5714–5739, 5897–5950; *N.W.* 20 Dec. 1875; 'Reminiscences of W.R. Young', PRONI T3382, pp. 11–15.

96 *B.N.L.*, 31 Jan. 1874.

97 James Musgrave to Gladstone, 10 Mar. 1886, Gladstone Mss. 44495, ff. 195–202. See also Dun, *Landlords and tenants in Ireland*, p. 175.

98 Quoted in Shaw-Lefevre, *English and Irish land question*, p. 148.

99 Dun, *Landlords and tenants in Ireland*, pp. 8–9. See also A.M. Sullivan, *New Ireland: political sketches and personal reminiscences of thirty years of Irish public life* (London, 15th edn, 1877), pp. 134–143; *C.C.*, 18 Dec. 1870.

100 *Reports on landlord–tenant relations*, pp. 97, 142, passim.

101 *Return showing, (1) for provinces and (2) in counties, the landed estates ... sold in one or more lots in the landed estates court for each of the five years prior to 1870, and up to the 1st of August 1870; and similar return for the remainder of the year 1870, and for each of the five years ending 31st December 1875 ...* H.L. 1876 (238), xi, 37, pp. 34–5, 48–50. Part of the thinking behind the encumbered estates act had been that smaller estates would be a more productive field for investment, and that the sale of estates in lots would enable those with 'a small amount of capital' to buy into the land system (see *Devon Report*, pp. 26–7). Of 3,428

purchasers up to April 1853, 2,225 (65 per cent) had been purchased at or under £2,000. *Returns from the court for the sale of incumbered estates in Ireland, up to the 1st day of April 1853* ... H.C. 1852–53 (390), xciv, 599, p. 2.

102 Sullivan, *New Ireland*, p. 141; W.E. Montgomery, *The history of land tenure in Ireland* (Cambridge, 1889), p. 113.

103 *Chelmsford Committee*, Qs1855–64, 1903–4.

104 Richey, *Irish land laws*, pp. 63–64.

105 Godkin, *The land war in Ireland*, p. 326.

106 *N.W.*, 8 Dec. 1870. See also speech of Gladstone, *Hansard*, 3, cxcic, 344–6 (15 Feb. 1870).

107 Godkin, *op. cit.*, p. 326; Richey, *Irish land laws*, p. 64.

108 *N.W.*, 10, 17 May 1872.

109 G. Shaw-Lefevre, *The purchase clauses of the Irish land acts* (London, 1882), p. 12. This inquiry also revealed that 'consolidation of farms was enforced in 520 cases'.

110 *N.W.*, 14 April 1874. See also *ibid.*, 25 Jan. 1870.

111 Richey, *Irish land laws*, p. 57.

112 Quoted in *N.W.*, 16 Feb. 1870.

113 *N.W.*, 11 July 1874.

114 *W.N.W.*, 23 Jan. 1869; *N.W.*, 21 Jan. 1870, 29 May 1875.

115 *C.C.*, 10 Dec. 1870.

116 *N.W.*, 19, 21, 26 Jan. 1870; 15 April 1874.

117 *Ibid.*, 8 Dec. 1870.

## Chapter 3

1 S.C. McElroy, *The Route Land Crusade, being an authentic account of the efforts made to advance land reform by the Route Tenants' Defence Association, the Antrim Central Tenant-Right Association, and the Ulster Land Committee.* (Coleraine, n.d.), p. 19.

2 O'Brien, *Parliamentary history of the land question*, pp. 88–103.

3 R.D. Collison Black, *Economic thought and the Irish question 1817–1870*, (Cambridge, 1960), p. 45.

4 *Ibid.*

5 E.R. Norman, *The catholic church and Ireland in the age of rebellion, 1859–1873* (London, 1965), ch. 4.

6 J.L. Hammond, *Gladstone and the Irish nation* (London, 1938), pp. 80–81; John Morley, *The life of William Ewart Gladstone* (2 vols, London, 1905), i, 924; Black, *Economic thought and the Irish question*, p. 58.

7 E.D. Steele, *Irish land and British politics, tenant-right and nationality 1865–1870* (Cambridge, 1974), pp. 55–61, 115.

8 For the various legislative proposals between 1852 and 1867, see O'Brien, *Parliamentary history of the land question*, pp. 88–130.

9 MacKnight, *Ulster as it is*, i, 80–81.

10 *Ibid.*, 90–1; Lyall, *Life of Dufferin*, pp. 156–7; *B.U.*, 5 Feb. 1867.

11 Black, *Economic thought and the Irish question*, p. 52.

12 See e.g. *B.U.*, 13 April, 14 May 1867.

13 For the election in the south see David Thornley, *Isaac Butt and home rule* (London, 1964), pp. 27–61. For a more detailed account of this and later elections in Ulster during this period, see Walker, *Ulster politics*. See also F. Thompson, 'Land and politics in Ulster, 1868–86' (PhD thesis, Queen's University, Belfast, 1982).

14 *B.N.L.*, 22 Sept. 1868.

15 Monsell's bill would have allowed presbyterian clergymen to officiate

at burials of presbyterians in episcopalian graveyards. This was an issue which excited intense interest among presbyterians.

16 Robert Montgomery, moderator of the presbyterian general assembly, to Lord Derby, 24 Feb. 1868, Disraeli Mss. B/IX/A/29; David Wilson, moderator of general assembly, to Disraeli, 6 Mar. 1867, *ibid.* B/IX/A/27d; Memorial to Disraeli, 4 Mar. 1868, *ibid.* B/IX/A/2b; Sir Frederick Heygate MP to Disraeli, 29 Feb. 1868, *ibid.* B/XXI/H563.

17 See Duke of Abercorn to Disraeli, 21 Nov. 1868, *ibid.* B/XIII/247; *B.U.*, 5 Dec. 1868.

18 This act prohibited processions which were likely to provoke disturbance and it was rigorously enforced against Orangemen in the north. It was not, and probably could not be, similarly enforced against Fenian processions in Dublin and other parts of the south. MacKnight, *Ulster as it is*, i, 142–7.

19 See Edward Taylor, Irish Tory chief whip, to Disraeli, 19 April 1868, Disraeli Mss. B/XX/T/112; *B.U.*, 24 Oct. 1867; *W.N.W.*, 16 May 1868.

20 The Orange leadership had been urging Orangemen to show restraint and not to defy the authorities. For the Orange and Conservative divisions in Belfast at this time, see also H. Patterson, *Class conflict and sectarianism, the protestant working class and the Belfast labour movement 1868–1920* (Belfast, 1980), pp. 1–6.

21 MacKnight, *Ulster as it is*, i, 129–131, 144; *B.U.*, 3, 7, 21, 31 Mar., 2, 7, April 1868; *W.N.W.* 7, 21, Mar., 20 June 1868; *L. Journ.*, 9, 16 June 1868; *T.C.*, 6 Mar., 10 April 1868.

22 *B.U.*, 15 Sept. 1868. See also open letter from Drew to Johnston, *ibid.*, 3 Oct. 1868.

23 *Ibid.*, 21 Mar. 1868.

24 *W.N.W.*, 12 Sept. 1868; *B.U.*, 25 July 1868.

25 See *L. Journ.*, 1 Sept. 1869; *W.N.W.*, 2 Oct. 1869.

26 Steele, *Irish land and British politics*, p. 97.

27 Thornley, *Butt and home rule*, pp. 31, 69.

28 *C.C.*, 25 Sept. 1869; *W.N.W.*, 2 Oct. 1869; *L. Journ.*, 16 Oct. 1869.

29 *W.N.W.*, 16 Jan. 1869.

30 See, e.g., *B.U.*, 17 Mar. 1868; Thornley, *Butt and home rule*, p. 70.

31 *L. Journ.*, 16 Oct. 1869.

32 *N.W.*, 21 Jan. 1870. See also *W.N.W.*, 20 Nov. 1869; *N.W.*, 15 April 1870.

33 *N.W.*, 21 Jan. 1870. See also speech of Rev. C. Porter at Larne, *ibid.*, 25 Jan. 1870.

34 *B.U.*, 29 July 1869.

35 *L. Stand.*, 23 Oct. 1869.

36 See e.g. resolutions at tenant meeting at Ballymoney, *C.C.*, 13 Feb. 1869. See also *B.U.*, 11 May 1869.

37 *W.N.W.*, 28 Aug. 1869.

38 *L. Journ.*, 25 Sept. 1869.

39 MacKnight, *Ulster as it is*, i, 214.

40 *B.U.*, 14, 17, Aug; *W.N.W.*, 14 Aug. 1869.

41 *W.N.W.*, 21 Aug. 1869. See also *L. Journ.*, 1 Sept. 1869; MacKnight, *Ulster as it is*, i, 214–15; McElroy, *Route land crusade*, p. 54. MacKnight makes the point that every single speaker at the Ballymena land conference of December 1869, one of the earliest and most important land meetings held in the province, had taken an active part in the Liberal campaign

in the Antrim by-election of 1869.

42  *C.C.*, 13 Feb. 1869; *W.N.W.*, 23 Oct. 1869; McElroy, *Route land crusade*, p. 31.

43  *W.N.W.*, 27 Nov. 1869.

44  Lord Lifford to Ed., *The Times*, repr. in *L. Journ.*, 1 Dec. 1869; speech of Lord George Hamilton to Middlesex Agricultural Society, *C.C.*, 9 Oct. 1869. See also *W.N.W.*, 30 Oct. 1869.

45  See e.g. *C.C.*, 25 Sept. 1869.

46  *L. Stand.*, 23 Oct. 1869; *L. Journ.*, 16 Oct. 1869.

47  Rev. N.M. Brown to Gladstone, 21 Feb. 1870, Gladstone Mss. 44425, f. 63; *L. Journ.*, 16 Oct. 1869; *L. Stand.*, 9 Feb., 9, 12, 19 Mar. 1870; *N.W.*, 5, 11, 14, 21 Mar., 18 April 1870.

48  McElroy, *Route land crusade*, p. 30.

49  *Ibid.*, p. 54; *W.N.W.*, 23 Oct. 1869.

50  *L. Journ.*, 3 Nov. 1869; *C.C.*, 6 Nov.; *W.N.W.*, 6 Nov. 1869.

51  McElroy, *Route land crusade*, p. 31; *W.N.W.*, 27 Nov., 4 Dec. 1869; *C.C.*, 27 Nov. 1869; *L. Journ.*, 20 Dec. 1869.

52  *C.C.*, 18, 25 Dec. 1869, 1 Jan. 1870; MacKnight, *Ulster as it is*, i, 214–218.

53  *W.N.W.*, 6, 13 Nov., 18 Dec. 1869.

54  *Ibid.*, 1 Dec. 1869.

55  *N.W.*, 24 Jan., 14 Feb. 1870; *C.C.*, 19 Feb. 1870.

56  *L. Journ.*, 8, 15 Jan. 1870; *L. Stand.*, 8, 12, 15, 19, 22, 29 Jan., 5 Feb. 1870; *N.W.*, 18, 20, 24, 31 Jan., 7, 9, Feb. 1870.

57  W.D. Henderson to Gladstone, 8 Mar. 1870, Gladstone Mss. 44425, f. 207. The associations listed by the local press as being present were — Coleraine, Route, Ballyclare, Ballymena, Newtownards, Portadown, Cookstown, Newtownlimavady, Comber, Derry, Castlefin, Letterkenny, Ballybofey, Armagh, Dungannon, Carrickfergus, Larne 'and other associations'. *N.W.*, 5 Mar. 1870.

58  *C.C.*, 6, 27 Nov. 1869; *W.N.W.*, 6, 27 Nov. 1879.

59  MacKnight, *Ulster as it is*, i, 217.

60  *B.F.P.* , 10 Feb. 1870.

61  Thornley, *Butt and home rule*, p. 80.

62  *L. Stand.*, 10 Feb; *C.C.* 19 Feb; *B.F.P.* 24 Feb. 1870.

63  *C.C.*, 19 Feb. 1870; *L. Stand.*, 19 Feb. 1870.

64  Dowse to Gladstone, 22 Feb. 1870, Gladstone Mss. 44425, f. 69.

65  *C.C.*, 26 Feb. 1870; *L. Stand.*, 23, 26 Feb. 1870; *N. Star*, 19 Feb. 1870.

66  *N.W.*, 17, 19 Feb. 1870.

67  *Ibid.*, 22–28 Feb. 1870.

68  J. Glover to Ed., *N.W.*, 24 Feb. 1870.

69  *N.W.*, 3, 23 Mar., 18 April 1870; *C.C.*, 5 Mar. 1870; *N. Star*, 19 Feb. 1870; *L. Stand.*, 26 Feb. 1870.

70  *N.W.*, 19 Mar. 1870.

71  *Ibid.*, 5 Mar. 1870.

72  W.D. Henderson to Gladstone, 8 Mar. 1870, Gladstone Mss. 44425, ff. 207–213. See also similar resolutions adopted at meeting of Route Tenant-Right Association and forwarded to Gladstone by Sir Shafto Adair, 5 Mar. 1870, *ibid.* 44425, ff. 185–7.

73  *L. Stand.*, 9, 19 Mar. 1870; *C.C.*, 26 Mar. 1870.

74  *Hansard*, 3, cc, 780, 28 Mar. 1870. See also James McKnight to Gladstone, 2 April 1870, Gladstone Mss. 44426, f. 68.

75  *Hansard*, 3, cc, 781, 28 Mar. 1870. The English MP who made the original proposal for this amendment was Assheton Cross, Tory MP for S.W. Lancashire.

76   *Ibid.*, 783–7, 29 Mar. 1870.

77   *Ibid.*, 1014–24, 31 Mar. 1870. Johnston was later presented with an address and a purse containing 600 sovereigns by the Ulster tenants in recognition of his services on their behalf during the passage of the bill. *C.C.*, 22 April 1871.

78   *C.C.*, 2, 16 April 1870; *B.F.P.*, 7 April 1870. See also the resolutions and sentiments expressed at a tenant-right conference in Ballymoney — at which twelve associations were represented — at the end of April, *N.W.*, 20 April; McElroy, *Route land crusade*, pp. 20–21.

79   *L. Stand.*, 20 June 1870; *C.C.*, 9 July 1870; *N.W.*, 9, 12 July 1870.

80   *N.W.*, 30 June 1870.

81   *L. Stand.*, 6 July; *C.C.*, 9 July 1870; McElroy, *Route land crusade*, p. 20.

82   *N.W.*, 18 April 1870.

83   *L. Stand.*, 9 July 1870. Ulster landlords were generally anxious for an early settlement of the question. See speech of the Duke of Abercorn in House of Lords, *N.W.*, 20 June 1870; Sir Frederick Heygate, Tory MP for Co. Derry to Disraeli, 'Ash Wednesday' 1870, Disraeli Mss. B/XXI/H/564.

84   *N.W.*, 9 Dec. 1870.

## Chapter 4

1   Isaac Butt, *A practical treatise on the new law of compensation to tenants in Ireland and the other provisions of the landlord and tenant act, 1870; with an appendix of statutes and rules* (Dublin 1871), p. 297. Much of the following paragraphs on the terms of the act is based on this work and also on R.R. Cherry (ed.), *The Irish land law and land purchase acts, 1860 to 1891 together with the rules and forms issued under each act* (2nd edn, Dublin 1893), pp. 149–202; J.E. Pomfret, *The struggle for land in Ireland, 1800–1923* (Princeton, NJ, 1930), pp. 71–96. For a useful discussion of the act, see Vaughan, *Landlords and tenants*, pp. 93–102.

2   Gladstone to Bright, 4 Dec. 1869, quoted in Morley, *Life of Gladstone*, i, 925.

3   Pomfret, *Struggle for land in Ireland*, p. 90

4   Richey, *Irish land laws*, p. 94.

5   Steele, *Irish land and British politics*, p. 313.

6   See Appendix IV for the statistics of cases under the act and for the sources. It should be pointed out that claims under the Ulster custom tended to be higher than under the other compensation clauses.

7   *L. Stand.*, 28 Sept. 1870.

8   Butt, *New law of compensation*, p. 342.

9   See e.g. *N.W.*, 20 Oct. 1870.

10  *Judicial Statistics (Ireland) 1871:–Part I. Police, Criminal Proceedings, Prisons — Part II. Common law, Equity, Civil and Canon law* [C.674], H.C. 1872, lxv, 235, p. 236. This was the only year in which the judicial statistics distinguished those claiming only under section I of the act. In succeeding years no distinction was made between claimants on the ground of tenant-right only and those who combined such claims with claims on other grounds. See Appendix IV, Table 4.

11  See e.g. *W.N.W.*, 8 April 1871.

12  See Appendix IV, Table 2.

13  *L. Stand.*, 17 May 1870.

14  *Chelmsford Committee*, Qs1866, 2100, 2328; *C.C.*, 30 Dec. 1871; *W.N.W.*, 23 Dec. 1871; *N.W.*, 1 Jan., 5 Aug., 2 Dec. 1874. Landlord spokesmen of course denied this, claiming that the

act had depreciated the value of property so far as the landlord was concerned (*Chelmsford Committee*, Qs443–50, 826–45, 857–861, 1250; *B.N.L.*, 21 June 1872, 7 July 1874). Few of them, however, cited actual sales to support this contention. An examination of the returns of the landed estates court suggests that the value of landed property was not seriously affected by the 1870 act; in the five years from 1865 until the end of 1869 the average number of years' purchase given for landed property in Ulster was 23.2, while in the five years 1871–75 the average was 24.15. The high average after 1870 was undoubtedly a result of the increasing prosperity of agriculture, but clearly there had been no great depreciation of property as a result of the land act of 1870. *Returns showing, (1) in provinces and (2) in counties, the landed estates ... sold in one or more lots in the landed estates court*, p. 5.

15  *Chelmsford Committee*, Q1932. See also Samuel McElroy's evidence, *Bessborough Commission*, Q4488.

16  *N.W.*, 2 Mar., 14 Sept. 1872.

17  *B.N.L.*, 11 Mar. 1872; *C.C.*, 26 Nov. 1870, 4 May 1872; *N.W.*, 2, 14 Mar., 23 Aug., 14 Sept. 1872; *Chelmsford Committee*, Qs798, 717, 2328; *Bessborough Commission* Qs5114, 40446.

18  See e.g. *Chelmsford Committee*, Qs1932–34; *Bessborough Commission*, Qs6059–61.

19  *Bessborough Commission*, Q14958.

20  *C.C.*, 4 May 1872; *N.W.*, 27 Dec. 1872, 12 Aug. 1874; *W.N.W.*, 9 Dec. 1876. See also Tuke, *Irish distress and its remedies*, p. 97; evidence of Thomas Shillington, *Bessborough Commission*, Q4986.

21  *N.W.*, 30 Jan., 26 July 1872; *Chelmsford Committee*, Qs2346, 2530.

22  *Chelmsford Committee*, Qs2458–62, 1674.

23  *Ibid.*, Qs1029–30.

24  *Bessborough Report*, pp. 13–14.

25  *Chelmsford Committee*, Qs437, 2388–2439, 2453.

26  *Bessborough Report*, p. 13. See also *Chelmsford Committee*, Qs437, 1024–30, 2380–2458; *Bessborough Commission*, Qs5469–71, 5941, 6091, 6549–50, passim.

27  Solow, *The land question*, p. 86.

28  The refutation is contained in Ó Gráda, 'The investment behaviour of Irish landlords'.

29  *Ibid.*

30  See above, p. 45.

31  Montgomery, *Irish land and Irish rights*, p. 10. See also address of F.J. Gervais to the electors of Ceseil, 24 Mar. 1873, Ellison-Macartney Papers/4.

32  *B.F.P.* , 6 Feb. 1873.

33  *N.W.*, 26 Feb. 1874.

34  *Bessborough Report*, p. 8. See also *Chelmsford Committee*, Qs1294–7.

35  *B.N.L.*, 23 Dec. 1872. See also *ibid.*, 19 June 1874; *Chelmsford Committee*, Qs794, 2518, passim.

36  *L. Journ.*, 13 Mar. 1872; *Chelmsford Committee*, Qs410–429, 825, 2525; Marquis of Hamilton to Disraeli, 26 Mar. 1872, Disraeli Mss. B/XXI/H37.

37  *L. Journ.*, 24 Feb., 2 Mar. 1872. See also *Chelmsford Committee*, Qs404, 1351–6, 1389, 2466.

38  *B.N.L.*, 14 July 1874; *Chelmsford Committee*, Qs404, 783–4, 2347–80.

39  *Chelmsford Committee*, Qs2525–6, 2513–4.

40  *Ibid.*, Qs219, 267; *Bessborough Commission*, Q6336.

41  *B.N.L.*, 5 May 1874.

42  See e.g. evidence of Robert Johnston, chairman of Down, *Chelmsford Committee*, Qs228, 237.

43  *T.C.*, 30 Jan. 1874.

44  *B.F.P.*, 8 Jan. 1874.

45  *W.N.W.*, 27 May 1871. See also *ibid.*, 8 April 1871; *C.C.*, 14 Jan. 1871.

46  *N.W.*, 1 Oct. 1872. See also *Chelmsford Committee*, Qs631–3, 692, 1634, 1673–4, 1842, 1920–3, 1997–2001, 2085–7, 2098.

47  See *N.W.*, 20 June 1872.

48  *Ibid.*, 27 June 1872.

49  *Ibid.*, 12 June 1872.

50  *Ibid.*, 26 June, 30 Dec. 1872.

51  *Ibid.*, 4 Jan. 1872; *C.C.*, 8 Nov. 1873.

52  *N.W.*, 2 Mar. 1874.

53  As, e.g., on the Leitrim estate, *ibid.*, 4 Jan. 1872. See also *ibid.*, 12 June 1872; resolutions at national land conferences in 1876, *W.N.W.*, 18 Mar., 28 Oct. 1876.

54  *Bessborough Commission*, Q5344. See also *ibid.*, Qs4573–7.

55  *C.C.*, 10 Aug. 1872; *N.W.*, 21 Dec. 1872.

56  See e.g. *C.C.*, 4 May 1872.

57  See e.g. *B.N.L.*, 17, 21, 25, 26 June 1872.

58  The figure of 41 years' purchase in this case was in fact misleading. Leitrim had let the land at £6 per annum but the occupant, as well as improving it, had reclaimed thirty acres of mountain land so that the holding was professionally valued at £19– 17s –6d. Thus the £250 compensation which Leitrim had to pay was not so much 41 years' rental at £6 as 14 years' rental at £19, the figure at which Leitrim was now able to let the holding. *Chelmsford Committee*, Qs672, 785, 1663, 1793–1810.

59  *N.W.*, 4, 7 June 1872. See also Sir Thomas Bateson to Marquis of Salisbury, 3 June 1872, Salisbury Mss. Ser. E.

60  *N.W.*, 21, 24, 26, 29 June, 5, 6 July 1872; *C.C.*, 22 June, 6 July 1872.

61  *B.N.L.*, 21 June, 1 July 1872; *N.W.*, 20, 24, 25 June, 6 July 1872.

62  *Chelmsford Report*, pp. iii–iv.

63  It should be remembered that up to 1870 a landed estates court conveyance gave the purchaser a clear title to the property, i.e. it conveyed to him the estate discharged of all rights which were not specifically referred to in the conveyance.

64  *L. Stand.*, 14 Dec. 1870; *N.W.*, 6, 8, 12, 16 Dec. 1870; *C.C.*, 17 Dec. 1870.

65  *W.N.W.*, 17, 24 June 1871; Butt, *New law of compensation*, pp. 479–86, ix–xxix.

66  *C.C.*, 8 July, 5 Aug. 1871; Donnell, *Land cases*, pp. 234–6.

67  *C.C.*, 5 Aug. 1871; *Chelmsford Committee*, Q1692.

68  Donnell, *Land cases*, p. 17; *Chelmsford Committee*, Q2334.

69  Donnell, *Land cases*, pp. 61–72; *Chelmsford Committee*, Q211; *Reports on landlord–tenant relations*, pp. 12, 102. John Young DL claimed that he had never even heard this question discussed before 1870. *N.W.*, 20 Dec. 1875.

70  *B.N.L.*, 15 Apr. 1872; Donnell, *Land cases*, pp. 251–7.

71  *B.N.L.*, 3 Apr. 1872.

72  Donnell, *Land cases*, pp. 198, 257–62; *N.W.*, 14, 15 Aug. 1872.

73  *N.W.*, 29 July 1872. It was believed that this case was brought forward as a test case by the landlords of Down and it led directly to the

formation of the Down Farmers' Association. *Bessborough Commission* Qs6233–4, 6335–6; W.J. Moore, Hon. Sec., Down Farmers' Union to Ed., *B.N.L.*, 24 Feb. 1874.

74 *B.N.L.*, 6 Apr. 1872; *Chelmsford Committee* Qs265–8; Donnell, *Land cases*, pp. 242–6.

75 *N.W.*, 18 Dec. 1872; *Bessborough Commission*, Qs6335–6.

76 See statement of Down Farmers' Association, *N.W.*, 30 Dec. 1872.

77 Speech at Ballycastle, *C.C.*, 3 Aug. 1872. For the *Burns v. Ranfurly* appeal see Donnell, *Land cases*, pp. 200–6.

78 *N.W.*, 8 Aug. 1874.

79 *B.N.L.*, 17 Feb. 1876. See also note 69 above.

80 *C.C.*, 5 Sept. 1874.

81 *Chelmsford Committee*, Qs1231–2.

82 The chairmen of Antrim (*Fleck v. O'Neill*), Donegal (*Weir v. Knox*), and Tyrone (*McGaghey v. Steward*), all took this view. *Chelmsford Committee*, Q2332; Donnell, *Land cases*, pp. 299–307.

83 *B.F.P.* , 6 Feb. 1873; Donnell, *Land cases*, pp. 377–80. This was almost certainly contrary to the intentions of Gladstone who, in introducing the bill, said that section 1 provided 'separately and completely' for holdings under the Ulster custom and that these would not 'as a rule fall within the provisions of the bill generally'. *Hansard*, 3, cxcix, 367–8, 15 Feb. 1870.

84 *Bessborough Commission*, Qs4631–9.

85 Case of *Browne v. Bruce*, *C.C.*, 1 Aug. 1874.

86 Donnell, *Land cases*, pp. 193–5.

87 See e.g. cases of *Carraher v. McGeough*, *Jolly v. Archdall*, and *Ogilby v. Coulter*, Donnell, *Land cases*, pp. 319–22, 327–8, 474–5.

88 *C.C.*, 6 Jan. 1872.

89 *B.N.L.*, 2 Jan. 1872; *Chelmsford Committee*, Q2333.

90 Donnell, *Land cases*, p. 272. See also for this question, Cherry, *Irish land acts*, p. 151.

91 *N.W.*, 3 June 1875. See also speech of J.W. Ellison Macartney, Conservative MP for Tyrone, in commons in 1879, *Hansard*, 3, ccxlv, 947, 8 May 1879; Cherry, *Irish land acts*, p. 152.

92 *Chelmsford Committee*, Qs217–220; *B.N.L.*, 18 Dec. 1872.

93 *Chelmsford Committee*, Q219.

94 *C.C.*, 31 Oct. 1874.

95 *W.N.W.*, 18 Nov. 1876.

96 *Ibid.*, 18 Nov. 1871. See also W.F. Bailey, *The Irish land acts, a short sketch of their history and development* (Dublin, 1917), p. 18.

97 Dowse, 'Memorandum', 4 Dec. 1880, Gladstone Mss. 44467, f. 104.

98 *N.W.*, 27 Oct. 1879.

99 *Chelmsford Committee*, Q228.

100 *W.N.W.*, 1 April 1876.

101 *Bessborough Commission*, Qs4545–4551, 6348–9. See also *B.F.P.*, 27 Nov. 1873.

102 Donnell, *Land cases*, p. 522; *N.W.*, 5, 6 July, 27 Oct. 1875.

103 *Bessborough Report*, p. 59.

104 *Ibid.*, p. 7.

105 See above, pp. 44-5.

106 Forster to Gladstone, 6 Dec. 1880, Gladstone Mss. 44158, f. 21; *Bessborough Report*, p. 8.

107 See e.g. evidence of Robert Johnston to the *Chelmsford Committee*, Qs278–80.

108 Donnell, *Land cases*, p. 317. Hamilton, like so many of the owners involved in these cases, was a recent purchaser in the landed estates court.

109 *C.C.*, 13 April 1872. See also Cherry, *Irish land acts*, p. 151. Claims arising from what were considered excessive increases of rents were common at land sessions throughout the province during the remainder of the 1870s.

110 Speech of Samuel Smyth at Moira, *N.W.*, 11 July 1874. See also *Bessborough Commission*, Qs8692–4, 6245; Richard Dowse, 'Memorandum', 4 Dec. 1880, Gladstone Mss. 44467, f. 105.

111 Speech of W. D. Henderson, *N.W.*, 19 Jan. 1872; *C.C.*, 1 Mar. 1879; *Bessborough Report*, p. 13.

112 George Young to Forster, 4 Dec. 1880, Gladstone Mss. 44467, f. 101. See also *Bessborough Commission*, Qs 4522, 4987–91, 5055, 5060, 5381–94, 5855, 6228–32, 6301–7, 6380, passim; and above, pp. 46-7.

113 *Bessborough Report*, p. 10.

114 *W.N.W.*, 13 Oct. 1877.

115 *N.W.*, 11 July 1874.

## Chapter 5

1 See e.g. *B.F.P.*, 3 Mar. 1870.

2 *L. Stand.*, 17 Aug. 1870.

3 *N.W.*, 15 Nov. 1870; *C.C.*, 17 Dec. 1870, 14 Jan. 1871: *L. Stand.*, 17 Dec. 1870.

4 *C.C.*, 23 Dec. 1871, 13 Jan. 1872.

5 *Ibid.*, 10, 31 Aug. 1872; *N.W.*, 24, 28, 29, 31 Aug. 1872.

6 *W.N.W.*, 30 Dec. 1871, 27 Dec. 1873; *N.W.*, 10 Feb. 1872, 5 Jan. 1874.

7 See below, pp. 110-11.

8 *N.W.*, 29 Sept., 1 Oct. 1870.

9 Among the affiliated associations were Ballymena, Ballyclare, Route, Lisburn and Magheragall in Antrim; Coleraine, Derry and Kennaught in Derry; Castlefin and Ballybofey in Donegal; Cookstown, Donemana and Dungannon in Tyrone; Saintfield, Banbridge and Newry in Down; and Portadown in Armagh.

10 William Montgomery thought that it 'might become as powerful and useful as ever was the Anti-Corn Law League'. Speech at Magheragall, *W.N.W.*, 18 Nov. 1871.

11 For this case see above, p. 92.

12 *N.W.*, 1 Jan. 1872; Donnell, *Land cases*, pp. 188–93.

13 *N.W.*, 15 Feb. 1872.

14 Speech at Newtownards Farmers' Association, *ibid.*, 15 June 1874.

15 *Menown v. Beauclerc* and *Austen v. Scott* were both fought on the question of leasehold tenant-right; the *Fleck v. O'Neill* case involved the question of the principle that 'input' was not necessary to entitle an outgoing occupier to claim under the Ulster custom.

16 Report of Samuel McElroy, secretary. *C.C.*, 15 Feb. 1873.

17 It was the Kennaught society which carried the question relating to landed estates court conveyances through the courts. It had also fought the *Austen v. Scott* case. See above, pp. 91-2.

18 *C.C.*, 23 Dec. 1871, 13 Jan. 1872.

19 *Ibid.*, 10, 31 Aug. 1872; *N.W.*, 24, 29 Aug., 25 Oct., 7 Nov., 21 Dec. 1872.

20 *W.N.W.*, 30 Dec. 1871; *B.N.L.*, 8 Jan. 1872; *N.W.*, 10 Feb., 24 May 1872, 14, 17, 18 Dec. 1875; *C.C.*, 11 April 1874.

21 For these cases see above, pp. 93-6.

22 W.J. Moore to 'Dear Sir', 22 May 1872, Moore Mss. D877/27a; *N.W.*, 20 June, 30 Dec. 1872; Speech of

Joseph Perry at Newtownards, *ibid.*, 15 June 1874; Speech of W.J. Moore at Saintfield, *ibid.*, 8 July 1874; *Bessborough Commission*, Qs6233, 6335–6.

23  *C.C.*, 4 Jan. 1873.

24  McElroy, *Route land crusade*, p. 23.

25  *N.W.*, 24, 26 Feb. 1873.

26  Thornley, *Butt and home rule*, p. 248; L.J. McCaffrey, *Irish federalism in the 1870s: A study in conservative nationalism* (Philadephia, PA, 1962), p. 12.

27  See e.g. *B.F.P.*, 30 Jan., 20 Feb. 1873; *C.C.*, 1, 15 Feb. 1873.

28  *B.F.P.*, 24 April 1873; *C.C.*, 26 April 1873.

29  The northern associations represented were the Route, Down, Dungannon, Coleraine, Cookstown, Ballyclare, Ballycastle, Maze, Kennaught, Ballymena, Castlefin, Newry, Tyrone, Omagh, Larne, Castlederg, Kilbrode, Donemana and Portadown associations.

30  *N.W.*, 21, 22 Jan. 1874; *C.C.*, 24 Jan. 1874; *B.F.P.*, 29 Jan. 1874; McElroy, *Route land crusade*, pp. 24–6.

31  See e.g. resolution of Lisburn Tenant Right Society, *N.W.*, 2 June 1875.

32  *Ibid.*, 30 July 1872; *C.C.*, 3 Aug. 1872, 4 Jan. 1873; *W.N.W.*, 18 Jan., 1, 15, 22 Feb., 8 Mar., 5 April 1873.

33  *W.N.W.*, 15 Feb. 1873.

34  McElroy, *Route land crusade*, p. 24.

35  *N.W.*, 8 July 1874.

36  *T.C.*, 7 Mar. 1873.

37  See e.g. *N.W.*, 16 July 1872.

38  Speech at Dromore, *ibid.*, 4 July 1872.

39  Speech at Moira, *ibid.*, 2 April 1874.

40  *W.N.W.*, 18 Nov. 1871; *N.W.*, 13 Nov. 1874; *ibid.*, 5 Jan. 1874; Thos McElderry to Ed., *C.C.*, 10 April 1880. The strength of the Tandragee membership no doubt resulted from the ongoing dispute about free sale on the Duke of Manchester's estate.

41  *N.W.*, 15 Apr. 1870; *W.N.W.*, 29 Nov. 1873. The *Northern Whig* attributed this to fear of landlord reprisals.

42  Dr Hume, chairman of the Crumlin Tenant Farmers' Association, claimed that it was 'eminently a tenant farmers' association … got up by farmers, sustained by farmers, conducted by farmers' (*ibid.*, 26 May 1877). Hume himself, it should be said, was a medical doctor.

43  *B.N.L.*, 27 Feb. 1874.

44  See above pp. 71-2.

45  See e.g. meetings of Castlefin, Down, Cookstown, Kennaught, Portadown, Lisburn and other associations. *N.W.*, 21, 24, 26, 29 June, 4, 5, 6 July 1872.

46  *N.W.*, 29 Dec. 1875.

47  *N.W.*, 6 Oct. 1870.

48  *N.W.*, 26 Feb. 1873. See also *ibid.*, 1, 2 Feb. 1872, 21 Jan., 17 July 1874, 6 Oct. 1874, passim; *W.N.W.*, 27 Dec. 1873; *C.C.*, 25 Feb., 8 Apr., 15 July 1871, passim.

49  *N.W.*, 26 Feb. 1873.

50  *L. Stand.*, 15 Jan. 1870.

51  *N.W.*, 20 Apr. 1870; *C.C.*, 25 Dec. 1869.

52  An attempt has been made to relate the sample to the general distribution of the movement; thus it consists of 12 officers from 6 associations in Antrim; 10 officers from 5 associations in Down; 4 officers from 2 associations in Armagh; 6 officers from 3 associations in Donegal; 7 officers from 4 associations in Derry; and 5 officers from 4 associations in Tyrone.

53 *Slater's Directory*, 1870; *Belfast and Ulster Directory*, 1874, 1877; *Return of the names of proprietors and the area and valuation of all properties in the several counties in Ireland*, pp. 97–141; the local press.

54 *N.W.*, 8 Jan. 1872; *W.N.W.*, 22 Dec. 1877.

55 *Bessborough Commission*, Qs6104–7, 6214.

56 *Ibid.*, Qs475–62, 4770–3, 4780–90, 4853; pp. 194–5; *N.W.*, 19 Jan. 1874.

57 *W.N.W.*, 6 Nov. 1869; *C.C.*, 1 Jan. 1870; *N.W.*, 29 Jan., 4 Apr. 1874.

58 *B.U.*, 30 May 1868. County cess was the tax levied for grand jury purposes. In the case of tenancies created before the 1870 act, it was exclusively payable by the occupying tenant; in tenancies created after the act, half was paid by the landlord and half by the tenant; and in the case of holdings valued at £4 and under, it was paid entirely by the landlord. Bailey, *Local and centralized government in Ireland*, pp. 17–18.

59 See *N.W.*, 30 Sept. 1870; *C.C.*, 6 May 1871. Grand juries were appointed by the county high sheriff. The presentment sessions were made up of members of the bench and cesspayers selected by the grand jury from a list of the highest cesspayers in the county. Bailey, *op. cit.*, pp. 15–16.

60 *C.C.*, 1 Mar. 1879. See also *L. Journ.*, 6 Mar. 1869; *N.W.*, 28 July, 29 Aug., 10 Oct. 1874; *C.C.*, 29 Mar., 31 May 1879.

61 It is fair to say that many of the tenants who supported such demands were primarily interested in reducing county expenditure and easing the burden of local taxation rather than in ending landed control or establishing a more democratic system of local government.

62 W.E. Vaughan and A. J. Fitzpatrick (eds), *Irish historical statistics, population 1821–1971* (Dublin, 1978), pp. 36–9. Twenty-eight towns in Ulster increased in size between 1851 and 1871; fifteen decreased.

63 *L. Stand.*, 12 Jan. 1870.

64 Rev. N.M. Brown, secretary of the Kennaught Farmers' Defence Association, credited Henderson with having done more than any other single individual to promote the development of the movement in Ulster. *W.N.W.*, 1 July 1871.

65 See tribute paid to Hume at meeting of Crumlin association in 1880, *N.W.*, 22 Jan. 1880.

66 Speech of Jackson B. Corbett, secretary of Newtownbreda association, *ibid.*, 2 Feb. 1875; Speech of Rev. Samuel Finlay of Kilraughts, *C.C.*, 15 Feb. 1873.

67 James McKnight of Derry, Hugh McCall of Lisburn, Dr Hume of Crumlin, John Harbison and William Glasgow of Cookstown, Rev. Dr Kinnear of Letterkenny and many other leading figures provided a certain continuity between the movement of the immediate post-Famine period and that of the 1870s.

68 Newtownards was typical in this respect, contributing a large sum annually to the grand jury in the shape of county cess and getting little in return. See *N.W.*, 29 May 1872, 21 Apr. 1875; *B.N.L.*, 7 Mar. 1872.

69 *L. Stand.*, 26 Jan. 1870.

70 *N.W.*, 10 Jan. 1879.

71 *L. Stand.*, 19 Jan. 1870.

72 Armour, *Armour of Ballymoney*, p. 4.

For a valuable assessment of Armour's career see introduction to J.R.B. McMinn (ed.), *Against the tide: a calendar of the papers of Rev. J.B. Armour, Irish presbyterian minister and home ruler 1869–1914* (Belfast, 1985).

73 James A. Rentoul, *Stray thoughts and memories*, ed. L. Rentoul (Dublin, 1921), pp. 18, 22–3, 26–7, passim.

74 *N.W.*, 3 Feb. 1874; *ibid.*, 20 Dec. 1875; 'Reminiscences of W.R. Young', p. 15. T3382.

75 *Chelmsford Committee*, Q797. This was a common Tory allegation; see e.g. *B.N.L.*, 21 June 1872, 14 July 1874.

76 *Chelmsford Committee*, Q795.

77 McElroy, *Route land crusade*, p. 53. It should be pointed out that in a number of cases the shopkeepers were also farmers themselves. For a valuable discussion of the electoral importance of shopkeepers and traders, see Hoppen, *Elections, politics and society*, pp. 55–60.

78 *C.C.*, 12 July 1879. See also speeches of Hugh McCall, a Lisburn businessman (*N.W.*, 14 Dec. 1870), and William Liddell, chairman of the Waringstown and Donacloney Tenant Farmers' Association, *W.N.W.*, 12 Jan. 1878.

79 *N.W.*, 16 Mar. 1870. See also speech of William Hurst, J.P. of Drumaness, *ibid.*, 8 July 1874.

80 *Ibid.*, 17 Mar. 1879; *C.C.*, 15 Mar. 1879.

81 *C.C.*, 12 July 1879.

82 *N.W.*, 21 Jan. 1874. See also *ibid.*, 12 May 1879.

83 *Ibid.*, 19 Jan. 1872, 21 May 1872, 16 June 1874; *L. Journ.* 6 Mar. 1869. See above, note 68.

84 *N.W.*, 14 Feb. 1870.

85 *Ibid.*, 31 Aug. 1872. See also *W.N.W.*, 4 Mar. 1876.

86 *L. Journ.*, 17 Apr. 1879; Godkin, *Land war*, pp. 304–10.

87 For the influence on the movement and on presbyterian opinion in the Route of ministers such as J.L. Rentoul and Samuel Finlay, see McElroy, *Route land crusade*, pp. 30, 53–4; *Armour of Ballymoney*, pp. 2–3. Presbyterian ministers were ideally placed to act as political brokers between the different presbyterian classes in Ulster. See Mogey, *Rural life in Northern Ireland*, p. 200; Sir John Ross, *The years of my pilgrimage, random reminiscences* (London, 1924), p. 5.

88 *N.W.*, 7 Feb. 1870; *L. Stand.*, 14 Dec. 1870; *N.W.*, 24 Jan. 1870, 21 Jan. 1875.

89 *N.W.*, 12 Jan. 1870. The *Whig* maintained that at least 95 per cent of presbyterian ministers were 'tenant–right advocates'. *Ibid.*, 28 Feb. 1874.

90 MacKnight, *Ulster as it is*, i, 219; Armour, *Armour of Ballymoney*, p. 105.

91 Speech at Ringsend, *C. Const.*, 25 Nov. 1882.

92 Armour, *op. cit.*, p. 42. See also speeches of Rev. Maxwell at Cookstown and Rev. A. Robinson at Ballymoney, *N.W.*, 9 Feb. 1870; *C.C.*, 27 Nov. 1869.

93 Latimer, *History of Irish presbyterians*, p. 448; *W.N.W.*, 16 Jan. 1869.

94 *C.C.*, 27 Nov. 1869.

95 For the continuing divisions between episcopalians and presbyterians after 1869, see A.J. Megahey, *The Irish protestant churches and social and political issues 1870–1914*, (PhD thesis, Queen's University, 1969), p. 41, passim; R. McMinn, 'Presbyterianism and politics in Ulster, 1871–1906', *Studia Hibernica*, xxi (1981), pp. 136–46.

96 *N.W.*, 3 Jan. 1874.

97 Hugh Shearman, 'Irish church finances after disestablishment', in *Essays in British and Irish history in honour of James Eadie Todd*, ed. H.A. Cronne, T.W. Moody and D.B. Quinn (London, 1949), pp. 278–302. See also P. M.H. Bell, *Disestablishment in Ireland and Wales* (London, 1969), pp. 196–205.

98 See e.g. *N.W.*, 28 Feb. 1874; Thomas McClure to Gladstone, 19 Sept. 1871, Gladstone Mss. 44431, f. 265.

99 Latimer, *op. cit.*, p. 505.

100 *Ibid.*, p. 537.

101 *Ibid.* For the social aspirations of well-to-do presbyterians and social attitudes of landed classes, see also Ross, *Years of my pilgrimage*, p. 3; A. Shanks, *Rural aristocracy in Northern Ireland* (Aldershot, 1988), pp. 29, 102, 115, 139.

102 Armour, *op. cit.*, p. 91.

103 Latimer, *op. cit.*, p. 504.

104 *N.W.*, 4 Feb. 1874.

105 Vaughan and Fitzpatrick, *Irish historical statistics*, pp. 52, 55; *B.F.P.*, 5 Sept. 1878; *W.N.W.*, 7 Sept. 1878.

106 Speech of John Eagleson, *N.W.*, 11 Feb. 1874.

107 *W.N.W.*, 7 Sept. 1878.

108 *N.W.*, 9, 17 Jan. 1874; *L. Stand.*, 20 Aug. 1870.

109 *L. Journ.*, 6 Mar. 1869.

110 *Ibid.*, 20 Feb. 1869.

111 *N.W.*, 15 May 1885; *L. Journ.*, 6 Mar. 1869. The catholics had an even greater grievance than the presbyterians, with only five catholic magistrates in Antrim and only one in Derry.

112 B.M. Walker, *Parliamentary representation in Ulster 1868–89, the formative years* (PhD thesis, Trinity College, Dublin, 1977), p. 71;

McMinn, 'Presbyterians and politics', p. 132. Apart from the particular grievance of being excluded from the bench, there was a fairly general dissatisfaction among presbyterians and catholics about the 'partiality' of the magistracy (W.F. Bailey, 'Magisterial reform; being some considerations on the present voluntary system, and suggestions for the substitution of an independent paid magistracy', *J.S.S.I.S.I.*, pt lxiii, viii, no. 8 (July 1885), pp. 595–605). This was a particular grievance with catholics in certain areas. See *N.W.*, 26 Feb. 1872; *L. Journ.*, 16 Jan. 1874.

113 Latimer, *op. cit.*, p. 448.

114 *L. Journ.*, 6 Mar. 1869. See also *W.N.W.*, 7 Sept. 1878.

115 *L. Journ.*, 6 Mar. 1869. See also Megahey, *The Irish protestant churches*, p. 44.

116 *N.W.*, 9 Jan. 1874.

117 *W.N.W.*, 7 Sept. 1878. See also *B.F.P.*, 29 Jan. 1874.

118 *N.W.*, 17 Sept. 1879.

119 *W.N.W.*, 7 Sept. 1878.

120 See e.g. the conference held under the auspices of the Ulster tenant-right associations in Ballymoney in December 1871, specifically on the subject of grand jury reform. *C.C.*, 9 Dec. 1871.

## Chapter 6

1 MacKnight, *Ulster as it is*, i, 25–9, 138–9. See also *N.W.*, 30 Jan. 1874.

2 MacKnight, *op. cit.*, i, 54.

3 *Ibid.*, 55–6, 114–15.

4 Walker, *Ulster politics*, pp. 58–9.

5 The increase depended on the number of £4 occupiers in each borough. The calculations in the

text are based on the figures given for 1865 and 1868 in Walker, *Parliamentary election results*, pp 102–11.

6   See e.g. Thomas Taylor to Earl of Belmore, 6 Mar. 1873, Belmore Mss. D3007/P/3; Stuart Knox to Belmore, 12 Mar. 1873, *ibid.* D3007/P/13.

7   Walker, 'Parliamentary representation in Ulster', pp. 122–3. Episcopalians in 1871 made up only 18.4 per cent of the population of Newry and 20.3 per cent of that in Derry.

8   For Saunderson's career, see Alvin Jackson, *Colonel Edward Saunderson, land and loyalty in Victorian Ireland* (Oxford, 1995).

9   *W.N.W.*, 18 July 1868; Philip Callan MP to Bishop Donnelly, 1, 4 July 1871, Dio (R.C.) 1/11a/9, 12; McGimpsey, 'Monaghan politics', pp. 157–79.

10  MacKnight, *Ulster as it is*, i, 155–69, 173–4; *W.N.W.*, 3, 10 Oct. 1868.

11  MacKnight, *op. cit.*, 1, 169.

12  *Ibid.*, 169–70.

13  *B.U.*, 24, 26 Nov. 1868.

14  *Ibid.*, 26 Aug. 1869; *N.W.*, 18 Feb. 1870; *L. Stand.*, 19 Feb. 1870.

15  Megahey, *The Irish protestant churches*, p. 64.

16  See e.g. *B.U.*, 7 April, 9, 11, 20 Aug., Sept., 21, 28 Nov. 1868.

17  Hoppen, *Elections, politics and society*, p. 267; Walker, *Ulster politics*, p. 64.

18  Walker, *Ulster politics*, p. 63; *N.W.*, 28 Feb. 1870; Bishop of Derry to Lord Abercorn, 19 Nov. 1868, Abercorn Mss. T2541/V.R. 288

19  *N.W.*, 28 Feb. 1870. See also Hoppen, *op. cit.*, p. 269.

20  Latimer, *History of the Irish presbyterians*, p. 513.

21  *N.W.*, 9 Jan. 1874. See also *W.N.W.*, 1 Aug. 1868.

22  *N.W.*, 14 Feb. 1870.

23  Walker, *Ulster politics*, p. 64.

24  Peter Gibbon, *The origins of Ulster unionism, the formation of popular protestant politics and ideology in nineteenth century Ireland* (Manchester, 1975), p. 93.

25  O'Brien, *Russell of Killowen*, p. 135.

26  *Northern Star*, 21 Nov. 1868.

27  *B.M.N.*, 16 Oct. 1868; *N.W.*, 7 April 1870.

28  Walker, *Ulster politics*, pp. 63–4.

29  See e.g. *B.U.*, 1, 3, 5 Dec. 1868; *N.W.*, 12 Mar., 7 Apr. 1870.

30  From 16 Nov. 1870 to1872, the *Ulster Examiner* was published as the *Daily Examiner*. From 1873 it became the *Ulster Examiner and Northern Star*.

31  Dorrian to Kirby, 28 Sept. 1865, Kirby Correspondence 1865, no. 216; same to same, 15 May 1868, *ibid.*, 1868, no. 161. For an authoritative account of Dorrian's political views and his involvement with the *Ulster Examiner*, see Ambrose Macauley, *Patrick Dorrian, Bishop of Down and Connor 1865–85* (Blackrock, 1987), pp. 203–18.

32  *N.W.*, 28, 29 May, 7 June 1872.

33  *Ibid.*, 30 Oct. 1872; *D.E.* 24 July 1872.

34  *D.E.*, 23, 24, 25, 29 July 1872.

35  *L. Journ.*, 27 Feb., 30 June 1869; *W.N.W.*, 16 Jan. 1869; Macknight, *op. cit.*, i, 149, 185–7; Bishop McGettigan of Raphoe to Wm Monsell MP, 8 Mar. 1869, O'Hagan Mss. D2777/8/3.

36  The amnesty movement was never well organised in the north, but such meetings as were held attracted huge crowds of sympathisers. See *W.N.W.*, 9, 23 Oct. 1869; *L. Journ.* 7 July 1869; *B.M.N.* 4 Oct., 1869.

37  *B.M.N.* 17 Apr., 16 Aug., 30 Oct.

1872. See also *D.E.*, 30 Oct. 1872.

38 P. Bew and F. Wright, 'The agrarian opposition in Ulster politics 1848–87', in *Irish peasants: violence and political unrest, 1780–1914*, ed. S. Clark and J.S. Donnelly Jr (Manchester, 1983), pp. 203–4.

39 For Palles's career, see V.T.H. Delaney, *Christopher Palles, his life and times* (Dublin, 1960).

40 *L. Stand.*, 6 Nov. 1872. See also *ibid.*, 13, 23 Nov. 1872; Delaney, *op. cit.*, pp. 70–1.

41 *B.F.P.* , 5 Sept. 1872. See also *ibid.*, 14 Nov. 1872.

42 *B.N.L.*, 8, 9, 20 Nov. 1872.

43 The Derry electorate, according to a breakdown by the *Belfast News Letter*, included 600 Catholics, 600 presbyterians, 355 episcopalians and 87 other protestants. *B.N.L.*, 29 July 1872.

44 *Ibid.*, 21 Nov. 1872; *L. Stand.*, 23 Nov. 1872. Bishop Dorrian's paper, the *Daily Examiner*, continued to oppose Palles. See *D.E.*, 21, 25 Nov. 1872. The rather ambivalent attitude of the *Examiner*, and perhaps of many northern catholics, towards the Liberals was well illustrated in the issue of 26 Nov. 1872, in which the leading editorial once again gloated over the defeat of Palles in Derry, while the sub-leader rejoiced in the election to Belfast town council of three 'staunch Liberals' for the Smithfield ward. *Ibid.*, 26 Nov. 1872.

45 *L. Journ.*, 26 Nov. 1872; *L. Stand.*, 27, 30 Nov. 1872.

46 See *B.F.P.* , 28 Nov. 1872; *C.C.*, 30 Nov. 1872; *Daily News*, 25 Nov. 1872. See also *N.W.*, 27 Nov. 1872.

47 MacKnight, *Ulster as it is*, i, 295.

48 *Ibid.*, 218–19.

49 McElroy, *Route land crusade*, p. 30.

50 *B.N.L.*, 4, 18, 27 Jan., 18 Mar., 12 April 1872.

51 See e.g. *L. Journ.*, 13 Mar. 1869; *W.N.W.*, 21 Aug. 1869; *B.U.*, 21 Aug. 1869; *N.W.*, 18 Feb., 25 April 1870; *C.C.*, 1 July 1871; *D.E.*, 11 April 1872.

52 *W.N.W.*, 5 April 1873.

53 For the Hamilton and Corry domination of Tyrone, see Earl of Belmore, *Parliamentary memoirs of Fermanagh and Tyrone from 1613 to 1885* (Dublin, 1887), pp. 118–19.

54 For the high prices of tenant-right in Tyrone, see *N.W.*, 5 Nov., 3 Dec. 1870; *T.C.*, 19 Dec. 1873; Dun, *Landlords and tenants in Ireland*, p. 139; *Reports on landlord–tenant relations*, p. 11, passim.

55 See above p. 84.

56 *N.W.*, 8, 19 Jan., 8, 15 Feb. 1872; *L. Journ.*, 7 Feb. 1872.

57 *N.W.*, 26 June 1872. See also J.C. Lowry to Earl of Belmore, 18 April 1873, Belmore Mss. D3007/P/125.

58 See Newton's evidence to *Chelmsford Committee*, Qs783–871.

59 James Greer to Belmore, 21 Mar. 1873, Belmore Mss. D3007/P/61; R.C. Brush to Belmore, 5 April 1873., *ibid.* D3007/P/106.

60 *C.C.*, 20 April 1872. Newton's claim on this occasion and others wrongly created the impression that there was a landlord conspiracy against the act, whereas in fact most of the leading owners in Tyrone thought his impetuous involvement in land cases unwise and unfortunate.

61 Stuart Knox to Belmore, 21 Mar. 1873, Belmore Mss. D3007/P/56; Donnell, *Land cases*, pp. 200–6.

62 J.C. Lowry to Belmore, 18 April 1873, Belmore Mss. D3007/P/125.

63  *T.C.*, 7 Mar. 1873.

64  A meeting of the Independent Orange Association in Belfast in January 1870 was attended by representatives from Derry, Coleraine, Ballymoney, Ballymena, Randalstown, Carrickfergus, Banbridge and Newry (*L. Stand.*, 2 Feb. 1870). The members of the new association were said to be 'chiefly of the lower, middle, and working classes'. *C.C.*, 1 July 1872.

65  Dalway, who had already offended the traditional Orange interests by defeating the official Conservative candidate in Carrickfergus in 1868, was finally expelled for supporting Sir Shafto Adair in the Antrim by-election of 1869 (*W.N.W.*, 25 Sept., 20 Nov. 1869; *N.W.*, 6, 7 Jan., 25 April 1870; John Christie, District Master, Carrickfergus Loyal Orange Lodge to Ed., *N.W.*, 25 April 1870). Although Johnston was openly attacked by the Tory press, no Orangeman dared suggest his expulsion from the order, but an obsolete rule of the order prohibiting retailers of 'spirituous liquors' from holding office was revived to secure the expulsion of three of his most prominent supporters from the Grand Orange Lodge of Belfast. *N.W.*, 30 April 1870.

66  See Earl of Enniskillen to Belmore, 24 Mar. 1873. Belmore Mss. D3007/P/38.

67  G.V. Stewart to Earl of Belmore, 17 Mar. 1873, Belmore Mss. D3007/P/38. See also speech of Henry W. Chambre at Orange demonstration at Killyman, *W.N.W.*, 17 July 1869.

68  The objects of the 'Orange democracy' were said by the *Spectator* in 1869 to be 'freedom of election and a perpetual land settlement'. Quoted in *L. Journ.*, 13 Jan. 1869. See also *ibid.*, 9 Oct. 1869;

*W.N.W.*, 4 Sept., 11 Dec. 1869; *N.W.*, 23 Mar., 18 April, 30 May 1870; *C.C.*, 4 June 1870.

69  See James Greer to Belmore, 14 Mar. 1873, Belmore Mss. D3007/P/20; Lord Claud Hamilton to Macartney, 'Sunday', n.d., Ellison-Macartney Mss. 3; *U.E.*, 14 Mar. 1873.

70  *T.C.*, 14 Mar. 1873; *B.F.P.*, 20 Mar. 1873; *C.C.*, 22, 29 Mar. 1873; *B.M.N.*, 29 Mar., 3 April 1873.

71  For Macartney's meetings at Clogher, Cookstown, Dungannon, Fivemiletown, Coalisland and other centres, see *T.C.*, 28 Mar., 4 April 1873; *W.N.W.*, 29 Mar., 5 April 1873.

72  Sir Thomas Bateson to Belmore, 19 April 1873, *ibid.* D3007/P/126; R.C. Brush to Belmore, 9 April 1873, *ibid.* D3007/P/114; James Greer to Belmore, 9 April 1873, *ibid.* D3007/P/117.

73  *C.C.*, 12 April 1873; *W.N.W.*, 12 April 1873; *B.M.N.*, 9 April 1873.

74  *W.N.W.*, 5, 12 April 1873.

75  *C.C.*, 12 April 1873; *W.N.W.*, 19 April, 19 May 1873; *T.C.*, 30 May 1873.

76  Francis Ellis to Belmore, 9, 13 May 1873, Belmore Mss. D3007/P/129, 130; *W.N.W.*, 10, 17, 31 May 1873; H.W. Chambre to Macartney, 17 May 1873, Ellison-Macartney Mss. 10.

77  One writer has claimed that the ballot changed 'the shape of politics' in Ulster. But the ballot merely provided the means: there were other more fundamental causes. M. Hurst, 'Ireland and the ballot act of 1872', *Historical Journal*, viii, 3 (1965), p. 349.

78  Lowry to Belmore, 18 April 1873, Belmore Mss. D3007/P/125.

79  For the election in the south, see Thornley, *Butt and home rule*, pp. 176–204; L.J. McCaffrey, 'Home rule and

the general election of 1874', *I.H.S.*, ix, 34 (Sept. 1954), pp. 190–212.

80 See G. Moran, 'The advance on the north; the difficulties of the home rule movement in south-east Ulster, 1870–83', in *The borderlands, essays on the history of the Ulster–Leinster border* (Belfast, 1989), ed. R. Gillespie and H. O'Sullivan.

81 Thornley, *op. cit.*, p. 177; McGimpsey, 'Monaghan politics', pp. 316–18; *B.N.L.*, 23 Feb. 1874; R. Lucas, *Colonel Saunderson MP, a memoir* (London, 1908), pp. 59–60.

82 McElroy, *Route land crusade*, pp. 24–5, 27; *B.F.P.*, 29 Jan. 1874; *N.W.*, 22, 29–31 Jan., 3 Feb. 1874; *L. Journ.*, 28, 30 Jan. 1874; *L. Sent.*, 29 Jan. 1874.

83 The following paragraphs are based on an analysis of the electoral addresses and campaign speeches contained in the local press.

84 McCaffrey, *Irish federalism*, p. 18.

85 *B.N.L.*, 29 Jan., 3, 5 Feb. 1874. See also *L. Sent.*, 29 Jan. 1874; *T.C.*, 30 Jan. 1874.

86 See e.g. *N.W.*, 3–25 Feb. 1874.

87 *L. Journ.*, 11 Feb. 1874. See also *ibid.*, 9, 16 Feb. 1874; *N.W.*, 2, 6, 9, 14 Feb. 1874.

88 As e.g. in Down and Antrim. *B.N.L.*, 2–7 Feb. 1874; *N.W.*, 7, 10, 25 Feb. 1874.

89 The Tories had been anxious to bring about a reconciliation with Johnston not only because they feared a repetition of the events of 1868 in Belfast, but perhaps even more because of the damage he could do in the counties. See Sir Thomas Bateson to M. Corry, 24 Nov. 1874, Disraeli Mss. B/XXI/J/83; Michael Hicks Beach to Disraeli, 29 Dec. 1875, *ibid.* B/XXI/J/94a.

90 See e.g. *C.C.*, 31 Jan. 1874. See also *N.W.*, 31 Jan., 4 Feb. 1874; *B.F.P.*, 29 Jan. 1874.

91 Stuart Knox to Earl of Belmore, 12 Mar. 1873, Belmore Mss. D3007/P/13; Col. Taylor to Belmore, 12 Mar. 1873, *ibid.* D3007/P/14.

92 See *N.W.*, 28 June 1874.

93 *B.N.L.*, 29 Jan., 3, 5 Feb. 1874.

94 *L. Sent.*, 27 Jan. 1874; *B.N.L.*, 17, 23 Feb. 1874.

95 Wilson, formerly of Broughshane, County Antrim, had made a fortune in Australia, but on his return settled in England. A perennial problem facing the Liberal party in Ulster was that of finding suitable candidates with the money and the will to stand for election. See e.g. *C.C.*, 20 Mar. 1880.

96 *N.W.*, 10, 11 Feb. 1874; *B.F.P.*, 5, 12 Feb. 1874.

97 *N.W.*, 7 Feb. 1874.

98 *N.W.*, 13 Feb. 1874. See also Disraeli to Belmore, 28 Jan. 1874, Belmore Mss. D3007/P/137; Stuart Knox to Belmore, 29 Jan. 1874, *ibid.* D3007/P/138; Henry Corry to Belmore, 31 Jan. 1874, *ibid.* D3008/P/144.

99 *B.N.L.*, 14, 17, 18, 21 Feb. 1874; *L.Sent.*, 14, 17 Feb. 1874.

100 *N.W.*, 15 April 1874.

101 See *ibid.*, 16 Feb. 1874.

102 See *B.N.L.*, 3 Mar. 1874.

103 *N.W.*, 16, 23 Feb. 1874.

104 *W.N.W.*, 15 Sept. 1877.

105 McElroy, *Route land crusade*, p. 28.

106 The societies affiliated to the D.F.U. were Downpatrick, Saintfield, Killough and Ardglass, Moira, Newtownbreda, Killyleagh, Waringstown and Donacloney, Millisle, Newtownards, Castlewellan, Clough, Dromore, Gilford, Banbridge and Bangor.

107 *B.F.P.*, 8 June 1876; McElroy, *Route land crusade*, p. 61.

108 *N.W.*, 20 Jan., 4 Feb. 1875.

109 *Ibid.*, 28 Feb., 19 June 1874, 2 July 1875.

110 See e.g. speeches of W.D. Henderson to the Crumlin association and Rev. A. Robinson to the Antrim Central Tenant-Right Association. *N.W.*, 10 Mar. 1874; *W.N.W.*, 10 June 1876.

111 See speeches of Joseph Perry and Dr. Hume, *N.W.*, 24 June, 13 Aug. 1874.

112 *Ibid.*, 13 Nov. 1874.

113 A list of these bills is given in T.M. Healy, *A word for Ireland* (Dublin, 1886), p. 113.

114 *N.W.*, 21, 22 Jan. 1875; *B.F.P.*, 28 Jan. 1875.

115 See e.g. speech of Hugh Law in Derry, *N.W.*, 6 Oct. 1874. See also *ibid.*, 18 Nov. 1874, 23 Jan. 1875. The Ulster Liberal MPs had refused to attend the conference in Dublin.

116 *N.W.*, 10 April, 30 June, 3, 6 July 1875.

117 *W.N.W.*, 18 Mar., 23 Oct. 1876; *B.F.P.*, 2 Nov. 1876.

118 Butt was highly regarded by northern tenant-righters, who were deeply suspicious of the new developments in the home rule party from 1877. See *W.N.W.*, 13 April 1878; *B.F.P.*, 18 April 1878.

119 *W.N.W.*, 28 Sept. 1878.

120 *N.W.*, 4, 5 June 1875; *W.N.W.*, 2 Feb. 1878.

121 See e.g. debates on Crawford's 1875 bill and Macartney's bill of 1879. *N.W.*, 3 June 1875, 24 April 1879.

122 *W.N.W.*, 18, 25 Mar. 1876, 10 Aug. 1878; *B.F.P.*, 9 May, 8 Aug. 1878; *N.W.* 14 July 1879.

123 Apart from the bills introduced by their own members, the Ulster Conservatives were clearly prepared to support Smyth's leasehold bill in 1877, but this was blocked by the actions of the southern Irish and British Conservatives. *W.N.W.*, 26 May 1877.

124 *B.N.L.*, 2 Feb. 1877.

125 See Lord Londonderry to Beaconsfield, 15 Aug. 1878, Disraeli Mss. B/xxi/H/41.

126 Michael Hicks-Beach to Lord Abercorn, 26 May 1875. Abercorn Mss. T2541/V.R.330/19.

127 See e.g. Marquis of Hamilton to M. Corry, 13 Jan. 1880, Disraeli Mss. B/XXI/H/42.

128 Speech of Rev. A. Robinson at Bellaghy, *W.N.W.*, 4 Mar. 1876.

129 MacKnight, *Ulster as it is*, i, 330. See also *W.N.W.*, 5 Jan. 1878.

130 Quoted in MacKnight, *Ulster as it is*, i, 306.

131 *Ibid.*, 319–20.

132 *U.E.*, 1 Feb., 22 Aug. 1876. Cahill was editor of the *Examiner* from 1870 until 1877. See Macauley, *Dorrian*, pp. 202–18.

133 *L. Journ.*, 21 Aug. 1876.

134 *L. Sent.*, 15 Aug. 1876.

135 See e.g. *L. Journ.*, 28 Aug. 1876.

136 *W.N.W.*, 2 Sept. 1876. It seems to have been generally agreed that 'a large number of presbyterians' supported Wilson. *N.W.*, 10 Nov. 1879; *C.C.*, 15 Nov. 1879.

137 MacKnight to Gladstone, 9 Oct. 1877, Gladstone Mss. 44455, ff. 175–6.

138 Thornley, *Butt and home rule*, pp. 316, 349–58.

139 *U.E.*, 7, 12, 14 April 1877.

140 *Ibid.*, 24 Nov. 1877.

141 *W.N.W.*, 15 Dec. 1877; *C.C.*, 15 Dec. 1877; *B.F.P.*, 20 Dec. 1877. The *Ulster

*Examiner* by this stage was extending its attacks from the Liberal party to the tenant-right movement itself. *U.E.*, 16 Feb. 1878.

142 See e.g. *W.N.W.,* 25 May 1878.

143 *Ibid.* This election cost Londonderry some £14,000, a colossal sum even by the standards of the day. Vane Londonderry to Beaconsfield, 15 Aug. 1878, Disraeli Mss. B/XXI/C/37.

144 This of course was a mere electioneering ruse, and the bill was quickly stopped in the lords after the election.

145 *W.N.W.*, 11, 25 May, 8 June 1878; MacKnight, *Ulster as it is*, i, 348–9.

146 It was reckoned that at least 1,500 of the 3,000 catholic electors in the county voted for Castlereagh. *W.N.W.*, 25 May 1878; *N.W.*, 25 Feb. 1879.

147 See *C.C.*, 16 Nov. 1878; Lord Lurgan to Lord Waveney, 19 Nov. 1878. Adair Mss. D929/HA12/F4/14.

148 *W.N.W.*, 7 Dec. 1878.

149 *L. Sent.*, 17 Dec. 1878. See also for this election, *W.N.W.*, 21, 28 Dec. 1878; *L. Stand.*, 11 Dec. 1878; *C.C.*, 14 Dec. 1878; MacKnight, *op. cit.*, i, 354.

150 *W.N.W.*, 28 Dec. 1878; M. Wylie, Secretary, Ulster Liberal Society, to Lord Waveney, 24 Dec. 1878, Adair Mss. D2929/HA12/F4/14. Catholic–Liberal relations continued on a very uneasy basis during the following year with the university question in particular causing problems. See e.g. *U.E.*, 3, 5, 7 June, 30 Aug., 14, 21, 28 Oct. 1879.

151 See e.g. *L. Sent.*, 21 Dec. 1878.

152 See *B.N.L.*, 17 Dec. 1879. See also *N.W.*, 17 Nov., 16 Dec. 1879; *B.N.L.*, 13 Dec. 1879.

153 *U.E.*, 6 Dec. 1879; *N.W.*, 16 Dec. 1879. See also Thomas MacKnight to Gladstone, 5 Jan. 1880, Gladstone Mss. 44462, f. 21.

154 See e.g. *C.C.*, 20 Dec. 1879.

155 Hamilton to M. Corry, 13 Jan. 1880, Disraeli Mss. B/XXI/H/42. See also T. P. Hamilton to Marquis of Hamilton, 8 Jan. 1880, *ibid.* B/XXI/H/42a.

## Chapter 7

1 *B.F.P.* , 29 Mar. 1877.

2 *Agricultural statistics of Ireland for the year 1877* [C.1938], H.C. 1878, lxxvii, 511, p. 15. See also *W.N.W.*, 22 Sept. 1877.

3 *Agric. stats. for 1877*, pp. 71–3.

4 *Agricultural statistics of Ireland for the year 1880* [C.2932], H.C. 1881, xciii, 685, pp. 49–53.

5 *Agric. stats. for 1877*, pp. 71–3; *Agric. stats. for 1880*, pp. 49–53.

6 *Agricultural statistics of Ireland for the year 1878* [C.2347], H.C. 1878–9, lxxv, 587, p. 71. See also *B.F.P.* , 26 Sept. 1878.

7 *B.F.P.* , 26 Sept. 1878; *W.N.W.*, 21 Dec. 1878.

8 *N.W.*, 21 Dec. 1878.

9 *Agricultural statistics of Ireland for the year 1879* [C.2534], H.C. 1880, lxxvi, 815, pp. 15–17.

10 *N.W.*, 8, 22 July, 27 Aug., 15 Oct. 1879; *B.F.P.* , 11 Sept. 1879.; *C.C.*, 6 Sept. 1879; *T.C.*, 12 Sept. 1879; *B.N.L.*, 1 Oct. 1879.

11 *Agric. stats. for 1879*, pp. 74–5; *N.W.*, 16, 30 Aug., 2, 3, 22 Sept., 15 Oct. 1879. See also reports from the poor law inspectors to the local government board in *Appendix to the annual report of the local government board for Ireland, being the eighth report* …[C.2603-1], H.C. 1880, xxviii, 39, pp. 78–82, 86–91.

12 *Agric. stats. for 1880*, pp. 49–53.

13 *B.N.L.*, 30 Oct. 1879.

14 Barrington, 'Agricultural prices', p. 252. See also *L. Sent.*, 28 June 1879.

15 *N.W.*, 5 Sept. 1879. The situation was reported to be even worse by the end of October. See *B.N.L.*, 30 Oct. 1879.

16 Tillage prices generally were on a par with the average for 1871–6. Barrington, 'Agricultural prices', pp. 252–3.

17 See *C.C.*, 6 Sept. 1879; *N.W.*, 11 Oct. 1879; *A.G.*, 24 Oct. 1879; *L. Stand.*, 12 Nov. 1879.

18 Tuke, *Irish distress and its remedies*, p. 82. Barbara Solow claims that the value of all crops in Ireland fell from £36.5 million in 1876 to £22.7 million in 1879 (Solow, *The land question*, p. 126) while W.E. Vaughan puts the fall in the value of total agricultural output from 1876 to 1879 at £8 million. W. E. Vaughan, 'An assessment of the economic performance of Irish landlords, 1851–81' in *Ireland under the union, varieties of tension: essays in honour of T. W. Moody*, ed. F.S.L. Lyons and R.A.J. Hawkins (Oxford, 1980), p. 199.

19 *N.W.*, 25 Aug. 1879, 12 Feb. 1880, 20 Feb. 1882.

20 See *Correspondence relative to measures for the relief of distress in Ireland, 1879–80* [C-2483], H.C. 1880, lxii, 157, p. 4.

21 *N.W.*, 3, 4 Sept. 1879; *Agric. stats. for 1879*, pp. 74–5; *Appendix to the eighth annual report of the local government board*, pp. 78–82, 86–91.

22 *Prelim. report of assistant commissioners*, p. 2; *Annual report of the local government board for Ireland, being the eighth report* …[C.2603], H.C. 1880, xxviii, l, p. 7; *N.W.* 17 Sept. 1879.

23 *Prelim. report of assistant commissioners*,

pp. 1–2. See also tenant petition to John Hancock, agent of Lurgan estate, 1 Nov. 1879, Hancock Mss. D1600/3/4; *Richmond prelim. report*, p. 7; *C.C.*, 31 Jan. 1880; *B.N.L.*, 30 Jan., 3 Mar. 1880.

24 *N.W.*, 10 Feb. 1880.

25 *Return of members in receipt of relief in the several unions in Ireland on the 1st day of January, the 1st day of March, and the 1st day of June in 1878, 1879 and 1880*, H.C. 1880 (420–Sess. 2), lxii, 289, pp. 2–3.

26 *Ibid.*, pp. 4–5, 20–1; Report of Donegal County Committee, 28 Oct. 1880 in *The Irish crisis of 1880: proceedings of the Dublin Mansion House Relief Committee 1880* (Dublin, 1881; hereafter cited as *M.H.C. report*), p. 326; Tuke, *Irish distress and its remedies*, pp. 38–40.

27 See Tuke, *Irish distress*, pp. 7, 13; Hugh Law's speech in House of Commons. *N.W.*, 11 Feb. 1880.

28 *N.W.*, 5 Mar. 1880; *M.H.C. report*, pp. 45–7, passim. Even the earlier more restricted outdoor relief had been opposed by ratepayers in some areas. See e.g., *L.G.*, 7, 21 Oct. 1879.

29 *M.H.C. report*, Appendix IV.

30 Tuke, *Irish distress*, pp. 9–10.

31 *Ibid.*, pp. 31–2.

32 *Ibid.*, p. 23. Tuke estimated that the failure of these two sources alone, i.e. the harvest work in Scotland and England and the summer work for young people in the Lagan, deprived the 1,000 families in the Gweedore district of some £16,000 in 1879. The loss of seasonal work in England also affected smallholders in the mountain districts in Armagh, Down and other counties, though the numbers involved were not nearly as great as in Donegal. *Prelim. report of assistant*

*commissioners*, p. 3; *N.W.*, 28 Jan. 1880.

33  *M.H.C. report*, pp. 224, 295–6.

34  *Ibid.*, pp. 53, 296–7.

35  *T.C.*, 20 Feb., 5 Mar. 1880; *N.W.*, 16 Feb. 1880; *M.H.C. report*, pp. 228, 266–7, 297.

36  *M.H.C. report*, pp. 55, 226, 263–4.

37  *Ibid.*, pp. 222–3; *N.W.*, 16 Feb. 1880.

38  *Agric. stats. for 1871*, p. xxvii; *Agric. stats. for 1881*, p. 38; Barrington, 'Agricultural prices', p. 252.

39  'Memorandum on the state of Ireland', July 1879, Disraeli Mss. B/XII/D/39; *The Times*, 17 Sept. 1879. See also *M.H.C. report*, p. 12.

40  *N.W.*, 25, 31 Oct., 8, 10 Nov. 1879.

41  *Correspondence relative to measures for relief and distress*, p. 5.

42  *Ibid.*, pp. 6–8. Only eight unions in Ulster were scheduled as distressed districts at this stage and these were all in Donegal. Later several unions in Cavan and Fermanagh were added to the list.

43  *Ibid.*, pp. 15, 23. The Conservative government later authorised the advance of an additional £250,000 from the Irish church surplus fund, and a further £750,000 was allowed by Gladstone's government in August.

44  *Return of all applications from landed proprietors and sanitary authorities in scheduled unions for loans under the notices of the commissioners of public works in Ireland … with result of applications to the 20th day of March 1880, arranged by baronies*, H.C. 1880 (154), lxii, 209, pp. 207. Serious allegations were later made as to the manner in which much of this money was spent, claims being made that landlords confined the employment to their usual staff and rarely employed the really destitute; that in some cases they employed only those who owed them rent, stopping their wages to help pay off the arrears; and that in others they borrowed the money at 1 per cent simply to reinvest it at 4 per cent or to re-loan it to their tenants at 4–7 per cent. See *N.W.*, 24 Dec. 1880. See also Healy, *A word for Ireland*, p. 126; *M.H.C. report*, pp. 256–8; MacKnight, *Ulster as it is*, i, 387; Davitt, *Fall of feudalism*, p. 233. Of the money applied for in Ulster, over £60,000 was for Donegal, nearly £20,000 for Cavan and about £4,000 for Fermanagh.

45  *M.H.C. report*, p. 43.

46  *Correspondence relative to measures for the relief of distress*, pp. 18–19, 21–4; *M.H.C. report*, pp. 43–44. The amount eventually allowed under this procedure up to 9 July 1881 was £276,344. *Return showing the amount allowed for relief works in Ireland …* H.C. 1881 (274), lvii, 705, p. 1.

47  *Eighth annual report of local government board*, p. 12; *M.H.C. report*, pp. 45–6.

48  *Eighth annual report of local government board*, pp. 13–14; *Appendix to the annual report of the local government board for Ireland, being the ninth report … 35 & 36 Vic., c.69* [C.2926–1], H.C. 1881, xlvii, 305, pp. 126–9; *Return showing the unions and electoral divisions scheduled by the local government board for Ireland under the Seeds Supply (Ireland) Act, 1880.* H.C. 1880 (299-Sess. 2), lxii, 339, p. 1. See also Tuke, *Irish distress*, pp. 44–5; *N.W.*, 26 Feb., 1, 3, 8 Mar. 1880.

49  *M.H.C. report*, pp. 1, 27, 32, 73; Donnelly, *Land and people of nineteenth century Cork*, p. 262.

50  Report of Donegal central committee, 28 Oct. 1880 in *M.H.C. report*, pp. 325–7.

51  *M.H.C. report*, p. 311.

52  See e.g. *W.N.W.*, 3 Nov. 1877, 21 Dec. 1878.

53  *C. Chron.*, 23 Aug. 1879. See also *B.F.P.* , 5 Feb. 1880; *N.W.*, 15 Aug. 1879, 22 Jan. 1880; Montgomery, *Irish land and Irish rights*, p. 10; J.H. Staples, *Solutions of the land question in Ireland* (London and Belfast, 1881), pp. 16–17; and evidence of Rev. Charles Quinn P. P., president of Camlough Tenant-right Association, and James McAleena, a Castlewellan auctioneer, to *Bessborough Commission*, Qs5708–9, 6391.

54  See James Crossle to Sir William Verner, 24 April 1880, Verner Mss. D236/488/1, p. 351; Crossle to Verner, 22 May 1880, *ibid.*, p. 356.

55  Letter to Ed., *T.C.*, 17 Oct. 1879.

56  *N.W.*, 24 Oct. 1879; J.A. Pomeroy to Montgomery, 16 Dec. 1879, Montgomery Mss. D627.275a.

57  Plunket to W.H. Dyke, 28 Oct. 1879, Disraeli Mss. B/XX/ch/42. Knox was the second son of the Earl of Ranfurly and was formerly Tory MP for Dungannon (1851–74).

58  There were, for example, only three major land meetings in Donegal, the most distressed of the Ulster counties, during the whole of the period from July 1879 to June 1880 — in contrast to forty-six meetings in Galway and sixty-two in Mayo during the same period. *Return of all agrarian crimes and outrages ... in the counties of Galway, Mayo, Sligo and Donegal from 1st February 1880 to 30th June 1880; of the number of meetings called for the purpose of promoting the land agitation ... within the same counties since 30 June 1879 ...* H.C. 1880 (327-sess.2), lx, 291, p. 2.

59  The abolition of the existing system 'of rents and landlordism' was advocated at home rule meetings in Draperstown, Belfast and Newry, the last two addressed by Parnell; but the tenant-right press denied that these were representative of tenant opinion in the province. *N.W.*, 16, 18 Oct.; *C.C.*, 18 Oct. 1879.

60  See e.g. the resolutions at the meetings at Toomebridge, Carndonagh, Camlough and Ballymoney. *B.F.P.* , 14 Aug. 1879; *N.W.*, 13 Aug., 29 Oct., 15 Dec. 1879, 13 Feb. 1880.

61  Speech of Andrew Wilson at Saintfield, *N.W.*, 9 Sept. 1879. See also speeches of Rev. Charles Quinn at Camlough and Richard Allen at Portadown, *ibid.*, 15 Dec. 1879, 26 Feb. 1880.

62  *N.W.*, 2 Dec. 1879. See also *ibid.*, 20 Aug., 3 Sept., 2, 4, 11, 18 Oct. 1879; *C.C.*, 6 Sept. 1879. Only the *Ulster Examiner* thought that in view of the depression in agriculture no rents should be paid. *U.E.*, 2 Sept. 1879.

63  *Return of all agrarian outrages reported by the Royal Irish Constabulary between the 1st January 1879 and the 31st January 1880 ...* H.C. 1880 (131), lx, 199, pp. 40–55, 90–1.

64  'Memorandum from Chief Secretary: Reports from resident magistrates re. renewal of peace preservation acts, Jan. 1880', Disraeli Mss. B/XII/D/40a.

65  See e.g. James Crossle to Sir William Verner, 24 April 1880, Verner Mss. D236.488.1, p. 351; C.F. Smith, *James Nicholson Richardson of Bessbrook* (London, 1925), p. 65.

66  Tuke, *Irish distress*, pp. 4–10. See also James Crossle to A.R. Jackson, 25 Nov. 1880, Verner Mss. D236/488/1, p. 496.

67  J.A. Pomeroy to Montgomery, 13

Oct. 1879, Montgomery Mss. D627/283.

68 Pomeroy to Montgomery, 16 Dec. 1879, *ibid.* D627/286a.

69 See e.g. correspondence between Lord Robert Montague and his County Antrim tenants (Pinkerton press cuttings, D1078/P/1, D1078/F/29; *B.F.P.* , 18, 24 Dec. 1879) and campaigns conducted by tenants on the Salters estate (*C.C.*, 11 Oct. 1879), the Kildowney estate in Down (*N.W.*, 18, 29 Nov., 29 Dec. 1879) and the Kilmorey estate, where the tenants explicitly warned Kilmorey that he could not depend on their votes in the future unless 'some material and tangible sympathy' was shown to them in the matter of rents (*ibid.*, 9 Dec. 1879).

70 For press comments on the failure of northern landlords in this respect, see *B.F.P.* , 2, 23 Oct. 1879; *N.W.*, 11 Aug., 8 Sept., 18 Oct., 7 Nov. 1879; *L. Stand.*, 12 Nov. 1879; *U.E.*, 6 Sept., 16 Oct. 1879; *A.G.*, 19 Sept., 24 Oct. 1879; *C.C.*, 6 Sept. 1879.

71 *The Times*, 30 Sept., 10 Nov. 1879. See also Montgomery to Thompson, Aug. 1879, Montgomery Mss. D1121/5.

72 *N.W.*, 23, 24, 29 Dec. 1879, 14 Jan., 16 Feb., 8 Mar. 1880; *B.N.L.*, 27 Jan. 1880; *B.F.P.* , 26 Feb. 1880; *T.C.*, 13 Aug. 1880; J.A. Pomeroy to H. Montgomery, 5, 16 Dec. 1879, Montgomery Mss. D627/285, 286a.

73 *Return of the names of landowners and sanitary authorities who have obtained loans under the provisions of the Relief of Distress (Ireland) Acts, 1880 ...* H.C. 1881 (99), lvii, 653, pp 2, 15–17. For complaints about the misuse of the loans, see above, note 44.

74 *Ibid.*, p. 16; James Musgrave to

Gladstone, 10 Mar. 1886, Gladstone Mss. 44495, ff. 201–2. See also *N.W.*, 1 Jan. 1880.

75 See e.g. Tuke's comments on landlords about Belleek in Fermanagh, Tuke, *Irish distress*, p. 6. For the general indebtedness of Irish landlords, see L.P. Curtis, 'Incumbered wealth: landed indebtedness in post-famine Ireland', *American Historical Review*, lxxxv (1980), pp. 332–67.

76 Over one-third of the total money borrowed in the distressed districts of Ulster was borrowed by three landlords — Lord Leitrim, the Musgraves and the Marquis Conyngham. *Return of names of landowners and sanitary authorities who obtained loans under the relief of distress acts*, pp. 15–16.

77 *N.W.*, 14 Jan. 1880.

78 Charlemont to Hugh Boyle, n.d. [Spring, 1880], Charlemont Mss., D266/367/31; Lifford to Ed., *The Times*, 17 Mar. 1880; Tuke, *Irish distress*, pp. 18, 31.

79 Quoted in Tuke, *Irish distress*, p. 4.

80 J.A. Pomeroy to Montgomery, 17 April 1880, Montgomery Mss. D627/297a: James Watt to Montgomery, 22 Mar. 1880, *ibid.* D627/29a.

81 See e.g. criticisms of *N.W.*, 14 Jan. 1880 and *B.F.P.* , 29 Jan. 1880.

82 *B.N.L.*, 20 July 1879; *N.W.*, 2, 6, 16, 19 Aug. 1879; *T.C.*, 29 Aug., 5 Sept. 1879; *L.G.*, 16 Sept. 1879.

83 *N.W.*, 18, 29 Nov. 1879; James Crossle to William Stewart, 28 Nov. 1881, Verner Mss. D236/477/2, pp. 277–8. See also *N.W.*, 9 Dec. 1879; *B.F.P.* , 30 Oct. 1879.

84 J.A. Pomeroy to Montgomery, 20 Sept. 1879, Montgomery Mss. D627/282.

85  J.A. Pomeroy to Montgomery, 5
    Sept. 1879, *ibid.* D627/281b; *N.W.*, 1
    Nov. 1879.

86  *T.C.*, 29 Aug.; *N.W.*, 24, 25 Oct. 1879;
    *C. Const.*, 25 Oct., 1 Nov. 1879.

87  *L.G.*, 20 April, 22 June 1880.

88  Charlemont to Hugh Boyle, 24 (Feb.
    1880), Charlemont Mss. D266/367/
    13; J.A. Pomeroy to Montgomery, 5
    Sept. 1879, Montgomery Mss.
    D627.281b.

89  John Hancock's circular to tenants
    on Lurgan estates in Armagh, *N.W.*,
    14 Nov. 1879.

90  *N.W.*, 31 Oct. 1879, 17 Dec. 1880.

91  Pomeroy to Montgomery, 5 Sept.
    1879, Montgomery Mss. D627/271b.

92  *T.C.*, 23 Jan. 1880; *C. Const.*, 16 Aug.
    1879; *N.W.*, 27 Aug., 10 Oct. 1879.

93  J.H. Staples to Ed., *N.W.*, 19 Nov.
    1879. See also *Prelim. report of assistant
    commissioners*, p. 2; *B.N.L.*, 25 Sept.
    1879. Charges on the Abercorn
    estate and on Sir John Marcus
    Stewart's Tyrone estate, for example,
    amounted to over 40 per cent of
    the total rental in each case. Curtis,
    'Incumbered wealth', p. 357, n. 60.

94  O'Neill allowed remissions of 7.5
    to 15 per cent, saying that it was
    impossible for him to offer more
    because the charges on his estate
    swallowed up half the rents (*C.
    Const.*, 1 Nov. 1879). The remissions
    were estimated to have cost him
    some £4,000 out of a total rental of
    £45,000 (Dun, *Landlords and tenants*,
    pp. 111–12). The charges on the
    Verner estates — including a
    jointure of £1,200 to Verner's
    mother and mortgage interest of
    nearly £3,000 — amounted to over
    £4,000 out of a total rental of about
    £12,000. Out-letter books of James
    Crossle, D236/488/2, p. 277; D236/
    488/3, pp. 312–3.

95  Lifford to Ed., *The Times*, 10 Nov.
    1879; J.A. Pomeroy to H.
    Montgomery, 16 Dec. 1879,
    Montgomery Mss. D627/286a;
    statement of James Price to his Co.
    Down tenants, *N.W.*, 9 Sept. 1879;
    reply of Lord Robert Montague to
    memorial from the tenants on his
    Ballymoney estate, *B.F.P.*, 24 Dec.
    1879.

96  *N.W.*, 9 Sept. 1879; *C.C.*, 27 Sept.
    1879. See also statement of Aubrey
    de Vere Beauclerc to his County
    Down tenants. *U.E.*, 11 Oct. 1879.

97  *T.C.*, 17 Oct. 1879; *C. Const.*, 20, 27
    Sept., 4 Oct. 1879; 'An Ulster
    landlord' to Ed., *N.W.*, 21 Nov. 1879;
    speech of J. Corry, MP for Belfast,
    in House of Commons, *N.W.*, 6
    Feb. 1880; 'An Ulster agent' to Ed.,
    *B.N.L.*, 29 Oct. 1879.

98  See e.g. *N.W.*, 14 Jan. 1880; *B.F.P.*, 29
    Jan. 1880.

99  The number of evictions in Ulster
    increased from 88 in 1878 to 172 in
    1879 to 251 in the first six months
    of 1880 (497 for the whole of 1880).
    The average for the period 1870–78
    had been 121. Not only were
    evictions up in 1879 but
    readmissions were down — from
    an average of 21 per cent during the
    period 1870–78 to 4 per cent in
    1879. *Return of evictions in each of the
    years 1849–80, p. 4; Return ... of cases
    of eviction which have come to the
    knowledge of the constabulary in each
    quarter of the year ended the 31st day of
    December 1880 ...* H.C. 1881 (2), lxxvii,
    713, pp. 2–3.

100 *C. Const.*, 31 Jan. 1880. See also
    report from *Saturday Review* in *N.W.*,
    29 Dec. 1879.

101 *N.W.*, 14, 24 Jan. 1880. See also *B.F.P.*,
    29 Jan. 1880; MacKnight, *Ulster as it
    is*, i, 361. On the other hand, many
    landlords resented the sometimes

blatant attempts made by tenants to use the crisis to their own advantage and to pressurise landlords into rent reductions which, in many cases, the landlords believed were unnecessary. See Earl of Charlemont to Hugh Boyle, 15 Nov. 1880, Charlemont Mss. D266/367/ 47; statement of Robert E. Ward of Bangor Castle to his tenants, *N.W.*, 7 Nov. 1879.

102 *U.E.*, 28 Oct. 1879.

103 *N.W.*, 3 Sept. 1879; *B.F.P.*, 14 Aug. 1879.

104 See e.g. tenant meetings at Toomebridge, Camlough, Kilmore. *B.F.P.*, 14 Aug. 1879; *N.W.*, 6 Sept., 15 Dec. 1879, 13 Feb. 1880. For tenant-right meetings, see *N.W.*, 24 Jan., 12, 20 Feb. 1880.

105 See e.g. *B.F.P.* , 4 Dec. 1879.

106 *N.W.*, 14 June, 11 Oct. 1879, 24 Jan. 1880; *B.F.P.* , 30 Oct. 1879; *L.G.*, 13 Jan. 1880.

107 Dorrian to Kirby, 24 Nov. 1879, Kirby correspondence 1879, no. 510; *U.E.*, 30 Aug. 1879. See also resolutions passed at tenant meetings in Draperstown and Camlough in favour of the Land League programme of peasant proprietorship, *ibid*, 6, 16 Sept., 16 Dec. 1879; *N.W.*, 6 Sept., 15 Dec. 1879.

108 *U.E.*, 28 Oct. 1879.

109 *Bessborough Commission*, Q5718–19; *L.G.*, 30 Mar. 1880.

110 *C.C.*, 10 Jan. 1880.

111 C.C. O'Brien, *Parnell and his party 1880–90* (corrected impression, Oxford, 1968), Ch. 1.

112 MacKnight, *Ulster as it is*, i, 373.

113 For Biggar and Fay's joint address, see *U.E.*, 13 Mar. 1880.

114 *B.N.L.*, 19 April 1880.

115 The ensuing discussion of the issues in the election is based on the addresses and reports of the speeches of the candidates contained in the local press.

116 This bill, it may be remembered, established the presumption of law with regard to tenant-right in favour of the tenant, abolished estate rules, and affirmed leasehold tenant-right.

117 See *B.F.P.* , 18 Mar. 1880.

118 Land reform, home rule, foreign policy, the record of the Tory government and nonconformist burials were the main issues discussed in the borough contests.

119 Dickson actually lost the seat on petition but his son was elected in his place by exactly the same majority.

120 *L. Sent.*, 6 April 1880; *C. Const.*, 10 April 1880; *B.N.L.*, 5, 14 April 1880; *N.W.*, 17 April 1880.

121 Henry Johnston to C.H. Brett, 4 April 1880, Brett Mss. D1905/2/ 247/4.

122 *N.W.*, 17 June 1880. See also *ibid.*, 16, 21 April 1880; *C.C.*, 10 April 1880.

123 *C.C.*, 10 April 1880; *C. Const.*, 3 April 1880; *L. Sent.*, 30 Mar. 1880. For an unflattering portrait of Bruce by his grandson, see H.J. Bruce, *Silken Dalliance* (London, 1946), pp. 17–33.

124 The petition was, however, dismissed. *N.W.*, 4 June 1880; *B.N.L.*, 5, 7 June 1880.

125 Wright, *Two lands on one soil*, pp. 447–9.

126 See e.g. speeches of Knox, Lewis and Mulholland, *B.N.L.*, 9, 15, 19, 25 Mar. 1880.

127 In Antrim there were estimated to be 7,000 presbyterian electors, 2,000 catholic and about 1,800 episcopalian electors in an electorate of just over 11,000 (S.C.

McElroy to Ed., *N.W.*, 1 April 1880); in Down, 40 per cent of the total population were presbyterians so that they presumably made up half or more of the electorate. Vaughan and Fitzpatrick, *Irish historical statistics*, p. 58.

128 *N.W.*, 8, 9, 15 April 1880. Many of the tenant-right societies had fallen into a state of neglect by 1880. *Ibid.*, 15 April, 5 June 1880.

129 *Ibid.*, 9, 12, 15 April; *B.N.L.*, 30 June 1880.

130 *B.N.L.*, 9 April 1880.

131 *Ibid.*, 1 June 1880. See also *N.W.*, 12, 14, 15 April; *B.F.P.* , 8, 15 April, 3 June 1880.

132 *B.N.L.*, 24 Mar., 6 April; *C. Const.*, 28 Feb; *N.W.*, 20–26 Feb., 25, 26 Mar., 1 April 1880.

133 The importance of this in influencing tenant votes should not be underestimated. See e.g. reports from Seaforde, Dromore and Warrenpoint polling stations in *N.W.*, 15, 17 April 1880. See also *ibid.*, 3 May; *B.F.P.* , 27 May 1880.

134 For Armagh, see *A.G.*, 19 Mar. 1880; *N.W.*, 22 Mar. 1880; *B.N.L.*, 18, 30 Mar., 8 April 1880; Earl of Charlemont to Boyle, 21, 30, 31 [March 1880], Charlemont Mss. D266/367/17, 18, 19. For divisions in Tyrone, see David Plunkett MP to M. Corry, 27 Mar. 1880, Disraeli Mss. B/XII/K11; *B.N.L.*, 10 April, 1 June 1880; *T.C.*, 16 April 1880.

135 See e.g. *B.N.L.*, 10 April 1880.

136 See T.P. Hamilton to Marquis of Hamilton, 8 Jan. 1880, Disraeli Mss. B/XXI/H/42a.

137 See e.g. *N.W.*, 18 Mar. 1880; *B.F.P.* , 25 Mar. 1880; *B.N.L.*, 6 May 1880.

138 See e.g. *C. Const.*, 17 April 1880. Polling in the Ulster counties started on 6 April and by that date the Liberals were showing a net gain of 77 seats in Britain. *B.N.L.*, 8 April 1880.

139 *B.N.L.*, 14 April, 2 June 1880.

## Chapter 8

1 Davitt, *Fall of feudalism*, p. 239.

2 *Ibid.*, pp. 241–4; Paul Bew, *Land and the national question in Ireland, 1858–82* (Dublin, 1978), pp. 99–104; O'Brien, *Parnell and his party*, ch. 1.

3 *N.W.*, 6 May 1880. See also *ibid.*, 3, 17 May; *B.F.P.* , 30 Sept. 1880.

4 *N.W.*, 3 June, 1 July 1880.

5 See e.g. *ibid.*, 17 May 1880; *B.F.P.* , 30 Sept. 1880

6 *N.W.*, 21, 27 July, 7 Aug. 1880; *C.C.*, 31 July 1880; *B.F.P.*, 29 July, 5, 12 Aug. 1880.

7 *N.W.*, 18 Aug. 1880.

8 *C.C.*, 21 Aug. 1880; *N.W.*, 27, 28 Aug., 6, 21, 25 Sept.; *B.N.L.*, 6 Sept. 1880; *T.C.*, 1 Oct. 1880; *B.F.P.* , 2, 30 Sept. 1880.

9 McElroy, *Route land crusade*, p. 35; *C.C.*, 16 Oct. 1880.

10 *Agric. stats. for 1880*, p. 53.

11 Barrington, 'Agricultural prices', pp. 251–2.

12 *B.N.L.*, 9 Sept. 1880.

13 *Agric. stats. for 1881*, p. 53.

14 Barrington, 'Agricultural Prices', p. 252.

15 *Agric. stats. for 1878*, pp. 34–5; *Agric. stats for 1880*, pp. 34–5.

16 *N.W.*, 12 Aug. 1880; *Agric. stats. for 1880*, pp. 84–6.

17 *Agric. stats. for 1880*, pp. 49–53.

18 *B.F.P.* , 12 Aug. 1880.

19 *B.F.P.* , 12 Aug. See also *C.C.*, 15 May 1880.

20 'Reports of County Inspectors of the R.I.C. on the condition of Ireland', forwarded by G.E. Hillier, Inspector-General, RIC, 28 Oct. 1880, Harcourt Mss. W.V.H. 17/2. Other county inspectors spoke in similar terms of the plight of the small farmers.

21 *Ibid.*; 'Summaries of reports of resident magistrates throughout Ireland on the state of the country', Oct. 1880, *ibid.* See also reports of resident magistrates in Cavan, Derry and Donegal.

22 *T.C.*, 5 Nov. 1880.

23 *N.W.*, 31 July 1880.

24 See *N.W.*, 4, 6, 9 Aug. 1880; *C.C.*, 7 Aug. 1880.

25 The *Coleraine Chronicle* admitted in November that the independent action taken by tenants to secure remissions of rent had taken the tenant-right leaders by surprise. *C.C.*, 13 Nov. 1880.

26 Donnelly to H. de F. Montgomery, 28 Dec. 1880, Montgomery Mss. D627/297e. See also G.W. O'Brien to Forster, 4 Nov. 1880, Gladstone Mss. 44157, f. 196.

27 *L.G.*, 30 Mar. 1880; Irish National League papers (hereafter cited as INL papers), 1/73; *N.W.*, 24 Aug. 1880; *T.C.*, 27 Aug. 1880.

28 For the stimulus given to the league campaign in the south by these events see Bew, *Land and the national question*, pp. 119–21; O'Brien, *Parnell and his party*, pp. 49–54.

29 *N.W.*, 2 Nov. 1880.

30 *B.N.L.*, 22 Oct. 1880.

31 *Ibid.*, 27 Sept. 1880; *N.W.*, 4 Oct. 1880. Other meetings were held in October at Craughaughrim in Donegal, at Donegal town, at Bailieborough and Bawnboy in Cavan and at Cullyhanna in Armagh.

32 'Summaries of reports of resident magistrates throughout Ireland on the state of the country', [late] Oct. 1880, Harcourt Mss. W.V.H. 17/2. The RMs had been asked to include details of league meetings and league branches in their districts, and as far as one can gather from their replies and from the local press there were at the end of October two league clubs in Cavan, two in Armagh, at least two in Donegal, five in Derry and one in Fermanagh.

33 *N.W.*, 2 Nov. 1880. A preliminary meeting had been held at Dungannon in October. *B.N.L.*, 22 Oct. 1880.

34 *T.C.*, 12 Nov. 1880; INL papers, 1/8, 74; C.S.O., R.P. 1880, 27322; *I.R.*, 11 Nov. 1880.

35 These paragraphs are based mainly on the following sources: Irish National League papers, cartons 1 and 10; C.S.O., R.P. 1880 and 1881; Land League papers, National Library Ireland, Mss. 17,708, 17,709; the local press.

36 *C. Const.*, 9 Oct., 4 Dec. 1880. See also *Newtownards Chronicle*, 4 Dec. 1880, 1 Jan. 1881.

37 Livingstone, *The Fermanagh story*, p. 261.

38 Among the branches in Donegal were Carndonagh, Craughaughrim, Falcarragh, Clonmany, Moville and Inishowen; in Derry, Loup and Magherafelt, Derry, Maghera, Ballinderry, Innishbrush and Draperstown.

39 The Mayobridge branch was reported to have over 1,000 members (*N.W.*, 8 Dec. 1880). In the branch reports from Ulster contained in the Land League papers in the National Library —

these include reports from only ten branches in the province — membership ranged from 86 in the Ballinderry branch in Derry to 590 in the Shantonagh branch in Monaghan, with most of the remainder having between 300 and 500 members. Land League papers, Ms. 17,708.

40  The league presence was felt in every part of Fermanagh, but it was particularly well organised in the north and west of the county. See Mervyn Archdale to W.E. Forster, 21 Mar. 1881, C.S.O., R.P. 1881, 11500; J.N. Thornfield to T. H. Burke, Undersecretary, Dublin Castle, Oct. 1881, *ibid.*, 34385.

41  For main areas of tenant-right activity, see above, pp. 105-6.

42  Livingstone, *The Monaghan story,* p. 334.

43  *N.W.*, 24 Dec. 1880. See also Clifford Lloyd, *Ireland under the Land League, a narrative of personal experiences* (Edinburgh and London, 1892), ch. 1.

44  *U.E.*, 1 Jan. 1881; *T.C.*, 12, 19 Nov. 1880.

45  J.S. Macleod RM, 'Memorandum on state of the barony of Inishowen', 6 Nov. 1880, C.S.O., R.P. 1880, 27322.

46  See below, p. 214.

47  Ward to Capt. Arthur Hill, 27 May 1881, Saunderson Mss. T2996/11/1. Ward was the youngest son of the 3rd Viscount Bangor and brother-in-law of Hill who owned the Gweedore estate.

48  The meetings at Sessiagh, Blacklion, Mayobridge, Belturbet, Castlewellan, Rostrevor, Crossmaglen and many others were all presided over by catholic clergymen.

49  Donnelly to Hugh Montgomery, 28 Dec. 1880, Montgomery Mss. D627/2973.

50  Dorrian to Kirby, 1 Nov. 1880, Kirby Correspondence, 1880, no. 477. See also same to same, 14 April 1880, 30 June 1880, *ibid.*, 1880, nos 193, 312; Macauley, *Dorrian,* pp. 328–34, 340–4.

51  Letter to organisers of an 'indignation meeting' in St Mary's Hall, Belfast to protest against the prosecution of the Land League leaders, *N.W.*, 18 Nov. 1880; Dorrian to Kirby, 1 Nov. 1880, Kirby correspondence, 1880, no. 477.

52  Major J. Blair, RM, Co. Monaghan, to T.H. Burke, 10 Dec. 1880, C.S.O., R.P. 1880, 31216. See also *B.N.L.,* 13 Nov., 10 Dec. 1880.

53  Speech of Michael Davitt at Saintfield, *N.W.*, 24 Dec. 1880. See also Davitt's speech at Downpatrick in January 1881, C.S.O., R.P. 1881, 5487.

54  I.N.L. papers, 1/84. See also speech of P. J. Sheridan at Bawnboy, 30 Oct. 1880, *ibid.,* 1/7; speech of John Pinkerton at Loughguile, Dec. 1880, Pinkerton press cuttings, D1078/P/1; resolution at meeting at Maghera, *L. Stand.*, 8 Dec. 1880; speeches of Father Peter Quinn and C.J. Dempsey at Keady, *N.W.*, 21 Dec. 1880; speeches of Jeremiah Jordan and James Maguire at Holywell, *I.R.*, 30 Dec. 1880, and many others.

55  C.S.O., R.P. 1880, 31216.

56  C.S.O., R.P. 1881, 9406. The *Impartial Reporter* saw this as evidence that 'the Land League in Fermanagh is different to the Land League in other counties', but this was to some extent true for the whole of Ulster. *I.R.,* 17 Mar. 1881.

57  *I.R.*, 30 Dec. 1880. See also speech of Bernard Campbell at Dungannon, Head Constable J. Devane to Inspector General RIC, 21 Oct. 1880, C.S.O., R.P. 1880, 26366.

58 A. Carleton to Inspector General, 11 Dec. 1880, C.S.O., R.P. 1880, 31216.

59 Speech of Francis Sheppard, *N.W.*, 24 Dec. 1880.

60 League speakers frequently tailored their speeches to their audiences. Speeches in, for example, north-west Donegal were normally more critical of British administration and generally less temperate than speeches in, for example, Co. Down where the local leaders made a particular effort to keep their words and actions 'moderate and very much within the law'. Michael McCartan to Patrick W. Russell, 23 May 1881, Russell Mss. A3.

61 *Down Independent* report in C.S.O., R.P. 1881, 5487.

62 Montgomery to Forster, 13 March 1881, C.S.O., R.P. 1881, 9406.

63 Speech of John McKee and resolution at Maghera, *L. Stand.*, 8 Dec. 1880. See also speech of Joseph Biggar at Loughguile, *N.W.*, 23 Dec. 1880.

64 Livingstone, *The Fermanagh Story*, p. 259.

65 *N.W.*, 10 Nov. 1880; *I.R.*, 11 Nov. 1880. See also speech of John Dillon at the same meeting.

66 Speeches of Joseph Biggar at Dungannon (*N.W.*, 2 Nov. 1880) and James O'Kelly, MP for Roscommon at Scotstown, Dec. 1880, C.S.O., R.P. 1880, 31216.

67 C.S.O., R.P. 1880, 31216.

68 *Ibid*. See also speech of John Pinkerton at Loughguile, Pinkerton press cuttings, D1078/P/1.

69 Speech at Pomeroy, *N.W.*, 11 Dec. 1880.

70 Bateson to Salisbury, 30 Dec. 1880, Salisbury Mss. E. Bateson owned estates in Derry and Down, was MP for Devizes and a former MP for County Derry.

71 R. Harvey RM to T.H. Burke, 10 Feb. 1881, C.S.O., R.P. 1881 9406; H. Montgomery to W.E. Forster, 13 Mar. 1881, *ibid*.

72 See Livingstone, *The Fermanagh story*, pp. 259–61.

73 *I.R.*, 24 Dec. 1880.

74 Rev. D.C. Abbott to Montgomery, 18 Dec. 1880, Montgomery Mss. D627/428/7.

75 Livingstone, *The Fermanagh story*, p. 260. See also *C.C.*, 4 Dec. 1880; *Newtownards Chronicle*, 4 Dec. 1880; *L. Stand.*, 7 April 1881.

76 Minutes of Fermanagh G.O.L., Dec. 1880, D1402/1 (see also *ibid.*, 5 May, 17 Nov. 1881); A. McClelland, 'The later Orange order', in *Secret societies in Ireland*, ed. T. Desmond Williams (Dublin, 1973), p. 130.

77 *N.W.*, 22 Jan. 1881.

78 *C.C.*, 4 Dec. 1880.

79 Speech of David McAteer at Dungannon, *N.W.*, 2 Nov. 1880.

80 C.S.O., R.P. 1880, 31216; John Harbinson to Lord O'Hagan, 4 Jan. 1881, O'Hagan Mss. D2777, ADD/50.

81 Hugh McKeever to Thomas Brennan, 23 May 1881, Land League papers, ms. 17,709.

82 See MacKnight, *Ulster as it is*, i, 361.

83 See e.g. Bishop Donnelly of Clogher to Hugh Montgomery, 5 Dec. 1880, Montgomery Mss. D627/327G.

84 Crossle to A.R. Jackson, 25 Dec. 1880, Verner Mss. D236/488/1, p. 518.

85 J.A. Pomeroy to Montgomery, 14 Dec. 1880, 7 Jan. 1881, Montgomery Mss. D627/299a, 302; Dun, *Landlords and tenants in Ireland*, pp. 141–2.

86 Cairns to Beaconsfied, 3 Dec. 1880, Disraeli Mss. B/xx/Ca/272.

87 *Return of the number of agrarian offences in each county in Ireland reported to the constabulary office in each month of the year 1880* ...H.C. 1881 (12), lxxvii, 619, p. 4; *Return of the number of agrarian offences in each county in Ireland ...in each month of the year 1881* ... H.C. 1882 (8), lv, 1, p. 4. After January the number fell to 20 in February and 14 in March, the lowest figure for 1881. *Ibid.*, pp. 5–6.

88 In November–December 1880 only five agrarian offences were reported in Fermanagh as against, for example, 15 in Antrim which, although the county least affected by the Land League, had the fourth highest number of outrages for these months. *Return of all agrarian outrages which have been reported by the Royal Irish Constabulary between the 1st day of November 1880 and the 30th day of November 1880* ... H.C. 1881 (6-I), lxxvii, 409; p. 77; *Return of all agrarian outrages ... between the 1st day of December 1880 and the 31st day of December 1880* ... H.C. 1881 (6-II), lxxvii, 487, p. 107.

89 R. Harvey RM to T.H. Burke, 1 April 1881, C.S.O., R.P. 1881, 11500. See also F. McGuire, Sub-Inspector RIC to H.G. Cary, County Inspector, 27 March 1881, *ibid.*; W.C. Trimble to W.E. Forster 22 Oct. 1881, C.S.O., R.P. 1881, 44241.

90 I.N.L. papers, 1/7.

91 See e.g. reports of league speeches in INL papers, ctn 1.

92 See e.g. speech of Daniel McSweeney, president of the Falcarragh branch of the league at Gortahork in March 1881. INL papers, ctn 10.

93 It is hardly necessary to point out that serious outrages had occurred in Ulster — usually for the same reasons — well before the advent of the league. See e.g. *Return of agrarian outrages reported between 1 Feb. and 31 Oct. 1880*, pp. 71–87.

94 An analysis of the 195 offences gives the following results — 6 cases of assault; 13 of incendiarism; 133 of intimidation by letter or notice, 18 of intimidation otherwise; 12 of damage to property; 9 of firing into dwellings; 1 of resistance to legal process. The remaining three were clearly family disputes. *Return of agrarian outrages for December 1880*, pp. 61–77; *Return of the number of agrarian offences in each county in each month of 1881*, p. 4.

95 *C.C.*, 12 Feb. 1881.

96 See e.g. J. S. Macleod RM, 'Memorandum on state of the barony of Inishowen', 6 Nov. 1880, C.S.O., R.P. 1880, 27322.

97 *Return of agrarian outrages for December 1880*, p. 77.

98 James Crossle to A.R. Jackson, 5 Dec. 1880, Verner Mss. D236/488/1, pp. 506–508; *N.W.*, 9 Dec. 1880.

99 C.S.O., R.P. 1880, 31452.

100 James Crossle to A.R. Jackson, 5 Dec. 1880, Verner Mss. D236/488/1, pp. 506–8.

101 Speeches of Joseph Biggar at Bawnboy (30 Oct. 1880, INL papers, 1/7) and James Maguire and Lynnott at Holywell, *I.R.*, 30 Dec. 1880. See also speech of Edward McHugh at Killeavy, *N.W.*, 4 Oct. 1880.

102 Only 13 of the 150 outrages reported in Ulster in November and December of 1880 were in any way related to land grabbing. *Return of agrarian outrages for November 1880*, pp. 46–53; *Return of agrarian outrages for December 1880*, pp. 61–77.

103 *Ibid.*

104 Speech of John Dillon at Pomeroy, 10 Dec. 1880, INL papers, 1/409.

105 Speech of Joseph Biggar at Cavan, 4 Nov. 1880, *ibid.*, 1/8.

106 See e.g. speeches of Michael Boynton at Carndonagh, 4 July 1880, and John Dillon at Pomeroy, 10 Dec. 1880, *ibid.*, 1/73, 1/409.

107 *Return of agrarian outrages reported between 1 Feb. 1880 and 31 Oct. 1880*, pp. 71–87; *Return of agrarian outrages for November 1880*, pp. 46–53; *Return of agrarian outrages for December 1880*, pp. 61–77; *Return of agrarian offences in each county in each month of 1881*, pp. 4–15.

108 See speech of Col. McLaughlin, president of the Derry branch of the league, at Cruchaughrim in Donegal in July 1881 — 'I call rent a tax. Let this tax be collected with the bayonets even at your throats' (4 July 1881, INL papers, 1/85). Professor Paul Bew has shown that 'rent at the point of the bayonet' was one of the most important tactics employed by the league in the south, but it does not appear to have been as extensively or at least as openly advocated in Ulster, where landlords were in a much stronger position. See Bew, *Land and the national question*, pp. 121–6.

109 See e.g. speech of Michael Boyton at Carndonagh, 4 July 1880, INL papers, 1/73.

110 *N.W.*, 24 Aug. 1880. See also *B.N.L.*, 27 Aug. 1880.

111 As, e.g., on W.F. Littledale's Deburren estate near Newry (*N.W.*, 8 Oct., 11 Nov. 1880), the Hamill estate at Killeavy (*ibid.*, 11, 24 Nov. 1880), the Wilson estate at Edentubber in Armagh (*ibid.*, 2, 3 Dec. 1880), the Hassard estate outside Swanlinbar

(*I.R.*, 30 Dec. 1880) and others.

112 See Irish Land Committee, *The land question, Ireland, No. 1. Notes upon the government valuation of land in Ireland, commonly known as Griffith's valuation* (London and Dublin, 1880), pp. 36–7. The Irish Land Committee estimated that the valuation in the three southern provinces would have to be increased from 10 to 25 per cent to bring it into line with the valuation in Ulster.

113 *C.C.*, 15 May 1880; resolution at league meeting at Saintfield, *N.W.*, 24 Dec. 1880. See also e.g. speeches of Biggar at Ballycastle (*B.F.P.* , 2 Dec. 1880); A. J. Kettle at Dromore, Co. Tyrone (*N.W.*, 31 Dec. 1880); Matthew Maguire at Clogher (*ibid.*) and others.

114 Report from *Down Independent*, Feb. 1881 in C.S.O., R.P. 1881, 5487.

115 *N.W.*, 11 Nov., 2 Dec. 1880.

116 *C.C.*, 4 Dec. 1880; *N.W.*, 15 Dec. 1880.

117 C.S.O., R.P. 1881, 41062.

118 Somerset Ward to Capt. A. Hill, 28 May 1881, Saunderson Mss. T2996/11/2.

119 Ward to Hill, 27 May 1881, *ibid.* T.2996/11/1.

120 R.W. Kirkpatrick, 'Origins and development of the land war in mid-Ulster, 1879–85', in Lyons and Hawkins (ed.), *Ireland under the union*, p. 222.

121 Hugh Montgomery to W.E. Forster, 13 Mar. 1881, C.S.O., R.P. 1881, 9406.

122 Montgomery to E.W. Hamilton, 30 Nov. 1880, Gladstone Mss. 44467, ff. 76–7.

123 Bateson to Salisbury, 30 Dec. 1880, Salisbury Mss. E.

124 *C.C.*, 13 Nov. 1880.

125 *N.W.*, 24 Nov., 7, 21–4, 31 Dec. 1880; Tenant's memorial to Lord Lurgan, 25 Nov. 1880, Hancock Mss. D1600/3/5.

126 Resolution at meeting of Downshire tenants, *N.W.*, 14 Dec. 1880. Similar resolutions were passed by tenant meetings on the Wallace, Shane's Castle and Connor estates and others.

127 Speech of Rev. S.D. Burnside at meeting of Downshire tenants, *ibid.*

128 *Ibid.*, 14 Dec. 1880. Tenants on the Co. Down estate of Ion Trant Hamilton (*ibid.*, 18 Dec. 1880), the Downshire Hilltown estate (*ibid.*, 23 Dec. 1880), the Killoquin, McNeill and Lawrence estates in Antrim (*C.C.*, 18 Dec. 1880, 1 Jan. 1881; *B.F.P.*, 6 Jan. 1881), Sir N.A. Staple's Lissan estate in Tyrone (*C.C.*, 8 Jan. 1881), and on the Irish Society's Culmore estate (*N.W.*, 24 Nov. 1880) all agreed to withhold rents until concessions were made.

129 *N.W.*, 29 Nov., 7, 22, 31 Dec. 1880.

130 James Pomeroy to Hugh Montgomery, 7 Feb. 1881, Montgomery Mss. D627/306.

131 Crossle to A.R. Jackson, 5 Dec. 1880, 2 Feb. 1881, Verner Mss. D236/488/1, pp. 506, 576. See also Crossle to Jackson, 25 Nov. 1880, *ibid.*, pp. 495–7; Crossle to Jackson 18 Feb. 1881, 28 May 1881, *ibid.* D236/488/2, pp. 10–11, 144.

132 Somerset Ward to Capt. A. Hill, 28 May 1881, Saunderson Mss. T2996/11/2.

133 de Ros to Beaconsfield, 7 Jan. 1881, Disraeli Mss. B/XXI/D/236.

134 See above, pp. 197. The Antrim Central Tenant-right Association received a number of requests from different associations urging it to hold public meetings. McElroy, *Route Land Crusade*, p. 35.

135 *N.W.*, 17–27 Nov., 3–31 Dec. 1880; *B.F.P.* , 2–30 Dec. 1880. The majority of these meetings were held under the auspices of different tenant-right associations.

136 As, e.g., at Moira (*N.W.*, 25 Nov.), Tullyhogue (*ibid.*, 27 Nov.), Drumillar (*ibid.*, 3 Dec.), Moneymore (*ibid.*, 11 Dec.), Kilmore (*B.F.P.* , 6 Jan. 1881), Aghadowey (*C.C.*, 22 Jan. 1881).

137 See *N.W.*, 8, 23 Dec. 1880; Rutherford, *An Ards farmer*, pp. 55–6.

138 Montgomery, 'Irish land and Irish rights', p. 11.

139 Forster to Gladstone, 2 Dec. 1880, Gladstone Mss. 44158, f. 3. See memorial from Ulster Liberals to Forster, 1 Dec. 1880, *ibid.* ff. 7–8. See also *C.C.*, 15 Jan. 1881; *B.F.P.* , 13, 20 Jan. 1881.

140 Speech of Mr Headley at Comber, *N.W.*, 29 Dec. 1880. See also resolutions at meetings in Monaghan, Loughgall, Bangor, Coleraine and Ballyclare.

141 Speech of James Parker at Moneymore, *ibid.*, 11 Dec. 1880.

142 *N.W.*, 31 Dec. 1880.

143 Bew and Wright, 'Agrarian opposition in Ulster', pp. 193–4, 214–16. See also Wright, *Two lands on one soil*, pp. 467–8.

144 See e.g. resolutions passed at Land League meeting in Maghera and tenant-right meeting at Moneymore early in December 1880. *L. Stand.*, 8 Dec. 1880.

145 A number of those on the platform at a meeting organised by the Farney Tenants' Defence Association in Carrickmacross in December 1880, for example, also played a prominent role in a meeting organised by the Land League in the same town about a

month later. Livingstone, *The Monaghan story*, p. 336.

146 Pinkerton press cuttings, D1078/P/ 1. See also speech of George Darragh T.C. at Holywell (*I.R.*, 30 Dec. 1880) and speech of John Morton at Downpatrick (Report from *Down Independent* in C.S.O., R.P. 1881, 5487).

147 *N.W.*, 11 Nov. 1880.

148 *Ibid.*, 16 Dec. 1880.

149 *Ibid.*, 23 Dec. 1880.

150 See e.g. speech of Thos Meek at Moneymore, *ibid.*, 11 Dec. 1880; speech of William Gault at Ballyclare, *C.C.*, 22 Jan. 1881; letter of Rev. J.B. Huston, chairman of Aghadowey Tenant Farmers' Association to *C. Const.*, 20 Nov. 1880.

151 *N.W.*, 10 Dec. 1880. See also speech of James O'Kelly at Ballyshannon, *B.N.L.*, 27 Sept. 1880.

152 Speech of Davitt at Downpatrick, C.S.O., R.P. 1881, 5487; speech of Biggar at Mayobridge, *N.W.*, 22 Nov. 1880.

153 Speech at Ballycastle, 30 Nov. 1880, Pinkerton Press Cuttings D1078/P/1.

154 *B.F.P.*, 30 Sept. 1880; *W.N.W.*, 25 Sept. 1880. See also *B.F.P.*, 4 Nov. 1880.

155 *N.W.*, 25 Dec. 1880. See also speeches and resolutions at Monaghan, Tullyhogue and Kilrea, *ibid.*, 23, 27 Nov., 30 Dec. 1880.

156 *C.C.*, 6 Nov. 1880.

157 Speech at Comber, *N.W.*, 29 Dec. 1880. See also Dickson's speeches at Kilrea, *ibid.*, 3 Nov., 30 Dec. 1880.

## Chapter 9

1 The Irish Land Committee published at least 14 pamphlets. See bibliography.

2 The executive members of the committee were all southerners. The *Newsletter* urged the Ulster proprietors to present their own evidence to the land commission, clearly implying that the land committee had no real constituency in the north. *B.N.L.*, 6 Sept. 1880. For the difference of opinion, see below, pp. 244-5.

3 See e.g. 'Letters to Mr Forster on the state of the country', Cabinet memorandum, 8 Nov. 1880, Harcourt Mss. W.V.H. 17/2.

4 Earl of Donoughmore to W. E. Forster, 8 Oct. 1880, Harcourt Mss. W.V.H. 17.2.

5 *B.N.L.*, 30 Oct., 2, 12 Nov. 1880; *T.C.*, 5 Nov. 1880.

6 Speech of Lord Ranfurly at Dungannon, *T.C.*, 5 Nov. 1880.

7 *C. Const.*, 20 Nov., 4 Dec. 1880; *B.N.L.*, 10 Dec. 1880.

8 Abbott to Montgomery, 18 Dec. 1880, Montgomery Mss. D627/428/7.

9 See speech of Rev. Thomas Whaley at Donacloney, *N.W.*, 18 Oct. 1880; speech of Rev. Thomas Ellis at Clones, *L.G.*, 17 Aug. 1880; *B.N.L.*, 8 Dec. 1880.

10 Quoted in Lucas, *Colonel Saunderson M.P.*, p. 66.

11 See e.g. Earl of Charlemont to Hugh Boyle, 2 Nov. [1880], Charlemont Mss. D266/367/44.

12 This was not a totally new development. Orangemen had shown an interest in land reform in the election of 1880, and in Fermanagh it had already caused divisions in Orange ranks (see *L.G.*, 22 June, 6 July 1880). But the organisation as an organisation had

deliberately avoided taking a stand on the question, although it had tried earlier in some areas to present the agrarian crisis in sectarian terms. See Minutes of Fermanagh G.O.L., 20 Nov. 1879, D1402/1.

13 See *C.C.*, 19 July 1880.

14 Letter of Peel to Donacloney meeting, *B.F.P.*, 21 Oct. 1880; speech of Ross at Portadown, *N.W.*, 6 Nov. 1880. See also *C.C.*, 23 Oct. 1880.

15 See e.g. Earl of Donaghmore to Beaconsfield, 19 Dec. [1880], Disraeli Mss. B/XXI/D/287.

16 An Orange drumming party unsuccessfully tried to break up a tenant-right meeting at Loughall, Co. Armagh (*N.W.*, 18 Dec. 1880) and Orangemen attacked and broke up a meeting of the tenants of Sir Richard Wallace's estate being held at Megaberry, near Moira. *Ibid.*, 7 Dec. 1880.

17 Abbott to Montgomery, 18 Dec. 1880, Montgomery Mss. D627/428/7.

18 Minutes of Fermanagh G.O.L., 9 Nov. 1880. D1402/1.

19 See e.g. speech of Rev. Stewart Ross at Portadown, *B.N.L.*, 6 Nov. 1880; speech of Rev. R.R. Kane at Lurgan and resolution at Orange demonstration in Portadown in December, *ibid.*, 2 Nov., 18 Dec. 1880.

20 Minutes of Fermanagh G.O.L., 9 Nov., 9 Dec. 1880. D1402/1; *B.N.L.* 28 Dec. 1880. For Orange Emergency Committee, see below, pp. 226-7.

21 See Minutes of Fermanagh G.O.L., 20 Nov. 1880. D1042/1.

22 For the failure of the counter-demonstration at Scotstown for which only about 200 Orangemen turned up (as against an estimated 7,000 for the league meetings), see C.S.O., R.P. 1880, 31216; *N.W.*, 10 Dec. 1880. Only about 180 Orangemen responded to the call for a counter-demonstration at Derrygonnelly. C.S.O., R.P. 1880, 33079; *N.W.*, 23 Dec.; *B.N.L.*, 23 Dec. 1880.

23 See John Blakely, secretary of organising committee for Dromore meeting, to W.E. Forster, 27 Dec. 1880, C.S.O. R.P. 1881, 388. See also resolutions at league meeting in Downpatrick, C.S.O., R.P. 1881, 5487.

24 See e.g. RM, County Monaghan to T.H. Burke, 10 Dec. 1880, C.S.O., R.P. 1880, 31216. See also Lloyd, *Ireland under the Land League*, ch. 1.

25 *B.N.L.*, 17 Nov. 1880.

26 Speech of Somerset Ward at Saintfield, *ibid.*, 24 Dec. 1880. See also speeches of Rev. James Stewart at Aghadowey (*C. Const.*, 18 Dec. 1880); Rev. Stewart Ross at Belfast (*B.N.L.*, 17 Nov. 1880); John Hazlett at Ballinode (*ibid.*,16 Dec. 1880); Edward Wingfield Verner in Ulster Hall, Belfast (*ibid.*, 11 Nov. 1880).

27 The incident which sparked off the trouble on the Lough Mask estate was Boycott's refusal, as Lord Erne's agent, to agree to a 25 per cent abatement of rent — Erne had offered 10 per cent — and his subsequent attempt to enforce ejectment processes. But Boycott's authoritarian attitude towards the tenants had earlier built up a well of resentment on the estate (see Memorial from Lough Mask tenantry to Lord Erne, 12 Aug. 1879, Erne Mss. D1939/21/9/15), though Erne himself dismissed the charges made by the tenants against Boycott

as 'frivolous' (Erne to W.A. Day, 12 Dec. 1880, Boycott Committee Papers. D3681/4).

28 The expedition was limited to 50 labourers at the insistence of the government. *Florence Arnold-Forster's Irish journal*, ed. T.W. Moody and R. Hawkins (Oxford, 1988), pp. 55, 89. See also Forster to Gladstone, 8 Nov. 1880, Gladstone Mss. 44156, f. 216.

29 McClelland, 'The later Orange order', p. 131; Palmer, *Land League crisis*, pp. 228–31; *B.N.L.*, 18, 28 Dec. 1880, 25 April, 17 June 1881; *C. Const.*, 14 May 1881.

30 Livingstone, *The Monaghan story*, pp. 335–9.

31 For example, the Monaghan Property Defence Association (Livingstone, *The Monaghan Story*, p. 335), the Pomeroy Protestant Defence Association (*B.N.L.*, 3 Dec. 1880), and the Fermanagh Property Defence Association (C.S.O., R.P. 1881, 36236).

32 N.W., 12 Nov. 1880; A. Carleton to Inspector General, RIC, 7 Dec. 1880, C.S.O., R.P. 1880, 31216.

33 'Several hundreds of Orangemen' were brought by special train from Belfast for the counter-demonstration at Saintfield in December. Lloyd, *Ireland under the Land League*, p. i. See also *N.W.*, 24 Dec. 1880.

34 See e.g. *C.C.*, 4 Dec. 1880; *B.F.P.*, 6 Jan. 1881; speech of Thomas Dickson at Tullyhogue, *N.W.*, 27 Nov. 1880.

35 One or two tentative efforts were made to deter tenants from agitating by raising the spectre of a labourers' campaign against the tenants (see e.g. speech of Sir H.H. Bruce in parliament, *C. Const.*, 10 July 1880; *B.N.L.*, 13 Oct. 1880;

resolutions at Orange meeting in Coleraine, *C. Const.*, 24 Dec. 1880). Tenant-right and Land League meetings tried to meet this threat by passing resolutions in favour of the removal of labourers' grievances and by arguing that the interests of tenants and labourers were identical (see e.g. *B.F.P.*, 15 July 1880). Such token gestures of concern were hardly convincing, but the tactic of rousing the labourers against the tenants was too potentially dangerous — from the point of view of alienating the tenants and creating even greater social instability — for the landlords seriously to contemplate its systematic use. Nevertheless it was Orange labourers who provided the main component of the forces used against both league and tenant-right meetings.

36 *C. Const.*, 8 Jan. 1881; *C.C.*, 1, 8 Jan. 1881.

37 *C. Const.*, 5 Feb. 1881. See also Fermanagh G.O.L. Minutes, 9 Dec. 1880, D1402/1.

38 See e.g. speech of William Stewart Ross at Ballymena, *B.F.P.*, 23 Dec. 1880.

39 *B.N.L.*, 2, 6, 11 Nov. 1880.

40 *Ibid.*, 3, 16, 17, 18, 21 Dec. 1880; *C. Const.*, 8 Jan., 26 Feb. 1881.

41 Statement of Viscount Castlereagh at Comber (*N.W.*, 29 Dec. 1880); speeches of Andre Murray Ker at Monaghan and Col. Thomas Waring at Portadown (*B.N.L.*, 17, 18 Dec. 1880), and others.

42 See e.g. speeches of Col. Waring and Rev. R.R. Kane at Portadown (*ibid.*) and W. Forde Hutchinson JP at Ballymena (*C. Const.*, 26 Feb. 1881).

43 *B.N.L.*, 17 Dec. 1880.

44 *N.W.*, 8, 20 Dec. 1880; Circular from John Hancock to tenants on

Lurgan's estates, 14 Oct. 1880, Hancock Mss. D1600/3/5.

45  John Harbinson to Lord O'Hagan, 4 Jan. 1881, O'Hagan Mss. D2777 ADD/50.

46  Charlemont to Hugh Boyle, 6 [June 1880], Charlemont Mss. D266/367/33. Charlemont's debt to the Royal Exchange Assurance Company increased from £150,000 in 1851 to £205,000 in 1892. Cannadine, 'Aristocratic indebtedness', p. 637.

47  Annesley to William Shaw, 1 Sept. [1881], Annesley Mss. D1854/6/8, p. 17.

48  Crossle to Verner, 22 May 1880, Verner Mss. D236/488/1, p. 356. See also Crossle to R. Wynne Roberts, 23 Aug. 1880, *ibid.*, p. 417; Crossle to Miss Verner, 17 Aug. 1880, *ibid.*, p. 416.

49  Crossle to Jackson and Prince, 20 Sept. 1880, 24 Sept. 1880, *ibid.*, pp. 434, 439.

50  Crossle to William Hardy (solicitor, Armagh), 28 Jan. 1881, *ibid.*, p. 560. See also Crossle to Henry L. Kiely (solicitor, Dublin), 30 Jan. 1881, *ibid.*, p. 569; Crossle to A.R. Jackson, 1 Feb. 1881, *ibid.*, p. 573.

51  Gerard Ford to Montgomery, 20 May 1881, Montgomery Mss. T1089/195; Montgomery to Ford, 22 May 1881, *ibid.*, D627/322. There was at this time a deadlock in the Irish land market so that there was no possibility of landowners selling land to raise money. See Earl of Charlemont to Hugh Boyle, n.d., Charlemont Mss. D266/367/51.

52  This was the case with the Scottish Widows Company, which lent out no less than £1.2 million secured on Irish land between 1866 and 1880 (Cannadine, 'Aristocratic indebtedness', p. 646). The

Representative Body of the Church of Ireland, which had £3.5 million tied up in Irish estates in 1877–78, also called a halt to mortgaging operations at this time. Curtis, 'Incumbered wealth', pp. 340–2.

53  *T.C.*, 26 Nov. 1880.

54  Pomeroy to Montgomery, 9 Jan., 4 Feb. 1881, Montgomery Mss. D627/303, 305. See also Pomeroy to Montgomery, 7 Jan. 1881, *ibid.*, D627/302.

55  Crossle to Miss Verner, 17 Aug. 1880, Verner Mss. D236/488/1, p. 416; A. Nunan to Inspector General, RI, 3 Dec. 1880 [Copy], Gladstone Mss. 44158, f.54.

56  Earl of Charlemont to Hugh Boyle, [17 Dec. 1880], Charlemont Mss. D266/367/56. Charlemont was reporting Stuart Knox's analysis of the situation.

57  Charlemont to Boyle, 26 [Oct. 1880], 20 Nov. [1880], 16 Dec. 1880, Charlemont Mss. D266/367/42, 49, 57.

58  Pomeroy to Hugh Montgomery, 7 Feb. 1881, Montgomery Mss. D627/306; Circular from Montgomery to his tenants, 10 Feb. 1881, *ibid.* D627/307a.

59  Innes and Blacker offered 10 per cent, Richardson and Cope 15 per cent. *N.W.*, 2, 8, 10, 11 Dec. 1880.

60  *Ibid.*, 11, 13 Nov., 2, 3 Dec. 1880.

61  See James Crossle to A.R. Jackson, 25 Dec. 1880, Verner Mss. D236/488/1, p. 518.

62  *B.N.L.*, 8 Dec. 1880; Crossle to A.R. Jackson, 17 Jan. 1881, Verner Mss. D236/488/1, p. 546.

63  *B.N.L.*, 25 Dec. 1880.

64  See e.g. meetings of Downshire and Wallace tenants, *N.W.*, 7, 14 Dec. 1880.

65  *U.E.*, 1 Jan. 1881.

66  Brooke to Hugh Montgomery, n.d. [1881], Montgomery Mss. D627/307b; Charlemont to Hugh Boyle, 26 [Oct. 1880], 16 Dec. 1880, Charlemont Mss. D266/367/42, 57.

67  *B.N.L.*, 18 Dec. 1880. Livestock prices had recovered to some extent, but Wallace's tenants denied that the rents were less than Griffith's valuation for land alone, and claimed that in those cases where they were under Griffith's it was because the tenants had paid out large sums of money to Wallace's predecessor to have them fined down. See *N.W.*, 18, 30 Dec. 1880.

68  *B.N.L.*, 24 Dec. 1880. The tenants' explanation of the low average rent was that half the estate was mountain or moorland and that the rents on some parts of the estate were from 40s to 50s an acre. They also denied that the memorial was got up by only a minority of tenants. John Dinsmore to Ed., *N.W.*, 31 Dec. 1880.

69  *N.W.*, 24 Dec. 1880.

70  *Returns — I. of the number of civil bill ejectments ... tried and determined in each county in Ireland, for each of the four years ending the 31st day of December 1880 ...* H.C. 1881 (90), lxxxii, 685, pp. 4–5, 8–9; *Returns — I. of the number of civil bill ejectments ... during the year ended the 31st day of December 1881 ...* H.C. 1882 (151), lv, 225, pp. 2–5.

71  Of the total number of evictions in Ireland in Jan.–March 1881, 51 per cent took place in Ulster. *Return ...of cases of eviction which have come to the knowledge of the constabulary in each quarter of the year ended 31st December 1881 ...*H.C. 1882 (9), lv, 229, p. 2.

72  *Return of evictions in each of the years 1849–80*, pp. 18–23; *Return of evictions for each quarter of the year 1880*, pp. 2–5; *Return of evictions for each quarter of the year 1881*, pp. 2–5; *Return ... of cases of eviction ... in each quarter of the year ended the 31st day of December 1882 ...* [C.-3465], H.C. 1883, lvi, 99, pp. 3–7; *Return ... of cases of eviction ... in the quarter ended the 31st March 1883 ...* [C.3579], H.C. 1883, lvi, 107, pp. 2–3; *Return ... of cases of eviction ... in the quarter ended the 30th June 1883 ...* [C.3770], H.C. 1883, lvi, 111, pp. 2–3; *Return ... of cases of eviction ... in the quarter ended the 30th September 1883 ...* [C.-3892], H.C. 1884, lxiv, 407, p. 3; *Return ... of cases of eviction ... in the quarter ended the 31st Dec. 1883...* [C.-3892], lxiv, 411, p. 3.

73  Forster to Gladstone, 8 Nov. 1880, Gladstone Mss. 44157, ff. 213–14. See also speech of Edward Litton, Liberal MP for Tyrone, *Hansard*, 3, cclxi, c. 323 (12 May 1881).

74  Crossle to Keilty, 20 Nov. 1880, Verner Mss. D236/488/1, p. 489. See also Crossle to A. R. Jackson, 5 Dec. 1880, *ibid.*, p. 506.

75  Crossle to Jackson, 2 Oct. 1880, *ibid.*, p. 444.

76  There were 440 evictions in Ulster during the three months April–June 1881. Of the 179 evictions in Ulster in the first quarter of 1881, 92 per cent were carried out in February and March.

77  'Return showing number and particulars of evictions in Ulster 1 Jan–31 March 1881', marked 'private and confidential', April 1881, Harcourt Mss.

78  See above, p. 187.

79  McGeough's evictions alarmed other landlords in Armagh. See

Forster to J.N. Richardson, 14 Feb. 1881, Richardson Mss. D1006/3/1/9.

80  There was a 66 per cent rate of readmission (mainly as caretakers) in Ulster in both 1880 and 1881 as against a 55 per cent rate in each year in Ireland as a whole. Sources as cited in note 72.

81  See e.g. James Crossle Jr to William Hardy (solicitor), 11 April 1881, Verner Mss. D236/488/2, pp. 63–4; James Crossle to Sir W. Verner, 2 May 1881, *ibid.*, p. 102; Earl of Charlemont to Hugh Boyle, n.d., Charlemont Mss. D266/367/32.

82  See e.g. Lord Lurgan to James Coulter, Sec. of tenants' deputation, 27 Nov. 1880, Hancock Mss. D1600/3/5; Earl of Charlemont to Hugh Boyle, 15 Nov., 17 Dec. 1880, Charlemont Mss. D266/367/47, 56; Earl of Annesley to William Shaw, 28 Aug. 1881, Annesley Mss. D1854/6/8, p. 16.

83  Annesley to William Shaw, 12 May 1881, Annesley Mss. D1854/6/8, p. 2.

84  See e.g. James Crossle to Elliott, manager of Provincial (?) Bank, Monaghan, 24 Aug. 1880, Verner Mss. D236/488/1, p. 419.

85  See above, p. 43.

86  See e.g. Crossle to A.R. Jackson, 25 Nov. 1880, Verner Mss. D 236/488/1, p. 496.

87  Annesley to William Shaw, 12 May 1881, Annesley Mss. D1854/6/8, p. 2.

88  James Crossle Jr to A.R. Jackson, 28 Feb. 1881, Verner Mss. D236/488/2, p. 19. See also Crossle Sr to Jackson, 23 April 1881, *ibid.*, p. 88.

89  Crossle to Jackson, 5 Dec. 1880, *ibid.*, D236/488/1, p. 508. See also Crossle to Jackson, 18 Feb., 12 Mar. 1881, *ibid.*, D236/488/2, pp. 11, 37; J.A. Pomeroy to Hugh Montgomery, 4 Feb. 1881, Montgomery Mss. D627/305.

90  John Vincent, 'Gladstone and Ireland', *Proceedings of the British Academy,* lxiii (1977), p. 210; Hammond, *Gladstone and the Irish nation*, pp. 165, 188.

91  Forster to Gladstone, 7 May 1880, Gladstone Mss. 44157, f. 127; T. Wemyss Reid, *Life of the Rt. Hon. W.E. Forster,* 2 vols. (repr., with introd. by V. E. Chancellor, Bath, 1870, of 3rd edn, London, 1888), ii, p. 243; C. H. D. Howard (ed.), *Joseph Chamberlain: A political memoir 1880–1892* (London, 1953), p. 6.

92  Forster to Gladstone, 25 Oct. 1880, quoted in Wemyss Reid, *Life of Forster,* ii, p. 262.

93  Forster to Gladstone, 5 Nov. 1880, Gladstone Mss. 44157, f. 193. See also memorandum submitted by Forster to the cabinet, 15 Nov. 1880, Harcourt Mss. W.V.H. 12/2.

94  Cabinet memorandum, 23 Nov. 1880, 'Land Tenure Reform Committee resolutions', Harcourt Mss. W.V.H. 17/2; *Bessborough Report,* p. 19; *Richmond prelim. report,* pp. 7–9, 20–4.

95  Hammond, *Gladstone and the Irish nation,* p. 189; *The diary of Sir Edward Walter Hamilton, 1880–1885,* ed. D.W.R. Bahlman (2 vols, Oxford, 1972), i, p. 93; Vincent, 'Gladstone and Ireland', p. 215.

96  The first draft of the land bill as explained by Gladstone to the cabinet contained provisions for fair rents and free sale, but not fixity of tenure. Chamberlain, *Political memoir,* p. 15.

97  Forster to Gladstone, 5 Nov. 1880, Gladstone Mss. 44157, f. 193.

98  Ulster Liberal MPs' memorial to Forster, 1 Dec. 1880, *ibid.* 44158, ff. 7–8; Forster to Gladstone, 2 Dec. 1880, *ibid.*, f. 3. See also Forster to

Gladstone, 10 Jan. 1881, *ibid.*, f. 121;
W.E. Forster, 'Memorandum on the
Irish land bill', 27 Dec. 1880,
Harcourt Mss. W.V.H. 17/2.

99 *N.W.*, 22 Jan. 1881; *C. Const.,* 29 Jan.
1881.

100 *N.W.*, 13 Jan. 1881. Other members
of the government were subjected
to similar pressure by the Ulster
Liberals. See R.B. O'Brien, *The Life of
Charles Stewart Parnell, 1846–1891* (2
vols, London, 1989), i, 298.

101 Quoted in *B.F.P.*, 23 Dec. 1880.

102 Lord Derby in an article in
*Nineteenth Century* argued that the
land grievance was 'a bond of
discontent between Ulster and the
rest of Ireland' and in this sense a
danger to the union. Hammond,
*Gladstone and the Irish nation*, p. 217.

103 G. Shaw-Lefevre, 'Memorandum on
Irish land legislation', 3 Jan. 1881,
Harcourt Mss. W.V.H. 17/2. See also
Hamilton, *Diary*, i, 93–4; Arnold–
Forster, *Journal*, pp. 55, 89.

104 Both the British and Irish Tories
regretted the failure of Gladstone's
bill to do more in the way of
promoting facilities for purchase.
The Ulster Tories wanted the state
to advance the whole of the
purchase money to the tenants. See
e.g. *C. Const.*, 30 April 1881; *B.N.L.*,
13 June 1881.

105 Gladstone to Forster, 7 Dec. 1880,
Gladstone Mss. 44158, f. 34; *Hansard*,
3, cclxiii, 289–90, 7 July 1881;
Hammond, *Gladstone and the Irish
nation,* pp. 185–7.

106 Hammond, *op. cit.*, p. 167. See also
Arnold-Forster, *Journal*, p. 89.

107 See e.g. National Liberal Federation,
*4th Annual Report*, 25 Oct. 1881
(Birmingham, 1881), pp. 13–18.

108 Speech at Enniskillen, *B.N.L.* 1 Jan.
1881. See also *Bessborough Report,* p. 19.

109 *Hansard*, 3, cclx, 892–4 (7 April 1881).

110 *Ibid.*, cclxi, 1378–9 (26 May 1881).

111 *Ibid.*, cclxiv, 252, 258 (1 Aug. 1881).
For Bright's speech see *ibid.*, cclxi,
103 (9 May 1881).

112 *Ibid.*, cclx, 1166 (25 April 1881). See
also speeches of Lewis (*ibid.*, cclxi,
1386. 26 May 1881) and Bruce (*ibid.*
cclxiii, 307–8, 7 July 1881); Earl of
Charlemont to Hugh Boyle, n.d.,
Charlemont Mss. D266/367/51.

113 W.E. Forster, 'Memorandum on the
Irish land bill', 27 Dec. 1880,
Harcourt Mss. W.V.H.17/2.

114 *Hansard*, 3, cclxii. 1839 (1 July 1881).
See also *ibid,* 802–3 (17 June 1881);
T.P. O'Connor, *The Parnell movement*
(London, 1886), pp. 457–8.

115 Circular from Montgomery to his
tenants, 10 Feb. 1881, Montgomery
Mss. D627/307a; *B.N.L.*, 20 Oct.
1881. For the belief that rents
would not be seriously reduced see
also Montgomery to G. Ford, 15
April 1881, Montgomery Mss.
D627/316; Pomeroy to
Montgomery, 25 April 1881, *ibid.*
D627/318; Earl of Charlemont to
Hugh Boyle, 11 April 1880,
Charlemont Mss. D266/367/37;
Dun, *Landlords and tenants in Ireland*, p.
262; Hamilton, *Sixty years' experience
as an Irish landlord*, p. 353;
Montgomery, *Irish land and Irish rights*,
p. 24.

116 *B.N.L.,* 18 Aug. 1881. See also *C.
Const.*, 20 Aug. 1881.

117 *B.N.L.*, 9 July 1881. See also *ibid.*, 8, 9
April; *C. Const.*, 9 April, 7 May 1881.

118 For the division list see *Hansard*, 3,
cclxi, 928–32 (19 May 1881).

119 *B.N.L.*, 28 April 1881.

120 See e.g. speeches of Bruce (*Hansard*,
3, cclx, 1879, 5 May 1881),
Macnaghten (*ibid.* cclxi, 306, 317, 12
May 1881), Lewis (*ibid.*, 1386–7, 26

May 1881). Gladstone eventually conceded the point about allowing the landlord as well as the tenant access to the court. See *B.N.L.*, 9 April, 20 June 1881.

121 The Irish Land Committee published three pamphlets on the 3Fs, all of them extremely critical — *Lord Dufferin on the 3Fs* (London and Dublin, Jan. 1881); *Mr Gladstone and the three Fs* (London and Dublin, Feb. 1881); *Mr Bonamy Price on the 3Fs* (London and Dublin, Feb. 1881).

122 Cairns to Beaconsfield, 3 Dec. 1880, Disraeli Mss. B/xx/Ca/272. See also Edward Gibson to Beaconsfield, 9 Dec. 1880, *ibid.* B/xxi/G/66; Gibson to Sir Stafford Northcote, 21 Dec. 1880, Ashbourne Mss. T2955/B71/10.

123 Earl of Donoughmore to Ed., *The Times*, 12 April 1881. See also letter of Ion T. Hamilton, MP for County Dublin, *ibid.*

124 Speech of Marquis of Waterford, *Hansard*, 3, cclxiv, 306 (1 Aug. 1881); Earl of Limerick to Salisbury, 25 July 1881, Salisbury Mss. E; speech of Marquis of Lansdowne, *Hansard* 3, cclxiv, 291–2 (1 Aug. 1881); speech of Edward Gibson, *ibid.*, cclx, 1100 (25 April 1881). See also speech of Col. A.L. Tottenham, MP for County Leitrim, *ibid.*, 1364–90 (28 April 1881).

125 It is significant that even within Ulster it was the landlords in the strongest tenant-right areas who had been most ready to support reform. Those in the outer province where tenant-right existed only in a more attenuated form were slower to accept the demand for reform and showed least enthusiasm for the 1881 bill.

126 See e.g. Earl of Limerick to Salisbury, 25 July 1881, Salisbury Mss. E.

127 Donoughmore to Beaconsfield, 19 Dec. [1880], Disraeli Mss. B/xxiD/287.

128 *Hansard*, 3, cclx, 1373 (28 April 1881).

129 See e.g. speech of Edward Gibson, *Hansard*, 3, cclx, 1103 (25 April 1881); Lord Oranmore and Brown to Salisbury, 13 June 1881, 1 Aug. 1881, Salisbury Mss. E; Earl of Limerick to Salisbury, 25 July 1881, *ibid.*

130 *Hansard*, 3, cclxiv, 301 (1 Aug. 1881). See also speech of Earl of Dunraven, *ibid.*, 332.

131 Heads of bill, 26 Jan. 1880, Disraeli Mss. B/xii/D/47(i); W.F. Moneypenny and G.E. Buckle, *The Life of Benjamin Disraeli, Earl of Beaconsfield* (6 vols, London, 1910–20), vi, 510. The bill proposed to advance four-fifths of the purchase money to tenants as against the two-thirds allowed by the act of 1870.

132 Moneypenny and Buckle, *op. cit.*, vi, 582. See also Robert Blake, *Disraeli* (London, 1966), pp. 728–9.

133 Northcote to Edward Gibson, 23 Dec. 1880, Ashbourne Mss. T2955/B71/11.

134 *Land*, 23 April 1881, p. 242.

135 Cairns to Beaconsfield, 11 Dec. 1880, 15 Dec. 1880, Disraeli Mss. B/xx/Ca/273, 274. See also Northcote to Gibson, 17 Oct. 1880, Ashbourne Mss. T2955/B71/7; Gibson to Northcote, 21 Dec. 1880, *ibid.*, T2955/B71/10.

136 Salisbury to Beaconsfield, 20 Dec. 1880, Salisbury Mss. D/20/-. See also Lady G. Cecil, *Life of Robert, Marquis of Salisbury* (4 vols., London, 1921–32), iii, 42–3.

137 Beaconsfield to Salisbury, 27 Dec. 1880, Salisbury Mss. E; Salisbury to Beaconsfield, 2 Jan. 1881, *ibid.* D/

20/-; Northcote to Salisbury, 15 April 1881, *ibid*. E.

138 Edward Gibson's diary, 13 Aug. 1881, Ashbourne Mss. T2955/A1/1.

139 Copy of resolution of executive committee of Irish Land Committee, 16 Aug. 1881, Salisbury Mss. E.

140 Northcote to Gibson, 29 Aug. 1881, Ashbourne Mss. T2955/B71/15.

## Chapter 10

1  The outline of the terms of the act which follows is based mainly on Cherry, *Irish land acts*, pp. 217–343. Good short summaries are also contained in Solow, *The land question*, pp. 156–62; Pomfret, *The struggle for land in Ireland*, pp. 161–7.

2  The compensation clauses of the act of 1870 were amended and enhanced by sections 7 and 9 of the Act of 1881. Cherry, *Irish land acts*, pp. 240–4.

3  This clause was first proposed by Healy but eventually drafted by Charles Russell. See R. Barry O'Brien, *Fifty years of concessions to Ireland 1831–1881* (2 vols, London, 1885), ii, 400–2.

4  Pomfret, *The struggle for land in Ireland*, p. 166.

5  W. F. Bailey, 'The Ulster tenant-right custom', pp. 20–22; Cherry, *Irish land acts*, p. 226.

6  Bailey, *loc. cit.*, pp. 21–2. For *Adams v. Dunseath* case see below, p. 267.

7  *Return showing the number of agricultural holdings in Ireland and the tenure by which they are held by occupiers* [C. 32], H.C. 1870, lvi, 737, pp. 16–17.

8  Altogether 1,477 applications were made under the act to have leases declared void, 108 of them in Ulster (and 52 of these in Antrim). *Report of the Irish land commissioners for the period from 22nd Aug., 1884 to 22nd Aug. 1885* ...[C.-4625], H.C. 1886, xix, 467, p. 31.

9  *N.W.*, 15 April; *B.M.N.*, 8 April; *C.C.*, 16 April 1881. See also *N.W.*, 8 April; *I.R.*, 14 April 1881. This enthusiasm was not, however, shared by the *Ulster Examiner*. See *U.E.*, 9 April, 26 July 1881.

10 See, e.g. *B.F.P.* 23 June 1881. A definition was included in the original bill but Gladstone was always unhappy about it (see Hugh Law to Gladstone, 29 April 1881 and n.d. [April 1881], Gladstone Mss. 44765, ff. 18–19, 21), and finally decided against giving any specific directions to the court in the matter.

11 Quoted in MacKnight, *Ulster as it is*, i, 398–9. See also Rutherford, *An Ards farmer*, p. 59; speech of John Megaw, president of the Route Association, at Ballymoney, *B.F.P.*, 27 Oct. 1881.

12 O'Brien, *Recollections*, p. 322. See also Davitt, *Fall of feudalism*, p. 332; Healy, *Letters and leaders of my day*, i, 134.

13 *B.N.L.*, 31 Oct., 10 Nov. 1881.

14 Tenants were encouraged to do this by their legal representatives. The charges, according to the *Coleraine Chronicle*, ranged from 10s for a holding of £5 rental and under to £4 for a holding of £100 and over (*C.C.*, 15 Oct. 1881). Henry Macauley, a Coleraine solicitor, was reported in November to have already served notices on behalf of 1,500 tenants (*ibid.*, 12 Nov. 1881. See also Hugh Law to Gladstone, 28 Oct. 1881, Gladstone Mss. 44472, f.186). If the act was a boon to Irish tenants, it was clearly an even greater boon to Irish lawyers.

15  Diary and account book of John Dick, 4, 7, 11, 13, 18 Oct. 1881. D1014/4. Tenants on the Mercers' estate, the Somerset estate, Sir H. Bruce's Downhill and Clothworkers' estate, John Mulholland's Co. Down estate and many others followed the same procedure. *C.C.*, Oct.–Nov. 1881; *N.W.*, Oct. 1881–Jan. 1882.

16  See e.g. James Crossle to Lady Verner, 15 May 1882, Verner Mss. D236/488/3, p. 143.

17  Montgomery to G. Ford, 18 Nov. 1881, Montgomery Mss. D627/324.

18  Crossle to Verner, 22 Oct. 1881, Verner Mss. D236/488/2, p. 250.

19  *B.F.P.*, 10 Nov. 1881.

20  See *Return of the number of originating notices lodged in the court of the Irish Land Commission and in the civil bill courts of the counties up to and including the 28th day of January 1882* [C.3123], H.C. 1882, lv, 361, p. 5; *Land*, 28 Jan. 1881, p. 503.

21  The average reduction during the first year worked out at 22.6 per cent in Ulster, 2 percentage points higher than the national average. See Table 10.3.

22  Mina Lenox-Conyngham, *An old Ulster house and the people who lived in it* (Dundalk, 1946), p. 201; *C.C.*, 19 Nov. 1881; *N.W.*, 11, 24 July 1882.

23  Circular to the tenants of the Kilcar and Glencolumbkille states, 30 Nov. 1881, Gladstone Mss. 44495, f. 201; Charlemont to Hugh Boyle, n.d., Charlemont Mss. D266/367/67.

24  Hamilton, *Sixty years' experience as an Irish landlord*, p. 394. See also *ibid.*, pp. 374–5.

25  See Montgomery to G. Ford, 18 Nov. 1881, Montgomery Mss. D627/324. See also Montgomery to Ed., *N.W.*, 14 Jan. 1882.

26  Crossle to A.R. Jackson, 22 April 1882, Verner Mss. D236/488/3, pp. 94–5; Crossle to Lady Verner, 30 May, 5 Aug. 1881, *ibid.*, pp. 170–1, 233–4; Crossle to Lady Verner, 10 March 1882, *ibid.*, D236/488/2, p. 503; Crossle to Lady Verner, 22 July, 5 Aug., 14, 19, 26 Sept. 1882, *ibid.*, D236/488/3, pp. 215, 234–5, 309–14, 321–3, 337–9.

27  Annesley to Shaw, 17 June [1882], Annesley Mss. D1854/6/8, p. 28.

28  Crossle to Lady Verner, 5 Aug. 1882, Verner Mss. D236/488/3, p. 234. See also Crossle to Smith, 28 July 1882, *ibid.*, p. 227.

29  *B.N.L.*, 17 Feb. 1883.

30  *N.W.*, 2 Sept. 1882.

31  In the four years up to 21 Aug. 1885 there were 18,759 appeals and 10,049 of these were from Ulster. The results of the appeals over the four-year period showed a 2 per cent increase in the judicial rents appealed. *Report of the Irish Land Commissioners for the period 22 Aug. 1884–22 Aug. 1885*, pp. 21–4.

32  *Report of the Irish Land Commissioners for the period from 22nd August 1882 to 22nd August 1883, and as to proceedings under the Arrears of Rent (Ireland) Act, 1882, to the 27th October 1883* [C.3897], H.C. 1884, lxiv, 41, pp. 13, 27.

33  See e.g. James Crossle to Hugh Moore (solicitor, Omagh), 30 May 1882, Verner Mss. D236/488/3, p. 164. See also *B.N.L.*, 17 Feb. 1883.

34  *First report from the select committee of the House of Lords on land law (Ireland)* ... H.C. 1882 (249), xi, 1, p. 3.

35  *Report of the Irish land commissioners for the period from 22nd August 1881 to 22nd August 1882* [C.3413], H.C. 1882, xx, 265, pp. 8–13; *Report of the Irish land commissioners for the period 22 Aug. 1882–22 Aug. 1883*, pp. 7–11; *Report*

*of the Irish land commissioners for period from 22nd August 1883 to 22nd August 1884 ...* [C.4231], H.C. 1884–5, lxv, 53, pp. 7–17; *Report of the Irish land commissioners for the period 22 Aug. 1884–22 Aug. 1885*, pp. 7–20.

36  See e.g. *C. Const.*, 1, 22 April 1882.

37  As for Table 10.1.

38  As for Table 10.1.

39  Donnelly, *Land and people of 19th century Cork*, p. 297.

40  Forster to Hartington, 24 Nov. 1881 (copy), Harcourt Mss. II H/11. See also Forster to Harcourt, 24 Nov. 1881, *ibid*; Forster's speech in House of Commons, *Hansard*, 3, cclxvi (9 Feb. 1882), 323; *N.W.*, 4 Mar. 1882; Hugh Montgomery to Ed., *N.W.*, 14 Jan. 1882.

41  *N.W.*, 12 Jan, 18 Feb. 1882. See also speech of James Richardson to House of Commons, *ibid.*, 7 Mar. 1882.

42  *Ibid.*, 1 Mar., 24 May, 27 July 1882; *F.T.*, 9 Mar. 1882; Healy, *A word for Ireland*, p. 137. There were only a handful of cases on each of these estates.

43  *N.W.*, 6 Nov. 1882.

44  *Ibid.*, 12 July 1882; Healy, *A word for Ireland*, p. 137.

45  See below, pp. 259-60.

46  Irish Land Committee, *The working of the land law act* (Dublin, Feb. 1882), p. 13.

47  *C. Const.*, 17 Dec. 1881. See also *ibid.*, 31 Dec. 1881; *B.N.L.*, 17 Nov., 26 Dec. 1881; *F.T.*, 26 Jan. 1882.

48  *N.W.*, 4 Jan. 1882.

49  Irish Land Committee, *The working of the land act*.

50  See e.g. *ibid.*, p. 30 and resolutions passed at landowners' conference in Dublin, *N.W.*, 4 Jan. 1882.

51  Speech of Charles Russell in House of Commons, *N.W.*, 7 March 1882.

52  *Land*, 10 Dec. 1881, p. 342. See also J.A. Fox to Hugh Montgomery, 30 Jan. 1884, Montgomery Mss. D627/428/11; Thompson, *English landed society in the nineteenth century*, pp. 308–17.

53  *N.W.*, 7 Mar. 1882.

54  *Ibid.*, 24 June, 6 Dec. 1882. See also *ibid.*, 11 Jan., 27 July 1882.

55  *Ibid.*, 27 April 1882.

56  *Ibid.*, 18 Jan. 1882.

57  *Ibid.*, 4 Feb. 1882.

58  *Ibid.*, 23 Feb., 16 Nov. 1882.

59  *Ibid.*, 14 Aug. 1882.

60  Solow, *The land question*, p. 150; *N.W.*, 20 Feb. 1882. See also *Land*, 10 Dec. 1881, 8 July 1882, pp. 342, 457.

61  Montgomery to G. Ford, 3 Dec. 1881, Montgomery Mss. D627/326. See also Montgomery to Ed., *N.W.*, 14 Jan. 1882.

62  Arnold-Forster, *Journal*, p. 320; *N.W.*, 7 Mar. 1882.

63  *C. Const.*, 28 Oct. 1882; *Land*, 9 June 1883, p. 260. See also *F.T.*, 9 Mar. 1882.

64  *N.W.*, 4 Jan. 1882.

65  Agricultural prices went down by 28 per cent between 1871 and 1885. Barrington, 'Agricultural prices', p. 252.

66  Gladstone to Earl of Granville, 3 Feb. 1883, Gladstone Mss. 44546, f. 75.

67  The number of estates over which receivers were appointed by court order increased from 165 in 1881 to 689 in 1886. Curtis, 'Incumbered wealth', p. 358.

68  *Land*, 13 Aug. 1881, p. 16. The aggregate amount of sales in the

land court in Dublin had dropped from £1,737,222 in 1873 to £325,549 in 1880. In 1873 the average price realised was 22.25 years' purchase; in 1880 it was 16.5 years'. *Ibid.*, 10 Sept. 1881, p. 91.

69 *Ibid.*, 27 Jan. 1883, p. 408.

70 *N.W.*, 13 Feb. 1882; Rutherford, *An Ards farmer*, p. 62; Russell's speech at Enniskillen, *N.W.*, 11 July 1882.

71 Annesley to Shaw, 13 Mar. [1882], Annesley Mss. D1854/6/8, p. 23. See also same to same, 25 Aug. 1881, 8 Dec. 1881, 19 Feb. 1882, *ibid.*, pp. 15, 20, 22.

72 Annesley himself, for example, later approved of Shaw's 'not pressing those tenants who are willing, but for illness or other causes are not able to pay more than part of what they owe'; others, however, he wanted proceeded against 'as quickly and as severely as the law will allow'. Annesley to Shaw, 19 April [1882], *ibid.*, p. 24.

73 Crossle to Lady Verner, 6 Sept. 1882, Verner Mss. D236/488/3, pp. 287–8.

74 Crossle to Lady Verner, 1 May 1882, 6 Sept. 1882, *ibid.*, pp. 107, 288.

75 *Return of evictions in each of the years 1849–80,* p. 4; *Return of evictions on each quarter of the year 1880,* p. 5; *Return of evictions in each quarter of the year 1881,* pp. 2–5; *Return of evictions in each quarter of the year 1882,* pp. 3–5.

76 *Ibid.* The percentages readmitted as tenants were low in both years — 5.1 per cent in 1880–1, 4.1 per cent in 1881–2.

77 There were 689 evictions in 1883 as against 172 in 1879 and an annual average of 121 between 1870 and 1878.

78 Crossle to Lady Verner, 13 May 1882, Verner Mss. D236/488/3, p. 142; Crossle to Robert Lavery, 3 Oct.

1882, *ibid.*, p. 353; Crossle to Lady Verner, 12 Dec. 1883, 3 Oct. 1882, *ibid.*, p. 353; Crossle to Lady Verner, 12 Dec. 1883, *ibid.* D236/488/4, p. 97; Crossle to Rev. J. W. Taylor, 4 Feb. 1884, *ibid.*, p. 184. See also Earl of Annesley to Shaw, 1 Sept. [1881], Annesley Mss. D1854/6/8, p. 17.

79 Crossle to Towers, 6 Oct. 1882, Verner Mss. D236/488/3, p. 353.

80 Crossle to Stokes, 19 Nov. 1883, *ibid.*, D236/488/4, p. 55.

81 Pomeroy to Hugh Montgomery, 20 Nov. 1881, Montgomery Mss. D627/325.

82 The Conservative leaders in Britain refused even to argue such a case. See Lord Cairns to Sir Stafford Northcote, 16 Dec. 1881, Iddlesleigh Mss. vol. ix, 50021, f. 143. See also Northcote to Salisbury, 21 Nov. 1881, Salisbury Mss. E.

83 See e.g. H. Montgomery to G. Ford, 16 Aug. 1881, Montgomery Mss. D627/323.

84 *Land,* 10 Mar. 1883, p. 75.

85 *B.N.L.*, 23 Dec. 1881. See also speech of Edward Gibson, *F.T.*, 26 Jan. 1882.

86 See e.g. *C.C.*, 29 April 1882.

87 *First report from lands' select committee on land act,* pp. 5–8.

88 *N.W.*, 17 Mar., 13 April 1882; *Land,* 22 April 1882, p. 230. See also below, pp. 280-1.

89 Salisbury to Northcote, 17 April 1882, Salisbury Mss. D/56/59; Salisbury to Cairns, 5 May 1882, *ibid.* D/12/21.

90 Lord George Hamilton, *Parliamentary reminiscences and reflections 1868–1906* (2 vols, London, 1916 and 1922), i, 232–6; Hamilton to Salisbury, 15 Mar. 1883, Salisbury Mss. E.

91 *B.F.P.* , 10 Nov. 1881. See also *I.R.*, 3 Nov. 1881.

92 *Land*, 21 Jan. 1882, p. 489; Russell to Gladstone, 15 April 1882, Gladstone Mss. 44475, ff. 39–40.

93 *N.W.*, 25 Feb. 1882. See also resolutions passed at tenant meeting in Lurgan (*B.N.L.*, 16 Dec. 1881), at meetings of Portaferry Tenant Farmers' Defence Association (*C.C.*, 17 Dec. 1881), Randalstown Tenant Right Association (*N.W.*, 4 Jan. 1882), Armagh Tenant Farmers' Association (*ibid.*, 17 Jan. 1882), and at tenant conferences in Belfast and Derry (*ibid.*, 21, 26 Jan. 1882) and numerous other meetings throughout the province.

94 *N.W.*, 26 Jan. 1882. See also speeches of John Megaw and Thomas Swann at tenant conference in Belfast (*N.W.*, 21 Jan. 1882) and resolutions at meetings of Ringsend and County Armagh associations and other tenant meetings (*ibid.*, 3, 6, 11, 12, 17 Jan. 1882); Forster to Hartington, 24 Nov. 1881, Harcourt Mss. II H/11.

95 Speech of Rev. A. Robinson at Ballymena, *N.W.*, 2 Oct. 1882.

96 Cherry, *Irish land acts*, pp. 253–5; Healy, *A word for Ireland*, pp. 133–5. For the facts of the case see *N.W.*, 1 Mar. 1882.

97 *Land*, 25 Mar. 1882, p. 141.

98 Spencer to Gladstone, 9 Mar. 1883, Gladstone Mss. 44310, f. 29. See also Lifford to Salisbury, 8 July 1882, Salisbury Mss. E. The fact that the decision came so late in the day (the principle had already been repudiated in hundreds of earlier cases before the land courts), the complexity and vagueness of the opinion pronounced by the court of appeal, and the repudiation of it by Gladstone in parliament all probably contributed to this end. MacKnight rightly claimed that the case belonged to 'the metaphysics of the land question'. MacKnight, *Ulster as it is*, ii, 6.

99 See Bailey, 'The Ulster tenant-right custom', pp. 21–2.

100 Russell to Gladstone, 15 April 1882, Gladstone Mss. 44475, ff. 40–1.

101 *N.W.*, 29 June 1882.

102 *B.N.L.*, 9 Dec. 1881; *F.T.*, 12 Jan. 1882. See also *B.N.L.*, 2, 20, 26 Dec. 1881.

103 *N.W.*, 9, 10 Mar., 22 April, 25 Feb. 1882.

104 *Ibid.*, 25 Feb. 1882.

105 See e.g. McElroy, *Route land crusade*, p. 38; speech of McElroy at Ballymoney (*N.W.*, 25 Feb. 1882); memorial from Ulster tenant-right associations to chief secretary (*ibid.*, 2 Oct. 1882); *St James' Gazette* quoted in *Ferm. Times*, 12 Jan. 1882. Up to August 1882, 38 per cent of the decisions given by the sub-commissioners in Ulster were appealed. See above pp. 253-4.

106 See e.g. resolutions passed at meetings of County Armagh Tenant Farmers' Association (*N.W.*, 17 Jan. 1882), Aghadowey Tenant Farmers' Society (*ibid.*, 8 Feb. 1882), Route Association (*ibid.*, 25 Feb. 1882), and Coleraine Tenants' Defence Association (*ibid.*, 28 Mar. 1882) and at tenant conferences in Belfast and Derry (*ibid.*, 21, 26 Jan. 1882).

107 Spencer to Harcourt, 2 Aug. 1882, Harcourt Mss. IV/A/2/67.

108 *Report of Irish land commissioners for the period 22 Aug. 1881–22 Aug. 1882*, p. 5; *N.W.*, 27 April, 15 Nov. 1882.

109 See e.g. speech of Dr R.H. Dodd, a Derry solicitor with wide experience of tenant cases, at Coleraine, *N.W.*, 29 April 1882.

110 Statement of G.M. Trevelyan, Forster's successor as Irish chief secretary, *ibid.*, 4 Oct. 1880.

111 See e.g. resolutions passed at tenant conferences in Ballymena and Coleraine (*ibid.*, 2, 9 Oct. 1882); at meetings of Portglenone, Ballycarry, Randalstown, Co. Armagh, Saintfield, Ballyclare, Lecale associations and many others (*ibid.*, Oct.–Nov. 1882). See also memorial from Ulster tenant-right associations to chief secretary (*ibid.*, 4 Oct. 1882).

112 See e.g. meetings of Armagh tenants' association, Portglenone association, the Limavady branch of the County Derry Liberal Union and tenant meeting at Tandragee, *ibid.*, 19 Oct., 7, 9 Nov. 1882; *C. Const.*, 25 Nov. 1882.

113 *N.W.*, 29 Nov. 1882.

114 See T.A. Dickson to Gladstone, 30 Mar. 1882, Gladstone Mss. 44474, f. 351; *N.W.*, 27 Mar. 1882.

115 A treasury minute issued in July 1882 estimated that rents on some 70 per cent of all estates in Donegal were in arrear. *N.W.*, 5 July 1882.

116 Crossle to Lady Verner, 1 May 1882, Verner Mss. D236/488/3, pp. 106–8.

117 This is so directly contrary to the assumption underlying so much that has been written about this period that one feels obliged to reiterate that not a single clause in the act suggested that tenants in arrears were ineligible to apply under it.

118 *N.W.*, 27 April 1882. See also Charles Russell to Gladstone, 15 April 1882, Gladstone Mss. 44475, f. 39.

119 Speech at Saintfield, *N.W.*, 24 April 1882.

120 *N.W.*, 7 Mar. 1882. See also memorial to Gladstone signed by 120 MPs including all the Ulster Liberal MPs, *ibid.*, 22 Mar. 1882.

121 *I.R.*, 15 Dec. 1881.

122 *N.W.*, 10 Mar. 1882. See also speech of Lord George Hamilton, *ibid.*, 23 May 1882; *Land*, 8 July 1882, p. 457.

123 Cherry, *Irish land acts*, pp. 341–3.

124 Dickson to Gladstone, 22 April 1882, Gladstone Mss. 44475, ff. 51–3.

125 *N.W.*, 20 May 1882. The state's contribution was to come out of the Irish church fund.

126 See e.g. Crossle to Lady Verner, 30 May, 26 June, 22 July 1882, Verner Mss. D236/488/3, pp. 168, 196, 215–6; Crossle to William Hardy, 24 July 1882, *ibid.*, p. 218.

127 See e.g. speech of John Givan, Liberal MP for Monaghan, in House of Commons. *N.W.*, 14 July 1882. See also speech of Trevelyan, *ibid.*, 15 June 1882. See also *ibid.* 7, 20 July 1882.

128 See Harold Rylett to Ed., *N.W.*, 30 Sept. 1882. See also *ibid.*, 21 Nov. 1882.

129 See e.g. *ibid.*, 8 Aug. 1882; *Land*, 8 July 1882, p. 457.

130 *Return of payments made to landlords by the Irish land commission, pursuant to the 1st and 16th sections of the arrears of rent act …* [C.4059], H.C. 1884, lxiv, 97, p. iv.

131 *Return showing the number of agricultural holdings and the tenure by which they are held*, pp. 16–17.

132 See e.g. tenant conferences in Belfast and Derry in January 1882, *N.W.*, 21, 26 Jan. 1882.

133 *Ibid.*, 25 Feb., 16, 18 March 1882.

134 Russell to Gladstone, 15 April 1882, Gladstone Mss. 44475, ff. 40–1; Todd's speech at meeting of Raphoe Tenants' Defence Association at St Johnston, *N.W.*, 15 May 1882. See also speeches of Samuel McElroy at Ballymoney and

Thomas Shillington at Tyrone Ditches, *ibid.*, 25 Feb., 29 May 1882.

135 McElroy, *Route land crusade,* p. 39.

136 Spencer to Gladstone, 9 Mar. 1883, Gladstone Mss. 44310, ff. 24–30.

137 The Liberals were determined after the arrears act to disabuse Irish tenants of any notion that the 1881 act would be further amended. See e.g. Spencer to Gladstone, 9 Mar. 1883, Gladstone Mss. 44310, ff. 24–5.

138 *B.F.P.* , 15 Dec. 1881; *C.C.*, 31 Dec. 1881.

139 See e.g. *N.W.,* 12 Oct. 1882; speeches of Hans McMordie at Broughshane and Saintfield (*ibid.*, 1, 24 April 1882), and resolutions of Route association at meeting in May 1882. McElroy, *Route land crusade,* p. 36.

140 Speech of Samuel Black at Broughshane, *N.W.*, 1 April 1882.

## Chapter 11

1 O'Brien, *Parnell and his party*, pp. 69–74; F.S.L. Lyons, *Charles Stewart Parnell* (London, 1977), pp. 164–77; Bew, *Land and the national question*, pp. 185–97; Davitt, *Fall of feudalism*, pp. 331–40.

2 See e.g. league meetings at Derry (*L. Journ.*, 18 April 1881), Omagh (*B.N.L.*, 21 April 1881), Cookstown (*ibid.*, 14 June 1881), Hilltown (*C. Const.*, 3 Sept. 1881), Boho (*I.R.*, 13 Oct. 1881), and Toome (*B.N.L.*, 19 Oct. 1881). Protestant support for the league and co-operation between the league and the tenant-right movement were already diminishing even before the land bill was introduced, as league meetings began from late January 1881 to give increasing prominence to resolutions condemning the government's policy of coercion

and in some instances attacking the Ulster Liberal MPs. See e.g. league meetings at Claudy and Park in Derry. *L. Journ.*, 4 Mar. 1881.

3 *I.R.*, 11 Aug. 1881.

4 See e.g. *B.F.P.* , 20 Oct. 1881; *I.R.*, 22 Sept., 20 Oct. 1881; *C.C.*, 1 Oct. 1881.

5 *T.C.*, 16 Sept. 1881. See also *Land*, 17 Dec. 1881, p. 366.

6 *C.C.*, 22 Oct. 1881; *B.F.P.* , 27 Oct. 1881; *N.W.*, 22 Oct. 1881; *I.R.*, 27 Oct. 1881.

7 *B.N.L.*, 20 Oct. 1881.

8 Earl of Belmore to Lord Cowper, 7 Nov. 1881, C.S.O., R.P. 1881, 44241.

9 Dorrian to Kirby, 8 Nov. 1881, Kirby correspondence, 1881, no. 405.

10 *F.T.*, 2 Feb., 16 Mar. 1881; *N.W.*, 3 Feb., 7 Apr. 1882; *I.R.*, 27 Oct. 1881; James Crossle to Lady Verner, 26 Jan. 1882, Verner Mss. D236/488/2, p. 406.

11 J.A. Pomeroy to Hugh Montgomery, 20 Nov. 1881, Montgomery Mss. D627/325.

12 T.P. O'Connor, *Memoirs of an old parliamentarian* (2 vols, London, 1929), i, 236.

13 Dickson in his campaign made frequent references to the Burns case and the attempt to destroy leasehold tenant-right on the Ranfurly estate in 1872–3, which was still widely remembered in Tyrone. See above, pp. 146–7.

14 More originating notices to have rents fixed under the act were served in Tyrone in 1881–2 and in the 5 years up to Aug. 1886 than in any other Ulster county. *Report of Irish land commissioners for the period 22 Aug. 1881–22 Aug. 1882*, p. 8; *Report of the Irish land commissioners for the period from 22 Aug. 1885 to 22 Aug. 1886* [C.4899], H. C. 1886, xix, 503, p. 10.

15  *B.N.L.*, 25 Aug. 1881; *T.C.*, 26 Aug. 1881; O'Connor, *Memoirs*, i, 236.

16  *I.R.*, 1 Sept. 1881. See also *ibid.*, 15 Sept. 1881; *C.C.*, 10 Sept. 1881.

17  See Knox's address, *T.C.*, 26 Aug. 1881 and speeches at Fintona, Strabane, Beragh, Omagh and New Mills, *ibid.*, 26 Aug., 2, 9 Sept. 1881.

18  *T.C.*, 2, 16 Sept. 1881; Davitt, *Fall of feudalism*, p. 332; *C.C.*, 10 Sept. 1881.

19  The result was — Dickson 3,168; Knox 3,084; Rylett 907.

20  Davitt, *Fall of feudalism*, p. 332. See also Healy, *Letters and leaders*, i, 134; O'Connor, *Memoirs*, i, 236.

21  Gladstone to Forster, 8 Sept. 1881, Gladstone Mss. 44159, f. 1; Forster to Gladstone, 11 Sept. 1881, *ibid.*, ff. 5–7. See also Harcourt to Gladstone, 10 Sept. 1881, Harcourt Mss. IIA/5; Reid, *Life of Forster*, ii, 334–8.

22  See James Crossle to Sir W. Verner, 8 Sept. 1881, Verner Mss. D236/488/2, p. 232. A recent analysis of the voting estimates that whereas in 1880 Litton got 34 per cent of the protestant votes, in 1881 Dickson's share was 44 per cent. Bew and Wright, 'Agrarian opposition', p. 217.

23  One result of the Land League agitation was the emergence of a local catholic lay leadership — mainly farmers, publicans, town traders and some professionals — who were later to play an equally active part in the politically more successful National League campaign (see police reports on progress of Irish National League, INL papers, ctns 6 and 9). This development in itself tended to push the catholic clergy into a greater accommodation with the nationalist party, and Parnell clinched their support by giving them a dominant role in the county conventions. O'Brien, *Parnell and his party*, pp. 128–132.

24  See Bew and Wright, 'Agrarian opposition', p. 216.

25  *U.E.*, 15, 19 Nov. 1881; *B.F.P.*, 1 Dec. 1881.

26  *U.E.*, 6 Dec. 1881.

27  There were conflicting reports in the different papers as to how the catholics voted in this election. The most balanced assessment and probably the correct one was that of the *Coleraine Chronicle* (10 Dec.) which estimated that the catholic vote had split, with less than 500 catholic votes (out of 1,200) going to Wilson.

28  See Porter to Gladstone, 9 Dec. 1881, Gladstone Mss. 44473, f. 146.

29  *T.C.*, 12 Aug. 1881. See also *C. Const.*, 19 Nov. 1881.

30  See e.g. speeches of W.J. Hurst at Dromore (*N.W.*, 11 Jan. 1882), T.A. Dickson at Armagh and Derry (*ibid.*, 17, 26 Jan. 1882), J. Givan at Belfast (*ibid.*, 21 Jan. 1882) and Samuel Black at Ballymoney (*ibid.*, 25 Feb. 1882).

31  *N.W.*, 3 Jan., 15–23 Mar., 13, 27 Apr., 18 May: *I.R.*, 29 Dec. 1881; *C.C.*, 11 June 1882; Livingstone, *The Monaghan story*, p. 340.

32  See above, p. 268. The arrears question in mid-1882 also stimulated considerable activity in Ulster; see e.g. C.S.O., R.P. 1882, 29945.

33  *Land*, 15 Apr. 1882, p. 208. See Northcote to Salisbury, 13 Mar. 1882, Salisbury Mss. E.

34  *N.W.*, 3, 5 May, 1 Aug. 1882; MacKnight, *Ulster as it is*, ii, 8; O'Connor, *Parnell movement*, pp. 483–4; Salisbury to Cairns, 3 May 1882, Salisbury Mss. D/12/20.

35  Salisbury to Lord George Hamilton, 6 Aug. 1882, Salisbury Mss. D/27/4.

For an account of this crisis and the almost exclusively party considerations which dictated its course see A. Jones, *The politics of reform 1884* (Cambridge, 1972), pp. 60–5.

36 See *Land*, 2 Sept. 1882, p. 60; Lord George Hamilton to Sir Stafford Northcote, 3 Aug. 1882 (Iddesleigh Mss., vol xxix, B.M. Add. Mss. 50041, ff. 105–6); Lord Lifford to Salisbury, 18 July 1882 (Salisbury Mss. E); Abercorn to Salisbury, 23 July, 9 Aug. 1882 (*ibid.*); Lord Fitzwilliam to Salisbury, 29 July 1882 (*ibid.*); Cairns to Salisbury, 6 Aug. 1882 (*ibid.*) and others.

37 John Gorst to Northcote, 8 Aug. 1882, Iddesleigh Mss., vol. xxix, B.M. Add. Mss. 50041, ff. 107–8. See also Cecil, *Life of Salisbury*, iii, 51–4.

38 Gladstone to Granville, 21 May 1883, Gladstone Mss. 44546, f. 116.

39 Irish Land Commission memorandum, 9 Mar. 1883, *ibid.*, 44310, ff. 32–3. See also Spencer to Gladstone, 9 Mar. 1883, *ibid.*, ff. 24–5.

40 *B.N.L.*, 27 Jan. 1883.

41 This became the policy of the Ulster Land Committee in 1885. *N.W.*, 10 Oct., 10 Nov. 1885.

42 T.A. Dickson MP, *A plea for the formation of an Irish land bank …* (London, 1884), p. 19. See also *N.W.*, 5 Apr. 1882; Arnold-Forster, *Journal*, p. 451.

43 See e.g. Michael McCartan to Patrick W. Russell, 6 Feb. 1881, Russell Mss. A1; John Pinkerton's speech at Ballymoney, 18 Nov. 1882, Pinkerton press cuttings. D1078/P/1.

44 Biggar to John Miskelly, 7 Nov. 1882, PRONI, T1160/1.

45 See reports on progress of Irish National League, INL papers, ctns 6 and 9.

46 J.H. Davies to E.G. Jenkinson, assistant under-secretary, 5 Feb. 1883, *ibid.*, ctn 9; A. Butler to Jenkinson, 10 Feb. 1883, *ibid.*

47 Return to E.G. Jenkinson showing progress of Irish National League up to the end of Jan. 1883. INL papers, ctn 6; A. Butler to Jenkinson, 10 Feb. 1883, *ibid.*, ctn 9.

48 This branch was 'composed principally of the hands of the Bessbrook mills', hence the unusually large membership. J.H. Davies to Jenkinson, 5 Feb. 1883, *ibid.*, ctn 9.

49 Report from R. Garrett, co-inspector of Armagh, 1 Feb. 1883, *ibid.*, ctn 6.

50 Reports on progress of National League, *ibid.*, ctns 6 and 9.

51 An attempt to form a National League branch in Monaghan town in December had 'completely failed', INL papers, ctn 6. For the Monaghan election, see J. Magee, 'The Monaghan election of 1883 and the invasion of Ulster', *Clogher Record*, viii, no. 2 (1974), pp. 147–66; McGimpsey, 'Monaghan politics', pp. 428–95.

52 See O'Connor, *The Parnell movement*, p. 487.

53 MacKnight, *Ulster as it is*, ii, 34.

54 *N.W.*, 19–21 June 1883.

55 *B.N.L.*, 18 June 1883.

56 The actual figures were — Healy 2,376; Monroe 2,011; Pringle 270.

57 *N.W.*, 5 July 1883. See also *B.N.L.*, 2 July 1883.

58 Healy, *Letters and leaders*, 1, 192.

59 *Land*, 7 July 1883, p. 301.

60 *Weekly News and Ulster Examiner*, 7 July 1883, quoted in Magee, *loc. cit.*, p. 156.

61 Monroe to Salisbury, 10 July 1883, Salisbury Mss E. See also *B.N.L.*, 2, 3 July 1883.

62 *N.W.*, 3 Aug. 1885. See also *B.M.N.*, 26 Aug. 1885.

63 R.E. Beckerson, 'Report on progress of Irish National League from 1 Oct. to 31 Dec. 1883', 10 Jan. 1884 (I.N.L. papers, ctn 6). For the concentration of league speakers on the land question see e.g. speeches of William O'Brien and T.D. Sullivan at Omagh (*Weekly Freeman's Journal*, 6 Oct. 1883), Sullivan at Rouskey (*ibid.*), Healey and Biggar at Roslea (*ibid.*, 20 Oct. 1883) and Davitt in St. Mary's Hall, Belfast (*B.M.N.*, 10 Nov. 1883.).

64 See e.g. speeches of William O'Brien, Jeremiah Jordan and T.D. Sullivan at Omagh, *Weekly Freeman's Journal*, 6 Oct. 1883.

65 Speech at meeting of central branch of league in Dublin, *ibid.*, 10 Nov. 1883. See also copy of letter from Parnell to Harrington some months later (*ibid.*, 14 June 1883). Parnell at this stage advised that meetings should be held only in strongly nationalist areas of Ulster.

66 Bew and Wright, 'Agrarian opposition', pp. 221–2.

67 See e.g. resolutions of the Grand Orange Lodge of Ireland, *F.T.*, 22 June 1882.

68 *C. Const.*, 11 Nov. 1882. See also *B.N.L.*, 13 July 1883; Lucas, *Colonel Saunderson MP*, pp. 66–7.

69 MacKnight, *Ulster as it is*, ii, 38.

70 O'Connor, *Parnell movement*, pp. 492–3.

71 For the development of the nationalist campaign in Ulster see Magee, 'The Monaghan election', pp. 158–65; Courtenay Boyle, 'Memorandum on National League',

24 Jan. 1884, Gladstone Mss. 443111, ff. 22–26. A loyalist account of the campaign is given in J. Wallace Taylor, *The Rossmore incident* (Dublin, 1884), pp. 5–28.

72 See Spencer to Gladstone, 23 Nov. 1883, Gladstone Mss. 44310, f. 168; Courtenay Boyle, 'Memorandum on Derry riots', Nov. 1883, Harcourt Mss. W.V.H. 17/2; Spencer to Harcourt, 29 Feb. 1884, Harcourt Mss. IVA/5/16.

73 A young Orangeman by the name of Giffen was killed when the military charged part of the Orange crowd with fixed bayonets. *Weekly Freeman*, 5 Jan. 1884.

74 See Trevelyan to Gladstone, 8 Nov. 1881, Gladstone Mss. 44335, f. 135; Spencer to Gladstone, 30 Sept. 1883, *ibid.* 44310, f.151

75 Quoted in R. Kee, *The green flag, a history of Irish nationalism* (London, 1972), p. 100.

76 Speech at Killylea, *B.N.L.*, 13 July 1881. See also editorial and report of speech of Lord Arthur Hill at Lambeg, *ibid.*, 13 July 1883; and *F.T.*, 3 Aug. 1882. Rossmore himself was expelled from the bench for irresponsibly provoking a confrontation at Roslea. For the Roslea incident and Rossmore's dismissal from the bench see Courtenay Boyle, 'Memorandum on the Rossmore incident', 28 Jan. 1884, Gladstone Mss. 44311, ff. 13–211; Lord Rossmore, *Things I can tell* (London, 1912), pp. 240–9; Taylor, *Rossmore incident*, pp. 11–14, 29n.

77 See A.B. Cooke, 'A Conservative party leader in Ulster: Sir Stafford Northcote's diary of a visit to the province, October 1883', *Proceedings of the Royal Irish Academy*, vol. 75, Sect. C, no. 4 (1975). See also

Northcote to Viscount Crichton, 20 Oct. 1883, Erne Mss. D1939/21/10/5.

78 *Weekly Freeman*, 8 Dec. 1883.

79 INL papers, ctn 6. See also Spencer to Gladstone, 30 Sept. 1883, Gladstone Mss. 44310, f. 151; Courtenay Newtown, 'Memorandum on National League', 24 Jan. 1884, *ibid.*, 44311, f. 24.

80 R.E. Beckerson, 'Report on progress of Irish National League, 1 Jan.–30 June 1884', 18 July 1884, INL papers, ctn 6. This growth continued during 1884 and 1885. R.E. Beckerson, 'Reports on progress of Irish National League, 1 July–31 Dec. 1884, and 1 Jan.–30 June 1885'. *Ibid.*

81 For a more detailed account of these events see F. Thompson, 'The Ulster Liberals and the general election of 1885' (MA dissertation, Queen's University, 1973), pp. 18–28.

82 The Liberal decline has often been attributed to the enfranchisement of the agricultural labourers in 1884. Yet the increase in the electorate was more than treble the total number of adult agricultural and general labourers in the province, many of whom remained unenfranchised at any rate. For the reform acts of 1884–5 and the difficulties of registration, see N. Blewett, 'The franchise in the United Kingdom, 1885–1918', *Past and Present*, no. 32 (December, 1965), pp. 27–56; B.M. Walker, 'The Irish electorate, 1868–1915', *I.H.S.*, xviii (March, 1973), pp. 359–66.

83 *N.W.*, 3 Aug. 1885.

84 See e.g. *ibid.*, 8, 10 June, 15 Oct. 1885.

85 See e.g. *ibid.*, 11 Nov. 1885.

86 MacKnight, *Ulster as it is*, ii, 76.

87 *N.W.*, 24 Aug. 1885.

88 Pomfret, *The struggle for land in Ireland*, p. 250.

89 *B.N.L.*, 10 Nov. 1885.

90 Armour, *Armour of Ballymoney*, p. 72.

91 *N.W.*, 29 Sept. 1885.

92 *Ibid.*, 22 July 1885.

93 See Thompson, 'The Ulster Liberals and the general election of 1885', pp. 29–32.

94 *Ibid.* The following two paragraphs are based mainly on this source.

95 See e.g. *B.N.L.*, 12, 19 Nov. 1885.

96 *Ibid.*, 2 Nov. 1885; *N.W.*, 16 Nov. 1885.

97 R. MacGeagh to James Bryce, 5 Feb. 1886, Bryce Mss. U.B. 44. This analysis was made in the wake of another Liberal defeat in a by-election in Mid-Armagh early in 1886, which marked a further stage in the transfer of Liberal votes to the Conservative party. See Thompson, 'The Armagh elections of 1885–6', pp. 375–8.

98 *N.W.*, 14 April 1886. See D.C. Savage, 'The origins of the Ulster Unionist party, 1885–6', *I.H.S.*, xii (1961), pp. 197–205. The Liberals had already turned down James Bryce's suggestion that they should instead 'press for adequate safeguards for Ulster'. R. MacGeagh to Bryce, 13 Mar. 1886, Bryce Mss. U.B.44.

99 Gladstone's proposals would have allowed tenants to buy their farms at 20 years' purchase.

100 See J. Crossle Jr to A.R. Jackson, 7 Dec. 1886, Verner Mss. D236/488/5, p. 1011; W.T. Small to Hugh Montgomery, 5 Jan. 1886, Montgomery Mss. D627/341F; Montgomery's statement to tenants, 15 Jan. 1886, *ibid.* D627/341G.

101 J. Crossle Jr to A.R. Jackson, 7 Dec. 1886, Verner Mss. D236/488/5, p. 1011; Solow, *The land question*, pp. 181–4. The 'plan of campaign' in Ulster is discussed in L.M. Geary,

*The plan of campaign 1886–1891* (Cork, 1986), pp. 50–3, which, however, underestimates its impact on the province. See E. Keown, 'The plan of campaign in Ulster, 1886–7' (BEd dissertation, St Mary's College, Belfast, 1996).

102 For the attitudes of the landlords to the land bill of 1887, see Alvin Jackson, *The Ulster party, Irish Unionists in the house of commons, 1884–1911* (Oxford, 1989), pp. 133–7.

103 Bonn, *Modern Ireland*, pp. 110–11; Solow, *The land question*, pp. 178–81. Solow estimates that rents by the early 1890s were 28 per cent down on their 1881 level.

104 Montgomery to Thompson, 29 Sept. 1892, Montgomery Mss. D1121/9.

105 S.C. McElroy, 'Statement on compulsory sale of land in Ireland', 3 Aug. 1892, Uncat. Bryce Mss. U.B. 143; T.W. Russell, *Ireland and the empire, a review 1800–1900* (London, 1901), pp. 165–71.

106 Russell, *Ireland and the empire*, pp. 144–6, 190–1. Tenants complained that where the landlord exercised his right of pre-emption the land commission fixed the price below what could have been obtained on the open market. Pomfret, *The struggle for land*, p. 215.

107 A. Jackson, 'Irish Unionism and the Russellite threat, 1894–1906', *I.H.S.*, xxv (1987), p. 379.

108 Bonn, *Modern Ireland*, pp. 99–100; Russell, *Ireland and the empire*, pp. 192–3.

109 Bonn, *Modern Ireland*, p. 121; Geary, *The plan of campaign*, pp. 50–1.

110 Bryce to Gladstone, 24 July 1892, Bryce Mss. 12, f. 57.

111 Jackson, 'Irish Unionism and the Russellite threat', pp. 381–9; Jackson, *The Ulster party*, p. 146.

112 For the Russellite campaign, see Jackson, 'Irish Unionism and the Russellite threat', pp. 390–402; Paul Bew, *Conflict and conciliation in Ireland, Parnellites and radical agrarians* (Oxford, 1987), pp. 86–91. See also J.R.B. McMinn, 'Liberalism in North Antrim, 1900–14', *I.H.S.*, xxiii (1982), pp. 19–20.

113 Bew, *Conflict and conciliation*, pp. 89–91.

114 Solow, *The land question*, pp. 192–3.

115 Jackson, *The Ulster party*, pp. 230–1; Bonn, *Modern Ireland*, pp. 147–9. See also Bew, *Conflict and conciliation*, p. 11.

116 Jackson, *The Ulster party*, pp. 266–73.

117 For Glendinning's victory, see McMinn, 'Liberalism in North Antrim', pp. 23–7.

## Conclusion

1 Bruce had taken eviction proceedings against Robinson after the latter had criticised Bruce in his role as chairman of County Derry grand jury. *W.N.W.*, 14 Jan. 1871; *C.C.*, 14 Jan. 1871.

2 *C.C.*, 27 Nov. 1869.

3 See e.g. Latimer, *History of Irish presbyterians*, pp. 537–8; Armour, *Armour of Ballymoney*, pp. 78–9, passim.

## Appendices

1 P. M.A. Bourke, 'The agricultural statistics of the 1841 census of Ireland: A critical review', *Economic History Review*, 2nd series, xviii (1965), 376–381; *Appendix to the minutes of evidence taken before her majesty's commissioners into the state of the law and practice in respect of the occupation of land in Ireland*, pt iv, [672], H.C. 1845, xxii, 162, pp. 280–3.

2  *Returns of agricultural produce in Ireland in the year 1848* [1116] , H.C. 1849, xlix, 1. This return shows a balance of only 2,380 holdings falling outside the provincial boundary, and these have been added to the totals in the different categories for 1845. There were also in the 1845 returns some 9,500 joint tenancies which were not classified.

3  I am grateful to my colleagues Dr Harry McKeown and Dr Peter McPolin for carrying out these calculations.

# Bibliography

## 1 MANUSCRIPT MATERIAL

I PUBLIC RECORD OFFICE OF NORTHERN IRELAND

Abercorn papers. Viceregal papers of 1st Duke of Abercorn, T254/V.R.

Annesley papers. Papers of 5th Earl of Annesley, D1854/6.

Ashbourne papers. Papers of Edward Gibson, 1st Baron Gibson, T2955.

Belmore papers. Papers of 4th Earl of Belmore, D3007/P.

Boycott Committee papers. Correspondence received by committee established to raise subscriptions for Captain Charles C. Boycott, D3681/1–27.

Brett papers. Papers of Charles H. Brett, Belfast, D1905/2/142, 247.

Charlemont papers. Papers of 3rd Earl of Charlemont, D266/367.

Clogher Diocesan papers. Papers of catholic diocese of Clogher, D10(RC)1.

Diary and account book of John Dick, secretary of tenants' association, Broadisland estate, County Antrim, D1014.

Ellison-Macartney papers. Papers of J.W. Ellison Macartney and Rt Hon. W.G. Ellison-Macartney.

Erne papers. Papers of 3rd Earl of Erne, D1939/21.

Minutes of Fermanagh County Grand Orange Lodge, D1402.

Hancock papers. Papers of John Hancock, agent of Lurgan estates, D1600.

Land Commission papers, Verner estate, Tyrone, LR 0184 AL.

Miskelly papers. Letters belonging to John Miskelly, a leading member of the Belfast branch of the National League, T1160.

Montgomery papers. Papers of Hugh de Fellenberg Montgomery, D627, D1121/2–12, T1089.

Autobiographical memoir of A.J.H. Moody, provision merchant, Coleraine, T2901/4/1.

Moore papers. Papers and newspaper cuttings of W. J. Moore, secretary of Down Farmers' Union, D877/27.

O'Hagan papers. Papers of Thomas O'Hagan, 1st Baron O'Hagan, D2777.

Pinkerton papers. Papers and newspaper cuttings of John Pinkerton, D1078.

Richardson papers. Papers of J.N. Richardson, Bessbrook, D1006.

Rossmore papers. Papers of 3rd Baron Rossmore, T2929.

Russell papers. Papers of P.W. Russell, Ballistrue, Downpatrick.

Saunderson papers. Papers of Colonel Edward Saunderson, T2996.

Verner papers. Out-letter books and correspondence of James Crossle, agent of Verner estates, D236/488/1–5.

Reminiscences of W.R. Young, T3382.

II  ELSEWHERE

Bryce papers. Papers of James Bryce (Bodleian Library, Oxford)

Chief Secretary's Office, Registered Papers, 1880–81 (State Paper Office, Dublin).

Disraeli papers. Papers of Benjamin Disraeli, 1st Earl of Beaconsfield (Hughenden Manor, High Wycombe, Buckinghamshire).

Gladstone papers. Papers of W.E. Gladstone (British Museum).

Harcourt papers. Papers of Sir William Harcourt (Bodleian Library, Oxford).

Iddesleigh papers. Papers of Sir Stafford Northcote, 1st Earl of Iddesleigh (British Museum).

Irish Land League and Irish National League papers, 1878–88 (State Paper Office, Dublin).

Land League papers (National Library of Ireland, Mss. 17,708–9).

Salisbury papers. Papers of 3rd Marquis of Salisbury (Christ Church, Oxford).

## 2.  NEWSPAPERS AND JOURNALS

*Armagh Guardian*

*Ballymena Advertiser*

*Ballymoney Free Press*

*Banner of Ulster*

*Belfast Morning News*

*Belfast News Letter*

*Coleraine Chronicle*

*Coleraine Constitution*

*Downpatrick Recorder*

*Fermanagh Times*

*Impartial Reporter*

*Land* (English agricultural and property journal)

*Lisbellaw Gazette*

*Londonderry Journal*

*Londonderry Sentinel*

*Londonderry Standard*

*Newtownards Chronicle*
*Northern Star*
*Northern Whig*
(London) *Times*
*Tyrone Constitution*
*Ulster Examiner* (*Daily Examiner* 16 Nov. 1870–1872)
*Weekly Freeman's Journal*
*Weekly Northern Whig*

# 3 PARLIAMENTARY PAPERS AND OFFICIAL PUBLICATIONS

I HANSARD'S PARLIAMENTARY DEBATES, 3RD SERIES

II AGRICULTURAL STATISTICS AND RETURNS OF AGRICULTURAL PRODUCE

*Returns of agricultural produce in Ireland in the year 1848* [1116], H.C. 1849, xlix, 1.
*The census of Ireland for the year 1851, pt ii: Returns of agricultural produce in 1851* [1589], H.C. 1852–3, xciii, 1.
*Returns of agricultural produce in Ireland in the year 1854* [2017], H.C. 1856, liii, 1.
*The agricultural statistics of Ireland for the year 1861* [3156], H.C. 1863, lxix, 547.
*The agricultural statistics ... 1871* [C 762], H.C. 1873, lxix, 375.
*The agricultural statistics ... 1876* [C 1749], H.C. 1877, lxxxv, 529.
*The agricultural statistics ... 1877* [C 1938], H.C. 1873, lxxvii, 511.
*The agricultural statistics ... 1878* [C 2347], H.C. 1878–9, lxxv, 587.
*The agricultural statistics ... 1879* [C 2534], H.C. 1880, lxxvi, 815.
*The agricultural statistics ... 1880* [C 1932], H.C. 1881, xciii, 685.
*The agricultural statistics ... 1881* [C 3332], H.C. 1882, lxxiv, 93.
*The agricultural statistics ... 1882* [C 3677], H.C. 1883, lxxvi, 825.

III RETURNS OF EVICTIONS

*Return by provinces and counties (compiled from returns made to the inspector-general, Royal Irish Constabulary), of cases of evictions which have come to the knowledge of the constabulary in each of the years from 1849 to 1880, inclusive.* H.C. 1881 (185), lxvii, 725.
*Return (compiled from returns made to the inspector-general of the Royal Irish Constabulary) of cases of eviction which have come to the knowledge of the constabulary in each quarter of the year ended the 31st day of December 1880, showing the number of families evicted in each county in Ireland during each quarter, the number readmitted as tenants, and the number readmitted as*

*caretakers.* H.C. 1881 (2), lxxvii, 713.

*Return ... of cases of eviction ... in each quarter of the year ended 31st December 1881 ...* H.C. 1882 (9), lv, 229.

*Return ... of cases of eviction ... in the quarter ended 31st December 1882 ...* [C 3465], H.C. 1883, lvi, 99.

*Return ... of cases of eviction ... in the quarter ended 31st March 1883 ...* [C. 3579]. H.C. 1883, lvi, 107.

*Return ... of cases of eviction ... in the quarter ended 30th June 1883 ...* H.C. [C 3770]. H.C. 1883, lvi, 111.

*Return ... of cases of eviction ... in the quarter ended 30th September 1883 ...* [C 3892], H.C. 1884, lxiv, 407.

*Return ... of cases of eviction ... in the quarter ended 31st December 1883 ...* [C 3892], H.C. 1884, lxiv, 411.

IV  RETURNS OF AGRARIAN OFFENCES

*Return of all agrarian outrages reported by the Royal Irish Constabulary between the 1st day of January 1879 and the 31st day of January 1880, giving particulars of crime, arrests, and results of proceedings.* H.C. 1880 (131), lx, 199.

*Return of all agrarian outrages ... between the 1st day of February and the 31st day of October 1880 ...* H.C. 1881 (6), lxxvii, 273.

*Return of all agrarian outrages ... between the 1st day of November 1880 and the 30th day of November 1880 ...* H.C. 1881 (6-I), lxxvii, 409.

*Return of all agrarian outrages ... between the 1st day of December 1880 and the 31st day of December 1880 ...* H.C. 1881 (6-II), lxxvii, 487.

*Return of the number of agrarian offences in each county in Ireland reported to the constabulary office in each month of the year 1880, distinguishing offences against the person, offences against property, and offences against the public peace, with summary for each county for the year.* H.C. 1881 (12), lxxvii, 619.

*Return of the number of agrarian offences in each county in Ireland reported to the constabulary office in each month of the year 1881 ...* H.C. 1882 (8), lv, 1.

V  JUDICIAL STATISTICS

*Judicial statistics (Ireland) 1871: Part I. Police, criminal proceedings, prisons: Part II. Common law, equity, civil and canon law* [C 674], H.C. 1872, lxv, 235.

*Criminal and judicial statistics (Ireland), 1872: Part I. Police, criminal proceedings, prisons: Part II. Common law, equity and civil law* [C 851], H.C. 1873, lxx, 247.

*Criminal and judicial statistics ... 1873 ...* [C 1034], H.C. 1874, lxxi, 251.

*Criminal and judicial statistics ... 1874 ...* [C 1295], H.C. 1875, lxxxi, 259.

*Criminal and judicial statistics ... 1875 ...* [C 1563], H.C. 1876, lxxix, 273.

*Criminal and judicial statistics ... 1876 ...* [C 1822], H.C. 1877, lxxvi, 261.
*Criminal and judicial statistics ... 1877 ...* [C 2152], H.C. 1878, lxxix, 265.
*Criminal and judicial statistics ... 1878 ...* [C 2389], H.C. 1878–9, lxxvi, 279.

VI  REPORTS OF THE IRISH LAND COMMISSIONERS

*Report of the Irish land commissioners for the period from 22nd August 1881 to 22nd August 1882* [C 3413], H.C. 1882, xx, 265.
*Report of the Irish land commissioners for the period from 22nd August 1882 to 22nd August 1883, and as to proceedings under the Arrears of Rent (Ireland) Act, 1882 to the 27th October 1883* [C3897], H.C. 1884, lxiv, 41.
*Report of the Irish land commissioners for the period from 22nd August 1883 to 22nd August 1884 ...* [C4231], H.C. 1884–5, lxv, 53.
*Report of the Irish land commissioners for the period from 22nd August 1884 to 22 August 1885 ...* [C4625], H.C. 1886, xix, 467.
*Report of the Irish land commissioners for the period from 22nd August 1885 to 22nd August 1886* [C4899]. H.C. 1886, xxi, 503.

VII  REPORTS OF THE COMMISSIONERS OF NATIONAL EDUCATION

*Eighth report of the commissioners of national education in Ireland for the year 1841* [398], H.C. 1842, xxiii, 339.
*Eighteenth report ... 1851,* vol. ii [1583], H.C. 1852–3, xliii, 1.
*Twenty-eighth report ... 1861* [3026], H.C. 1862, xx, 249.
*Thirty-eighth report ... 1871* [C 599], H.C. 1872, xxiii, 253.
*Forty-eighth report ... 1881* [C 3243], H.C. 1882, xxiv, 77.

VIII  OTHER PARLIAMENTARY PAPERS

*Report of the commissioners appointed to take the census of Ireland for the year 1841, with plates, appendix etc.* [504], H.C. 1843, xxiv, 1.
*Report from her majesty's commissioners of inquiry into the state of the law and practice in respect of the occupation of land in Ireland* [605], H.C. 1845, xix, 1.
*Appendix to the minutes of evidence taken before her majesty's commissioners into the state of the law and practice in respect of the occupation of land in Ireland,* pt iv [672], H.C. 1845, xxii, 162.
*Returns from the court for the sale of incumbered estates in Ireland, up to the 1st day of April 1853, of number of petitions lodged for the sale of estates; number of petitions fiated by the commissioners; number of petitions dismissed; total produce of sales in each county; number of conveyances executed; total amount paid out ...* H.C. 1852–53 (390), xciv, 599.

*Report of her majesty's commissioners appointed to inquire into the incumbered estates court, and into the expediency of continuing it, or transferring its powers to the court of chancery: together with an appendix, containing evidence and returns*, H.C. 1854–55 (1938), xix, 527.

*Census of Ireland for the year 1851, pt iv: Report on ages and education* [2053], H.C. 1856, xxix, 1.

*Census of Ireland for the year 1851, pt vi: General report* [2134], H.C. 1856, xxxi, 1.

*Census of Ireland for the year 1861, pt. ii: Report and tables on ages and education*, vol. i [3204-I], H.C. 1863, lvi, 1.

*Census of Ireland for the year 1861, pt v: General report* [3204-IV], H.C. 1863, lxi, 1.

*Reports from poor law inspectors on the wages of agricultural labourers in Ireland* [C35], H.C. 1870; xiv, 1.

*Reports from poor law inspectors in Ireland as to the existing relations between landlord and tenant in respect of improvements on farms, drainage, reclamation of land, fencing, planting etc.; also, as to the existence (and to what extent) of Ulster tenant-right in their respective districts, etc.* [C31], H.C. 1870, xiv, 37.

*Return showing the number of agricultural holdings in Ireland and the tenure by which they are held by occupiers* [C32], H.C. 1870, lvi, 737.

*Returns of the total value of lands sold in the incumbered estates court and landed estates court, Ireland: of the total number of evictions which have taken place in each county in Ireland during the three years ended 31st December 1869: and, of the average value of cattle, etc., in the years 1850, 1860 and 1869*, H.C. 1870 (101), lvii, 302.

*Thirty-ninth report from the board of public works, Ireland: with the appendices, for the year 1870–1* [C383], H.C. 1871, xvi, 307.

*Report from the select committee of the house of lords on the Landlord and Tenant (Ireland) Act, 1870; together with the proceedings of the committee, minutes of evidence, appendix and index*, H.C. 1872 (403), xi, 1.

*Return of the number of estates sold by the landed estates court during each of the last ten years, showing the total amount of purchase money, the valuation, and the rental of the estate sold, and the number of years purchase in each case*, H.L. 1874 (228), xvi, 139.

*Census of Ireland, 1871, pt. i: Area, houses and population, also the ages, civil condition, occupations, birthplaces, religion, and education of the people – vol. iii, province of Ulster ... Summary tables and indexes* [C964 – I to X], H.C. 1874, lxxiv, pt i, 1.

*Return of the names of proprietors and the area and valuation of all properties in the several counties in Ireland, held in fee or perpetuity, or on long leases at chief rents*, H.C. 1876 (412), lxxx, 395.

*Summary of the returns of owners of land in Ireland, showing, with respect to each county, the numbers of owners below an acre, and in classes up to 100,000 acres and upwards, with an aggregate acreage and valuation of each class*, H.C. 1876 (422), lxxx, 35.

*Return showing, (1) in provinces and (2) in counties, the landed estates held in fee, fee-farm for lives renewable for ever, or for terms of years of which sixty shall have been unexpired, sold in one or more lots in the landed estates court for each of the five years prior to 1870, and up to the 1st of August 1870; and similar return for the remainder of the year 1870, and for each of the five years ending 31st December 1875* ... H.L. 1876 (238), xi, 37.

*Return of the amount awarded to tenants at land sessions in Ireland, exclusive of costs, under the Landlord and Tenant (Ireland) Act, 1870, since the passing of that measure up to the 31st day of December 1875, with totals and gross totals; etc.* H.C. 1877 (194), lxix, 593.

*Annual report of the local government board for Ireland, being the eighth report under the Local Government Board (Ireland) Act, 35 & 36 Vic., C. 69* [C 2603], H.C. 1880, xxviii, 1.

*Appendix to the annual report of the local government board for Ireland, being the eighth report* ... [C 2603-1], H.C. 1880, xxviii, 39.

*Return of all agrarian crimes and outrages ... in the counties of Galway, Mayo, Sligo, and Donegal from 1st February 1880 to 30 June 1880; and of the number of meetings called for the purpose of promoting the land agitation reported by the constabulary within the same counties since 30th June 1879* ... H.C. 1880 (327 ... sess. 2), lx, 291.

*Returns of the amount of purchase money realised by the sale of estates in the landed estates court (Ireland) each year, from 1870 to 1879, both inclusive: and, of the number of sales effected in the said court from the 1st day of November 1879 to the 1st day of June 1880* ... H.C. 1880 (303), lx, 377.

*Correspondence relative to measures for the relief of distress in Ireland, 1879–80* [C2483], H.C. 1880, lxii, 157.

*Return of all applications from landed proprietors and sanitary authorities in scheduled unions for loans under the notices of the commissioners of public works in Ireland, dated the 22nd day of November 1879, and the 12th day of January 1880 respectively; with result of applications to the 20th day of March 1880, arranged by baronies.* H.C. 1880 (154), lxii, 209.

*Return of numbers in receipt of relief in the several unions in Ireland on the 1st day of January, the 1st day of March, and the 1st day of June in 1878, 1879 and 1880*, H.C. 1880 (420 – sess. 2), lxii, 289.

*Return showing the unions and electoral divisions scheduled by the local government board for Ireland under the Seeds Supply (Ireland) Act 1880*, H.C. 1880 (299 – sess. 2), lxii, 339.

*Preliminary report from her majesty's commissioners on agriculture* [C2778], H.C. 1881, xv, 1.

*Preliminary report of the assistant commissioners for Ireland* [C2951], H.C. 1881, xvi, 841.

*Report of her majesty's commissioners of inquiry into the working of the Landlord and Tenant (Ireland) Act, 1870, and the amending acts; with the evidence, appendices, and index* [C2779], H.C. 1881, xvii–xix.

*Appendix to the annual report of the local government board for Ireland, being the ninth report under the Local Government Board (Ireland) Act, 35 & 36 Vic., c.69* [C2926-1], H.C. 1881, xlvii, 305.

*Return of the names of landowners and sanitary authorities who have obtained loans under the provisions of the Relief of Distress (Ireland) Act 1880, distinguishing those obtained at the reduced rate of interest, showing the dates of application and of sanction, the amount of the loans, the description of works, together with the dates of first advantages and gross amounts of money issued on account of such loans, to the 31st day of December 1880, inclusive, arranged by counties and baronies.* H.C. 1881 (99), lvii, 653.

*Return showing the amount allowed for relief works in Ireland, the amount authorised to be expended, and the amount expended up to the present date.* H.C. 1881 (274), lvii, 705.

*Returns – I. of the number of civil bill ejectments, distinguishing ejectments on the title from those for non-payment of rent, tried and determined in each county in Ireland, for each of the four years ending the 31st day of December 1880 ... and, – II of the number of actions of ejectment in superior courts commenced, distinguishing ejectments on the title from ejectments for non-payment of rent; and those tried and determined in each county in Ireland for each of the four years ending the 31st day of December 1880 ...* H.C. 1881 (90), lxxvii, 685.

*Census of Ireland, 1881, pt i: Area, houses, and population: also the ages, civil or conjugal condition, occupations, birthplaces, religion and education of the people: vol. iii, province of Ulster* [C3204 – I to X], H.C. 1881, lxxviii, 1.

*First report from the select committee of the house of lords on land law (Ireland); together with the proceedings of the committee, minutes of evidence, and appendix,* H.C. 1882 (249), xi, 1.

*Report of the intermediate education board for Ireland for the year 1881* [C3176], H.C. 1882, xxiv, 17.

*Return of payments made to landlords by the Irish Land Commission, pursuant to the 1st and 16th sections of the arrears of rent act; and also a return of rent charges cancelled pursuant to the 15th section of the act* [C4059], H.C. 1884, lxiv, 97.

## 4 PRINTED DOCUMENTS

Bahlman, D.W.R. (ed.), *The diary of Sir Edward Walter Hamilton, 1880–1885*, 2 vols (Oxford, 1972).

Cooke, A.B., 'A Conservative party leader in Ulster: Sir Stafford Northcote's diary of a visit to the province, October 1883', *Proceedings of the Royal Irish Academy*, vol. 75, sect. C, no. 4 (1975), pp. 61–84.

Corish, P.J. (ed.), 'Irish College, Rome: Kirby papers, guide to material of public and political interest, 1862–1883', *Archivium Hibernicum, Irish Historical Records*, xxx (1972), pp. 25–115.

Howard, C.H.D. (ed.), *Joseph Chamberlain: a political memoir 1880–1892* (London, 1953).

McMinn, J.R.B., *Against the tide: a calendar of the papers of Rev. J.B. Armour, Irish presbyterian minister and home ruler 1869–1914* (Belfast, 1985).

Moody, T.W. and R. Hawkins (eds), *Florence Arnold-Forster's Irish Journal* (Oxford, 1988).

PRONI, Education facsimiles, *The Great Famine* (n.d.).


## 5 WORKS OF REFERENCE

Bateman, John, *The great landowners of Great Britain and Ireland* (4th edn, London, 1883; repr. Leicester, 1971).

*Belfast and Ulster directory* (Belfast, 1874, 1877, 1881).

Black, R.D.C., *A catalogue of pamphlets on economic subjects published between 1750 and 1900 and now housed in Irish libraries* (Belfast, 1969).

*Dod's parliamentary companion* (London, annually).

*McCalmont's parliamentary poll book of all elections 1832–1918*, ed. J. Vincent and M. Stenton (8th edn, Brighton).

Mitchell, B.R. and P. Deane, *Abstract of British historical statistics* (Cambridge, 1962).

Mulhall, M.G., *The dictionary of statistics* (4th edn, London, 1909).

*Slater's directory of Ireland* (London, 1870).

Vaughan, W.E. and A.J. Fitzpatrick (eds), *Irish historical statistics, population 1821–1971* (Dublin, 1978).

Walker, B.M. (ed.), *Parliamentary election results in Ireland 1801–1922* (Dublin, 1978).

# 6 CONTEMPORARY AND NEAR CONTEMPORARY PUBLICATIONS

I  PAMPHLETS

Bryce, James, *England and Ireland, an introductory statement* (London, 1884).

Dickson, T.A., *A plea for the formation of an Irish land bank, to expand and develop the purchase clauses of the Irish land acts, and facilitate the transfer of land from landlord to tenant* (London, 1884).

George, Henry, *The Irish land question: what it involved and how alone it can be settled; an appeal to the Land Leaguers* (London and Glasgow, 1881).

Hill, Lord George, *Facts from Gweedore* (repr., with introduction by E. Estyn Evans, Belfast, 1971, of 5th edn, 1887).

Irish Land Committee, *The land question, no. i. Notes upon the government valuation of land in Ireland, commonly known as Griffith's valuation* (London and Dublin, 1880).

Irish Land Committee, *The land question, no. ii. The anarchy in Ireland* (London and Dublin, 1880).

Irish Land Committee, *The land question, no. iii. Facts and figures* (London and Dublin, 1880).

Irish Land Committee, *The land question, no. iv. French opinion on the Irish crisis* (London and Dublin, 1880).

Irish Land Committee, *The land question, no. v. Arrested progress* (London and Dublin, 1881).

Irish Land Committee, *The land question, no. vi. Lord Dufferin on the 3Fs* (London and Dublin, 1881).

Irish Land Committee, *The land question, no. vii. Mr Gladstone and the 3Fs* (London and Dublin, 1881).

Irish Land Committee, *The land question, no. viii. Mr Bonamy Price on the 3Fs* (London and Dublin, 1881).

Irish Land Committee, *The land question, no. ix. Mr Gladstone's commissioners and Mr Gladstone* (London and Dublin, 1881).

Irish Land Committee, *The land question, no. xiv. The working of the land law act* (Dublin, 1882).

Joule, B. St J.B., *A letter to Mr James H. Tuke; an answer to the statements made by him in his pamphlet, Irish distress and its remedies* (London, 1881).

Kinnear, J.B., *Ireland in 1881* (London, 1881).

Montgomery, H. de F., *Irish land and Irish rights* (London, 1881).

National Liberal Federation, *4th annual report* (Birmingham, 1881).

Shaw-Lefevre, G., *The purchase clauses of the Irish land acts* (London, 1882).

*Speeches, delivered by the Rt Hon. W. E. Gladstone at Leeds, October 7th and 8th, 1881* (London, 1881).

Staples, J.H., *Solutions of the land question in Ireland* (London and Belfast, 1881).

Tuke, J.H., *Irish distress and its remedies, a visit to Donegal and Connaught in the spring of 1880* (4th edn, London, 1880).

II  MEMOIRS, DIARIES, BIOGRAPHIES, AND OTHER WORKS

Bailey, W.F., 'Magisterial reform; being some considerations on the present voluntary system, and suggestions for the substitution of an independent paid magistracy', *J.S.S.I.S.I.*, pt lxiii, viii, no. 8 (1885), pp. 595–605.

Bailey, W.F., 'The Ulster tenant-right custom: its origin, characteristics, and position under the land acts', *ibid.*, x (1894), pp. 12–22.

Bailey, W.F., *Local and centralised government in Ireland, a sketch of the existing systems* (London and Dublin, 1888).

Belmore, Earl of, *Parliamentary memoirs of Fermanagh and Tyrone from 1613 to 1885* (Dublin, 1887).

Bonn, M.J., *Modern Ireland and her agrarian problem* (Dublin, 1906).

Butt, Isaac, *Land tenure in Ireland; a plea for the Celtic race* (3rd edn, London, 1866).

Butt, Isaac, *A practical treatise on the new law of compensation to tenants in Ireland and other provisions of the landlord and tenant act, 1870; with an appendix of statutes and rules* (Dublin, 1871).

Cherry, R.R. (ed.), *The Irish land law and land purchase acts, 1860 to 1891, together with the rules and forms issued under each act* (2nd edn, Dublin, 1893).

Corry, S.R. Lowry, 4th Earl of Belmore, *The history of two Ulster manors and of their owners* (Revised edn, London, 1903).

Coyne, W.P. (ed.), *Ireland, industrial and agricultural* (Dublin, 1902).

Davitt, Michael, *The fall of feudalism in Ireland: or the story of the Land League revolution* (London and New York, 1904).

Donnell, Robert, *Reports of one hundred and ninety cases in the Irish land courts; with preliminary tenant-right chapter* (Dublin, 1876).

Doyle, Lynn, *An Ulster childhood* (London, 1921).

Dublin Mansion House Relief Committee, *The Irish crisis of 1880: proceedings of the Dublin Mansion House Relief Committee 1880* (Dublin, 1881).

Dun, Finlay, *Landlords and tenants in Ireland* (London, 1881).

Fitzgerald, Percy, *The story of the incumbered estates court* (London, 1862).

Godkin, James, *The land war in Ireland* (London, 1870).

Grimshaw, T.W., 'A statistical survey of Ireland, from 1840 to 1888', *J.S.S.I.S.I.*, pts lxviii, ix (1888), pp. 321–61.

Grimshaw, Thomas, 'President's address', *ibid.*, x (1890), pp. 439–48.

Gwynn, Stephen, *Highways and byways in Donegal and Antrim* (London, 1899).

Hamilton, Lord Ernest, *Forty years on* (London, n.d.).

Hamilton, Lord George, *Parliamentary reminiscences and reflections 1868–1906*, 2 vols (London, 1916–1922).

Hamilton, John, *Sixty years' experience as an Irish landlord: memoirs of John Hamilton D.L. of St. Ernan's, Donegal* (London, 1894).

Healy, T.M., *A word for Ireland* (Dublin, 1886).

Healy, T.M., *Letters and leaders of my day*, 2 vols (London, 1928).

Latimer, W.T., *A history of the Irish presbyterians* (Belfast, 1902).

Lloyd, Clifford, *Ireland under the Land League, a narrative of personal experiences* (Edinburgh and London, 1892).

Lucas, R., *Colonel Saunderson MP, a memoir* (London, 1908).

Lyall, Sir Alfred, *The life of the Marquis of Dufferin and Ava* (London, 1905).

McElroy, S.C., *The Route land crusade, being an authentic account of the efforts made to advance land reform by the Route Tenant's Defence Association, the Antrim Central Tenant-right Association, and the Ulster Land Committee* (Coleraine, n.d.).

MacKnight, Thomas, *Ulster as it is, or twenty-eight years' experience as an Irish editor*, 2 vols (London, 1896).

Mawhinney, G. and E. Dunlop (eds), *The autobiography of Thomas Witherow 1824–1890* (Draperstown, 1990).

Mill, J.S., *Chapters and speeches on the Irish land question* (London, 1870).

Montgomery, H. de F., 'The present aspect of the Irish land question', *Macmillan's Magazine*, xxxii (May, 1875), pp. 33–41.

Montgomery, W.E., *The history of land tenure in Ireland* (Cambridge, 1889).

Morley, John, *The life of William Ewart Gladstone*, 2 vols (London, 1905).

Morris, W. O'Connor, *Letters on the land question of Ireland* (London, 1870).

Murphy, J.N., *Ireland, industrial, political and social* (London, 1870).

O'Brien, R.B., *The parliamentary history of the Irish land question from 1829 to 1869; and the origin and results of the Ulster custom* (London, 1880).

O'Brien, R.B., *Fifty years of concessions to Ireland 1831–1881*, 2 vols (London, 1885).

O'Brien, R.B., *The life of Charles Stuart Parnell 1846–1891*, 2 vols (London, 3rd edn, 1899).

O'Brien, R.B., *The life of Lord Russell of Killowen* (London, n.d.).

O'Brien, William, *Recollections* (London, 1905).

O'Connor, T.P., *The Parnell movement* (London, 1886).

O'Connor, T.P., *Memoirs of an old parliamentarian*, 2 vols (London, 1929).

Reid, T.W., *Life of the Rt Hon. W.E. Forster*, 2 vols (repr. with introduction by V.E. Chancellor, Bath, 1970, of 3rd edn, London, 1888).

Rentoul, J.A., *Stray thoughts and memories*, ed. L. Rentoul (Dublin, 1921).

Richey, A.G., *The Irish land laws* (2nd edn, London, 1881).

Ross, Sir John, *The years of my pilgrimage, random reminiscences* (London, 1924).

Rossmore, Lord, *Things I can tell* (London, 1912).

Russell, T.W., *Ireland and the empire, a review 1800–1900* (London, 1901).

Rutherford, J.C., *An Ards farmer: or, an account of the life of James Shanks, Ballyfounder, Portaferry* (Belfast, 1913).

Shaw-Lefevre, G., *English and Irish land questions, collected essays* (2nd edn, London, 1881).

Sullivan, A.M., *New Ireland: political sketches and personal reminiscences of thirty years of Irish public life* (London, 15th edn, 1877).

Taylor, J.W., *The Rossmore incident: an account of the various nationalist and counter-nationalist meetings held in Ulster in the autumn of 1883* (Dublin, 1884).

Trench, W.S., *Realities of Irish life* (London, 1868).

## 7   LATER WORKS

Adams, J.R.R., *The printed word and the common man: popular culture in Ulster 1700–1900* (Belfast, 1987).

Akenson, D.H., *The Irish education experiment, the national system of education in the nineteenth century* (London, 1970).

Armour, W.S., *Armour of Ballymoney* (London, 1934).

Atkinson, N., *Irish education, a history of educational institutions* (Dublin, 1969).

Bailey, W.F., *The Irish land acts, a short sketch of their history and development* (Dublin, 1917).

Bardon, J., *A history of Ulster* (Belfast, 1992).

Barrington, Thomas, 'A review of Irish agricultural prices', *J.S.S.I.S.I.*, pt ci, xv (1927), pp. 249–80.

Beckett, J.C., *The making of modern Ireland 1603–1923* (London, 1966).

Bell, J., 'The improvement in Irish farming techniques since 1750: theory and practice', in *Rural Ireland: modernisation and change*, ed. P. O'Flanagan *et al.* (Cork, 1987), pp. 24–41.

Bell, P.M.H., *Disestablishment in Ireland and Wales* (London, 1969).

Best, G., *Mid-Victorian Britain 1851–75* (revised edn, St Albans, 1973).

Bew, P., *Land and the national question in Ireland, 1858–82* (Dublin, 1978).

Bew, P., *Conflict and conciliation in Ireland, Parnellites and radical agrarians* (Oxford, 1987).

Bew, P. and F. Wright, 'The agrarian opposition in Ulster politics, 1847–87', in *Irish peasants: violence and political unrest, 1780–1914*, ed. S. Clark and J.S.

Donnelly Jr (Manchester, 1983), pp. 192–229.

Black, R.D.C., *Economic thought and the Irish question 1817–1870* (Cambridge, 1970).

Blake, R., *Disraeli* (London, 1966).

Blewett, N., 'The franchise in the United Kingdom, 1885–1918', *Past and Present*, no. 32 (December, 1965).

Bourke, P.M.A., 'The agricultural statistics of the 1841 census of Ireland; a critical review', *Economic History Review*, 2nd ser., xviii (1965), pp. 376–91.

Boyce, D.G., *Nineteenth century Ireland, the search for stability* (Dublin, 1990).

Boyce, J.W., 'Industrial conditions in the nineteenth century', in *Ulster since 1800, a social survey*, ed. T.W. Moody and J.C. Beckett (London, 1957).

Boyle, J.W., 'A marginal figure: the Irish rural labourer', in *Irish peasants; violence and political unrest 1780–1914*, ed. S. Clarke and J.S. Donnelly Jr (Manchester, 1983), pp. 311–38.

Bruce, H.J., *Silken dalliance* (London, 1946).

Burnett, J., *Plenty and want, a social history of diet in England from 1815 to the present day* (Harmondsworth, 1968).

Cannadine, D., 'Aristocratic indebtedness in the nineteenth century; its administration', *Economic History Review*, 2nd ser., xxx (1977), pp. 624–50.

Cecil, Lady G., *Life of Robert, Marquis of Salisbury*, 4 vols. (London, 1921–32).

Clarkson, L.A., 'Population change and urbanisation, 1821–1911', in *An economic history of Ulster, 1820–1939*, ed. L. Kennedy and P. Ollerenshaw (Manchester, 1985), pp. 137–57.

Conyngham, M.L., *An old Ulster house and the people who lived in it* (Dundalk, 1946).

Cooke A.B. and J. Vincent, *The governing passion, cabinet government and party politics in Britain 1885–86* (Brighton, 1974).

Cornford, J.P., 'The parliamentary foundations of the Hotel Cecil', in *Ideas and institutions of Victorian Britain*, ed. R. Robson (London, 1967), pp. 268–311.

Cousens, S.H., 'Emigration and demographic change in Ireland, 1851–1861', *Economic History Review*, xvii, no. 2 (1961), pp. 275–88.

Cousens, S.H., 'The regional variations in population changes in Ireland, 1861–81', *ibid.*, xvii (1964), pp. 301–21.

Crawford, W.H., 'Landlord–tenant relations in Ulster, 1609–1820', *Irish Economic and Social History*, ii (1975), pp. 5–21.

Crawford, W.H. and B. Trainor (eds), *Aspects of Irish social history* (Belfast, 1969).

Crossman, V., *Local government in nineteenth century Ireland* (Belfast, 1994).

Crotty, R.D., *Irish agricultural production, its volume and structure* (Cork, 1966).

Cunningham, M.W., 'Victoria College: the early years', *Pace*, x, no. 2 (1978–9), pp. 3–7.

Curtis, L.P., 'Incumbered wealth: landed indebtedness in post-famine Ireland', *American Historical Review*, lxxxv (1980), pp. 332–67.

Daly, M.E., *The Famine in Ireland* (Dundalk, 1986).

Delaney, V.T.H., *Christopher Palles, his life and times* (Dublin, 1960).

Donnelly, J.S. Jr, *The land and the people of nineteenth century Cork: the rural economy and the land question* (London, 1975).

Donnelly, J.S. Jr, 'The Irish agricultural depression of 1859–64', *Irish Economic and Social History*, iii (1976), pp. 33–54.

Donnelly, J.S. Jr, 'Landlords and tenants', in *A new history of Ireland: Ireland under the union, 1801–70*, ed. W.E. Vaughan (Oxford, 1989), pp. 332–49.

Donnelly, J.S. Jr, 'Excess mortality and emigration', *ibid.*, pp. 350–56.

Evans, E. Estyn, 'The prehistoric and historic background', in *Land use in Northern Ireland*, ed. L. Symons (London, 1963), pp. 24–44.

Falk, B., *'Old Q's' daughter, the history of a strange family* (London, 1937).

Fitzpatrick, D., 'The disappearance of the Irish agricultural labourer, 1841–1912', *Irish Economic and Social History*, vii (1980), pp. 66–92.

Foster, R.F., *Lord Randolph Churchill, a political life* (Oxford, 1981).

Geary, L.M., *The plan of campaign, 1886–1891* (Cork, 1986).

Gibbon, P., *The origins of Ulster Unionism, the formation of popular protestant politics and ideology in nineteenth century Ireland* (Manchester, 1975).

Grant, J., 'The Great Famine and the poor law in Ulster: the rate-in aid issue of 1849', *I.H.S.*, xxvii, no. 105 (1990), pp. 30–47.

Gwynn, W.B., *Democracy and the cost of politics in Britain* (London, 1962).

Hammond, J.L., *Gladstone and the Irish nation* (London, 1938).

Hoppen, K.T., 'Landlords, society and electoral politics in mid-nineteenth century Ireland', *Past and Present*, no. 75 (1977), pp. 62–93.

Hoppen, K.T., *Elections, politics and society in Ireland 1832–1885* (Oxford, 1984).

Hoppen, K.T., *Ireland since 1800: Conflict and conformity* (London, 1989).

Hurst, M., 'Ireland and the ballot act of 1872', *Historical Journal*, viii, no. 3 (1965), pp. 326–52.

Jackson, A., 'Irish Unionism and the Russellite threat, 1894–1906', *I.H.S.*, xxv (1987), pp. 376–404.

Jackson, A., *The Ulster party, Irish Unionists in the house of commons 1884–1911* (Oxford, 1989).

Jackson, A., *Colonel Edward Saunderson: land and loyalty in Victorian Ireland* (Oxford, 1995).

Jones, A., *The politics of reform 1884* (Cambridge, 1972).

Kee, R., *The green flag, a history of Irish nationalism* (London, 1972).

Kennedy, B.A., 'The tenant-right agitation in Ulster, 1845–50', *Bulletin of the Irish Committee of Historical Sciences*, no. 34 (Nov. 1944), pp. 2–5.

Kennedy, L., 'The rural economy, 1820–1914', in *An economic history of Ulster 1820–1939*, ed. L. Kennedy and P. Ollerenshaw (Manchester, 1985), pp. 1–61.

Kinealy, C., *This great calamity, the Irish Famine 1845–52* (Dublin, 1994).

Kirkpatrick, R.W., 'Origins and development of the land war in mid-Ulster, 1879–85', in *Ireland under the union, varieties of tension: essays in honour of T. W. Moody*, ed. F.S.L. Lyons and R.A.J. Hawkins (Oxford, 1980), pp. 201–35.

Lane, P.G., 'The encumbered estates court, Ireland, 1948–9', *Economic and Social Review*, iii (1971–2), pp. 413–53.

Lane, P.G., 'An attempt at commercial farming in Ireland after the Famine', *Studies*, lxi (1972), pp. 54–66.

Lee, J., *The modernisation of Irish society, 1848–1918* (Dublin, 1973).

Livingstone, P., *The Fermanagh story, a documented history of the County Fermanagh from the earliest times to the present day* (Enniskillen, 1969).

Livingstone, P., *The Monaghan story, a documented history of the County Monaghan from the earliest times to 1976* (Enniskillen, 1980).

Lyons, F.S.L., *Ireland since the famine* (London, 1971).

Lyons, F.S.L., *Charles Stewart Parnell* (London, 1977).

Lyons, F.S.L., *Culture and anarchy in Ireland 1890–1939* (Oxford, 1979).

Macauley, A., *Patrick Dorrian, Bishop of Down and Connor, 1865–1885* (Blackrock, 1987).

McCaffrey, L.J., 'Home rule and the general election of 1874', *I.H.S.*, ix, no. 34 (1954), pp. 190–212.

McCaffrey, L.J., *Irish federalism in the 1870s: a study in conservative nationalism* (Philadelphia, PA, 1962).

McClelland, A., 'The later Orange Order', in *Secret societies in Ireland*, ed. T.D. Williams (Dublin, 1973), pp. 126–37.

McDowell, F.M., *Other days around me* (Belfast, 1972).

McDowell, F.M., *Roses and rainbows* (Belfast, 1972).

McIvor, J.A., *Popular education in the Irish presbyterian church* (Dublin, 1969).

McMinn, J.R.B., 'Presbyterianism and politics in Ulster, 1871–1906', *Studia Hibernica*, xxi (1981), pp. 127–46.

McMinn, J.R.B., 'Liberalism in North Antrim, 1900–1914', *I.H.S.*, xxiii, no. 89 (1982), pp. 17–29.

Magee, J., 'Catholic education in Ireland, 1800–1920', in *Aspects of catholic education* (Belfast, 1971), pp. 14–29.

Magee, J., 'The Monaghan election of 1883 and the invasion of Ulster', *Clogher Record*, viii, no. 2 (1974), pp. 147–66.

Maguire, W.A., *The Downshire estates in Ireland 1801–1845, the management of*

*Irish landed estates in the early nineteenth century* (Oxford, 1972).

Miller, D.W., *Queen's rebels, Ulster loyalism in historical perspective* (Dublin, 1978).

Mogey, J.M., *Rural life in Northern Ireland* (London, 1947).

Mokyr, J., *Why Ireland starved: a quantitative and analytical history of the Irish economy, 1800–1850* (London, 1985).

Moneypenny, W.F. and G.E. Buckle, *The life of Benjamin Disraeli, Earl of Beaconsfield*, 6 vols (London, 1910–20).

Moody, T.W. and J.C. Beckett (eds.), *Ulster since 1800, a political and economic survey* (London, 1955).

Moran, G., 'The advance on the north; the difficulties of the home rule movement in south-east Ulster, 1870–1883', in *The borderlands, essays on the history of the Ulster–Leinster border*, ed. R. Gillespie and H. O'Sullivan (Belfast, 1989), pp. 129–42.

Morrison, H.S., *Modern Ulster, its character, customs, politics and industries* (London, 1920).

Norman, E.R., *The catholic church and Ireland in the age of rebellion 1859–1873* (London, 1965).

O'Brien, C.C., *Parnell and his party, 1880–90* (corrected impression, Oxford, 1968).

O'Day, A., *The English face of Irish nationalism, Parnellite involvement in British politics 1880–86* (Dublin, 1977).

O'Donovan, J., *The economic history of livestock in Ireland* (Cork, 1940).

Ó Gráda, C., 'Agricultural head rents, pre-famine and post-famine', *Economic and Social Review*, v, no. 3 (1974), pp. 385–92.

Ó Gráda, C., 'The investment behaviour of Irish landlords 1850–75; some preliminary feelings', *Agricultural History Review*, xxiii (1975), pp. 139–55.

Ó Gráda, C., *Ireland before and after the Famine, explorations in economic history, 1800–1925* (Manchester, 1988).

Ollerenshaw, P., 'Industry 1820–1914', in *An economic history of Ulster 1820–1939*, ed. L. Kennedy and P. Ollerenshaw (Manchester, 1985), pp. 62–108.

O'Neill, T.P., 'The Famine and its consequences', in *Ulster since 1800, a social survey*, ed. T.W. Moody and J.C. Beckett (London, 1957), pp. 35–43.

Palmer, N.D., *The Irish Land League crisis* (New Haven, CT, 1940).

Patterson, H., *Class conflict and sectarianism, the protestant working class and the Belfast labour movement, 1868–1920* (Belfast, 1980).

Perren, R., 'The landlord and agricultural transformation, 1870–1900', *Agricultural History Review*, xviii (1970), pp. 36–51.

Pomfret, J.E., *The struggle for land in Ireland, 1800–1923* (Princeton, NJ, 1930).

Robinson, O., 'The London companies as progressive landlords in nineteenth century Ireland', *Economic History Review*, 2nd ser., xv, no. 1 (1962–3), pp. 103–18.

Robinson, O., 'The London companies and tenant-right in nineteenth century Ireland', *Agricultural History Review*, xviii (1970), pp. 54–63.

Savage, D.C., 'The origins of the Ulster Unionist party, 1885–6', *I.H.S.*, xii, no. 47 (1961), pp. 185–208.

Savage, D.C., 'The Irish Unionists, 1867–1886', *Eire–Ireland*, ii, no. 3 (1967).

Shanks, A., *Rural aristocracy in Northern Ireland* (Aldershot, 1988).

Shearman, H., 'Irish church finances after disestablishment', in *Essays in British and Irish history in honour of James Eadie Todd*, ed. H.A. Cronne, T.W. Moody and D.B. Quinn (London, 1949), pp. 278–302.

Smith, C.F., *James Nicholson Richardson of Bessbrook* (London, 1925).

Solow, B.L., *The land question and the Irish economy 1870–1903* (Cambridge, MA, 1971).

Spring, D., *The English landed estate in the nineteenth century: its administration* (Baltimore, MD, 1963).

Steele, E.D., *Irish land and British politics, tenant-right and nationality 1865–1870* (Cambridge, 1974).

Thompson, F., 'The Armagh elections of 1885–6', *Seanchas Ard Mhaca: Journal of the Armagh Diocesan Historical Society*, viii, no. 2 (1977), pp. 360–85.

Thompson, F., 'Attitudes to reform: political parties in Ulster and the Irish land bill of 1881', *I.H.S.*, xxiv, no. 95 (1985), pp. 327–40.

Thompson, F., 'The landed classes, the Orange Order and the anti-Land League campaign in Ulster 1880–1881', *Eire–Ireland*, xxii, no. 1 (1987), pp. 102–21.

Thornley, D., *Isaac Butt and home rule* (London, 1964).

Turner, M.E., 'Towards an agricultural prices index for Ireland, 1850–1914', *Economic and Social Review*, xviii (1987), pp. 123–36.

Turner, M.E., 'Output and productivity in Irish agriculture from the Famine to the great war', *Irish Economic and Social History*, xvii (1990), pp. 62–78.

Vaughan, W.E., 'Landlord and tenant relations in Ireland between the Famine and the land war, 1850–1878', in *Comparative aspects of Scottish and Irish economic and social history, 1600–1900*, ed. L.M. Cullen and T.C. Smout (Edinburgh, 1977), pp. 216–26.

Vaughan, W.E., 'An assessment of the economic performance of Irish landlords, 1851–81', in *Ireland under the union, varieties of tension: essays in honour of T.W. Moody*, ed. F.S.L. Lyons and R.A.J. Hawkins (Oxford, 1980), pp. 173–99.

Vaughan, W.E., 'Agricultural output, rents and wages in Ireland, 1850–

1880', in *Ireland and France 17th–20th centuries: towards a comparative study of rural history*, ed. L.M. Cullen and F. Furet (Paris, 1980), pp. 85–97.

Vaughan, W.E., 'Potatoes and agricultural output', *Irish Economic and Social History*, xvii (1990), 79–92.

Vaughan, W.E., *Landlords and tenants in mid-Victorian Ireland* (Oxford, 1994).

Vincent, J., *The formation of the British Liberal party 1857–1868* (London, 1966).

Vincent, J., 'Gladstone and Ireland', *Proceedings of the British Academy*, lxiii (1977), 193–238.

Walker, B.M., *Ulster politics, the formative years 1868–86* (Belfast, 1989).

Walker, B.M., 'The Irish electorate, 1868–1915', *I.H.S.*, xviii, no. 71 (March, 1973), 359–406.

Whyte, J.H., *The independent Irish party 1850–9* (Oxford, 1958).

Wright, F., *Two lands on one soil: Ulster politics before home rule* (Dublin, 1996).

## 8 UNPUBLISHED THESES

Feingold, W.L., 'The Irish boards of poor law guardians 1872–86, a revolution in local government' (PhD thesis, University of Chicago, 1974).

Keown, E., 'The plan of campaign in Ulster, 1886–7' (BEd dissertation, St. Mary's College, Belfast, 1996).

Kirkpatrick, R.W., 'Landed estates in mid-Ulster and the Irish land war, 1879–85' (PhD thesis, Trinity College, Dublin, 1976).

McGimpsey, C., 'To raise the banner in the remotest north: politics in County Monaghan 1868–83' (PhD thesis, University of Edinburgh, 1982).

Megahey, A.J., 'The Irish protestant churches and social and political issues 1870–1914' (PhD thesis, Queen's University, Belfast, 1969).

Thompson, F., 'The Ulster Liberals and the general election of 1885' (MA thesis, Queen's University, Belfast, 1973).

Thompson, F., 'Land and politics in Ulster, 1868–86' (PhD thesis, Queen's University, Belfast, 1982).

Vaughan, W.E., 'A study of landlord and tenant relations in Ireland between the famine and the land war, 1850–78' (PhD thesis, Trinity College, Dublin, 1973).

Walker, B.M., 'Parliamentary representation in Ulster 1868–86, the formative years' (PhD thesis, Trinity College, Dublin, 1977).

# Index